India Studies in Business and Economics

The Indian economy is considered to be one of the fastest growing economies of the world with India amongst the most important G-20 economies. Ever since the Indian economy made its presence felt on the global platform, the research community is now even more interested in studying and analyzing what India has to offer. This series aims to bring forth the latest studies and research about India from the areas of economics, business, and management science. The titles featured in this series will present rigorous empirical research, often accompanied by policy recommendations, evoke and evaluate various aspects of the economy and the business and management landscape in India, with a special focus on India's relationship with the world in terms of business and trade.

More information about this series at http://www.springer.com/series/11234

Seema Purushothaman · Sheetal Patil

Agrarian Change and Urbanization in Southern India

City and the Peasant

Seema Purushothaman
Azim Premji University
Bengaluru, Karnataka, India

Sheetal Patil
Azim Premji University
Bengaluru, Karnataka, India

ISSN 2198-0012 ISSN 2198-0020 (electronic)
India Studies in Business and Economics
ISBN 978-981-10-8335-8 ISBN 978-981-10-8336-5 (eBook)
https://doi.org/10.1007/978-981-10-8336-5

© Springer Nature Singapore Pte Ltd. 2019
This work is subject to copyright. All rights are reserved by the Publisher, whether the whole or part
of the material is concerned, specifically the rights of translation, reprinting, reuse of illustrations,
recitation, broadcasting, reproduction on microfilms or in any other physical way, and transmission
or information storage and retrieval, electronic adaptation, computer software, or by similar or d ssimilar
methodology now known or hereafter developed.
The use of general descriptive names, registered names, trademarks, service marks, etc. in this
publication does not imply, even in the absence of a specific statement, that such names are exempt from
the relevant protective laws and regulations and therefore free for general use.
The publisher, the authors and the editors are safe to assume that the advice and information in this
book are believed to be true and accurate at the date of publication. Neither the publisher nor the
authors or the editors give a warranty, expressed or implied, with respect to the material contained
herein or for any errors or omissions that may have been made. The publisher remains neutral with regard
to jurisdictional claims in published maps and institutional affiliations.

This Springer imprint is published by the registered company Springer Nature Singapore Pte Ltd.
The registered company address is: 152 Beach Road, #21-01/04 Gateway East, Singapore 189721,
Singapore

Foreword

In Defense of the Small Farmer in an Urbanizing World

Indian small farmers face a tragic dilemma today. On the one hand, it has become extremely hard to survive merely on agricultural incomes to reproduce themselves and their families. On the other, a decent sustainable alternative in terms of non-farm work simply does not exist yet for the vast majority. The existing alternatives in terms of rural non-farm work or urban informal work are neither sufficiently remunerative nor do they come with acceptable working conditions. Farmers can neither leave agriculture nor stick to it. Increasingly, therefore, to make both ends meet, it has become common for farmers and agricultural workers to invest the only alienable resource that they possess—labour power—in a portfolio of different occupations and livelihoods that span across what used to be fairly deep divides such as agricultural–non-agricultural, rural–urban, simultaneous landowner (rural)–tenant (urban) existence. Along with the two distinct classes of workers and farmers, there is a new class of farmer-workers. The continued survival of this class is premised on continuously traversing between these previously distinctive spaces in the process of acquiring a largely 'coerced' subjectivity and hybridity that help them deal with unavoidable economic distress. This book is a deep exploration of this dilemma and the resultant hybridity among farmers from different regions of the Karnataka state by analysing the making of farm livelihoods across one of these divides—villages and their interaction with different kinds of urban spaces. There are other important facets that this book explores that pertain to the interaction between villages and urban spaces with deleterious consequences for existing rural institutions and sustainable ecologies.

As the Indian economy continues to register the highest growth rates among all economies across the globe, a simple question needs to be continuously posed. Who is benefiting from this growth and what is the redistributive nature of this growth vis-à-vis different groups/classes that have made this growth possible? From various qualitative and quantitative studies that are available, it is now evident that the growth process in India is very different from the early growth process in East

Asian countries in the mid-twentieth century. Growth has been inequality—heightening with the major beneficiaries being the capitalist, managerial and professional classes located in urban spaces (mainly large cities) creating an enclave-like growth process that marginalises the urban and rural majorities (including small farmers, workers and farmer-workers). These growth beneficiaries too draw from a portfolio of options—investments and job opportunities in existing cities, expansion of these activities into greenfield sites that were hitherto considered rural or semi-urban areas or into the global economy. These classes voluntarily seek hybridity and mobility in pursuit of higher profits and incomes. Existing institutions and ecologies (including agricultural ones) are to be conquered and modified to make these pursuits possible.

When these two very different modalities of existence are juxtaposed, a more realistic picture of the Indian economy emerges. Indian lives across the spectrum are in a state of continuous flux, though most of these lives have experienced extreme distress while a small group of others have prospered extremely This raises a critical question—What is the way forward? How do we imagine a space/economy that can bring together these two modalities not as a predatory form of growth of one modality over the other, but as one that preserves and extends institutions that provide spatial and income mobility to a majority, while preserving sustainability along the ecological and livelihood dimensions? This book provides an exploration of these possibilities by analysing the small farmers/workers and their engagements with cities and towns in their near vicinity and afar in the state of Karnataka.

The dominant top-down view of Indian agriculture is that it is a repository of various inefficiencies. Landholdings are distributed suboptimally because of the existence of too many small and marginal farmers. Farmers tend to adopt technologies and input use practices that reduce productivity. Labour in Indian agriculture is either underemployed or unemployed. Markets (product, labour and credit) are interlinked and therefore can possess uneven power asymmetries. This results in a suboptimal agricultural growth performance that has harmful implications for food security of the urban populations and in the production of other raw materials that are essential for an improved growth performance of the overall economy. Yet, the state cannot act on these inefficiencies because of the political constraints that prevail in the Indian democracy. Instead, the state is forced to make populist concessions such as providing price support, cheap credit, production and consumption subsidies or loan waivers to farming communities that then prolong this state of affairs. This produces a different kind of an impasse in the minds of the top-down policymakers—while productivity-enhancing alternatives are available, they cannot simply be deployed because of the pressures and constraints of functioning in an electoral democracy.

Against such a backdrop, the authors of this book, Seema Purushothaman and Sheetal Patil, offer a very different story of small farmers located in a larger context of rapid urbanisation and tease out their current and potential contributions to the Indian economy. They rightly criticise the dominant narratives on Indian agriculture for their lack of engagement with the complexity and variety of different

Foreword

agricultural settings, different institutional configurations and a range of ecological conditions. They offer trenchant criticisms of frameworks that offer 'one-size-fits-all' prescriptions that ignore the specificities, nuances, political economies and different histories of the vast tapestry that is the Indian agricultural landscape. Any attempt to formulate effective agricultural policy ought to take these specificities into account, while keeping certain ideals in mind.

Using ideas from many thinkers but mainly drawing on the work of Alexander Chayanov (a Russian agronomist of the early twentieth century), they ask for a fundamental and radical rethinking of the small farmer and her current and future contributions towards producing an equitable and sustainable society. In a global context of fragile ecologies and impending climate change, they offer the possibility that a sustainable future depends in part on generating sustainable agriculture that draws from the existing and past ecumenical practices of small farmers that can be further strengthened through the setting up of various institutional support structures.

Various studies show multiple benefits of smallholder agriculture. Small famers tend to produce rich *in situ* biodiversity through constant experimentation that is essential for the food security of future generations. Although they are not rewarded for this, this is a deep service that small farmers render to the rest of society. Using an insight from Chayanov, several authors also argue that small farmers tend to be more productive on a piece of land through more intensive cultivation based on hands-to-mouth ratios that different family farms face. This adds to the need for land reforms and various support structures that small farmers ought to be provided with. Small farmers that are not caught in an orbit of 'forced commerce' also tend to choose cropping patterns and practices of input use that are compatible with existing ecologies and food security needs of proximate populations. This sort of a decentralised 'micropolis' understanding of agriculture with appropriate rescaling also provides one of the key components of a potential solution to the global problem of climate change and unsustainable economic pursuits. This is the tradition that the current book is located in. Yet, the book goes beyond this tradition and makes important contributions to various literatures in agrarian, urban, rural–urban and ecological studies.

In Western European and East Asian capitalist development trajectories, there was a shrinking of the small farmer community either through waves of what Marx referred to as primitive accumulation (e.g. England) or through a more gradual absorption of farmers into the urban labour force (e.g. post-WWII Japan and South Korea). In the Indian case (and to a much lesser extent, in the Chinese case) and other countries that are growing today with large rural populations, such absorption seems much less likely. Numerous studies have pointed out that economic growth during the last 30 years (neoliberalism) has not been employment generating. This creates the tragic dilemma that was posed above. In order to understand how small farmers are coping with this dilemma, positing of a unitary urban–rural dynamic will not suffice. Urban itself is heavily differentiated and so are rural settings. One of the innovations of this book is that it sets up these interactions in the state of

Karnataka by positing four distinct urban processes and multiple village settings that interact with these urban processes.

Neither the urban nor the rural setting is essentialised in this account. Each setting is produced by unique histories (precolonial, colonial/princely states and different post-colonial emphases), political economies, ecologies, rich institutional settings and state policies (e.g. irrigation). While the entry point for the study is different types of urban, the rural settings that interact with these different urban types are also laid out in careful detail. Methodologically, this is innovative and of value to future researchers. For instance, in selecting the urban settings, different types of urban processes are discussed—a large/primate city setting (Bangalore), a small town located at a distance (50–60 KMs) but dependent on the large city (Ramanagara), an agro-dynamic urban setting (Mandya) and a remote setting that belonged to the very different economic, political and cultural ecology of the erstwhile Hyderabad State that has also seen a recent spurt in irrigation (Yadgir). Villages around these different urban types are selected for intensive study to show that the small farmers and the environments they face are unique and cannot be subsumed under generalised urban and rural settings. Given the above-mentioned combination of multiple determinations, each village setting is also unique. Through this diversity, there is the presentation of the economic and behavioural aspects of Chayanovian small farmers that are theorised in the contexts of their larger environments. This nuanced presentation not only adds richness to their account but gives deep credence to the idea that agricultural policy needs to take into account subtle realities that are only visible when actual field-level dynamics are studied and understood carefully.

The tragic dilemma posed above can be resolved by combining several imperatives. First, agriculture could be strengthened by making it more compatible with the surrounding ecological processes and strengthening the institutional structures around it. This could also be combined with a movement away from the growth-/productivity-oriented agricultural model as well as populist state policies. This would require a fine-grain understanding of the agricultural and urban processes at work in different contexts across the country and a careful formulation of decentralised policy imperatives and support structures. Various kinds of co-operation can be imagined and implemented after taking into account sociocultural and political specificities of different contexts. This would be a bottom-up imperative that would ease the pressures caused by economic distress and other push factors emanating in this sector. Second, a job-oriented, labour-intensive economic growth model can be implemented that takes into account the labour abundance in India and strives to provide a living wage along with decent working conditions. This would strengthen positive pull factors in urban economies.

A combination of the above two resolutions can lead to a strong fallback position for small farmers, who may choose to stay in farming or leave it on their terms. Of course, this is a resolution that will not win the favour of the classes in the growth enclave that have entrenched themselves in positions of influence and power over the last 30 or so years. This is the deep struggle that needs to be waged in order to defend the interests of small farmers. In this fight, there is no need to choose an exclusive option. The countryside and the city can each be remunerative for the participants or a symbiotic combination of the two. Moreover, the ecological contradiction of the metabolic rift (e.g. deep separation of sites of production and consumption as well as production and disposal of waste) that is produced and intensified in capitalism through the separation of the city and countryside can also be addressed through a more creative conceptualisation of the interactions between the city and the countryside.

Seema and Sheetal do not offer a simple solution to the precarity of small farmers. They underscore the point that any enduring solution to the dilemma of the small farmer needs to ensure certain basic livelihood needs and capabilities of these farmers, while simultaneously addressing questions of ecological sustainability and economic viability of farming as a process. Addressing the central questions that the world is facing today such as climate change or deep inequalities may be inextricably intertwined with addressing and providing a clear path of sustainability for the small farmer.

Amherst, USA
June 28, 2019

Vamsi Vakulabharanam
Department of Economics
University of Massachusetts Amherst

Preface

Urbanisation is an anthropogenic process set in motion since the beginning of human civilisation. Some ancient cities and civilisations sustained longer than others did. Yet, the ideal type of urbanisation remains an open question. Answer to this may provide a clue to the longevity of human civilisation. History of civilisations indicates that the connection between the two lies in the agro-ecological impacts of urbanisation.

Proximate impacts of urbanisation like pollution and congestion are visible. Lesser noticed are the impacts on rural landscapes and communities. While displacement of farmers for converting land to non-agricultural use has been discussed to some extent, the impact of urbanisation on farmers who remain in the job is seldom looked into. Reasons for lack of attention to this impact of urbanisation span across the diversity in the way urbanisation happens, the small and scattered individual existence of farm households and the complex embeddedness of production and consumption as well as farm and non-farm activities in today's farm household. The book attempts to unravel this maze of complexity and diversity amidst a notable persistence of small farms—a large but invisible presence in Indian agriculture.

Relative to the magnitude of the problem, this book is a modest attempt and does not claim to address either all possible urbanisation processes or all complexities of farm livelihood. Diversity in the urbanisation front is captured in four study sites set in South India's Karnataka State, chosen based on the urbanisation parameters. The complexity of agrarian status unravelled in these sites appears similar in certain aspects but varies in yet others. While gleaning pointers from the above variation, it was evident that governance—especially the long-term welfare orientation of governance—played a crucial role in the coexistence of persistence and distress among small farms. This made us venture into the archived history of governing agricultural land and revenue, before unpacking prevalent complexities. Unexpectedly, this led to paleontological information too, as some farm practices were found to be more enduring in a changing market and technology. Thus, a simple enquiry on how the city impacts the peasant in its periphery turned into a multi-pronged transdisciplinary research around urbanisation and agrarian change.

Analysing primary information on four study sites from multiple angles not only unveiled the pattern in the status of smallholders, but also elicited the factors that can aid sustainability of a smallholder dominant agrarian society. Secure access to productive land as well as village commons along with diverse marketing options emerged as the primary tier of equally important factors. Deliberative local social institutions for multifaceted adaptive skilling of smallholders as well as off-farm rural jobs built on local agricultural produce constituted an equally significant second tier of interconnected factors.

Qualitative and quantitative approaches at a range of different scales made this writing endeavour challenging. It is structured in such a way that individual chapters would provide a flavour of the overall message. The last chapter presents a comparative analysis of the sites and the essence of what the book stands for.

The ideal outcome of this work, more than being of use in academic discussions, would be policymakers and development actors imbibing the message on why and how to harmonise the city–peasant relationship.

Bengaluru, India
July 2019

Seema Purushothaman
Sheetal Patil

Acknowledgements

Studying the intricate interface between urbanisation and agrarian communities, that too in the complex context of Karnataka state, and then writing on it, predictably needs a lot of help and support. The study was conceptualised in the beautiful and intellectually stimulating environs of the Indian Institute of Advanced Studies (IIAS), Shimla, during 2012, when the first author was there on a fellowship. This fellowship happened to be soon after completing a study on the policy impacts on small farmers of Karnataka and resulted in the conceptual foundation of a follow-up study on the larger question of the interface between urbanisation and farming.

The conceptual framework developed at IIAS was translated into empirical research in five districts of Karnataka state with support from the Research Center at Azim Premji University (henceforth referred to as 'the University'), Bengaluru. We acknowledge the support extended by the University in all stages of the study and writing the manuscript. The help rendered by our colleagues attached to the library, administration, finance, pantry, housekeeping, facilities and logistics departments of the University is gratefully acknowledged. Equally important was encouraging faculty colleagues, especially the inputs received from those in the School of Development.

We would like to profusely thank Siddhartha Lodha, who, apart from coordinating the entire project, was involved in data collection from both primary and secondary sources. Assistance rendered by Shridhar Bellubbi and Ashwatha Gowda in conducting participant interviews was crucial for building a quality database. Support extended by the District Institutes of Azim Premji Foundation at Yadgir and Mandya in hosting the field assistants is duly acknowledged. Grassroots Research and Advocacy Movement (Mysore) helped us with configuring the questionnaires for a tablet-based survey. Needless to say, co-operation from and interest shown by more than 200 respondents—both farmers and migrants—made the study a meaningful reality.

Many photographs in the book were captured in camera by Raghvendra Vanjari, our colleague at the University. Raghvendra's perseverance in gathering essential secondary data also is much appreciated. The illustrations on the study sites were meticulously drawn and revised multiple times by Juny Wilfred. Juny's skilful efforts made each illustration a comprehensive reflection of the study site. Jayalakshmi Krishnan patiently generated and custom-made maps for a spatial depiction of specific features of the study sites.

We were fortunate to have the keen and critical eyes of Rosa Abraham for her adept reviews of all chapters. Rekha Abel pitched in at the last stage, for an editorial review of the final draft. The challenge of converting primary and secondary information on a complex topic into a readable form would have been much more formidable without their editorial help. Appreciation is also due to Sham Kashyap, who helped us with the review of archives on Mysore and Hyderabad Karnataka regions.

During the study, we conducted three workshops to gather inputs and share our insights. The first workshop was in Yadgir—'Agricultural Dynamics and Strategies among Small holders of Yadgir' in June 2015. The other two workshops were in Bengaluru—'Agrarian Change and Urbanisation' in June 2016, and 'Family Farms in Urbanising Karnataka' in June 2018. We take this opportunity to thank the participants of the three workshops.

The support we received from the Departments of Agriculture and Water Resources, Krishi Vigyan Kendras, Raitha Samparka Kendras, Agricultural Prices Commission and Agricultural Produce Marketing Committees in various locations, and from the officials of the study taluks and villages, is gratefully remembered. Informative interactions with scholars and officials at the Universities of Agricultural Sciences in Bengaluru and Dharwad, College of Agricultural Sciences, B'Gudi (Yadgir), Karnatak University, Mysore University, National Institute of Advanced Studies, Institute of Social and Economic Change, and Water and Land Management Institute (Dharwad) brought richness to the discussions, especially those based on primary data.

Conversations with Teodor Shanin and Henry Bernstein in 2017, on the side of the BRICS conference on agrarian studies, significantly helped in sharpening the focus towards family farms. Suggestions on the study design and the book proposal from Amit Bhaduri and Gopal Kadekodi, as well as the comments on specific chapters from A. R. Vasavi, Radha Gopalan and K. N. Ganeshaiah, have been valuable. Vamsi Vakulabharanam's willingness to go through the chapters and pen a thoughtful foreword warrants special thanks and appreciation. We also take this opportunity to acknowledge the support provided by the entire team at Springer who patiently dealt with us till the last moment.

Lastly, but most importantly, the book would not have been complete without the strong support and co-operation from the families of both the authors. We extend our warm gratitude to our families and support staff at home.

Contents

1 Contemporary Agrarian Questions—An Introduction 1
  1.1 The Context 2
  1.2 Peasantry to Family Farms: Persistence or Metamorphosis? . . . 3
     1.2.1 Indian Peasant in the Time of Commercialisation
        and Urbanisation. 4
     1.2.2 Lower Equilibrium Among the Peasantry
        and Social Differentiation 6
  1.3 Agrarian Frameworks and Family Farms in India 8
     1.3.1 Indifference to Ecological Concerns 9
     1.3.2 Institutional Vacuum 11
     1.3.3 Approaching an Integrated Frame 13
  1.4 Agrarian Questions in Twenty-First-Century India 14
  1.5 Semantics and Typology 17
  1.6 Organisation of the Book 18
  References 21

2 Family Farms in Agrarian Literature—A Critique 25
  2.1 Smallholder as an Economic Entity 25
  2.2 Nature, Moral Economy and the Peasant 30
  2.3 Agrarian Institutions 33
  2.4 Agrarian Movements 36
  2.5 Food Regimes and Agrarian Political Economy 38
  2.6 Persistence and Diversity Amidst Adversities 40
     2.6.1 Persistence or Resilience? 40
     2.6.2 Dilemma of Transition 42
     2.6.3 Differentiated Persistence 44
     2.6.4 Adversities and Outcomes 46
  2.7 Summary 48
  References 49

xv

3	**Study Approach, Processes and Methods**		53
	3.1	Conceptualising the Study	53
	3.2	Typology of Urbanisation	54
	3.3	Exploring the Urban–Agrarian Interface	58
		3.3.1 Farmlands	58
		3.3.2 Village Commons	59
		3.3.3 Water	61
		3.3.4 Crops, Animals and Ways of Farming	62
		3.3.5 Occupation and Migration	63
		3.3.6 Markets	64
		3.3.7 Institutions	64
	3.4	Research Methodology	65
	3.5	Analytical Approach	71
	References		73
4	**Agrarian Ecology and Society in the Study Regions: A Historical Perspective**		77
	4.1	Emergence of Agricultural Settlements in the Study Regions	77
	4.2	Tracing the Rural–Urban Rift and Social Differentiation	81
	4.3	Political Economy of Land Relations in Mysore and Gulbarga	84
	4.4	Agrarian Context in the Study Sites	90
	4.5	Widening Divergence	94
	Annexure 4.1: Rulers and Invaders of Mysore and Hyderabad–Karnataka		97
	References		98
5	**Agriculture in the Era of Urbanisation**		101
	5.1	Indian Agriculture—a Journey from Food Famine to Livelihood Famine?	102
		5.1.1 Urbanisation and Farm Livelihoods	104
	5.2	Agriculture and Urbanisation in Karnataka	106
	5.3	Study Sites—a Brief Introduction	112
	References		115
6	**The City and the Peasant—Family Farms Around Bengaluru**		119
	6.1	Mega City of the Neo-Liberal Times	119
	6.2	Farmlands: Enduring Rapid Transformation	125
	6.3	Nature's Commons: Up for Acquisition and Encroachment	127
	6.4	Irrigation: The Tube Well—Energy Nexus	130
	6.5	Farming Systems: Feeding a Mega City and Sustaining Culture	131

	6.5.1	Flowers for and from the Garden City	132
	6.5.2	Eucalyptus in Peri-urban Bengaluru	133
	6.5.3	Animal Keeping Exclusively for Milk	134
6.6	Operational Expenses: Costly Outsourcing		135
6.7	Labour: Competing with Other Sectors		137
6.8	Selling Farm Produce: Options Around the City		140
6.9	Socio-economic Conditions: Better off with Loans?		143
6.10	Shifting to Urban Occupations		146
6.11	Institutions: Old Norms and New Networks		148
6.12	Farms Around a Megacity: Give Plenty and Take Little?		150
References			151

7 Family Farms Around Ramanagara ... 153

7.1	Small-Town Urbanism		153
7.2	Farmlands: Persisting Smallholdings		159
7.3	Nature's Commons: Forests, Grazing Lands and Water Bodies		160
7.4	Irrigation: Tanks, Sewage and Streams		162
7.5	Notable Farming Systems		165
	7.5.1	Silky Shine in Kanakapura	166
	7.5.2	Spread of Mango in Magadi	168
	7.5.3	Livestock—For Milk, Draught and Meat	169
7.6	Running Cost: Labour for Ragi and Small Capital for Silk		170
7.7	Labour: Balancing Farm and Non-farm Work		171
7.8	Selling Farm Produce: Private Traders and Regulated Markets		173
7.9	Socio-economic Conditions: High Farm Income and High Indebtedness		175
7.10	Migration from Farming: Recent and Unappealing		178
7.11	Institutions and Integration		178
7.12	Urbanisation with Smaller Agrarian Footprint		180
References			182

8 Agricultural Urbanism—Family Farms Around Mandya ... 183

8.1	Agriculture as a Driver of Urbanisation		183
8.2	Farmlands: With Dominant Communities		188
8.3	Nature's Commons: Lakes and Rivers		189
8.4	Irrigation: Confluence of Old and New Ingenuity		190
8.5	Farming: Canal Irrigated and Rain-fed Systems		194
	8.5.1	From Small Town to 'Sugar City'—Journey of Irrigated Mandya	195
	8.5.2	Coconut, Ragi and Livestock—A Long-Standing System in Rain-fed Areas	197
8.6	The Cost of Farming: Capital and Family Labour		198

8.7	Selling Farm Produce: Processing Units and Regulated Markets	200
8.8	Socio-economic Situation: Deceptive Prosperity	203
8.9	Migration: Stress and Aspirations	206
8.10	Agrarian Norms and Institutions	207
8.11	Family Farms in a Struggling Agricultural Economy	209
References		211

9 Family Farms in Yadgir District ... 213

9.1	Rural Agrarian Towns	213
9.2	Farmlands: Larger Parcels and Diverse Communities	219
9.3	Nature's Commons: Limestone Deposits and Deep Black Soils of Shorapur Doab	220
9.4	Irrigation: Favouring Intensive Crops	222
9.5	Farming Systems: Declining Jowar and Disappearing Groundnut	223
	9.5.1 Spread of Paddy in Semi-arid Yadgir	225
	9.5.2 Land of Cattle Fairs and Festivals	228
9.6	Running Cost: Increasing with Irrigation	229
9.7	Labour: Seasonal Circulation Between Farm and Non-farm Work	230
9.8	Women in Farm Households: Burdened and Discriminated	232
9.9	Regulated Markets: Dominating the Agricultural Marketing Scene	232
9.10	Socio-economic Situation: Mounting Debt and Distress	234
9.11	Farmer Migrants as Construction Workers in Cities	237
9.12	Social Institutions: Bound to Customs	240
9.13	Small Holdings in the Hinterlands: Rainfed Systems, Intensification and Persisting Migration	241
References		243

10 Withering Family Farms ... 245

10.1	The Study	245
	10.1.1 Invisibility of Small Family Farms	246
	10.1.2 Contexts and Regions in Focus	247
10.2	Trajectories of Regional Divergence: Nature or Governance?	248
	10.2.1 Agriculture and Development	249
	10.2.2 Agrarian Movements	251
	10.2.3 Farming Systems	251
10.3	Farmlands—Equity, Management and Conversion	253
	10.3.1 Land Distribution	254
	10.3.2 Leasing, Sharecropping and Contract Farming	256
	10.3.3 When Is Farmland Left Uncultivated?	257

	10.3.4	Women in Smallholdings	259
	10.3.5	Change in Agricultural Land Use—Transactions and Acquisitions	259
10.4		Ecological Commons—Forests, Village Lands and Water Resources	260
10.5		Irrigation: A Dangerous Treadmill	262
10.6		*Mandis, Santhes* and the Urban Niche Markets	266
10.7		Fragile Balance—Wages, Farm Income and Loans	269
10.8		To Farm or to Migrate?—The Dilemma	271
10.9		Local Institutions and Mobilisation for Adaptive Skilling	276
10.10		The City and the Peasant: Complementary, Competitive or Hegemonic?	277
References			280

Index 283

About the Authors

Seema Purushothaman is a Professor at Azim Premji University, Bangalore, India. She uses interdisciplinary approaches to study social, ecological and economic change in livelihoods and policies in India, investigating their linkage to food and agrarian crises. Her research spans across the concept and issues of sustainability in and around forests and family farms. Her primary teaching interest is in sustainability as a concept, as an agrarian concern, and from an economic perspective.

Sheetal Patil is a researcher at Azim Premji University, Bangalore, India. With formal training in engineering and computer application, her current research interest is in policy impact on agricultural sustainability and its assessment at the micro level. Using the lens of sustainability, she focuses on agrarian and related issues that range from natural resource management to food security, livelihood sustenance, alternate institutions, and safeguarding traditional and cultural knowledge.

Chapter 1
Contemporary Agrarian Questions—An Introduction

'Peasant' has been a favourite, if not romantic, topic of academic explorations. The boundaries that peasantry shared with others in society were stark and amenable to dichotomous treatments of deprivation and exploitation. Closely intertwined, nature and peasant were both exploited by landlords and industries. Surging economies distanced themselves from the primary sector in favour of propelling further growth while inflicting considerable social and ecological externalities on nature and the peasant alike. The accumulation of these conflicts in production landscapes created vast inequalities in outcomes, agency and voice, that often resulted in violent unrests. Thus, questions of justice, equality, dignity and human rights have been the subject of agrarian literature for a long time.[1]

As 'peasant' in its pure old-world imagery began to fade away, a more complex entity started emerging—the smallholder family farm. While other rural occupations like weaving, carpentry, leather and metalworks, backyard poultry, folk art, etc., disappeared almost entirely from the rural livelihood basket due to falling demand and competition from mass producing industries, crop cultivation and dairying survived as the last bastions of small-scale household production, coexisting with new non-farm activities.

These smallholder farm units are characterised by varied dimensions across agro-ecologies. Their physical scale of operation varies depending on land and inputs, preferred crops, animals as well as the diversity of their livelihood basket. The sizes of small farms could range from half an acre of homestead or terrace farm to two acres of plain irrigated field or about five acres of dryland agriculture. Though other characteristics such as choice of crops and intensity of input usage may vary among smallholders across different agro-ecologies, relative smallness in size *vis-a-vis* other farm units in the same landscape and involvement of the whole family in farming appear as universal features. Hence, we use the terms smallholders, small farmers, small-scale agriculturists or family farms interchangeably.

---

[1]For example, Hobsbawm (1973), Stokes (1978), Scott (1985), Patnaik and Dingwaney (1985), Kutty (1986), McMichael (2005) and Arnold (2005).

© Springer Nature Singapore Pte Ltd. 2019
S. Purushothaman and S. Patil, *Agrarian Change and Urbanization in Southern India*, India Studies in Business and Economics, https://doi.org/10.1007/978-981-10-8336-5_1

1.1 The Context

Nearly 85% of Indian farmers are small and marginal with operational landholding of up to two hectares depending on the agro-ecology. They produce about 40% of our food while operating on 45% of the cultivated area of the country.[2] Hence, though individually small, together they have a massive presence. About 100 million families working on 70 million hectares of land, smallholders in the country cannot be overlooked, whether as producers or consumers. Often, they are seen as unwieldy obstructions to large industrial projects, and at other times as too weak to be viable in farming.

Whether the small player in agriculture is to be encouraged (or not) is a decision that India is yet to make. The contradictions we find in policies—many schemes are coined in the name of the smallholder, but most directly or indirectly hurt them—stand testimony to this ambivalence.[3] These contradictions spell insecurity to the farm families who in turn have to explore other options to supplement their livelihoods. Thus, they form a significant portion of circular migrants to urban India's informal economy, contributing to its various sectors.

Amidst arguments for and against weaning millions of smallholders from this primary occupation, farmers' suicides have continued for more than two decades in some part of the country or the other. Despite the occasional noise made in the media, budgetary speeches, and academic literature about the continued distress of this constituency, their voice is seldom heard, and this is the case even where farmers' organisations have some say in policy lobbies. Out of both desperation and misinformation about market, technology and farming practices, farmers often inflict adversities on themselves and on their only asset—a piece of land—by compromising soil fertility and water quality. In seeking short-term profit maximisation, they take disproportionate risks, prodded by short-sighted policies and market signals.

Omnipresent but unnoticed by the mainstream society, smallholders contribute to support this populous nation's nutritional security and industrial raw materials, while moving in and out of their primary occupation. They defy existing binaries in terms of production versus consumption households, subsistence versus commercial forms of production, exclusive use of family versus hired labour, solely rural versus urban identity, as well as challenge set notions of efficiency, viability and sustainability. Yet, neither has academic literature conceptualised nor have policy frameworks recognised the unique challenges they face. The consumption-driven upper middle class across urban India, increasingly conscious about health and environment, appear to

---

[2]In 2015–16, India had 125 million (86% of total holdings) small and marginal landholders who cultivated 74 million hectares of agricultural land (47% of total operated area, Agriculture Census, 2015–16). As categorised by Agricultural Census, landholdings are of five classes: marginal (0.01–0.99 ha), small (1–1.99 ha), semi-medium (2–3.99 ha), medium (4–9.99 ha) and large (more than 10 ha).

[3]For instance, the coexistence of loan waivers declared by the State and a non-inclusive credt sector; heavy subsidisation of chemical inputs coexisting with schemes to popularise organic practices; huge public investment in irrigating rain-fed lands followed by State acquisition of the newly irrigated land for industries or infrastructure.

be oblivious of the potential contribution that small agriculturists can make towards safe and nutritious food and ecological resilience.

As a distinct, dynamic and complex socio-cultural entity, Indian family farms largely remain a reality without a conceptual framework. Having begun with an overview of the continued presence of small farmers and deliberating if and how they have changed over time, we move on to discussing notable academic approaches in use to understand and analyse this constituency and the currently relevant agrarian questions (Sects. 1.2, 1.3 and 1.4). In the penultimate Sect. 1.5, we elicit the semantics and typology of smallholders followed in this volume before sketching an outline of the study and the book in Sect. 1.6.

1.2 Peasantry to Family Farms: Persistence or Metamorphosis?

Is peasantry history? Is it persisting in some form or the other? Or has it evolved into a different socio-economic entity?[4]

From a purely subsistence venture dependent entirely on family labour and living under deprived conditions in the hinterlands as studied by Chayanov (1986 [1925]), Kautsky (1988), Georgescu-Roegen (1960) and others over time, 'peasants' morphed into units combining subsistence and profit pursuits; family and hired farm labour; and migrant and other non-farm employment. Looking at the literature on the peasantry of early twentieth century and at those on the farming community of the twenty-first century, we reckon that the 'peasant' has changed in its physical and social form while retaining several of the old features. What remains to be seen is whether this change has been beneficial or not for the small farmer constituency and the society as a whole.

Smallholders, unlike their peasant predecessors, own the land they till. They are not exploited by hefty direct taxes or rent and engage mostly, though not exclusively, family labour in farming. Though their livelihood basket is diverse, land-based production of crops and animal rearing appears integral. Thus, family farms have been trying to survive from Chayanovian times by combining varying levels of family labour, capital and technology. The characteristics persisting in family farms from those times include their relative small size, predominant use of family labour and technologies which are less capital-intensive, though farm size may not always indicate intensive use of inputs or technology. Nevertheless, most smallholders seem to lurk at the bottom of the socio-economic pyramid, with visible lack of dignity. Given the constraints faced by the landed poor to move between and within occupations and places, often they are socio-economically more deprived than the landless. As rural prosperity bypassed smallholders struggling for critical capital, their emergence as the new poor of the rural landscape and as the potential axle of agrarian movements

---

[4]We do not intend to engage with the classical peasant transition or capitalisation debate that is successfully accomplished in Lerche (2013).

has been well espoused in Gupta (1998, 2005). Wherever agriculture did not prosper, the landless were the first to migrate. Land grant schemes and, to a lesser extent, land reforms strategy enabled some landless families to join the fray as new small farmers.

This constituency, though widely present in rural India, appears diverse in character in terms of history, drivers and responses across regions. They pose a complex problem that disciplinary or ideological lenses find tough to conceptualise and difficult to ignore. If usage of the term 'peasantry' for todays small/marginal farmer sounds like a misnomer, it is not because it ceases to indicate an entity of the past (Hobsbawm 1994), but because of the connotation of 'exclusive subsistence' that the term wields. But, as Roseberry's (1982) admonition goes, despite an apparent metamorphosis, the concept of 'peasant' resists being discarded, given the continued relevance of many historical movements around it and the potential persistence of their social status. Shah and Harriss-White (2011) attempt to unveil the complexity of the present-day peasant and hint at the role of the State in hindering a conventional capitalist transition of the peasant in India. Before delving into the larger context around the status of Indian small farmers, below we present a characterisation of the Indian smallholder in todays society.

1.2.1 Indian Peasant in the Time of Commercialisation and Urbanisation

Defying conventional predictions, smallholders in India continue to exist in large numbers. This unintended reality is the result of various factors.[5] Their persistence as a class-in-itself is despite the fact that many smallholders abandoned the sector altogether and joined the army of workers producing and maintaining Indian cities. While very few small farmers scale up by ploughing in investment from other sources, the vast majority remain small farmers who are also vulnerable as consumers. **As non-farm livelihoods are uncertain and ad hoc in most places, they still have to use their access to cultivable land in order to insulate the household from food insecurity.**

This necessity to hold on to the piece of nature that they have legitimate access to becomes critical when the ever-growing and ever-changing demands of a liberalised urbanised economy push them into the fold of urban poor. Thus, 'persistence' of smallholdings is just the desperate existence in close interaction with other sectors of the economy, safeguarding their access to land in order to manage the consumption expenditures of the family amidst visible inflationary trends and increasing dependence on markets for everything.

Nutritional and health requirements and the food culture of workers in any sector of the economy depend on retaining their links with land. As a result, many, if not most, non-farm workforce also maintain partial identity as farmers—either just owning a

---

[5]Recommendations to urge smallholders abandon farming since their scale is unviable and to join the urban informal sector are not uncommon, e.g. Panagaria (2019).

1.2 Peasantry to Family Farms: Persistence or Metamorphosis?

piece of land that is left fallow, or leasing out arable land, or engaging in part-time or seasonal farming on own or leased land. It is common practice for families living in labour camps near construction sites in cities to bring food grains from their villages. Apart from this culinary connect, retaining their land and house in the village also facilitates children's schooling and provides shelter for other dependent members of the family.

Thus, far from transforming into active agents in capitalist enterprises, peasants joined the labour force in the urban informal sector partially or completely. This does not appear to be out of choice, rather an outcome of gambling with capitalisation. This counterfactual of capitalist transformation involved disproportionate financial risk in borrowing capital and adopting new technologies. There are ample examples of smallholders trying to enter the capitalist cycle, accumulating debt because of a price dip and/or crop loss, and landing the whole family in distress.[6]

Thus, reaping profits and accumulating surplus that is sufficient enough to be ploughed back for scaling up the farm or to be diverted for non-farm investment or to feed higher levels of consumption appears to be an exception rather than the norm for smallholders. Failure of smallholdings to generate adequate capital surpluses in an economy with majority of its' workers in the small-scale primary sector meant that agriculture's contribution to economic growth declined sharply, while other sectors' expanded.

Given the above circumstances, diversity within any small farm is a challenge as livelihoods have to be diversified beyond farming and related activities. Small farmers may also lease out their own land and move in and out of active farming and in and out of their native place, making diversity (e.g. livestock keeping or mushroom farming) a difficult proposition. Between seasonal crop cycles, most of them join the army of unskilled labour in non-farm sectors located usually in urban or peri-urban areas. Apart from the vagaries of the non-farm informal sector, these farm families have to survive multiple challenges—social and political marginalisation, land acquisition, volatile neoliberal markets and unpredictable climate. While attempting to switch from their primary occupation, increasing numbers of farm families end up either as urban poor or in extremely distressed rural situations. Still, as a constituency they seem to defy polarisation of any sort—whether it is in the above outcomes, or in terms of political affiliation, in practices adopted, or in the objective of agriculture pursued.

The new age agrarian normative of maximising production and profit, and ignoring agro-ecological features along with the associated traditional caution of minimising monetary risk and crop loss, triggers undue turbulence in the peasant economy. **Had all of them embraced capitalist ways of agriculture, small farms would not have persisted as they are now, as continuous pursuit of capital would have meant completely surrendering their livelihoods to gambling with the uncertainties of price and production.** Choice of non-farm livelihood options without totally dissolving the smallholding can often help farmers achieve a better balance between effort and returns. For the majority of farmers engaged in multiple activities, the

---

[6]See Ramamurthy (2011) for the caste politics dimension to such tragedies in capitalist transition.

experience has been one of a livelihood juggler, delicately balancing to survive on the brink, barely avoiding severe distress. How do we characterise such an existence of a large community? We discuss that in the following section.

1.2.2 Lower Equilibrium Among the Peasantry and Social Differentiation

Emerging from the discussion so far is the fact that persistence of smallholders in most cases does not mean prosperity or that smallholders persist without monetary incentives required in a market economy. They appear to be in lower levels of equilibria as in the downward transitions discussed in Chayanov (1986 [1925]).[7] These lower equilibria among present-day smallholders are driven by (a) increased cost of farming due to lack of access to fair markets for inputs, outputs and credit, (b) lack of technical know-how on locally suited best practices, (c) disproportionate impact of climatic variations and (d) disappearing village commons and reduced size of livestock affecting the availability of green manure and organic inputs leading to declining land productivity. These are in addition to other factors such as a general lack of dignity of farming as an occupation in a rapidly urbanising society, sectoral trade-offs adversely impacting agriculture and difficulty in discarding the identity attached to land and place.

The above-mentioned factors facilitate conditions opposite to 'involution'—a cultural-anthropological concept linked to the higher equilibria found within traditional farming as in Java (Geertz 1963). The involution process in Java was a case of increased labour intensity in wet paddies that increased output per land area without increasing output per head. With constant returns to scale for a long time, this pattern inhibits economic growth even with an increase in production per unit area. Geertz's agricultural involution referred to intensification, rather than change, by rice farmers who were driven by the demands of the Dutch rulers and internal demands due to population growth. Rice farmers persisted at higher equilibrium that was attained through changes in agro-ecology with new crops and incommensurate agricultural outcomes. Indian small farmers in general (though too vast and diverse a category to club together) persist for a long time with lower intensity of production. In India, where alien technologies made an entry amidst shrinking size of smallholdings, similar involution outcomes can be cited (Sanyal and Bhattacharya 2009; Bowles and Harriss 2010).

---

[7]Equilibrium here refers to the long-term status of peasant farms. Chayanov locates these at the intersection of satisfaction and drudgery. He discussed how the balance between satisfaction in consumption and drudgery in production is affected by family size and the ratio of working members to non-working members. Equilibrium graphs constructed for factors that were not amenable to precise measurement such as willingness to put in greater efforts and desire to maintain a constant level of well-being showed downward transition towards a lower equilibrium with more drudgery and less satisfaction.

1.2 Peasantry to Family Farms: Persistence or Metamorphosis?

If we consider the larger social scale, commercialisation can help large farms even without modern technology (Dhanagare 1983). When both commerce and technology favour large holdings and capitalist farmers, then agrarian society develops a deep cleavage with marginal, small and some of the resource strapped middle-sized holdings tending to fall far below the large and capitalist farms. Accentuating this cleavage within agrarian society is the clear urban–rural divergence in development focus. Policies, with or without explicit linkage to farming, also play a role in triggering or aiding this spatial and social differentiation pauperising smallholdings by adversely impacting agro-ecology.[8] Technological interventions without price security reinforced the continuation of lower equilibria by way of indebtedness.

Exhaustion of soil fertility and soil moisture levels have an adverse impact on not just farm output but also on the food and health security of the household. Conservation policies preventing extraction of fuelwood from forests led to the widespread use of cattle manure as fuel, depriving agricultural soils of free and valuable amendments.[9] Felling of forests for hydroelectric projects while depriving agricultural soil of such amendments also irreversibly replaced sturdy crops with input-intensive species. If these were the impacts of the two extreme cases of conservation and felling of forests, policies on non-forest commons also changed farming irreversibly. Privatisation and enclosure of non-forest village commons curtails fodder availability, thereby discouraging livestock keeping as a viable source of manure and draught power for the fields. Recent data points to such direct and indirect ecological drivers of farmer proletarianisation and out-migration in parts of re-emerging economies. Gray (2011) talks about this phenomenon in Africa, Massey et al. (2010) in Nepal and Afifi and Warner (2008) internationally.

Thus, vanishing village commons and groundwater exploitation by the resourceful (especially while catering to urban demand) along with the spread of industrial dairy and poultry farming resulted in a drastic erosion of diversity within farm holdings and farming communities. Crop cultivation now heavily dominates smallholdings that earlier raised fish, animals and birds in tandem with crops—mixed/integrated farming in today's parlance. Wherever such disempowerment of smallholdings and resultant rural-social differentiation was prevented, small farms survived, although at a lower equilibrium. The absence of institutional mechanisms that help them move beyond these lingering drawbacks binds these family farms to unsustainable reproductive conditions. Other small growers who did not have access to new technologies or resources and did not completely convert to new agricultural practices retained the ecological advantage (e.g. biodiversity and soil quality) though again at a lower equilibrium. Thus, those who saved themselves from debt, liquidity crisis, crop loss and the eventual liquidation of their land were also struggling with price fluctuations and could not increase their production levels.

---

[8]Purushothaman et al. (2012) present the diversity of policies that impact farmers.

[9]Denying access to forests and common lands across India constrained the availability of grazing areas, farmyard manure and fuelwood for smallholdings. *Soppinabettas* of hilly regions of Karnataka (Purushothaman and Dharmarajan 2005) is a case in point.

Unlike purely accumulation-oriented enterprises that are relatively easy to scale up, a small farm as production unit is an *in situ* composite of diverse elements of nature, culture, occupations and social institutions. As a complex mode of production by, for and of the masses, it defies both the need for and feasibility of scaling up, while continuing to be an integral part of the economy.

A more recent discussion is on feminisation of small farms resulting mainly from out-migration of men in search of jobs—also a manifestation of the persisting lower equilibria.[10] Primarily responsible for fetching water and fuelwood, and preparing and serving food for the family and guests, women of farm families have been ecologically better informed. This intimate understanding of ecology needed for agriculture is being swept away in the flood of new crops, varieties and technologies amidst lack of information on their impacts and required precautions. This so far has not been argued convincingly in the literature any further than the socio-economic dimensions (Agarwal 1995; Pattnaik et al. 2017). Nonetheless, family farms stand as the last frontier of knowledge, skills and culture attuned to specific agro-ecologies. **If integrated into the mainstream economy without damaging the local social–ecological fabric, their adaptive potential, currently lying unnoticed behind the lower equilibria, holds promise for a metamorphosis of the rural society, shedding old prejudices and amalgamating social progress on multiple scales.**

Having brought out the complexities that characterise the smallholder and the context of their persistence, we turn next to notable academic approaches towards this constituency.

1.3 Agrarian Frameworks and Family Farms in India

Agrarian literature from India is rich in sociological, anthropological and economic analysis of peasant societies. These studies treat peasants as a broad group, engaged primarily in agriculture with mostly family labour and production for subsistence, though wage labour and commercial production are not completely ruled out by many. In fact, the body of the literature on agrarian frameworks for the Indian context is comparable to the peasant studies that came out of Eastern Europe and Russia in the late nineteenth and early twentieth centuries.

Many of them, though anchored in a specific disciplinary domain and/or an ideological school, do not shy away from adopting other approaches in social sciences to validate their arguments. Notable among these are Epstein (1973), Dhanagare (1983), Thorner (1982), Harriss-White (2012) and Patnaik (1990) among others. They elucidate what went on in the peasant societies in different parts of pre- and early independent India and provided theoretical explanations. Showcasing conflicting views about pro-peasant arguments, together they fall short of unpacking the

---

[10]Recent study by National Institution for Transforming India (NITI Aayog) indicates a reversal of feminisation (Chand et al. 2017). But in rain-fed areas with huge circular migration, the reversal anyway did not happen, resulting in feminisation of agrarian distress (Pattnaik et al. 2017).

entire complexity of the most common agricultural entity in today's India. A critical volume of work found around production relations and tenancy arrangements in feudal India (Mukhia 2008; Omvedt 1981; Basole and Basu 2011a, b; Patnaik 1990) does not fully disentangle the complexity of the Indian smallholder. Also, despite such an abundance of the literature around peasant exploitation, given the way agro-social relations have been changing in the neoliberal era, their contemporary relevance is questionable.

Widespread oral leasing between landless and smallholders and reverse leasing of smallholdings by the resourceful are now common. Though land rights are more transparent in most parts of urbanising India, smallholders continue at the bottom of the social pyramid for want of options for either scaling up farming or moving out for good, except when forced evictions happen.[11] We try to disambiguate this complex identity in the context of conspicuous changes happening along the gradients of urbanisation and agro-ecology.

Given the options available to the landless and smallholders, the former seem to have more flexibility in availing farm and non-farm labour employment. Leasing arrangements between smallholders and the landless, or between smallholders who migrate and those who do not, often take the form of equal sharing of cost and produce, avoiding exploitative monopoly rent. Agricultural census or other official records may not show these multiple modes of land leasing since formal tenancy has been officially abolished, and these arrangements lack formal agreements.[12] This is not to ignore the corporate contract farms that may resemble the exploitative tenancy of feudal times, but with the landowner as the exploited. In any lease arrangement made exclusively for commercial purpose, rent seeking behaviour of the tenant could adversely impact the long-term productivity of the farm.

The gaps hitherto left unattended by agrarian literature include those pertaining to ecological aspects and institutional dynamics. The next two sections provide a brief general review of the literature on peasant farming from these two perspectives, before an in-depth examination of the literature on the Indian family farmer in the next chapter.

1.3.1 Indifference to Ecological Concerns

Farming unlike most production processes and livelihood options is *directly* dependent on nature. Hence, a healthy agro-ecosystem in terms of quality of soil, water and biodiversity of the production landscape determines the security of farming as a livelihood option. For a small family farm, despite the small size, nature is more than

---

[11] Estimates show that since India's independence, 42 million people have been displaced in different development projects and 60% of them were farmers. Fernandes (1999), Roy (1999) and Kothari (1996) dwell upon development-induced displacement in India.

[12] NITI Aayog is proposing a model act to legalise land leasing for agriculture. Discussion paper on the proposed lease law can be found here—http://niti.gov.in/writereaddata/files/document_publication/NITIBlog2_VC.pdf.

a means of production. It embodies values beyond the utilitarian—values that are difficult to capture in the use and non-use values that environmental economics attribute for 'provisioning' and 'cultural' services offered by farmlands. These environmental values and services should have urged farmers to take up sustainable practices. However, more often than not, they fail to do so. This apparent paradox of a dearth of sustainability consciousness among nature-dependant farmers can be attributed to many factors.

Farmers' approach to farming is dictated by what is happening in the rest of society—in terms of uncertainties in farming along with the rural–urban and farm–nonfarm divergence. Also notable is the divergence among farmers in their approach to sustainability. Different farmers have different objectives that could be either to maximise or sustain family income per unit area or to sustain farm livelihood in the long term. If the farming community appears to have mutually divergent objectives in farming, policy strategies generally emphasise only one of the many objectives of farming—short-term profit. The non-farming, non-rural section of the population pulls the financial, academic and policy levers in the direction of short-term profits, overlooking other equally relevant objectives.

Lack of concern about agro-ecology in today's society needs to be contrasted with the urban adoration for charismatic wildlife, its hypocritical engagement with climate change discourse, and its emergent concern about food safety and health. We just saw that policy thrust on short-term profit and societal ambivalence together managed to ignore agro-ecology and to worship profit as the motive in farming. Thus, ecological destruction of vast production landscapes went unnoticed as a burgeoning population of non-rural consumers, who prefer to avoid soiling their hands, continued to demand cheap staples and 'high-value' farm products.[13] Health concerns are now inducing urban consumers to gradually turn towards safe food, thereby nurturing certified green corporate units with commercial origins in distant places. This concern of consumers is yet to be translated as a perceivable signal to family farms for engaging in sustainable practices.

More alarming than the ecological indifference and ignorance of an urbanising consumerist society is the missing focus of ecological concerns in the avalanche of the literature in agrarian social sciences, agricultural economics and even in core agricultural sciences. When we look at early Marxian deliberations on agrarian relations, we see that agro-ecological arguments are scanty. *Capital* refers to the impact of industrial agricultural development on soil fertility (Vol. 1, Part 4, Chap. 15, Sect. 10), but as is known, it does not celebrate the merit of small family farms. Agricultural economics does not internalise the long-term social–ecological costs of managing a farm purely for short-term profits and hails economies of scale. Ellis (1993) addresses some of the ignored dimensions in agricultural economics such as the relationship to environmental resources, but most others (Goodwin 1997; Subba Reddy et al. 2012 for instance) choose to overlook these as if the economics of agriculture has nothing to do with the health of soil, water or biodiversity.

---

[13] 'High value' here generally refers to the exotic and input-intensive nature of the produce, apart from steeper prices relative to traditional local products.

1.3 Agrarian Frameworks and Family Farms in India

Sociological and anthropological studies explicitly linking ecological elements to agrarian socio-economic issues (e.g. Vasavi 1999) stop short of projecting such inter-linkages as central to agrarian livelihoods. However, we do recognise the existence of such literature in the international academic world (a significant body of scholarship on the agro-ecological dimension, including that on the metabolic rift that Marx gestures at—Altieri 2002; Moore 2000; Schneider and McMichael 2010; IAASTD 2009 etc.), as well as Indian popular literature on the deterioration of agro-ecological fabric (e.g. Shiva 2015).

A bibliometric analysis of agricultural research in the country at the graduate and doctoral level over a period of five years reveals a meagre 8% of content related to agro-ecology.[14] There are as many as 89 organisations under Indian Council of Agricultural Research (ICAR) and National Agricultural Innovation Project. Five journals published by the Indian Council of Agricultural Research also show similar coverage of ecological topics in the same five-year period. In the field of agrarian social sciences and agricultural sciences, respectively, on the other hand over the same period, 39 and 24% of articles with some ecological content appeared in three major peer-reviewed international journals.[15]

In the next chapter, we critique selected literature from both within and outside India to showcase the ecological indifference highlighted in this section, while acknowledging the few that actually engage with this concern. While ecological indifference in the society at large could be a result of institutional and cultural changes in an urbanising society, the same in science and policy implies lack of responsibility towards agrarian reality.

1.3.2 Institutional Vacuum

Economic systems are founded on formal and informal institutions. If we accept that small family farms are a distinct economic entity, but different from exclusively capitalist firms (Chayanov 1986 [1925]; Georgescu-Roegen 1960), then institutional considerations appear inevitable for a meaningful discourse of their changing character.

Institutions around farming should be dynamic and adaptive so as to cope with new challenges that emerge from changing economic conditions, social relations and technology. Established social norms could prevent harsh distress among vulnerable smallholders in times of food inflation, climate variability and volatile agricultural markets. Dynamic agrarian social institutions can prevent the permanent crossing over of vulnerable farm families to the class of landless footloose labour.[16] These

---

[14]Based on information from the Indian National Agricultural Research System for the period from 2010 to 2014.

[15]The *Journal of Peasant Studies* and *Journal of Agrarian Change* were chosen for agrarian social sciences and *Agricultural Systems* for agricultural sciences.

[16]Needless to say, here we refer to normative agricultural institutions (e.g. customary sharing of seed, labour and information; food and fodder banks, etc.), while acknowledging the discriminatory

include institutions that nurture agricultural improvements through experimentation and evaluation of locally suitable farm practices to ensure availability of inputs and food produce for the needy. Agricultural skilling of a community is an ongoing process through such shared, collective and continuous process. Stone (2007) finds deskilling the key reason for the distress caused by wide spread adoption of BT cotton in Telangana.

At present, for most small farmers, the choice seems to be between either being somewhat less poor for a short while by exclusively catering to the market but bankrupt/proletariat in the long run, or being less rich than potentially possible in the short run by sustainably surviving above the poverty line in the long term. Both these options involve engagement with non-farm options and hence possession of skills other than farming. The second option of sustainable survival excludes maximisation of capital accumulation but does not rule out capital formation altogether and in fact might allow for varying peaks of accumulation over time.

Possessing non-farm skills helps to avoid being trapped in farming for various reasons, despite vulnerabilities (for instance, see involution in Sect. 1.2.2), and staying or moving out of farming becomes an informed choice. For those millions of farm holdings that continue to engage in small farming as their major occupation, land provides access to basic entitlements as envisaged in their choice of sustainable survival. Occupational migration in such a situation will then be decided by the availability of new and preferred choices instead of a transition towards pauperisation. An analysis of the role of various institutions in enabling sustainable choices for small farms is missing in agrarian academics.

The institution here includes collective know-how to ensure that farming is free from occupational hazards (e.g. exposure to hazardous chemicals and unviable financial commitments) and to understand how new technologies can be collectively evaluated for social–ecological impacts. In the absence of informal norms and institutions, evaluative community interactions on farming will not happen, resulting in the downward loop of deskilling and undue risk-taking.

If smallholders had a say in the technology that is being developed supposedly for them, would they have asked for different ones? Why is it that while, in general, there is huge budgetary support for formal agricultural science, time tested traditional agricultural knowledge is left to the mercy of voluntary organisations? Is it possible to craft new agrarian social institutions to tackle this anomaly? If so, how do we prevent discriminatory tendencies? Such possibilities are unexplored by agrarian academics. Agricultural science and technology often get caught in a self-serving mode (research for its own sake) without small farmers or agrarian relations in their sight.[17]

---

and exploitative institutions of tenancy, bonded labour and untouchability as hallmarks of feudal agricultural societies.

[17] For instance, *raita teerpu* (Farmers' Jury) conducted in Karnataka during 2009, critiqued agricultural research for not taking into account farmers' concerns http://www.raitateerpu.com/documents/and_the_verdict%20is_.pdf.

Even while acknowledging the tentativeness involved in any generalisation of farmers' responses arising from the trade-offs involved in their choices, as also due to the divergence in farmers' objectives that we came across earlier in the chapter, crafting appropriate institutions for adaptive agrarian skilling is discerned to serve the cause of producers and consumers alike.

The institutional lacunae found in agrarian literature urge us to look at how institutional economics deals with such contexts. The concerns of Old Institutional Economics (Commons 1957, building on Veblen) regarding the internal and external challenges that trigger institutional changes remains to be explored in the context of the small farm constituency. External challenges arising out of economic growth in terms of market relations and technology and internal challenges arising from the problems and conflicts of interest between different types of small farms constitute the much-needed institutional queries in a changing social–ecological scenario.

1.3.3 Approaching an Integrated Frame

Incorporating institutional imperatives and ecological prudence while discussing the diverse and interwoven aspects of smallholder farming is rare. Whatever limited progress has been made towards an integrative analysis comes largely from anthropological literature, whereas agricultural sciences and economics appear to have contributed the least. Does this imply that agricultural sciences in its preoccupation with researching highly resource-intensive technology considers the conceptualisation of family farms an academically obsolete or infeasible pursuit? Our effort here is to showcase the extent of trans-disciplinary academic expeditions possible in the agrarian domain.

Macroeconomic statistics of production, procurement, food and input subsidies, exports, and research investment may indicate the growth status of the agricultural sector, but do not reveal the institutional drivers behind distress in family farms. These drivers may not emerge from a disaggregated analysis—perhaps of regional/micro-scale case studies—unless the data goes beyond numbers of production, productivity and profit.[18] Perhaps, the '*political economy of uncaring*' lamented by Vasavi (2012), apart from the blindness of macroeconomic frameworks towards non-capitalistic realities (Sanyal 2007) on the ground, is responsible for this. Thus, if agriculture is being judged only by profit without the voices and plight of collective institutions involved, family farms may be totally absent in any societal vision.

If economics fails the institutional needs of smallholders, other agrarian theories, in their objective and focused historical efforts to segregate 'demons' and 'victims' (in terms of land, class and capital), overlook peasantry as 'people'. Interestingly, the

---

[18] A country-level subsectoral analysis of Indian agriculture spanning 27 volumes, titled 'State of the Indian farmer' (CSDS 2014), talks about the 'sector' than the farmers, farm holdings or farm families. Based on data gathered from various sources (that actually mention ecological impacts and sustainability concerns), it recommends measures like intensive irrigation, without engaging with their long-term impacts.

question of small farmers as families can circumvent the subordination of long-term public 'good' by short-term private profit and societal food security. While avoiding a static identity, this will also allow the movement of families towards and out of small farm holdings as a partial or exclusive livelihood option.

While standard economics would not find such an approach tenable, those from history, sociology, anthropology and political sciences are preoccupied with binaries and dichotomous tensions over land, capital and class. Thus, agrarian academics appear uncomfortable with the blurring and merging of boundaries within and between the socio-political classes and nature. Ecologists, still preoccupied with protected areas, find the smallness of family farms unworthy of their attention—conservation objectives appear threatened in a social–ecological system consisting of too many smallholdings.

Keeping in mind the above mismatch between academics and the complex reality of family farms, and the fact that the latter cannot be a monolithic uniform entity, we gravitate towards Georgescu-Roegen's argument that there are cross-cutting strengths among the smallholders like efficiency in input–output conversion. Nonetheless, he cautions that energy efficiency by itself may not imply or explain the existence of ecologically conscious small-scale cultivators. Small farms, taken all together, can be significant contributors to the environmental concerns arising from negative externalities of modern farming (health hazards from residues of synthetic fertilisers and pesticides as well as that of salinisation caused by intensive irrigation).

Nevertheless, a large number of non-capitalist subsistence smallholdings are adhering to ecologically sensible practices. This is facilitated by the availability of the required biomass, know-how, culinary preferences, and health concerns. Relatively, these may be more resilient to market volatility, as all their risks are not solely addressed by farming and they may not have entailed huge monetary obligations. Thus, unlike exclusively capital oriented holdings, these dual-purpose small units could persist longer despite the absence of real incentives and with temporary suspension of farm operations during adversities. Facilitating agencies, local networks, and institutions, that generate positive social capital for information sharing and skilling, as also for rural food security, help them tide over climatic, market and labour crises.

1.4 Agrarian Questions in Twenty-First-Century India

Given that agricultural skills and agrarian institutions are vanishing, will the first half of the twenty-first century be known for the disappearance of family farms in India? This could very well be the overarching question on agrarian change. This disturbing question, along with the diversity and persistence of family farms despite adversities, was the primary motivation for this study.

1.4 Agrarian Questions in Twenty-First-Century India

Complexity

The varying size and components among the large number of family farms, the diverse nature of their drivers, the varied impacts of land reforms, green revolution and economic liberalisation on them, along with their varying colonial–post colonial past—all of these make the Indian small farmer a uniquely complex constituency to explore. Yet, it may appear unrealistically normative to think of an integrative frame in the manner elaborated in the previous section where social–ecological changes as well as livelihoods have equal and connected stakes. This book is an integrative endeavour in approaching the complexity of small farms of different regions in the context of invasive urbanisation.

Open questions, contradictions and trade-offs

There are obvious questions nested within the overarching aim of the book. Looking at the uncertain future of family farms amidst pervasive urbanisation processes, we ask the questions—When do families opt to continue in small farming as an occupation? When do they decide to move out? What determines both these transitions? Given the significant presence of smallholders, the ecological questions appear to be twofold—(i) sustainability of smallholdings for food, livelihood, health and cultural identity of farmers and (ii) food and ecological security and welfare of the society as a whole. With the continued persistence of smallholdings despite non-declining distress among farmers, addressing these questions could inform possible ways of synergising economic growth with prosperity in small farms so that rural welfare objectives can be harmonised with development objectives.

The conflicts between the welfare and development objectives are manifested, according to Vasavi (2012) in (a) agricultural growth rates propped up by the 'expertocracy'—missions, commissions and reports; (b) policies devoid of democratic scrutiny[19] and (c) State-level interventions and populist schemes without conceptualising the role of smallholdings. As State interventions rarely take into account the nuances of the social fabric, and when they do it is entirely based on statistical estimates at larger scales, it is no surprise that farming as livelihood and as a way of life remains disjointed from the big budget policies around research, technology and credit that successive governments introduce.

Increase in public expenditure for new technologies continues to chase new seeds, fertilisers, pump sets, bore wells, etc., while expenditure on State procurement of agricultural produce is declining with liberal imports and scanty investment in crafting suitable institutions. The mere integration of small farm economy with larger macroeconomic changes may not completely accomplish the integration of welfare and development objectives. Vulnerability is reinforced through skewed distribution of resources (land, water and capital), exploitative agrarian relations, economic and political marginalisation, and ecologically harmful technology (Vasavi 1999).

---

[19]For instance, the way in which Knowledge Initiative in Agriculture and Biotechnology Regulatory Authority bill came into being has been criticised for complete absence of transparency and democratic process (Kuruganti 2008).

Another trade-off that we need to consider, apart from the welfare versus development one that we just mentioned, is the one between the micro and macro scales. The effort here is to see how the micro can be linked with the macro—this in itself is a challenging task, mainly because standard models of both development and small-scale farming may not be able to establish linkages with the multiple lived realities of farmers. We recognise that trying not to miss both 'the wood' and 'the tree' (the farm and food economies at the global scale on the one hand and the small-scale agriculturist on the other hand) is a major challenge. In order to keep important agrarian concerns within sight, we may need to zoom in and out of smallholdings linking them to agricultural economy at a larger scale as and when needed.

Imperatives in engaging with small family farms

Merely debating over the above trade-offs can gloss over the issue that farm families grapple with—meeting basic welfare needs. In times of high food inflation and low farm gate prices, the kind of market-driven farming that is undertaken with or without the guidance of local agricultural officials but guided invariably by the local input trader-cum-money lender as 'forced commerce' (Bhaduri 1986) gives no guarantee for adequacy in quantity and quality of food availability, health care and education for the farm family. If the family holds a below poverty line (BPL) card, then the Public Distribution System (PDS) may provide partial food security (without meeting nutritional and cultural needs). This dependence imparts legitimacy to public expenditure in food imports, and ironically, in the process it destabilises the very same 'forced commerce' that smallholders were persuaded into.

Apart from the 'triviality' of primary food producers themselves suffering from food insecurity, distress in small farms also has wide economic repercussions. Family farms supply quality workforce and generate sustained demand for consumer goods and services from other sectors. Taking the small agriculturist seriously can thus serve the economy, while catering to rural well-being and the production ecosystem. Even a century after Chayanov's analysis of prerevolution Russia and Scott's (1998) depiction of West Africa showing the peasant as an independent dual entity as producer–consumer, this does not find a worthy place in any conceptual treatment of Indian agrarian sector.

As we saw in Sect. 1.1, for most smallholders, cultivating their small piece of land is important for various reasons including available skill sets and inherited values. Smallholder families, engaged mostly in low-income non-farm occupations, generally lease their land out or do sharecropping. Even for them, this link to land is crucial and reassuring both for supplementing income and food and for reproducing the identity of farmer, place and kinship. **It is not really necessary to maximise surplus production from unit area of land in either of the above two cases (of partial and of significant engagement in farming). Hence, in such smallholder communities with unambiguous land rights, the agrarian question moves away from land, capital and class to the needs of food, identity, occupational choice and living environment.**

When rural agriculture takes on an exclusive commercial focus, one of the possible outcomes is distress, manifested as turbulence in the personal and social lives of farmers 'when collective social reproduction of the society is made subordinate to individual economic production' as noted by Vasavi (1999) on Bidar, Karnataka. This is an instance where the expected invisible potential of markets to work towards a larger common good fails to serve the food, ecological and livelihood security of the farming community in the short run and weakens the societal fabric in the long term. Farmers in many parts of rural India fall prey to socio-psychological disorders leading to conflicts within and between families and communities.[20]

Lastly, strictly speaking from an agro-ecosystems' perspective, it may be ideal to have larger and fewer farms that are biodiverse and sustainable in their practices and input use. In reality, when land and agricultural landscapes are viewed as production machines for feeding the conspicuous urban consumption and infinite profit seeking of the neoliberal economy, large farms tend to be ecologically blind reinforcing the trade-off with cultural diversity, distributional equity and relative economic efficiency.

Recognising the variation among people and geographies, the emerging central tenet is that family farms will continue to be necessary for the society at large. Nonetheless, we cannot be presumptuous about their productivity in terms of land and labour. **If numerous small farms behave unsustainably, we need to look for the causes originating in institutional gaps and failures leading to the skewed distribution of skills, capital and science.[21] However, we contest the notion that own land, labour and capital are the only relevant means of production for them. Village commons, self-enterprise and informal institutions are equally necessary.** This argument forecloses certain ways of thinking like perfect substitutability between resources needed by each farm and that well-being of small farms lies in gambling in distant and uncertain markets.

1.5 Semantics and Typology

Thinking about family farms, we imagine a landholding not too large for a small-scale farm nor too small for a production unit that is appropriate for any region and can handle the diversity of farm components. The typology of peasantry in the literature includes three categories: (1) Chayanov's (1986 [1925]) categorisation according to their transition paths—downward, upward, differentiation, levelling and upward with levelling[22]; (2) forms of peasant production characterised by Friedman (1980) as independent household production, sharecropping and a form that combines the first two; (3) Bharadwaj's (1985) categorisation into (a) very small cultivators includ-

---

[20]Based on a rural psychological analysis of farmer suicides, Nagthan et al. (2011) brings forth the primacy of indebtedness leading to personal stress and intra-family conflicts.

[21]These factors, especially institutional gaps, contribute to extractive behaviour than the financial impatience of the poor reflected in high discount rates referred to in economics.

[22]Transition in terms of drudgery of production and satisfaction of consumption mentioned in Chayanov, noted in foot note 7.

18   1 Contemporary Agrarian Questions—An Introduction

ing the landless/deficit households; (b) small cultivators who produce just enough for subsistence; (c) medium cultivators with enough surplus and responding to market stimuli; and (d) cultivators with substantial surplus, setting the conditions of exchange.

Among the possible vocabulary emerging from the above—peasant, middle peasant, petty commodity producer, small-scale farmer, etc.,—'agriculturist' seems to be the closest to our imagination (depicted in Sect. 1.1), imbibing a range of identities from the 'peasant' (subsistence oriented producer) to 'farmer' (market oriented producer), and excluding the large holders working exclusively for surplus and accumulation. The terms—small farmer, family farms or peasant—used in this book invariably refer to those families engaged in farming with or without other occupations alongside, producing both for the family and the market, using mostly family labour, but occasionally hiring wage labour as needed. **In summary, our target constituency is the family farm in contemporary India, engaging in primary production to feed both the market and the family, using both traditional and modern practices, and possessing a dynamic livelihood basket while continuing to uphold farming as the primary occupation.**

With varying relative relevance across global geographies, presently we find coexistence of the 'peasant' in the Chayanovian sense with the small and middle peasant of Lenin's Russia as well as the rural proletariat in Marxian typology. Certain distinct features of these constituencies seem to have partially merged into what can now be identified as 'small farmer' holdings, whose average scale of operation depends on the agro-ecological context. We identified smallholdings in different agro-ecologies based on what makes the farmer a small player using relative per capita land operated, proportion of family labour and proportion of marketed surplus, as the criteria.

How can we describe and predict changes in and impacts on such small farm(er)s while taking into account their strengths, weaknesses as well as overlaps, contradictions and synergies with others in the sector (as well as in other sectors)? This question is debated in the book, based on a field study in the State of Karnataka during 2013–17.

1.6 Organisation of the Book

Accepting the facts of continued significance, increasing diversity and complexity (such as objectives, scale and development trade-off) of smallholders in this introductory chapter, in the following chapters we examine the repercussion of the ecological–institutional gaps in the study sites. We adopt a framework wherein agrarian economy lies embedded in the social–ecological system of a production landscape. **In other words, this book is not about boosting the growth of the agricultural economy; rather, it explores how and when agriculture can be a sustainable option in the small farmers' livelihood basket, while catering to the welfare needs of the society. That said, this book is also not about going back to a rustic peasant life of basic subsistence; rather, it acknowledges the fact that more and more smallholders are joining the twin club of partial or ex-peasants and a floating**

1.6 Organisation of the Book

labour force. It is about re-envisioning the conditions necessary for fair and sustainable ways of peasant reproduction, moving beyond the fetishism of accumulation of land/capital or the exploitation of labour. This requires an adaptable approach that bridges agrarian theories with ground reality to reveal the central facets of family farms in times of urbanisation driven by economic growth.

A conceptual first step in this chapter has been to use Chayanovian pathways in order to link frameworks from economics (e.g. Georgescu-Roegen 1960) to ecology (e.g. Toledo 1989). This instils confidence in the following assumptions: (a) both ecological and human resources in small farms, as well as the occupation itself are significant, though this does not imply a permanent or exclusive affiliation to farming and (b) long-term functionality of family farms can ensure livelihood and subsistence security with cultural compatibility, when non-farm options are ad hoc in the short run and skill dependent in the long run.

Chapter 2 (Family Farms in Agrarian Literature: A Critique) is devoted to a more detailed discussion on specific literature on family farms, keeping in view the major gaps—ecological and institutional—identified here, in this chapter.

Having described the constituency and identifyingied the research needs, Chap. 3 (Study Approach, Processes and Methods) sketches the conceptualisation and process adopted for the three-year-long (April 2013 to July 2016) field study. It includes the rationale for selection of study sites and respondents and juxtaposes the study sites in a typology of the peri-urban interface. Major analytical approaches looking at social networks, local discourses and archival materials are also explained in this chapter.

Chapter 4 (Agrarian Ecology and Society in the Study Regions—A Historical Perspective). The interplay of ecology, society and governance in the persistence, sustainability and/or transition of farm families is an interesting story. Connecting this story with contemporary market reality will help us take a closer look at how primary producers became consumers in two historical regions different in not just agro-ecology but more so in the history of governance and the society. It lays the ecological–historical context including that of domestication and spread of crops. The chapter attempts to link this with the co-evolutionary patterns in crops raised, dietary habits, etc., while tracing policies and governance around land, urbanisation, food and agriculture in the two regions.

Gleaning from a large canvas of historical information, this chapter reveals the political ecological backdrop of societies in the study sites. It reveals how the patterns of landownership and agriculture changed over time across social groups in the two contrasting study regions. Later on, as neoliberal economic policies unfolded, the regions diverged further in the power-play within their social categories, consumption habits and culture.

Chapter 5 (Agriculture in the Era of Urbanisation) introduces the recent status of agriculture and agrarian society in India and the State of Karnataka. The discussion starts with secondary data on urbanisation, agriculture, farm holdings and farmers and includes a general picture of peri-urban life—land use, water, occupations and migration. It then discusses perceptions from systematic group interactions conducted to finalise the study sites.

The next four chapters (Chaps. 6–9) present the results of the empirical study conducted in four sites (selected by the process described in Chap. 3) and are the foundation of our arguments. These chapters focus on the changing status of small farmers in the backdrop of urbanisation unfolding in their vicinity. Each of the four chapters contains context-specific deliberations on the linkage between small family farms and the social–political–economic contexts that support or hinder their existence. The chapters are essentially built on primary data and narratives collected from individual interactions with farmers and farmer migrants. This site-specific chapterisation helps us weave a bottom-up pattern of drivers and causes of vulnerability among family farms. Apart from analysing changes in farmers' lives based on individual interviews in each site, they also look at social networks, gender, migration and markets specifically and briefly.

Chapter 6 (The City and the Peasant: Family Farms Around Bengaluru) introduces the first study site located in the peripheries of the metropolitan city of Bangalore. The physical, social and economic details of small farms dotting the outskirts of the urban sprawl are revealed here. Peri-urban farming around Bangalore is notable for stretches of eucalyptus and polyhouses with high-value flowers and vegetables in different directions. Constantly dealing with the pull and push from the city's neoliberal character, the opportunities and challenges facing small farmers find place here in a balanced overview of Bangalore's impacts. While the city's neoliberal character poses several pressures on these peripheries, these farms also take advantage of easy access to non-farm opportunities without giving-up agriculture, and alternate production practices for safe food in response to nascent trends in urban consumption. Multiple challenges and opportunities in the margins of a megacity together weave the nature of farmers who will sustain their professions in the future.

Chapter 7 (Farming Farms Around Ramanagara). Without being a fast-growing city, smaller towns foster a different kind of relationship with farmers in their vicinity. Generally, these towns may be historically significant in some way or the other—as an army base of the colonial or precolonial times or hosting a large-scale industry, and the like. Small towns exhibit the dual character of a rural centre and the economic pull of a city in the making. Old traditions of sericulture and new trends of fruit crops coexist in the periphery of the small town of Ramanagara. How this helps farmers in its periphery and how they fare relative to farmers in other urban peripheries is a fascinating story.

Chapter 8 (Agricultural Urbanism: Family Farms Around Mandya). Urbanisation in this study site is unique in that it facilitates both forward and backward linkages with local production systems. In the locales of Mandya, the interdependency of agrarian livelihoods with local enterprises and industries (sugarcane for production of sugar and jaggery, coconut for oil extraction, paddy for rice mills and mulberry for sericulture) is a characteristic feature.

Based on the experiences of family farms in this region, this chapter highlights the possibilities of integrating farm livelihoods into the urbanisation process without completely hampering the socio-cultural and ecological fabric of the place that is aided by formal and informal institutions and strategies. The chapter advocates a regional agricultural economy for less inequitable development in line with the discussion on regional agricultural economy in Purushothaman and Patil (2017).

Chapter 9 (Family Farms in Yadgir District). Although no part of Karnataka is untouched by urbanisation, remote towns by themselves impact farming slowly and differently. Farms located in the hinterlands face different challenges compared to their counterparts in more urbanised regions. Yadgir, located in north-east Karnataka, is one such remote region characterised by the coexistence of dryland stretches of pulses and cotton with vast and expanding patches of irrigated paddy. This chapter presents both the advantages and disadvantages that this dual farming system poses for small farmers in the interior agrarian regions in terms of changes in formal and informal institutions, farming practices, agro-ecology and occupations.

Chapter 10 (Withering Family Farms) serves the twin purpose of summarising key learning from previous chapters and distilling the key messages including the future of family farms in Karnataka, amidst growing number of expanding cities.

The book broadly tries to address the questions: Are we seeing a metamorphosis or disappearance of the peasant? How is socio-cultural transition keeping pace with the changing alignment between landownership and social categories in different agro-ecologies? How does this pattern influence farming, food and cultures that contribute to agrarian welfare in an era of neoliberal economy and urbanisation? Based on the answers and insights from the study in Karnataka, the book hopes to inform the debate on whether smallholders as a 'class-in-itself' will continue and transform without being a 'class-for-itself'.[23] This will give a clear message on why it is imperative to strive for sustainable family farms, and establish that it is necessary to go beyond their inevitable persistence amidst pretentious societal altruism.

References

Afifi, T., & Warner, K. (2008). *The impact of environmental degradation on migration flows across countries* (UNU-EHS Working Paper No. 5).

Agarwal, B. (1995). *A field of one's own: Gender and land rights in South Asia*. Cambridge University Press.

Altieri, M. (2002). Agroecology: The science of natural resource management for poor farmers in marginal environments. *Agriculture, Ecosystems & Environment, 93*, 1–24.

Annon (2014). *State of Indian farmers*. Centre for the Study of Developing Societies.

Arnold, D. (2005). Agriculture and 'improvement' in early colonial India: A pre-history of development. *Journal of Agrarian Change*, 505–525.

Basole, A., & Basu, D. (2011a). Relation of production and mode of surplus extraction in India: Part I—Agriculture. *Economic & Political Weekly, 41*(14), 41–58.

Basole, A., & Basu, D. (2011b). Relation of production and mode of surplus extraction in India: Part II—Informal industry. *Economic & Political Weekly, 41*(15), 63–79.

Bhaduri, A. (1986). Forced commerce and agrarian growth. *World Development, 14*(2), 267–272.

Bharadwaj, K. (1985). A view on commercialisation in India agriculture and the development of capitalism. *The Journal of Peasant Studies, 12*(4), 7–25.

---

[23]Following Marx's observation of urban proletariat first becoming a class-in-itself by mutually sharing grievances before standing together for themselves against the capitalists.

Bowles, P., & Harriss, J. (2010). *Globalisation and labour in China and India: Impacts and responses*. New York: Palgrave Macmillan.

Chand, R., Srivastava, S., & Singh, J. (2017). *Changing structure of rural economy of India: Implications for employment and growth* (Discussion Paper). NITI Aayog. Retrieved March 7, 2018, from http://niti.gov.in/writereaddata/files/document_publication/Rural_Economy_DP_final.pdf.

Chayanov, A. (1986 [1925]). *The theory of peasant economy*. Madison: University of Wisconsin Press.

Dhanagare, D. (1983). *Peasant movements in India 1920–50*. Delhi: Oxford University Press.

Ellis, F. (1993). *Peasant economics: Farm households in agrarian development*. Cambridge University Press.

Epstein, S. (1973). *South India: Yesterday, today and tomorrow*. London: Macmillan.

Fernandes, W. (1999, November). Displacement: What is all the fuss about? *Humanscape*.

Friedman, H. (1980). Household production and the national economy: Concepts for the analysis of agrarian formations. *The Journal of Peasant Studies, 7*, 158–184.

Geertz, C. (1963). *Agricultural involution*. University of California Press.

Georgescu-Roegen, N. (1960). Economic theory and agrarian economics. *Oxford Economic Papers, 12*(1).

Goodwin, J. (1997). *Agricultural economics*.

Gray, C. (2011). Soil quality and human migration in Kenya and Uganda. *Global Environmental Change, 21*(2), 421–430.

Gupta, A. (1998). *Postcolonial development: Agriculture in the making of modern India*. Durham, NC: Duke University Press.

Gupta, D. (2005). Whither the Indian village: Culture and agriculture in rural India. *Economic and Political Weekly, 40*(8), 751–758.

Harriss-White, B. (2012). Capitalism and the common man: Peasant and petty production in Africa and South Asia. *Agrarian South: Journal of Political Economy, 1*(2), 109–160.

Hobsbawm, E. (1973). Peasants and politics. *Journal of Peasant Studies, 1*(1), 3–22.

Hobsbawm, E. (1994). *Age of extremes: The short twentieth century 1914–1991*. London: Michael Joseph.

Kautsky, K. (1988). *The agrarian question* (Vol. 1). Zwan Publications.

Kothari, S. (1996). Whose nation? The displaced as victim of development. *Economic and Political Weekly*.

Kuruganti, K. (2008). Targeting regulation in Indian agriculture. *Economic and Political Weekly, 43*(48).

Kutty, K. (1986). *Peasantry in India*. Abhinav Publications.

Lerche, J. (2013). The agrarian question in neoliberal India: Agrarian transition bypassed? *Journal of Agrarian Change, 13*(3), 382–404.

Massey, D., Axinn, W., & Ghimire, D. (2010). Environmental change and out-migration: Evidence from Nepal. *Population Environment, 32*(2), 109–136.

Mclntyre, B. D., Herren, H. R., Wakhungu, J., & Watson, R. T. (Eds). (2009). *Agriculture at a crossroads: Synthesis report*. Synthesis Report–A Synthesis of the Global and Sub-Global IAASTD Reports, International Assessment of Agricultural Knowledge, Science and Technology for Development.

McMichael, P. (2005). Reframing development: Global peasant movements and the new agrarian question. *Canadian Journal of Development Studies, 27*(4), 471–486.

Moore, J. (2000). Environmental crises and the metabolic rift in world-historical perspective. *Organization and Environment, 13*(2), 123–157.

Mukhia, H. (2008). Peasant production and medieval Indian society. *Journal of Peasant Studies*, 228–251.

Nagthan, S., Poddar, R., Kunnal, L., Basavaraja, H., & Banakar, B. (2011). A probe into socio-economic and psychological profile of farmers' suicide in Karnataka. *Karnataka Journal of Agricultural Sciences, 24*(2), 157–160.

References

Omvedt, G. (1981). Capitalist agriculture and rural classes in India. *Economic and Political Weekly, 16*(52).

Panagaria, A. (2019). Confront the harsh reality: The only way we can really help farmers is to take most of them out of farming. *Times of India.* Accessed on January 17, 2019 at https://timesofindia.indiatimes.com/blogs/toi-edit-page/confront-the-harsh-reality-the-only-way-we-can-really-help-farmers-is-to-take-most-of-them-out-of-farming/.

Patnaik, U. (1990). *Agrarian relations and accumulation: The 'mode of production' debate in India.* New Delhi: Sameeksha Books.

Patnaik, U., & Dingwaney, M. (1985). *Chains of servitude: Bondage and slavery in India.* Sangam Books.

Pattnaik, I., Lahiri-Dutt, K., Lockie, S., & Pritchard, B. (2017). The feminisation of agriculture or the feminisation of agrarian distress? Tracking the trajectory of women in agriculture in India. *Journal of the Asia Pacific Economy.* https://doi.org/10.1080/13547860.2017.1394569.

Purushothaman, S., & Dharmarajan, P. (2005). Upland paddies, foliage hillocks and multistoried horticulture: An ecologically sustainable agroecosystem. *Asia-Pacific Agroforestry Newsletter, 27,* 11–13.

Purushothaman, S., & Patil, S. (2017). Regional economies and small farmers in Karnataka. *Economic and Political Weely, 52*(46), 78–84.

Purushothaman, S., Patil, S., & Kashyap, S. (2012). Agrarian crisis and policy links: A framework for Karnataka, India. In D. McNeill, I. Necheim, & F. Brouwer (Eds.), *Land use policies for sustainable development: Exploring integrated assessment approaches* (pp. 167–190). Cheltenham, UK: Edward Elgar.

Ramamurthy, P. (2011). Rearticulating caste: The global cottonseed commodity chain and the paradox of smallholder capitalism in South India. *Environment and Planning, 43*(5), 1035–1056.

Roseberry, W. (1982). Peasants, proletarians, and politics in the Venezuelan Andes, 1875–1975. In R. Weller & S. Guggengeim (Eds.), *Power and protest in countryside* (pp. 106–131). Durham: Duke University Press.

Roy, A. (1999, June 4). The greater common good. *Frontline.*

Sanyal, K. (2007). *Rethinking capitalist development: Primitive accumulation, governmentality and post-colonial capitalism.* New Delhi: Routledge India.

Sanyal, K., & Bhattacharya, R. (2009). Beyond the factory: Globalisation, informalisation of production and the new locations of labour. *Economic and Political Weekly, 44*(22), 35–44.

Schneider, M., & McMichael, P. (2010). Deepening, and repairing, the metabolic rift. *Journal of Peasant Studies, 37*(3), 461–484.

Scott, J. (1985). *Weapons of the weak: Everyday forms of peasant resistance.* Yale University Press.

Scott, J. (1998). Taming nature: An agriculture of legibility and simplicity. In J. Scott (Ed.), *Seeing like a state* (pp. 262–306). Yale University Press.

Shah, A., & Harriss-White, B. (2011). Resurrecting scholarship on agrarian transformation. *Economic and Political Weekly, 41*(39), 13–18.

Shiva, V. (2015, February 19). Yield vs wealth, measure for measure. *Asian Age.*

Stokes, E. (1978). *The peasant and the raj.* Cambridge: Cambridge University Press.

Stone, D. (2007). Agricultural deskilling and the spread of genetically modified cotton in Warangal. *Current Anthropology, 48*(1), 67–102.

Subba Reddy, S., Raghy Ram, P., Neelakanta Sastry, T., & Bhavani Devi, I. (2012). *Agricultural economics.* Oxford and IBH Publishers.

Thorner, A. (1982). Semi-feudalism or capitalism? Contemporary debate on classes and modes of production in India. Part 3. *Economic and Political Weekly, 17*(51), 2061–2066.

Toledo, V. (1989). The ecological rationality of peasant production. In M. Altieri & S. Hecht (Eds.), *Agroecology and small farm development.* Boca Raton, FL: CRC Press.

Vasavi, A. (1999). Agrarian distress in Bidar: Market, state and suicides. *Economic and Political Weekly,* 2263–2268.

Vasavi, A. (2012). *Shadow spaces: Suicides and the predicament of rural India.* Three Essay Collective.

Chapter 2
Family Farms in Agrarian Literature—A Critique

This chapter presents glimpses of the treatment of smallholders in noted agrarian literature. As the notion of the smallholder is multi-dimensional, multi-scalar and also multi-regional, the volume of published work is extensive. Consequently, categorising this body of work is challenging. Yet, we have tried to organise relevant and well known studies in a manner that will be useful while reading the rest of the book. This chapter will uncover the ecological and institutional gaps identified in the previous chapter while trying to unearth pertinent questions that remain unaddressed. This is a selective, chronological review of literature relevant to agrarian dynamics in the backdrop of urbanisation and is not intended to be exhaustive. Most relevant studies on peri-urban interface have been reviewed in our earlier work (Purushothaman et al. 2016). In the interest of brevity, studies relevant for selected peri-urban locations will be taken up during site-specific discussions in the later chapters.

2.1 Smallholder as an Economic Entity

This section mainly relies on Chayanov 1986 [1925], Georgescu-Roegen (1960) and Schultz (1964a, b) among others for unpacking smallholders as an economic entity.

The first serious look at small farmers as a distinct economic entity was in the *Theory of Non-Capitalist Economic Systems* by A. V. Chayanov (AVC from now on) in the early twentieth century. While the principles of Production and Organisation School to which AVC belonged cannot be applied in totality to times and places far distant from early twentieth century Russia, we can nevertheless find arguments and approaches in the school relevant to our constituency—the Indian smallholder.

Though family farms are still significant in India, their continued presence may not be attributable to any of those criteria such as self-exploitation and unconstrained availability of land as espoused by Chayanovian school. This inapplicability of Chayanovian approach to the Indian context critiqued by Patnaik (1976) attributes

---

© Springer Nature Singapore Pte Ltd. 2019

S. Purushothaman and S. Patil, *Agrarian Change and Urbanization in Southern India*, India Studies in Business and Economics,
https://doi.org/10.1007/978-981-10-8336-5_2

it to the differentiation found among the peasant equivalent class in India. However, the only limitation we find is the fact that Indian smallholder is generally distant from even the 'impure peasant' (peasant employing hired labour) that Chayanov refers to. **Compared to peasants in Chayanovian Russia, consumption needs of contemporary small farmers in an urbanising Indian society are more persuasive and bondage to land much less intense, where nominal profits may not suffice.**

The challenge in applying this model to the Indian context also arises from the following: (i) it is impossible to completely dissociate capital from today's peasant, i.e. the family farmer (AVC allowed incursion of capital only in broad institutional recommendations for the peasant society and a few analytical occasions), (ii) there are blurred boundaries and forms of social/demographic differentiation, an aspect which is not obvious in today's family farms and (iii) there is a weakening influence of consumption-drudgery balance and consumer–worker ratio on the scale of production owing to the present prevalence of land scarcity and non-farm options for livelihoods. Yet we see that even in the absence of a nominal profit and with an increasing engagement in non-farm sector, most smallholders retain their links to land and agriculture in their native village.

The Chayanovian approach helps us recognise the smallholding as an economic unit despite its non-profit, non-capital elements. It helps us to formally substantiate non-farm occupations and differential optima in analytical terms and argues that the subjective decisions of peasant family are central to economic analyses *vis-á-vis* the arithmetic of bookkeeping. AVC identifies factors that affect choice between farm and non-farm options (mainly crafts and trade), as well as choice within farm elements such as crops and animals. He also establishes the futility of imputing wages to labouring on own land due to the role of family labour in increasing the rent forming factors, its flexibility and the element of satisfaction. The approach also questions the economic rationale in computing rent for own land, irrespective of the prevalence or absence of leasing as a practice.

Bottom-up handling of social realities and recommendation of vertical co-operatives that are scale-neutral for organising production are relevant now, when family farms coexist with growing economies. **The appeal of AVC's approach is that it does not embrace the 'only small is beautiful' position, while rejecting the 'larger is necessarily more effective' assumption.** It is also difficult to ignore the rigour behind the empirical pursuits with simple statistical analysis of detailed data from *guberniyas* collected by committed farm officers of *Zemstvos*, uncaring of academic labels and political threats.

AVC's observations implied the inevitable correlation of low agricultural growth to high growth in national income (Chayanov 1986 [1925]—Chap. 6) proving itself true even after almost a century. This resonates with Marxian 'irrationality'[1] argument regarding capitalist agriculture and can be seen extended in the broader binary of 'need' and 'greed' economy of Sanyal (2007). Thus, despite the dissimilarity of

---

[1]"… rational agriculture is incompatible with the capitalist system (although the latter promotes technical improvements in agriculture) and needs either the hand of the small farmer living by his own labour or the control of associated producers". (Marx (1894) Vol. III, Part 1, Chap. 6—Capital).

Indian smallholder from the Russian peasant of early twentieth century, we find that the Chayanovian school resonates with the family farms of twenty-first-century India.

Georgescu-Roegen's (1960) work was probably the first academic work that used the Chayanovian model to argue in favour of small farms, based on optimal scale, time and energy in production. Georgescu-Roegen considered formal academic efforts incapable of fully understanding small farmers, pointing to the fact that individuals become academic professionals only when they settle in towns/cities leaving their rural and agrarian roots, thus preventing a realistic understanding of the complex rationale of small farms. Georgescu-Roegen's (1960) seminal piece on agrarian economic theory takes the cue from Chayanovian studies before resorting to energy efficiency for a comparison of peasant and capitalist farming. However, Georgescu-Roegen's energy argument by itself may not justify the existence and support for present-day small farms, not even on environmental grounds. Even if all smallholders across the globe turn to sustainable practices, the total achievable reduction in energy use will be meagre, compared to the energy-guzzling sectors like transportation, construction or manufacturing. Thus, even though Georgesçu-Roegen's (1971) entropy analysis proves the ecological advantage of smallholdings, that by itself is not enough to obtain economic and political support for small farmers. His work does not go beyond energy to other realms of agrarian concerns or biological diversity, as for instance in Guha and Martinez-Alier (1997), who follow Georgescu-Roegen and Chayanov in their work.

Thus, while both AVC and Georgescu-Roegen present the economic rationale of peasant, both reveal the existence of an ecological blind spot in classical as well as modern capitalist and Marxian approaches in explaining the economic rationale of the peasant. For a long time thereafter, we would not see any serious theoretical engagement on small-scale farming as an economic entity inclusive of environmental aspects.

Around the time when Georgescu-Roegen was establishing peasantry as an entropy-efficient economic entity, there arose some notable concern about small farms. Anthropologist Geertz's (1963) study of intensified Javanese agriculture led to the concept of agricultural 'involution'—a risk identified by extending the concept from cultural anthropology. It implied change without progress, persisting social patterns failing to transform and tending to intensify existing inefficient practices. With constant returns to scale for a long time, this pattern inhibits economic growth even with an increase in production per unit area. Critiqued by many, but difficult to ignore, the involution debate (see Chap. 1, Sect. 1.1.2 where we discussed lower equilibrium among the peasantry) was linked to the entry of sugarcane as a smallholder cash crop along with rice production in Java, resulting in conditions similar to Chayanovian self-exploitation and resulting in less than proportionate outcomes. **By the second half of last century, an academic world without much appreciation of smallholdings attained a widespread fear of 'involution'. This gave rise to a general impression that small farms may be inevitable for historical reasons, but it may neither be essential nor be desirable to sustain them.**

We need to look at how the persistence of family farms in today's India relates to this fear. Involution even now could be a lurking danger (Sanyal and Bhattacharya 2009) seen as the outcome of small farmers sustaining without any remarkable surplus, for long. But the present-day small farm only partially depends on the small piece of land, with part of family income sourced from non-farm employment. Thus, farming cannot be judged in isolation given the intricate linkage it has with several elements mentioned in the previous chapter such as food, health, culture and identity. Constant returns to scale, a common manifestation of involutionary tendencies in present-day smallholdings may not be too undesirable, as long as it enables basic security for comfortably tiding over risks in the non-farm engagements of the family. **Despite the absence of accumulated surplus, family farms provide a platform to anchor stable, demand-driven economic growth, without inflicting distressful impacts of food inflation on-farm families, while securing cultural identity, nutritional security, institutions and biodiversity.**

American economist Schultz's (1964a, b) work on transforming agriculture was available to the English-speaking world prior to the translated work of Chayanov from Russia. Schultz's work extends the discussion on potential strengths and weaknesses of smallholdings. Shultz, like Chayanov, found 'traditional' agriculture in a low-level economic equilibrium (see Footnote 6 in Chap. 1) though his identified reason was stagnancy either in the state-of-the-art or in aspirations, or both. Shultz's case studies on Guatemalan and Indian agriculture examined this puzzling equilibrium and concluded that the observed income poverty was not due to significant inefficiencies in factor allocations, nor was it reflective of survival below subsistence as most such families were engaged in non-farm occupations. Shultz's conclusion that the factors on which the agrarian economy is dependent are incapable of producing more holds true for today's small farms. For today's small farmers agriculture seems to be essential for long-term food, livelihood and cultural security, but not sufficient for a dignified life.

Confident that low income communities can increase agricultural production substantially by efficient allocation of available resources, Shultz classifies the farm into three types: (a) traditional farm—in an equilibrium of its own, (b) modern farm—also in equilibrium, least gap between technology arrival and adoption and (c) transitional farms—in dis-equilibrium owing to the gap between price of technology change and productivity. He then substantiates the argument about how agriculturists engaged in traditional farming appear to have unutilised time[2] and attributes it to the low marginal productivity (MP—defined as change in output by employing just one more unit of a particular input, usually labour) of this kind of labour, taking note also of the low MP of capital in these farms. While discussing underemployment in modern agriculture, he points towards factor market imperfections and limited technical substitutability of factors. Banking on data on labour and cropped area during the influenza epidemic of 1918–1919 in India, he refutes the doctrine that agricultural labour in countries like India often has zero MP.

---

[2]Though Chayanov refers to this as 'leisure', Shultz does not cite this as probably the Russian economist's work was not yet available in English.

2.1 Smallholder as an Economic Entity

Analysing the potential for transformations in traditional agriculture to fuel economic growth, Shultz rejects several hypotheses arguing that those are based, at best, on half-truths and to some extent, as responses to the physiocratic and classical legacy of economic thought.[3] These include the hypotheses that opportunity of growth from agriculture is the least attractive of all sectors; that in poor countries agriculture can contribute substantial capital and labour (at zero opportunity cost as there is considerable labour with zero MP) to the industrial sector[4]; that farmers do not respond to normal economic incentives or often respond perversely and that large farms are essential to minimise production cost. Shultz relies on three well-argued assumptions before handling the above hypotheses: income elasticity of demand for food is higher in poorer countries; instability in agriculture is the result of a growing economy; and the possibility of adapting agriculture to a fast growing economy.

Shultz quotes Mitrany (1951) to refute the idea of reduced production cost in larger farms found in Marxian and classical economics studies alike. His observation that scale in traditional agriculture is aligned with factor proportionality is more appealing than the usual tendency to align it with indivisibility of available technology. The real indivisibility he cites is of the farmer entrepreneur, who nonetheless ventures partially into off/non-farm jobs in present times.

While Schultz devotes one chapter to the need for '*low priced sources of permanent increase in incomes*', he, like most of his contemporary economists, misses the cost minimisation potential of sustainable practices altogether. Even traditional agriculture, which his book is about, is defined as something static, compared to modern or transitional farms, and in need of complete transformation. Yet, like Chayanov and Georgescu-Roegen, Shultz too shows that small farms (though traditional) are as efficient (if not more) as large farms in production terms. He identifies capital investment accompanied by education in general, and education on farming in particular, as crucial steps to improving production levels. Land expansion is considered neither feasible nor necessary. He presents interesting comparisons of Japan, USA, Israel, Mexico and India, though this is often critiqued as casual empiricism (Raj 1990) in the absence of an explicit long-term conceptual perspective.

It is interesting to find that Shultz's (1964b) recommendations resonate with what Bhaduri (1983) concludes for peasants. In order to usher in capitalistic transformation of 'backward agriculture' in a pre-capitalistic agrarian society, Bhaduri urges for imaginative markets and affordable loans (for consumption as well as production) to peasants. **What is difficult to accept in these studies by Bhaduri and Shultz is**

---

[3]The physiocrats believed in the axiom that agriculture alone is productive as it paid the workers (subsistence), the entrepreneurs (their earnings) and generated a surplus. They believed that industry and trade were sterile. Classical economists on the other hand, relying on principles of capital accumulation, Malthusian population and law of diminishing returns in agriculture, argued that agricultural landowners could absorb benefits of economic growth, attributing it to Ricardian rent when land is fixed.

[4]Shultz' rejection of this hypotheses could be read along with what Sanyal and Bhattacharya (2009) find—agricultural involution as reason for large number of rural workforce and urbanisation of poverty, differing from the productivity argument.

the characterisation of all[5] small-scale agriculture as backward and the glossing over of their significance as nations' food basket and for their adaptive strengths to environmental and market variations. In their opinion, the aggregate resource base and marketed surplus from small growers are not comparable to that of the large landholders, indirectly implying the dispensability of this constituency. The fact that small farms are responsible for more than 40% of food produce for a diverse population of about 1.2 billion and from about half the total cultivated area of the country cannot be ignored.

2.2 Nature, Moral Economy and the Peasant

Recognising that the smallholder is an economic entity, though different from other profit seeking units, we will look for perspectives beyond economics. Family farms' rationale in retaining inherited connect to land, community and place can be unravelled only after understanding their closeness to nature and non-material values. This discussion refers to many authors namely Desai (1979), Friedman (1978), Lipton (1991), Scott (1998) and Kumarappa (1945) among others.

Literature discussed hitherto does not elucidate the role of ecology in a meaningful existence of smallholders in India. How do ecological implications change if—(i) family farms transition into larger or more capital intensive production units with better stakes in the market, (ii) farms successfully meet consumption needs and other day-to-day expenditures of the family, (iii) family farms over years of constant or slightly increasing returns to scale, complemented by other factors (education and non-farm income), move out of farming? How does ecology play out in these positive changes or in the downward transition of budding small-scale proprietors into pauperised or semi proletarianised peasants? We engage with these questions in our field sites.

Sociologist Desai's (1979) work is a rare early instance where ecological aspects find some place among the corroborating factors for 'pauperisation' of Indian peasants, along with imperialist rule and feudal production systems. His reference was to the exclusionary forest laws that prevented entry into and extraction from the forests. This exclusion forced farmers to use cattle dung for fuel, depriving their land of manure. Chap. 1, Sect. 1.2 mentions how both conservation and development policies alike deprive farmers of their natural resources. **Soil exhaustion (along with already undernourished family labour) led to productivity decline in turn leading to undernourished livestock, further impacting health of the family and their land. This 'ecological rent' that the poor farmers end up paying appears similar to the Chayanovian 'hunger rent', since even the consumption needs of the family usually met from village commons remain affected.**

---

[5]Like other modes of agricultural production, smallholders could also be inefficient, but the large chunk of diverse holdings together makes such generalisation problematic for India.

2.2 Nature, Moral Economy and the Peasant

Friedman (1978), the food system analyst turned sociologist, was responsible (along with sociologist McMichael) for changing the agrarian discourse to include cultural and political-ecological angles. Thus, towards the last two decades of the twentieth century, we find the emergence of serious interest in small farmers by sociologists concerned about the breaching of the food-culture-ecology continuum by business and political interests (e.g. Araghi (2009) and McMichael (2009) in Akram-Lodhi and Kay).

Lipton's (1991) discussion of coalition theory—of distributive coalitions for collective goods in agriculture—could be expanded to include common lands—village forests, grazing lands, water bodies, etc.—that are crucial for smallholdings. In fact, the omission of ecological dimension in most agrarian frameworks also means overlooking the deprivation in access to village common lands attributable to the erosion of agro-ecological institutions. Sen (1991) discusses the ecological and distributional risks in expanding non-agricultural sector in scattered pockets of rural landscapes, the livelihood effect of which is overshadowed by the talk of generating industrial employment.

Scott's (1998) work on 'taming nature' (Chap. 8 in 'Seeing like a State') makes up for the ecological gap in his earlier work on moral economy (1977). Here he brings out the complex functionality of tropical farms, defying the penchant for order, scale and short term gains in modern agricultural science. The realisation of depleted nutrients in rural soils consequent to continuous export of agricultural produce to cities triggered the first import of fertilisers into Britain, in the form of bones from battlefields and guano from Peru (Moore 2000; Schneider and McMichael 2010). The clear association of such a town-country nutrient gap was already being extended to a larger and more dynamic human-nature divide in modern society (see Foster (1999) for a discussion on the social and environmental paradox).

This multifaceted discourse on agrarian sustainability has been missing in Indian literature, despite expanding urbanism and persisting agrarian distress. Though Foster along with others enriched the eco-Marxist and environmental sociology schools of thought significantly, such concerns in Indian literature is confined to the interface of forests and tribes in the background of economic growth (see Mollinga (2010) for a detailing of silence in Indian literature on agriculture, water and tribals). Recognising this lacuna, this book will present varied social–ecological ruptures on the ground without attempting a detailed conceptual analysis of any one of them.

The moral economy framework floated by Marxist historian Thompson (1971) in the background of the eighteenth- and nineteenth-century peasant revolts in England was applied to South Asian context during the early twentieth century by Scott (1977). Interestingly, it is very close to the Indian work on 'economy of permanence' floated in 1945 by Kumarappa (1945). Scott's moral economy of peasants finds validity in individuals holding on to land so as to return occasionally to farming, keeping the identity of place and community intact. This is over and above the cultural and economic needs (both every day and long term, e.g. need for a permanent address or a proof of identity), especially for a migrant worker who may take decades to possess a dwelling of her own, let alone a piece of land in the city.

Kumarappa (1945) deals with the ecological rationale of farming in greater detail than the two studies on moral economy mentioned above. The loss of creative freedom in rural livelihoods espoused by Kumarappa is what recent literature on farmer deskilling in post-Green Revolution agriculture (e.g. Brodt (2001), Thrupp (1989)) largely laments about. **Agricultural skill or farmers' adaptive ability to decide on-farm practices based on experiments, evaluation and comparisons is a collective and long process. Losing relevance in the wake of exogenous decisions and introductions, scope for on-farm creative explorations and farmer's conviction on-farm practices became less prominent. Among others, the obvious fallout of this deskilling process was a growing materialistic vision of agriculture even in family farms.**

Pushing potential regional agrarian economies of permanence to numerous scattered profit seeking firms of unviable small scale and deskilled farmers happened without the required economic paraphernalia. This, according to Dhanagare (1983) and Bhaduri (1983), implies a fertile ground for social uprisings. **The already identified institutional lacunae (see Chap. 1, Sect. 1.2.2) indicates that nurturing the emergence of new social mechanisms of both the formal and informal kind may partially revive creative agricultural skills. While the universal normative of democracy and economic growth flourished across urban geographies, crafting of new rural institutions that can anchor dynamically changing agrarian societies failed to keep pace.**

While recounting discourses around different frames gazing at the changing complexity surrounding the smallholder, we cannot overlook the criticism by political scientist Brass (2000). Brass interpreted the re-emergence of the peasant in post-modern agrarian literature in the form of culture and peasant essentialisation, as depoliticising populism. To him, this post-modern project supports the middle peasants as also the moral economy theses and prevents socialist mobilisation among peasants. He also draws complementarity between neo-populism and right-wing ideology. Left-wing social movements in India among peasants are also critiqued in the same vein.

Desai's differentiation of farmers' movements into those by non-poor and land-owning farmers for their share of the fruits of development in contrast to those by poor but land-owning farmers mostly to defend their right to land and other ecological resources [seen in Omvedt (1981) and Dhanagare (1983)] may explain why farmers' organisations often fail to highlight smallholders' long-term issues and confine themselves to seeking symptomatic relief like loan waivers. If farmer organisations and political outfits are ambivalent about the root causes of natural resources deprivation in small farms, agricultural science and practice in India are no different.[6] Despite their continued reliance on land for subsistence and inherited values, profit emerges as the primary motive, making even cultural-ecological needs dispensable. This materialisation of agriculture could be both the cause and effect of an undernourished rural socio-cultural institutional environment.

---

[6]See Chap. 1, Sect. 1.2.1 for a brief bibliometric analysis.

In the absence of adaptive institutions, subsistence security continues to be paramount for small farm community even today as fair markets seem to overlook them amidst the clamour for free trade and cheap food. In the backdrop of an unlikely radicalisation of the scattered constituency of smallholders alongside the trend of neo-populism, the overhanging question is how can farmers escape the maze of multifaceted precariousness.

2.3   Agrarian Institutions

When farming was integral to culture and society and not just a profit-making venture, it had a symbiotic relationship with informal social institutions, instrumental in sustaining agricultural production systems. By virtue of being entirely based on common natural resources, small-scale holdings were dependent on these informal institutions. As profit gained supremacy, farming came to be dependent on more formal and external institutions ranging from research organisations bringing out seeds or agro-chemicals, types of markets to government line agencies. Nonetheless, farming continues to be part of societal culture in India with most festivals and rituals directly linked to agricultural seasons and events. This section looks at major studies around formal and informal institutions in Stone (2002, 2007), Bardhan (1989) and Chakravarthy (1991).

An important function or role of informal institutions was in developing agricultural skills suitable for the agro-ecology and consumption needs of the region, over time. The science of assessing, evaluating and experimenting for adaptation or rejection in many agrarian societies nurtured a well-guarded agro-ecological knowledge base. Dependence on input and output markets made informal institutions redundant, while the institutional base for newer practices continue to be a work-in-progress. This slow and regionally patchy evolution of an institutional scaffolding needed for modern agriculture is impacted by the pace with which newer technologies emerge. Without a suitable mechanism to build a strong local knowledge base on the pros and cons of new practices, deskilling came to stay in most agricultural belts. Farmers' deskilling in the aftermath of the spread of agricultural biotechnology is now well-studied (see for instance Stone 2002, 2007).

It is common to see farmers completely ignorant about the suitability and outcomes of the seeds and agro-chemicals they used, often availing borrowed capital. Socio-cultural knowledge as a resilient institution might be able to explain the dramatic emergence of collectives in sustainable agriculture, often supported by the State and mostly found in peri-urban areas. For instance, collectives in peri-urban Bengaluru are engaged in on-farm production and sharing of organic manure and pesticides using local biodiversity. Differential pace of such institutional change along the rural–urban gradient is noteworthy.

Notable focus on institutions in Indian agrarian literature is first found in Bardhan (1989). The book spans the Marxian production relations, new institutional economics on property rights and voluntary contracts and the imperfect information school analysing the currently missing elements in credit, insurance and future markets. The school of institutional economics anchored on imperfect information is closely linked to the transaction cost school. Spelling out the assumptions and concepts of equilibrium, Bardhan brings out implications for strategic behaviour under differential asymmetry of information. After comparing the three schools of institutional economics, Bardhan's book showcases institutions modelled from the imperfect information school for analysing the currently missing credit, insurance and futures markets.

Nonetheless, the trade-off between scale and transaction cost as noted in his introductory chapter can be contested. Lower transaction cost and higher production cost need not be true for small family farms, given the informal labour and input sharing norms prior to individualisation of farming. Related problem in Bardhan's discussion as well as in other theorists is the notion of farming solely as business and hence seeing only relatively formal institutions, though there are minor references to informal contracts like oral tenancy.

Bardhan (1989) concludes that institutions in agriculture are increasingly driven by the objective of economic growth as governments come under pressure from a neoliberal world. At the same time, it is increasingly becoming clear that provincial and lower tiers of governance can potentially break undesirable feedback loops in farm livelihoods. This conflict between the federal as well as centralised policies on the one hand and decentralised governance on the other viewed from the angle of dialectical materialism finds mention in Breman and Mundle (1991) indicating that centralised policy institutions align with major multinational companies more than their own decentralised counterparts.

According to Chakravarthy (1991), public good provisioning as a determinant of rural transformation needs the intervention of State institutions. This aspect of State's role in the much needed public good provisioning for rural transformation does not find place in most academic literature. This is reinforced by Lipton (1995)'s thesis that rural groups in developing regions, with increasing population and risks, tend to manage their public goods and private conflicts in such a way that the outcomes shift from low transaction cost solutions to non-co-operative prisoners' dilemma.

In the absence of enough and reliable information sharing among and between farmers and consumers, each farmer assumes that there is enough of soil fertility and water to extract infinitely while powerful ecological rent seekers like State and corporate bodies get undue share of common natural heritage (land for dams or airports, waste dump; forests for mining and water bodies for sewage). Consumers on the other hand, oblivious of the impacts of production activities, continue to demand cheaper farm produce for consumption and careless wastage.

The information gap from varying production contexts needs to be unpacked. Among Indian case studies, even the well acclaimed socio-economic analysis of two villages in Karnataka by anthropologist Epstein (1973) as well as other works, such as those of Srinivas (1976) and Harris (1991), do not do justice to the ecological and governance aspects. While finding disparity across regions and castes in the progress achieved by a large-scale irrigation project, Epstein was oblivious to the inherent sustainability impacts (including distributional) of canal irrigation, unlike

2.3 Agrarian Institutions

Mishra (1985) who critiqued the canal irrigation model itself for its limited traditional capital transformation among small growers. A Gandhian geographer, Mishra's work will be revisited when we discuss the study sites.

Stiglitz, in (Bardhan 1989), representing the school of institutional economics based on imperfect information clarifies how institutions such as sharecropping make sense from a peasant rationality perspective. Going beyond the transaction cost school of institutional economics, he looks at how sharecropping minimises externalities and fills the gap of insurance institutions. But sharecropping is, in reality, a more diverse set of arrangements than discussed here and serves diverse purposes beyond distributing risks—a function served by default. Sharecropping is more a mechanism to keep the land cultivated when the farmer wants or needs to engage in other occupations. This ensures partial food security, as they often transport food grains to the cities where they find informal employment when the family is in need of some money.

Stiglitz argues that the presence of large and smallholdings in a production landscape may not necessarily mean a completely perfect or imperfect competitive market. It is also implied that imperfect information may lead to the persistence of inefficient institutions necessitating State intervention for institutional change. We could use this argument to explain how in the absence of a clear understanding of smallholding ecosystems in science and policies, use of synthetic fertilisers became universally scale-neutral. Also implied is the role that the State has to perform in closing the adverse feedback loops already set in motion so as to sustain soil productivity and social well-being.

Thus, the institutional environment around smallholder farming appears to be responsible for the following functions: reducing costs, distributing risks, evolving knowledge, skills as well as providing basic security in food, capital, input and labour. The central question is—what combination of traditional and newly crafted social institutions, along with governmental and corporate strategies, can nurture a suitable institutional environment for sustaining small farmers in varied agrarian contexts?

The institutional literature on agrarian issues leaves many such questions still unanswered. Most studies do not seem to take into account ecological factors, market shocks, power (im)balances and differential capabilities of smallholders. These are in addition to other gaps in institutional theories identified by Polzin et al. (2016)—such as narrow definitions (e.g. as constraints or enablers of change), preconceptions of change itself (e.g. artificial selection or path dependency) and abstraction of social and behavioural institutions.

The diversity of informal institutions that used to prevail (and still do in some locales) to ensure food, land and occupational security gets buried in the flood of studies on class struggles and on property rights. Vasavi (1999) mentions some of these vanishing social institutions and compares them with contemporary mainstream institutions, especially the state-driven ones, in North Karnataka.

On the other hand, literature on the bipolar coexistence of capitalistic accumulation in large farms and peasant deprivation presents class tensions or struggles as the only solutions. Even as the class taxonomy is blurring and when creative responses (e.g. *La* Via *Campesina*,[7] LEISA (Low External Input Sustainable Agriculture) India Consortium,[8] natural farming collectives and producer companies in organic farming) are sporadically emerging, resistance would still be important as developmental governmentality tends to gloss over the need economy amidst the glamour of accumulative corporate interests. Nevertheless, it may not be the only or the first way out. That is where the 'builder' approach (Friedmann and McNair 2008), *vis–á–vis* the usual 'warrior approach' to social change, through locally embedded socio-political processes, deserves attention from agrarian theorists. Builder approach urges us to look for evolutionary tendencies in agricultural movements in the study sites to explore how movements represent and achieve small farmers' interests.

2.4 Agrarian Movements

Agrarian movements in colonial India have been many and heterogeneous (Vishwanath 1990), with diversity in causes and drivers. But similar upheavals have been rare in both green revolution and neoliberal India. Given that the indirect factors influencing agriculture are many and entangled, though their impact spreads across land, water and forest, both in the private and common property regimes, it is unclear against whom the peasant should revolt in a post-feudal neoliberal society.

Analysing peasant movements in India between 1920 and 1950, Dhanagare (1983) notes that growth of commercial farming in the absence of connectedness between market relations and capitalisation is conducive for peasant mobilisation. This linkage of peasant movements with commercialisation and capitalisation in agriculture is portrayed in the context of Punjab's farmer prosperity leading to social movements to defend ecological and human health. But it is unable to answer the lack of uprising among many smallholder communities despite volatile prices, perverse subsidies and forced land acquisition.

This 'structural possibility' of the changing nature of resistances and struggles was compared with Marxian theory of dynamic trajectory by Wright (1980). But more striking is Rudra's (1990) treatment of the potential social dynamics behind agrarian change. According to Rudra [in Patnaik (1990)], the two discerning classes in Indian agriculture are the landlords and the labourers (including marginally landed, landless and poor tenants). He observes that the insignificance of the rest of Indian farmers is due to the fact that they may not have enough contradictions and conflicts to trigger agrarian change and even goes on to State that the conflict of smallholders' interest

---

[7]Literally 'the peasant way'—an international movement founded in 1993 coordinates a coalition of 148 farmer organisations of small- and medium-scale producers, agricultural workers, rural women and indigenous communities from Asia, Africa, America and Europe. The member organisations advocate family farm-based sustainable agriculture. The term 'food sovereignty' was popularised by this group.

[8]Consortium established in India for enhancing information exchange about LEISA technologies. Information exchange is carried out through participatory capacity building processes and experience sharing by farmers.

2.4 Agrarian Movements

with that of State polices on prices and landownership is meek or muted at the level of the individual farmer. **The muted conflicts along with lack of clear contradiction with other social classes, made smallholders a forgettable part of the nation and academic interest, despite their large presence, notable persistence and visible marginalisation.**

Yet, there are suggestions to the contrary. Omvedt's (1981) paper on middle peasants or petty commodity bourgeoisie in a rural–urban as well as agriculture-industry continuum actually suggests that the new rural poor, being closer to proletarians than peasants, are a potential class to trigger an upheaval for various distributional rights. Omvedt's analysis uniquely informs how the constituency of peasant proletarians varies in their plight along the above continuum. This difference in plight is observed among the smallholding family farms in the peri-urban interface, rural production landscapes and forest peripheries. The new and growing 'process of (informed) social emancipation' (Breman et al. 1997) among the marginalised, across the above categories of smallholdings, could find explanation in the widespread precariousness of livelihoods seen in partial depeasantisation (Araghi 1995) co-existing with circular migration.

Struggles and resistances will be part of creative responses as we saw in previous section (Sect. 2.3). But these are strategically built around democratic egalitarianism and thus involve a more persistent engagement with the State through contextually innovative institutions of diverse nature (see Mishra (2006) for such a recommendation for Maharashtra). It may be worthwhile to integrate these possibilities into a framework around the future of small farms as part of the missing 'movements'. Insignificant social struggles and policy efforts to restore access to common lands for fulfilling household and social needs expose limitations in the emergence of such two-pronged approach. This does not ignore the occurrence of sporadic movements for public good provisioning [as mentioned in De Angelis 2003 cited in Akram-Lodhi et al. (2009)], such as struggles against mining companies or power plants in Orissa, Andhra Pradesh and Karnataka. The fact is while alienation of the extent and quality of commons has been near universal, peasant movements and policy change for the cause have been very few.

Despite the continued insecurity in subsistence and the threat of volatile but 'free' (though 'free' for whom and for what purpose is not always clear) trade and unfair prices, why are not peasant revolts impactful enough?[9] Is it that the farm families are less concerned about subsistence but more about wages, to meet increased expenses of

---

[9] As we write this book, there have been protests by Sikar farmers in Rajasthan for better prices, loan waivers and against rules on trading farm animals; Tamil Nadu farmers demanding drought-relief package, loan waiver and setting up of the Cauvery Management Board; Marathas (middle caste farming community in Maharashtra) for social welfare schemes; Patidars in Gujarat and Gujjars in Rajasthan demanding reservation in government jobs- http://www.thecitizen.in/index.php/en/newsdetail/index/1/7313/2016-3-months-of-non-stop-farmer-protests-across-india; and farmers' 'long march' in Maharashtra (Editorial, Economic and Political Weekly, 17 March 2018). None apparently targeted substantial issues around land, trade and markets. Though it may be premature to judge these as agrarian movements (George and Kumar 2017), they definitely make the governments turn towards agrarian issues. *Kisan Mukthi March* in Delhi (December 2018) brought out Manifesto of Indian Farmers, with 19 demands, the outcomes of which is yet to be known.

health care, communication and customary compulsions? Does the partial existence of small farmer as wage labour leave her with neither enough time nor interest to identify the adversary both far and near? Is it that they are subdued by a welfare State delivering minimum subsistence and health security, adhoc relief measures and electoral sops? Or is it that the victim is a scattered million powerless people with multiple but precarious livelihoods? Is it that society mistakes the organised struggles of propertied farmers for their pie in economic growth, in terms of irrigation, free power and higher product price, as 'peasant' revolts? Is it true that today's peasant struggle is to retain their stakes in natural resources—land, water and forests—and no longer about food security or fair trade? Such agrarian questions continue to emerge from different agro-ecological and political-economic contexts.

2.5 Food Regimes and Agrarian Political Economy

Agrarian structure is invariably linked to food regimes, the form in which the primary functions of a production system gets configured in a globalised neoliberal consumerist society. McMichael (2009) attempts to unpack the complex linking of agrarian structure to food regimes. Though his argument is not fully integrated into a bifurcated agrarian organisation (bifurcated into export-oriented capitalist farmers and domestic supply oriented small-scale farmers (Breman and Mundle (1991)), his analysis of the organic links between anti-globalisation movements (against accumulation by dispossession (in Harvey (2004) and Sanyal (2007) mainly around exploitation of wage labour) and peasant resistance to displacement, ecological injustice and disappearing food diversity aligns with the dichotomy. **Thus, towards the end of the first quarter of the twentieth century, we seem to be converging on the fact that the agrarian question is not a classical land or labour question, nor is it a neo-classical impatience of transforming a 'culture' into a 'business'.**

Instead, the question is identified as politics around accelerated circulation of food [e.g. 'growers and eaters', (Patel 2007)] with ethical, ecological and governance implications encompassing rights and sustainability issues. McMichael's position on this resonates with Sanyal's (2007) plea for a political society within the need economy that currently is a necessary prop for the capitalist development core. The export-driven path mainly around demand for non-traditional agricultural crops raises the relative surplus value of global agro-capital through capitalist farm sector together with agro-industries and a corporate food regime. This neoliberal economic structure from the days of de-ruralisation of the production landscape by 'great global enclosures' (Araghi 2009) shaped the agrarian change we see today through state-driven trade agreements (like WTO Uruguay round's agreement on agriculture).

The food route to agrarian change is not just through corporate food regimes but also through public food grain distribution (PDS) and procurement systems. While PDS makes available secure access to staples, it also means that food habits and cropping pattern across agro-ecologies are homogenised. **Food habits change**

2.5 Food Regimes and Agrarian Political Economy

according to what is cheaply available and cropping pattern follows the procurement policy aimed at cheap food. This impact of subsidised food supply pitches the consumer against the producer, while in reality, both these identities combine in the same entity for at least 117 million Indians who are marginal and small producers.[10]

World Food Summit in 1996 at FAO's headquarters in Rome defined food sovereignty as 'the right of peoples to healthy and culturally appropriate food produced through sustainable methods and their right to define their own food and agriculture systems'. Corporate and State food regimes together threaten the food sovereignty of communities, especially in backward and income poor regions. Considerations about large-scale displacement of small farmers and global ecological degradation remained unattended while food security concerns fought against hunger and famines. This led to the emergence of transnational food sovereignty movements such as *La Via Campasina* (mentioned as an example of creative response in Sect. 2.4). The movement emerged in response to global food trade favouring industrial agricultural production. It was in the interest of human right to access food and was intense in the countries where corporate food regimes were most prevalent. As a more nuanced argument beyond provision of food by any means, food sovereignty includes support for small-scale farmers and for collective farming practices rather than industrialising the sector. McMichael (2009) diagnosed the central point of contradiction between the corporate food regime under WTO ('food from nowhere') and food sovereignty movement's support to 'agroecology-based-localism'.

While peasantry is dislocated from food, livelihood and ecological security, and as large-scale farming in globalised agriculture faces ecological limits, agrarian structural change is being driven by the politics around food. Instances of food used as 'weapon' (e.g. food supply being used for negotiations with North Korea for avoiding wars) or as a 'bait' (e.g. during unrest in Syria and Yemen having millions of people dependent on food aid) are more common compared to food supply being used as a driver of a healthy welfare society.

Reappearance of agrarian reforms in policy discourses emphasises economic aspects of institutions (Ellis 2000)—the socio-economic setting in which rural poor seek sustainable livelihoods. The socio-economic context in which reforms are making a feeble reappearance has been criticised as deeply neo-classical in nature and neoliberal in orientation (Akram-Lodhi et al. 2009; O'Laughlin 2004) given its attribution of deprivation to an inappropriate set of choices made by farmers.

---

[10]Evaluation Study on Role of Public Distribution System in Shaping Household and Nutritional Security in India (NITI Aayog 2016) reports that 88% of marginal and smallholders are beneficiaries of subsidised food supply. The pro-consumer bias is reflected in Damodaran (2019).

2.6 Persistence and Diversity Amidst Adversities

2.6.1 Persistence or Resilience?

Family farms dominate global agriculture. Of the 475 million small family farms in the world, more than one-fourth are in India (FAO 2001, 2013; Lowder et al. 2016). China and India together account for 75% of smallholders of the world.[11] Agrarian academics compare very distant and unrelated contexts before sufficiently disambiguating the existing and evolving transformation path(s) in diverse Indian contexts. This impatience complements the ecological hollowness and institutional ambivalence in literature already identified. The oft-quoted rural development models are from Japan, Taiwan (World Development Report 2008) and South Korea (Breman and Mundle 1991). The discussion about co-existence of differentiated peasantry across capitalist and socialist countries of South Asia, alongside the processes of capitalist development in agriculture, reveals the pressure exerted on smallholdings to scale up. Is the persistence of Indian smallholder a case of mere continued existence? What are the probable factors contributing to their persistence? We use Sanyal (2007), Griffin (1976), chapters in Breman and Mundle (1991) among others for a discussion around these questions.

Political urge to pre-empt inflationary trends through imports seems to be more compelling than the thoughtful efforts needed to sustain the smallholder, though ironically they constitute a big chunk of the consumer base too. Scanty attention to appropriate cultivation practices, marketing and research for small family farms forces them to surrender to the market driven trend in selection of crops, animals and intensification, while continuing small-scale farming through generations. **They find themselves at a disadvantage even after producing a bumper crop, often due to glut in the market triggered by imports.[12] Thus, while increasing production by itself does not seem to be a worthwhile objective, what to produce and how to, seem to be unaddressed in small family farms.**

Yet, rather than political ignorance or technology, institutional unpreparedness has been identified as the reason behind non-capitalisation of the economies of the South (Griffin 1976). **Griffin explains how the package of capital and technology may not create surplus in agriculture even with free trade, except in an unequal society.** His argument reinforces the case for incentivising small farms towards building less unequal societies and offers an institutional explanation for the existence of a bifurcated structure of farm economy (Sanyal 2007; Akram-Lodhi and

---

[11] Persistence of smallholders in the east Asian context has been discussed in detail in Rigg et al. (2016).

[12] Farmer riots coinciding with bumper harvest were reported in many Indian States in June 2017 (see http://indianexpress.com/article/opinion/columns/farmers-riot-maharashtra-madhya-pradesh-socio-economic-growing-prosperity-4696779/ and http://www.thehindu.com/opinion/editorial/the-rot-in-farming/article18967114.ece).

2.6 Persistence and Diversity Amidst Adversities

Kay 2009), implying that a capitalistic farm economy needs an unequal society.[13] Griffin's recommendation ranged from distribution of concentrated landownership to 'market-based' land reforms in the developing country contexts that he focused on.

Supporting distributional fairness in agricultural changes like Griffin, Harris (1991) also observes that though growth in agriculture is essential for a non-involutionary expansion of non-farm sector in rural areas, unequal agricultural growth will prevent economic diversification. He cites cases of Korea and Taiwan for the role of early advances in rural infrastructure for decentralised development. Saith (1991) in the volume by Breman and Mundle on the other hand takes cue from stories of development success to argue that rural industrialisation may not necessarily be the answer. **Nonetheless, Saith, departing from Harris (1991) and Sen (1991), remarks that whenever non-farm sector grew in rural areas, institutional reforms for agrarian equality and development of other sectors of the economy have been satisfactory, minimising the ecological and distributional externalities.** Apart from the larger objective of employment generation and poverty alleviation, Saith foresees that rural industrialisation will be instrumental in ensuring equal wages, worker welfare and internal skill formation, apart from agricultural development through forward and backward linkages with local primary production.

Lipton's (1991) juxtaposition of the binaries and gradients of rural and urban with that of farm and non-farm is interesting for its current relevance. He sets out to show that surplus extraction from rural Africa for financing urban private production was instrumental in slowing down development in African countries. While this kind of rural surplus extraction for urban growth is relatively less in the Asian continent, where small farmers of the world congregate, it varies between and within the countries of Asia. Lipton attributes this variability to the 'State', as manifested in political decision making, administration, implementation and enforcement across different layers and agencies. To demonstrate this, he cites Asian experiences where urban sectors grew out of prolonged re-investment of their own surplus rather than extracting from meagre rural agrarian surplus, though it may not be the case in all phases and types of urban growth.

The void in agrarian literature (except Scott (1985) and Leonard (1977) for Africa) on the precariousness situated at the fulcrum of the three axes: rural–urban; farm-non-farm and state-centre, imply the necessity of merging the institutional dimension with an integrative social-political-ecological lens.

Sanyal's (2007) thesis of a mutually reinforced extractive tightly coupled economy can be utilised in this analysis too. The co-existence of the 'accumulation economy' of the capitalist make-up and the subsistence driven 'need economy' of the developing world depicted in Sanyal finds reflection in the 'Occupy' movement across the world in 2011.[14] It is probably for the first time after Chayanov that deserving attention

---

[13]Resembling Piketty's (2014) take on larger economy and society, deriving from the grand theory of capital and inequality—that says wealth grows faster than economic output, accentuating inequality.

[14]International socio-political movement against social and economic inequality and lack of real 'democracy' around the world. The movement began in 2011 in New York city and went-on in over

was given to 'subsistence ventures' as an 'economy' in itself, though Sanyal does not even highlight the agrarian need economy. His prominent departure from other development analysts in viewing primitive accumulation as everlasting potentially explains how post-colonial electoral democracy created exclusion and dispossession in place of exploited wage labour of previous times. This is also reflected in what Deshpande (2012) identifies as the need to address the dilemma in inherited modes of bracketing the non-economic constituents of the economy, thereby blinding the disciplinary vision and making the economy illegible.

Sanyal's characterisation of the need economy (that hosts the eco-cultural within), as outside capital but inside capitalism, can comfortably rationalise the assertions of demand for resources by the agrarian community for its expanded reproduction for continued persistence. In the case of small farmers, the political economy of exclusion (as against the economics of transition) strives to create an economic space based on a logic of 'need' rather than 'accumulation'. This politics of the governed though unique is disparate and plural. Coming close to involution (discussed in the Chap. 1 Sect. 1.1.2 and in this chapter in Sect. 2.1), it allows for a need-based political economy in producing for domestic consumption (Mencher 1978) without the expansionary thrust for an infinitely accumulating economy. This perspective can help us characterise various means and ends of *'ensuring the reproduction of conditions of existence of the need economy'* (Sanyal 2007), of small producers.

Globally, Indian economy is considered resilient in the face of shocks, avoiding hyper-inflations, large-scale debt crises or major adjustment 'recessions' and with reasonable credit rating. This is largely attributed to the monetised structure of the economy (that is not part of formal economic structure, e.g. limited digitisation of transactions and large presence of informal sector) that subdues the impacts of inflationary shocks, where wage earners in the unorganised sector bear disproportionate cost. **Smallholders, most of whom are also part-time occupational migrants to non-farm sectors building our cities and contributing to the above mentioned macro-economic resilience, bear with huge disparity (Sanyal 2007), both on-farm and off-farm. Thus, in many ways, India's economic resilience comes at the cost of resilience of family farms.**

2.6.2 Dilemma of Transition

Arguing that the perpetual wait for 'transition' to capitalist mode of production is meaningless as the 'need economy' is created and maintained by the 'accumulation economy' for the latter's benefit, Sanyal calls for a political society in the need economy to evoke 'developmental governmentalism'.[15] Sanyal reminds us of the lack of

---

951 cities across 82 countries. Galsius and Pleyers (2013) discuss background, structure, context and demands of this and similar global social movements.

[15] Referred to in previous discussions on moral economy earlier in the chapter (Sect. 2.2).

2.6 Persistence and Diversity Amidst Adversities

path dependency in the way economies are transitioning in the South. Thus, Sanyal's logic, going beyond the neo-Gramscians (passive revolution), can be extended to imply how agrarian progress is permanently restricted by the integral need for a non-capitalised periphery to maintain post-colonial capitalism.

Delving deeper into Dhanagare's admonition of commercialisation sans markets (Sect. 2.2), it may be useful to see what triggers commercialisation. Friedmann (1978) lays out the influences of commoditisation. While specifying the unit of production and social formation required for reproduction and transformation, she concludes that the central tenet of agrarian relations is the 'form of production'. According to her, '*personal and productive consumption of farm output resists commodification of peasantry*' while mobility of land, labour and credit encourages commoditisation. Most mobile factors are alien to 'peasants', as are competition and increasing accumulation for improving their means of production.

Mohan Rao (1991 in Breman and Mundle), in his chapter on commercialisation, points out that surplus accumulation and agricultural growth are dependent on the pace of market formation. The inadequacy in market formation hampering capitalist transformation of peasantry despite the fading away of a feudal society in rural India is well known [see similar reference in Bhaduri (1973), Dhanagare (1983)]. Mohan Rao debates this and compares the Godavari belt and South Korea to conclude that the pace of market formation together with distribution and governance of ecological resources determine transformation of peasantry.

Thus, while studies seem to rule out transition of smallholders as capitalisation, there is no emphatic statement on the prevalence of other modes of transition. De-agrarianisation, depeasantisation and proletarianisation are part of that discourse. Bryceson (2000) warns about de-agrarianisation when people increasingly depend on non-farm options for livelihood, commodifying their labour. **While there is evidence to show how farm distress is linked to such risks in livelihoods generated by the society, there are few serious interdisciplinary studies on how depeasantisation has its origins in ill-informed commercialisation. Commodification of nature and labour in the absence of land reforms is an outcome of an emphatic focus on land and capital intensive production efficiency.**

The risks originating in un-differentiated commercialisation across all farm holdings, according to Vasavi (2012), are three-fold: ecological (erosion of ecological specificity leading to dissonance of knowledge base or deskilling), economic (distant and unknown external markets) and personal (unsuitable, imbalanced nutrition, unhealthy contacts with chemicals; individualisation and feminisation). These tentative and contextual risks along with necessary subordination of small-scale farming are accentuated when public sector is surrendered to private capital. This surrender depends invariably also on what is societally perceived as 'improvement' (Stiglitz et al. 2010) or what constitutes developmental governmentality (Sanyal 2007). This societal perception will in turn determine whether small-scale agriculture will continue to be regarded as 'the enemy of economic growth', relegating farm level distress to 'shadow spaces' (Vasavi 2012).

Breman and Mundle (1991) deliberate rural proletarianisation in their edited volume on rural transformation in Asia. While taking note of the dominance of wage labour in agriculture (70% of the Indian workforce in 1990), they question the use of wage labour as the indicator of capitalisation in agriculture, as it actually indicates semi-proletarianisation. They note the challenge involved in disentangling the maze of agriculture, population and economic growth in order to trace future of the peasant. **This is what we try to attempt in the rural–urban continuum of Karnataka where we expect peasant proletarianisation to vary according to the nature of urbanisation and involution possibilities followed by a flow of labourers to non-farm sector**.

In the context of distributional equity, even in the analysis of international development, it has been a recognised need for the poor to secure access to a diverse set of productive assets including land (Ravillion and Van De Walle 2006). Once affirmative land distribution allows secure access to land, concerns about small credit, technical inputs or institutional platform for collective honing of skills, techniques and marketing will have to be addressed. Only then is it reasonable to expect that those who exit small farming are doing so out of choice and are not just the less 'efficient' or pauperised producers [Wood, in Akram-Lodhi et al. (2009)].

From the diverse paths of rural transformation found in literature, Breman and Mundle extract the consistent centrality of three elements in all cases of rural transformation: the omnipresent State, class struggle and changing levels of natural endowments as well as of productive forces like technology—this is a rare instance in literature of acknowledging natural conditions as a factor in agrarian transformation.

Alongside a tour of diverse vantage points in Breman and Mundle on agrarian transition in South Asia, it is worthwhile to visit Bernstein's (1996) arguments. Bernstein discerned that the potential successful transitions may not be possible, and even if possible, may not provide enough material security or political freedoms. He finds three angles to the transition question: political (class differentiation and tensions), production (changing conditions of production) and accumulation (to be extracted for the industries or for the city). While we agree with the above determinants of small farmer transition, we would like to examine if successful transition is indeed impossible.

For a conclusive overarching message on institutional and related aspects, we are benefitted by Lerche (2013) as well as Shah and Harriss-White (2011). Their arguments on transition of a different kind in India (with regional variation ranging from pre-capitalist communities, old and new semi-feudalistic tendencies to petty captialisation and semi-proletarianisation) amidst a diminishing role (except for short term populist measures) of the State and de-radicalisation of the constituency (especially with respect to the power dynamics around land and trade) will be deliberated in later chapters of the book discussing the study sites in Karnataka.

2.6.3 Differentiated Persistence

State, markets and ecology along with the extent of land, hired or family labour, inputs (own or purchased), credit availed as well as quantum or value of marketed surplus contribute to diversity within the peasantry, though the exact pattern of peasant differentiation varies with geographical and social denominations. Diversification within Indian small farms could be the result of either efforts towards accumulation or survival strategies (see chapters by Harris (1991) and Sen (1991) in Breman and Mundle), within smallholders.

Examining the political economy of land in the era of neoliberal globalisation, authors in Breman and Mundle identify a bifurcated agrarian structure in which an export-oriented agrarian subsector coexists with a subsector of peasants producing for domestic market. The latter, in itself, is subject to a process of differentiation. Relating these two agrarian structures in different countries and also finding many outliers, they conclude that bifurcation occurs differently in different contexts, especially with respect to the initial distributional aspects (land, labour, income and capital) and political/governance contexts as also with respect to the diversity in linkages between the modes of export and domestic trade. Thus, the classical agrarian questions on land, capital and labour acquire new foci of trade. The peasant subsector shows characteristic forward and backward linkages with the domestic economy both at subnational and other scales. The export-oriented and domestic market subsectors differ in their relative proportion of production for the market as also in the intensity of labour used *vis-á-vis* capital.

Without trying to fit pre-established models of class structure to help reflect reality as such, Breman and Mundle segregate peasants as net (surplus) producers from appropriators. This typology is attractive and problematic at the same time. Attractive since a small farm family has to be seen as a combination of production and consumption forces rather than exclusively or predominantly as a producer. Problematic because they engage with more than one production system and are also important consumers of all economic sectors. **Thus, it is not only that a family farm cannot be a net producer across sectors, but also cannot be so, even within the agricultural sector. Even selling an agricultural commodity by a farmer may not imply surplus production of that or other agricultural products required by the family.**[16]

With respect to technology in family farms, the tendency to classify technological changes into labour replacing (machinery) and land replacing (fertilisers, irrigation and pesticides) often lead researchers to favour the latter in the prevailing context of subdivision of holdings, land scarcity and population growth (Bray 1991). It needs to be examined if this is in fact a useful bifurcation of family farms, given the growing aversion to drudgery, and technological possibility of automation as also depleting biodiversity and increasing climate variability. **Moreover, land-saving technologies often end up as land damaging, undermining long-term livelihood security.**

In Akram-Lodhi and Kay (2009), we begin to see cultural, ecological, institutional and political-economic dimensions being woven into agrarian differentiation. The discourse here does not attempt to frame a large theory of these dimensions, but instead tends towards reflecting ground reality.

---

[16]Cash strapped families generally sell their farm produce demanded by the market confining family's consumption to cheaper produces and supply from the public distribution system.

2.6.4 Adversities and Outcomes

Persistence of peasantry appears as an exploited need economy chained to the peripheries of a fast growing urban economic core. Peasantry persists by tweaking the forms of production combining commerce with subsistence, hired with family labour and farm employment with non-farm wage labour. Neoliberal globalisation reversed land reforms and rolled back farm subsidies as much as political space allowed. The weak persistence as a need economy in the peripheries of an accumulation economy, within the uneven rural development on a world scale, has been a *'procedurally similar but historically specific'* process distinct from accumulation by dispossession and displacement (Akram-Lodhi et al. 2009).

Sen (1991) takes a closer look at agricultural instabilities till 1985. His analysis starts with the recognition that though both GDP and agricultural economy grew at rates higher than that of population after India's independence, the problem of how to increase per capita income in agriculture (keeping agricultural employment low) still haunts our planners. Sen pinpoints reasons: (a) growth in agriculture failed to result in significant increase in real income as input costs increased (b) employment in agriculture continues to be high and both (a and b) worsened since 1966 as attention moved to the formal sector (c) post-1966, growth in agricultural economy confined to pockets; while most parts of the country showed decline in farm income per head, widening the gap between rural and the urban societies (d) the initially embraced development model continued with long-term ecological degradation—pockets of affluence creating acute pollution while the less affluent who fed and maintained the affluent pockets, faced externalities in pollution and resource depletion. **Rural societies, with or without active non-farm sectors, were compelled to depend increasingly on a declining stock and diversity of grazing lands, water bodies and forests.** Thus, Sen sets the context from where we can see how rural transformation played out in India.

Thorner (1982) signifies the potential adaptation of exploitative tenancy arrangements to techno-economic changes in the society. Her comprehensive review of the debate around modes of production also brings to light the 'caste' gap in earlier literature on agrarian change in India, the dynamics between the axes of caste and class, and between industrial capitalism and agricultural capitalism. The only conclusive change that she notes in Indian agriculture is the shift from tenant exploitation for production to large-scale intensive farming with hired labour. **Thorner also concludes that capitalism by itself would not be able to address India's rural problems and highlights the need for studying the State's expected role and the lack of measures on the ground. Her analysis like many others of that time leaves out ecological impacts of different modes of production and of production relations around common and private lands and consequent impacts on livelihood security.**

In line with what Dhanagare and Bhaduri (among others) had argued, Akram-Lodhi et al. (2009) conclude that wherever there has been significant inter-sectoral linkages between the export-oriented and the peasant subsectors, rural poverty reduc-

2.6 Persistence and Diversity Amidst Adversities

tion has been visible (e.g. Vietnam and Brazil) though with varying degrees of inequality. On the other hand, where linkages between the two are weak (e.g. India), despite significant capital accumulation through high-value agricultural crops, the gains are weakly distributed and food insecurity deepened. Neoliberal export bias in crop selection and knee-jerk import of farm products can lead to crises not just in domestic production but also in nutritional security and food cultures. New food cultures push input intensive high-value agriculture through several agencies (including FAO and IFPRI) resulting in *'agriculture without farmers'* (in Teubal's words [in Akram-Lodhi et al. (2009)] or more aptly 'farms without agriculturists'. In India and the Philippines, internal demand expanded more than other countries like Pakistan and Egypt, but the emphasis by peasant producers on crops for exports in both countries fostered inter- and intra-sectoral differentiation even as food imports increased.

The export-oriented (or exclusively commercial) subsector is formed by MNCs' involvement in retail, seed inputs, chemicals and energy sectors. These organisations entered countrysides of the global south influencing decisions on what and how to grow. Thus, production may be carried out 'by' the peasantry but not 'for' the peasantry and by the logic of corporate capital (Araghi 2000) akin to what Bhaduri (1986) termed 'forced commerce'.[17] Those who did not enter this capitalist mode of production, competing with food imports and local capitalist farmers, were forced into forms of disguised wage labour/petty commodity production [critiqued in Harriss-White (2012), Banaji (2003)]. They ended up either as semi-proletariat 'foot loose labour' or 'reserve army of labour' in the 'planet of slums' (Davis 2006). The non-capitalist small holders appear to be endlessly roaming in a 'ship of fools' (Sanyal 2007)—a befitting metaphor for keeping peasants perpetually in a vulnerable persistence with token policy supports.

Production practices have always been subsumed by techno-commercial interests rather than ecological prudence needed for overall sustainability. Making the farm sector work for the secondary or tertiary sectors of the economy cannot change the character of its direct dependence on nature, nor the hog cycles[18] involved. The repercussions of this oversight invariably fall on the entire society in the long run, as ultimately all economic activities derive from or indirectly depend on the primary sector. What is further to be integrated into this is the strength that smallholdings bring with them in linking primary production with the secondary sector without trapping energy in very high entropy activities. We search for instances of vulnerabilities in the study sites and discuss their contexts in Chaps. 6–9.

---

[17] *Forced commerce* involved unequal exchanges and mutually reinforcing feedback loops between poverty and debt.

[18] Hog cycles are recurring and successive changes in production and/or prices over years extending from one peak (or valley) to the next peak (or valley) as a result of the inevitable gestation period involved in agricultural production to respond to price signals.

2.7 Summary

This chapter reviewed dominant agrarian literature in an attempt to identify their relevance to the contemporary Indian smallholder, while noting major gaps and oversights. In recognising the smallholder as an independent economic unit, the Chayanovian approach provided a unique, yet relevant, analytical frame for studying the Indian smallholder farmer. The chapter offers a critique of the ecological and institutional gaps in currently dominant agrarian frameworks. It also points out the casual treatment meted out to the complexity and diversity of small farms—a dominant social identity in India that has the potential to provide sustainable livelihoods for millions.

The structural reconfiguration of this constituency of smallholders into the 'reserve army of labour' discussed here is more or less supported by empirical studies [e.g. Byres (1996)]. The ecological and cultural dynamics of a bifurcated persistence into capitalised and resource-poor farms is still missing, especially the changes needed in policies and practices for transforming this agrarian structure towards sustainability. In the absence of any notable alternative development paradigms, capitalistic large holdings emerge as the only viable model. Resultant unimodal agriculture might have the following repercussions in the immediate future—(i) co-existence of rent-seeking intensive farming of high-value products, with rampant fallowing of staple growing dry lands resulting in surging food prices or import bills (ii) loss of ecological, agricultural, culinary and cultural diversity and (iii) distress land sales, land acquisitions and influx to urban slums widening the socio-economic inequalities. Thus, the agrarian question, instead of becoming a non-issue [on '*capitalisation bypassed in India*', see Lerche (2013)], has in the neoliberal globalisation era been transformed into a more complex multi-dimensional issue with systemic linkages between the local and global contexts of market, politics, culture and environment.

Neither capitalistic nor socialist frames would suffice to explain this semi- or non-capitalist economic entity anchored in dynamically changing social–ecological systems. It appears as if ecological factors made cursory appearance in empirical studies on Indian farming, albeit qualitative and marginal, without integration with central agrarian questions. In the field studies of economic historians and agrarian theoreticians, this integration is conspicuous by absence. **Thus, although we see agrarian studies occupying prime status among social sciences in India in terms of number of studies carried out, it falls short of an organic exploration around the omnipresent entity of smallholder whose culture and livelihood lie in tinkering nature's cycles for producing food for the larger society, from a small piece of land.**

In parallel, environmental studies on the impact of agri-business model on land, food, consumers and farmers left-out the politico-economic and cultural perspectives. The need for a fruitful convergence between these perspectives so as to inform policy debates is obvious. Whenever calamities occur, whether it is drought or incidence of suicides; knee-jerk attribution of their origin is to natural causes rather than societal role. This leads to proposing more capital and technology as solutions alongside populist fixes. **By camouflaging the real structural issues of land, natural resources and markets, populist policies make inequality tolerable and pre-empt mass**

2.7 Summary

uprisings. An illogical absence of vertical and horizontal linkages within and between farms and regional economies hides the actual cost of short term fixes.

Feeble reflection of smallholders in the large discourse hovering around agrarian relations and transition is a classic case of missing the trees for the wood. Conventional assumptions in social sciences about a 'landed' community as not-so-poor were not debunked till recently (Gupta 2005). One would expect social scientists to take up the cause of revealing the nexus between half-baked technologies and policies instrumental in agrarian deskilling, damaging the agro-ecological foundations of a dominant social identity of rural India.

We attempt to pick up important missing threads in revealing how family farms differ from capital accumulating business enterprises in ensuring a life beyond, but not excluding livelihood aspirations. This we do by acknowledging the diversity of interfaces between urban areas and smallholders. Based on a dialectical treatment of research questions, the field study follows a gradient of urbanisation within the south-western Indian State of Karnataka.

References

Akram-Lodhi, A., & Kay, C. (2009). The agrarian question: Peasants and rural change. In *Peasants and globalization. Political economy, rural transformation and the agrarian question*. London and New York: Routledge.

Akram-Lodhi, A., Kay, C., & Borras, S. (2009). The political economy of land and the agrarian question in an era of neoliberal globalization. *Peasants and Globalization, 214–238*.

Araghi, F. (1995). Global depeasantisation, 1945–1990. *The Sociological Quarterly, 36*(2), 337–368.

Araghi, F. (2000). The great global enclosure of our times. In F. Magdoff, F. Buttel, & J. Foster (Eds.), *Hungry for Profit: The agribusiness threat to farmers, food and the environment* (pp. 145–160). New York: Monthly Review Press.

Araghi, F. (2009). The invisible hand and the visible foot, Peasant, Dispossession, and Globalisation. In A. Akram-Lodhi & C. Kay (Eds.), *Peasant and globalisation. Political economy, rural transformation and the agrarian question* (pp. 111–147). London: Routledge.

Banaji, J. (2003). The fictions of free labour: contract, coercion, and so-called unfree labour. *Historical Materialism, 11*(3), 69–95.

Bardhan, P. (1989). *The economic theory of agrarian institutions*. Oxford: Oxford University Press.

Bernstein, H. (1996). Agrarian questions then and now. *The Journal of Peasant Studies, 24*(1/2), 22–59.

Bhaduri, A. (1973). A study in agricultural backwardness under semi-feudalism. *Economic Journal*.

Bhaduri, A. (1983). Cropsharing as a labour process, size of farm and supervision cost. *The Journal of Peasant Studies, 10*(2–3), 88–93.

Bhaduri, A. (1986). Forced commerce and agrarian growth. *World Development, 14*(2), 267–272.

Brass, T. (2000). *Peasants, populism, and postmodernism: The return of the agrarian myth*. Psychology Press.

Bray, F. (1991). Rice economies: The rise and fall of china's communes in East Asian perspective. In J. Breman & S. Mundale (Eds.), *Rural transformation in Asia* (pp. 193–217). Delhi: Oxford University Press.

Breman, J., Kloos, P., & Saith, A. (1997). *The village in Asia revisited*. Delhi: Oxford University Press.

Breman, J., & Mundle, S. (1991). *Rural transformation in Asia*. Oxford: Oxford University Press.

Brodt, S. (2001). A systems perspective on the conservation and erosion of indegenous agricultural knowledge in Central India. *Human Ecology, 29,* 99–120.

Bryceson, D. (2000). Peasant theories and smallholder policies: Past and present. *Disappearing Peasantry,* 1–36.

Byres, T. (1996). *Capitalism from above and capitalism from below: An essay in comparative political economy.* London: Macmillan.

Chakravarthy, L. (1991). Agrarian economies and demographic regimes in India 1951-81. In J. Breman & S. Mundle (Eds.), *Rural transformation in Asia* (pp. 338–401). Delhi: Oxford University Press.

Chayanov, A. (1986[1925]). *The theory of peasant economy.* Madison: University of Wisconsin Press.

Damodaran, H. (2019). *Agri trade policy: A belated move from pro-consumer to pro-producer.* The Indian Express, Feb 7, 2019.

Davis, M. (2006). *Planet of slums.* New York: Verso.

Desai, A. (1979). *Peasant struggles in India.* Oxford: Oxford University Press.

Deshpande, S. (2012). Capitalism, exclusion, transition: The politics of the present. *Economic and Political Weekly, 42*(16), 41–44.

Dhanagare, D. (1983). *Peasant movements in India 1920–50.* Delhi: Oxford University Press.

Ellis, F. (2000). *Rural livelihoods and diversity in developing countries.* Oxford: Oxford University Press.

Epstein, S. (1973). *South India: Yesterday, today and tomorrow.* London: Macmillan.

Food and Agriculture Organisation. (2001). Number and area of agricultural holdings by land size class—1990 and 2000 round.

Food and Agriculture Organisation. (2013). Number and area of agricultural holdings by land size class—1990 and 2000 round.

Foster, J. (1999). Marx's theory of Metabolic Rift: Classical foundations for environmental sociology. *American Journal of Sociology, 105*(2), 366–405.

Friedmann, H. (1978). World market, state, and family farm: Social bases of household production in the era of wage labor. *Comparative Studies in Society and History, 20*(4), 545–586.

Friedmann, H., & McNair, A. (2008). Whose rules rule? Contested Projects to certify 'local production for distant consumers. *Journal of Agrarian Change, 8*(2 and 3), 408–434.

Galsius, M., & Pleyers, G. (2013). The global moment of 2011: Democracy, social justice and dignity. *Development and Change, 44*(3), 547–567.

Geertz, C. (1963). *Agricultural involution.* University of California Press.

George, A., & Kumar, A. (2017). Class in itself? Caste for itself?: Exploring the latest phase of rural agitaions in India. In *The 5th International Conference of the BRICS Initiative for Critical Agrarian Studies.* Moscow, Russia.

Georgescu-Roegen, N. (1960). Economic theory and agrarian economics. *Oxford Economic Papers, 12*(1).

Georgesçu-Roegen, N. (1971). *The entropy law and the economic process.* Harvard University Press.

Griffin, K. (1976). *The political economy of agrarian change: An essay on the green revolution.* Palgrave Macmillan.

Guha, R., & Martinez-Alier, J. (1997). *Varieties of environmentalism: Essays North and South.* London (UK): Earthscan Publications Ltd.

Gupta, A. (2005). Whither the Indian village: Culture and agriculture in rural India. *Economic and Political Weekly, 40*(8), 751–758.

Harris, J. (1991). Ariculture/non-agriculture linkages and the diversification of rural economic activity: A South Indian case study. In J. Breman & S. Mundle (Eds.), *Rural transformation in Asia* (pp. 429–458). Delhi: Oxford University Press.

Harriss-White, B. (2012). Capitalism and the common man: Peasant and petty production in Africa and South Asia. *Agrarian South: Journal of Political Economy, 1*(2), 109–160.

Harvey, D. (2004). The 'New' imperialism: Accumulation by disposession. *Socialist Register* 63–87.

References

Kumarappa, J. (1945). *Economy of permanence*. Varanasi: Sarva Seva Sangh Prakashan.

Leonard, D. (1977). *Reaching the peasant farmer: Organising theory and practice in Kenya*. Chicago: Chicago University Press.

Lerche, J. (2013). The agrarian question in Neoliberal Indi: Agrarian transition bypassed? *Journal of Agrarian Change, 13*(3), 382–404.

Lipton, M. (1991). Agriculture, rural people, the state and the Surplus in some asian countries: Thoughts on some implications of three recent approaches in social sciences. In J. Breman & S. Mundle (Eds.), *Rural transformation in Asia* (pp. 93–126). Delhi: Oxford University Press.

Lipton, M. (1995). The Prisoner's Dilemma and coase's theorem: A case for democracy in less developed countries? In R. Matthews (Ed.), *Economy and democracy* (pp. 49–109). The British Association for the Advancement of Science.

Lowder, S. K., Skoet, J., & Raney, T. (2016). The number, size and distribution of farms, smallholder farms and family farms worldwide. *World Development, 87*(C), 16–29.

Marx, K. (1894). Capital: A critique of political economy.*Volume III: The process of capitalist production as a whole*. (F. Engels, Ed., 1959). New York: International Publishers.

McMichael, P. (2009). Food sovereignty, social reproduction and the agrarian question. In A. Akram-Lodhi & C. Kay (Eds.), *Peasant and globalisation: Political economy, rural transformation and the agrarain question* (pp. 288–311). London & New York: Routledge.

Mencher, J. (1978). *Agriculture and social structure*. Allied Publications.

Mishra, R. P. (1985). *Development issues of our time*. New Delhi: Concept Publishing Company.

Mishra, S. (2006). Farmers' suicides in Maharashtra. *Economic and Political Weekly*, 1538–45.

Mitrany, D. (1951). *Marx against the peasant*. Chapel Hill: University of North Carolina Press.

Mohan Rao, R. (1991). Commecialisation and agricultural growth in Asia: A comparative study of South Korea and Coastal Andhra. In J. Breman & S. Mundle (Eds.), *Rural transformation in Asia* (pp. 256–280). Delhi: Oxford University Press.

Mollinga, P. (2010). Boundary work and the complexity of natural resources management. *Crop Science, 50*, S1–S9.

Moore, J. (2000). Environmental crises and the metabolic rift in world-historical perspective. *Organization and Environment, 13*(2), 123–157.

NITI Aayog. (2016). *Evaluation study on role of public distribution system in shaping household and nutritional security in India, development monitoring and evaluation offfice*. New Delhi: NITI Aayog.

O'Laughlin, B. (2004). Rural livelihoods and diversity in developing countries. *Development and Change, 35*(2), 385–403.

Omvedt, G. (1981). Capitalist agriculture and rural classes in India. *Economic and Political Weekly, 16*(52).

Patel, R. (2007). *Stuffed and starved: The hidden battle for the world food system*. Brooklyn, NY: Melville House Publishing.

Patnaik, U. (1976). Class differentiation within the Peasantry—An approach to analysis of India agriculture. *Economic and Political Weekly, 11*(39), A82–A101.

Patnaik, U. (1990). *Agrarian relations and accumulation: The 'Mode of Production' debate in India*. New Delhi: Sameeksha Books.

Picketty, T. (2014). *Capital in twenty-first century*. Cambridge: Harvard University Press.

Polzin, F., von Flotow, P., & Klerkx, L. (2016). Addressing barriers to eco-innovation: Exploring the finance mobilisation functions of institutional innovation intermediaries. *Technological Forecasting and Social Change, 103*, 34–46.

Purushothaman, S., & Patil, S. (2017). Regional economies and small farmers in Karnataka. *Economic and Political Weely, 52*(46), 78–84.

Purushothaman, S., Patil, S., & Lodha, S. (2016, January). Social and environmental transformation in the Indian peri-urban interface—Emerging questions. *Azim Premji University, Working Paper Series 1*.

Raj, K. (1990). Bridging rural-urban Gap. *Economic and Political Weekly*.

Ravillion, M., & Van De Walle, D. (2006). Land reallocation in an agrarian transition. *The Economic Journal, 116*(514), 924–942.

Rigg, J., Salamanca, A., & Thompson, E. (2016). The puzzle of East and Southeast Asia's persistent smallholder. *Journal of Rural Studies, 43,* 118–123.

Rudra, A. (1990). Class relations in Indian agriculture. In U. Patnaik (Ed.), *Agrarian relations and accumulations: The 'mode of production' debate in India.* Sameeksha Trust, Bombay: Oxford University Press.

Saith, A. (1991). Asian rural industrialisation: Context, features, strategies. In J. Breman & S. Mundle (Eds.), *Rural transformation in Asia* (pp. 458–489). Delhi: Oxford University Press.

Sanyal, K. (2007). *Rethinking capitalist development: Primitive accumulation, governmentality and post-colonial capitalism.* New Delhi: Routledge India.

Sanyal, K., & Bhattacharya, R. (2009). Beyond the factory: Globalisation, informalisation of production and the new locations of labour. *Economic and Political Weekly, 44*(22), 35–44.

Schneider, M., & McMichael, P. (2010). Deepening, and repairing, the metabolic rift. *Journal of Peasant Studies, 37*(3), 461–484.

Schultz, T. (1964a). The doctrine of agricultural labor of zero value. *Transforming traditional agriculture* (pp. 58–70). Lyall Book Depot: Ludhiana.

Schultz, T. (1964b). *Transforming traditional agriculture.* Ludhiana: Lyall Book Depot.

Scott, J. (1977). *The moral economy of the peasant: Rebellion and subsistence in Southeast Asia.* Yale University Press.

Scott, J. (1985). *Weapons of the Weak: Everyday forms of peasant resistance.* Yale University Press.

Scott, J. (1998). Taming nature: An agriculture of legibility and simplicity. In J. Scott (Ed.), *Seeing like a state* (pp. 262–306). Yale University Press.

Sen, A. (1991). Shocks and instabilities in an agriculture-constrained economy: India 1964–85. In J. Breman & S. Mundle (Eds.), *Rural transformation in Asia* (pp. 490–522). Delhi: Oxford University Press.

Shah, A., & Harriss-White, B. (2011). Resurrecting scholarship on agrarian transformation. *Economic and Political Weekly, 41*(39), 13–18.

Srinivas, M. (1976). *Remembered village.* Berkeley: University of California Press.

Stiglitz, J., Sen, A., & Fitoussi, J. (2010). *Mis-measuring our Lives. Why the GDP doesn't add up.* The Report by the Commission on the Measurement of Economic Performance and Social Progress. New Press, New York.

Stone, G. (2002). Both sides now: Fallacies in the genetic-modification wars, implications for developing countries, and anthropological perspectives. *Current Anthropology, 43*(4), 611–630.

Stone, G. D. (2007). Agricultural deskilling and spread of genetically modified cotton in Warangal. *Current Anthropology, 48*(1), 67–102.

Thompson, E. (1971). The moral economy of the english crowd in the eighteenth century. *Past and Present, 50,* 76–136.

Thorner, A. (1982). Semi-feudalism or capitalism? Contemporary debate on classes and modes of production in India. Part 3. *Economic and Political Weekly, 17*(51), 2061–2066.

Thrupp, L. (1989). Legitimizing local knowledge: From displacement to empowerment for Third World people. *Agriculture and Human Value, 6,* 13–24.

Vasavi, A. (1999). Agrarian distress in Bidar: Market, state and suicides. *Economic and Political Weekly,* 2263–2268.

Vasavi, A. (2012). *Shadow spaces: Suicides and the Predicament of Rural India.* Three Essay Collective.

Vishwanath, L. S. (1990). Peasant movements in Colonial India—An examination of some conceptual frameworks. *Economic and Political Weekly, 25*(2), 118–122.

World Development Report. (2008). *Agriculture for development.* Washington, DC: The World Bank.

Wright, E. (1980). Class and occupation. *Theory and Society, 9*(1), 177–214.

Chapter 3
Study Approach, Processes and Methods

3.1 Conceptualising the Study

Recognising the gaps prevalent in the existing agrarian frameworks in general and the lack of focus on smallholders in particular, this study explores the dynamics of family farms in urbanising India, specifically in the southern State of Karnataka. The intention is to understand small farmer as an identity and small farming as a livelihood option, based on existing data and scholarship.

In order to develop a framework around the life of small farmers beyond their modes of engagement with land and labour, a careful integration of multiple, diverse and changing dimensions was felt needed. This integration (discussed in Chap. 1, Sect. 1.2) needs alternative approaches so as to answer questions like how and when can agriculture be a sustainable option for the family while ensuring welfare needs of the society.

Such an integrative framework is approached from the following premises. The first is that urbanisation processes connect the macroeconomy with agricultural regions in various ways. The second is that history of social and ecological changes influences agrarian outcomes in such interfaces. Thus, the study proceeds from understanding diversity in urbanisation towards analysing what it means to be a smallholder in different contexts (Fig. 3.1).

In such an approach involving multiple dimensions in the urban–agrarian interface, small farmers' persistence is seen as a constant, yet adaptive effort, evolving with changes in urbanisation, ecology and society. The study engages with two prominent and intertwined layers of the urban centre and small farms in their peripheries. **The hypothesis is that occupational shift from farming may not always be successful or result in better quality of life, nor will all farmers who get non-farm opportunities, move out of farming**. We see two major questions about small family holdings emerging from the above hypotheses on the rural–urban mosaic in the State of Karnataka:

© Springer Nature Singapore Pte Ltd. 2019
S. Purushothaman and S. Patil, *Agrarian Change and Urbanization in Southern India*, India Studies in Business and Economics,
https://doi.org/10.1007/978-981-10-8336-5_3

Fig. 3.1 Approaching family farms from urbanisation onwards

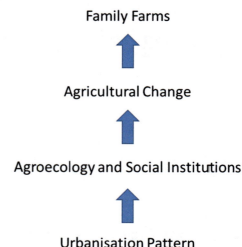

- with respect to land (ecological factors), economic factors, family conditions and exogenous drivers, when do people continue in small farming as a profession of their preference and when do they move out partially or completely from farming?
- what (policies, institutions, skills, etc.) facilitates or hinders the transition of smallholders into part-time farming (along with seasonal out-migration) or into a completely non-farm livelihood?

In addressing the above questions, while agrarian change in response to urbanisation in the immediate vicinity is the primary focus, the influence of distant but heavy urbanisation as well as of the larger political-economic dynamics on remote farmlands are also brought into analysis. Proximate or distant, urban centres interact with peri-urban agriculture directly or routed through common natural resources. These flows get influenced, either structurally or functionally, by a changing rural–urban dynamics (Fig. 3.2).

Such interactions between peri-urban farms and urban centres may be mutually overlapping in spatial and temporal scales without clear starting and ending points in both time and space. However, for empirical purposes, the study sites are chosen so as to reflect discernible diversity in urbanisation process. Sections below unravel this diversity and the elements to explore in their interface with agrarian land- and social scapes.

3.2 Typology of Urbanisation

Urbanisation process is heterogeneous in a spatially discontinuous gradient and ranges from small rural towns to metropolitan cities. At times urban spots or clusters

3.2 Typology of Urbanisation

appear within the rural and vice versa. This mosaic of rural and urban landscapes acts both as the cause and outcome of economic changes in the production landscapes.

The wave of urbanisation in the early period of independent India was driven by large public sector undertakings such as BEL, BHEL, HAL and HMT in Bengaluru, NTPC in Madhya Pradesh, Steel cities of Bhilai, Bokaro and Salem, and so on. Private corporate establishments too gave rise to new residential towns that later transformed to cities like Jamshedpur that grew around the Tata steel factory.

The second wave of urbanisation that occurred after independence in Bengaluru, Hyderabad and Noida was centred around information technology. In Coimbatore and Tiruppur, it was around export-oriented textiles and garments industries. There are also towns that emerged from agro-commercial expansion. These include the wheat economy of Harda (Madhya Pradesh), Bhatinda and Patiala (Punjab); the silk and sugar economy of Mandya region (Karnataka), fish trade in Vishakhapatnam (Andhra Pradesh), flourishing tea economy around Guwahati (Assam), apple and berries hub around Shimla (Himachal Pradesh), small towns fueled by cotton trade around Bhiwandi (Maharashtra), Anantapur (Andhra Pradesh) and Indore (Madhya Pradesh). Other towns such as Anand flourished around dairy-based products, while Varanasi and Ludhiana grew around a vibrant handloom economy and manufacture of woollen apparel, respectively. Agro-machinery manufacturing in Rajkot and chemical and fertilizer industries in Kanpur, also drove local processes of urbanisation.

Other common drivers of urban expansion found elsewhere include the education industry in Pune and Bengaluru, the tourism economy in the cities of Rajasthan and Goa, the pilgrims' hubs concentrated in and around Haridwar and Rishikesh, and major coastal cities around seaports such as Cochin, Kollam, Karwar, Mangalore and Gandhidham. All the above types of urbanisation have resulted in positive and negative farm and non-farm impacts.

In order to understand the various types and processes of urbanisation in the State of Karnataka, literature covering urban, peri-urban and rural studies was surveyed. This, alongside the insights gathered from our initial field studies, informed the urban

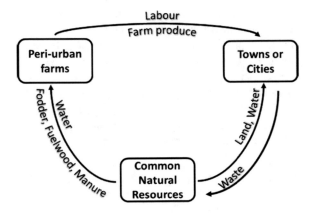

Fig. 3.2 Exchanges between peri-urban farms and urban centres

typology used in the book. While thinking of urbanisation as a driver of agricultural and agrarian change, we see certain emergent patterns and processes unfolding in distinct ways.[1] The key characteristics of the core urban space and its peripheral farmlands in four distinct categories are discussed below.

Recent but heavy urbanisation

Unlike regions that were historically marketing hubs in the erstwhile Mysore, some geographies act as new hubs of capital accumulation, population growth and infrastructural development. The timeline of evolution of this category of cities coincides with the years of neoliberal growth in the country and the information technology (IT) boom beginning in the 1990s. The influx of both foreign and domestic capital into such core development areas, together with cosmopolitan demand, signalled changes in farm practices both in their immediate surroundings as well as in relatively distant agrarian geographies. These spaces of concentrated economic growth demand more as well as newer farm products. Rapidly expanding urban population and land use, intensified farming in the immediate peripheries and livelihood shifts are hallmarks of this region.

Parts of the cities of Bengaluru, Hyderabad, Chennai, Delhi, Mumbai and Kolkata showcasing similar changes since the dawn of liberalisation era in the 1990s can be characterised as neo-urban (NU) landscapes. Rapid and extensive shifts in land use and occupations, surging land value, and inward migration of both skilled and unskilled labour characterise these neo-urban landscapes. For example, Pune city and its rapidly expanding and changing periphery together offer a more recent contender as a NU landscape. The regions where urbanisation was driven by state-run manufacturing and other institutions in the mid-twentieth century could be currently co-existing with the newly urbanised spaces, within the larger NU spatial context. In case of Bengaluru, areas surrounding the large public sector units such as Indian Space Research Organisation (ISRO), Hindustan Machine Tools Limited (HMT), Bharat Electronics Limited (BEL), Bharat Earth Movers Limited (BEML) and Hindustan Aeronautics Limited (HAL) that were established since independence, and some large private industries are such instances.

The fast-paced trajectory of growing economy and population in the NU landscapes overshadow and mutate the social–ecological fabric of the place, in more or less uniform fashion across such cities. Among all such NU cities, there is a characteristic homogenisation in the way roads, buildings, water bodies, gardens/parks and consumption pattern including food co-exist. It is not easy to find remnants of the old patterns of the above features in a NU landscape, though some elements of erstwhile culture and social relation are still embedded in the NU citizenry.

Peripheral farmlands of such cities attract migrants from different parts of the State as well as neighbouring States seeking work in the construction, manufacturing and service industries of the NU core. Farming in the peripheries of these hubs of intensive

---

[1] There exist other kinds of urbanisation processes in other parts of the globe. Here, we intend to keep the discussion to the process that is most relevant to effectively link it with the other layer of the study—agrarian change.

3.2 Typology of Urbanisation

urbanisation mainly caters to the demand for fresh produce (including dairy) by the inhabitants of the metropolitan city and its suburbs.

Slowly urbanising towns

Compared to NU spaces, slowly urbanising towns still retain some earlier features of the local agro-ecology and society. Development of these smaller towns may be slowly driven by weak and multiple drivers unlike a metropolis relying on neoliberal economic forces. Depending on proximity to a mega city, such a small town may eventually get subsumed within the larger socio-economic boundaries of a capital-accumulating NU core. Yet, it is not rare to find some remnants of pre-existing culture, food, trees and even old structures like buildings and markets here. Tumkur and Ramanagara towns not-so-far from Bengaluru city are examples under this category. These slowly urbanising areas may have also been influenced by medium-scale establishments run by the State, public corporate sector or the private corporate sector.

Extensive agricultural landscapes start right at the edge of these small towns. Land use change here would have been recent and driven by small residential layouts or industrial estates. These towns generally spread horizontally compared to the vertically growing urban areas with population surge within finite boundaries. Family members of the same households here would be engaged in diverse occupations. Smaller towns that turned multifunctional in the recent past are characterised within this urbanisation type.

Agro-urban spaces

Different from the above two spaces and processes, urbanisation could also be mainly in response to local economic drivers evolving organically from production activities of a region. A distinct feature of this kind of process is its direct linkage with the local production systems. It is not rare to see historical interdependency between enterprises built on local resources including skill sets of rural communities and agricultural production. Indian towns like Dibrugarh, Mandya and Kochi grew around tea, sugarcane/silk, and spices, respectively, over different timelines. A few primary sector processing industries together with agriculture that feed them result in accumulation of capital, political clout, improved infrastructure and a flourishing services sector in the agro-processing towns.

Rural towns

Different from the above three geographies that are urbanising in distinct paces and patterns, there are regions relatively far from the buzz of intense urbanisation. These are rural towns sans a dynamic demography. Nonetheless, these spaces service other rapidly urbanising spaces in various ways—supplying cheap labour or important dry land produces, while remaining largely unacknowledged and hidden with characteristically low human development parameters. Districts located in north-eastern Karnataka represent such agrarian hinterlands among the numerous rural towns sprawled across India.

The four processes mentioned indicate that these are not completely mutually exclusive. We will now look into the key elements through which the interactions of urbanisation with the agrarian landscape in the above fourfold typology are to be explored.

3.3 Exploring the Urban–Agrarian Interface

Exploring agrarian change in the above-described intertwined rural–urban landscapes envisages an eye for complexity amidst their most explicit features. The idyllic rural land- and social scape with distinct lifestyle and livelihoods has morphed into localities with visible influence of city's consumerism. Plastic garbage, bottled water, exotic food items, cosmetics, smartphones and motorbikes dot the 'bottom of the pyramid' villages now.[2] Yet, villagers continue to negotiate the tenacious tentacles of caste, gender and land ownership as also that of culture, politics and neo-capitalism. Growing urban neighbourhoods as potential destinations for their farm produce and non-farm employment, pose both problems and prospects for rural dwellers, especially the small holder. Such a scenario of hybrid lifestyles and problems seems to be more enduring rather than just a phase of transition. Notable agrarian changes under the influence of urbanisation explored in detail by the study are identified below.

The most visible change is in rural land use. Land use could change from natural landscape to agricultural production systems or from natural landscapes and agricultural use to non-agricultural uses. Changes in cropping pattern, cultivation practice, occupation and marketing happen in tandem with this change in land use. Changes in institutions and infrastructure also deserve attention but these could be both the cause and effect of other changes happening in and around the village society. Chapters 6–9 that focus on the study sites will deliberate empirical observations categorised and outlined below - farmlands, village commons, water, crops, animals and farm practices, migration, markets and institutions.

3.3.1 Farmlands

In any agrarian landscape, the major impact of urbanisation happening in the vicinity is land conversion away from agriculture. This conversion could be either voluntary or involuntary following an increase in land value. A hike in the exchange value of land in a growing economy encourages voluntary exit from small-scale farming. Many farmers in such places would sell their land for a good price and move to remote interiors where land value is less, saving some money in the process to spend on a family function, medical treatment or to pay off outstanding loans. Chances of reinvesting in agricultural land are very remote, given the uncertain cash flow in farming.

---

[2] 'Bottom of the pyramid' refers to rural areas as vast market for consumer goods (Prahlad 2012).

3.3 Exploring the Urban–Agrarian Interface

Compared to this voluntary conversion of agricultural land use, acquisition for construction of roads and other public purposes or for industries and huge infrastructural projects (like airports and the 'pay-and-use' speedways) entails compulsion. The latter often results in lasting conflicts due to a combination of inadequate and delayed compensation along with violation of human and livelihood rights. This can be seen in many cases like Karnataka Industrial Area Development Board and Information Technology Investment Region near Devanahalli, and Nandi Infrastructure Corridor Enterprise—the speedway around Bengaluru (Balakrishnan 2017), Science city in Chitradurga,[3] Special Investment Region in Dholera as well as Sardar Sarovar Narmada Nigam Limited along the banks of Narmada (Varghese 2016; NIE 2013). These conflicts happen alongside national dialogues on fair processes of acquisition and resettlement.[4]

Even when financial compensation is reasonable and paid without much delay, why do acquisition processes result in conflicts with farmer landowners? Firstly, farm families rarely possess skills that earn them a secure job in any of the upcoming non-farm ventures, even though employment for project affected families generally is an important precondition to secure legal permission for farmland acquisition. Secondly, most smallholders are not exposed to dealing with financial capital and fail to prudently manage the amount of compensation received. Most end up spending the compensation money in ceremonies, medical treatment, in paying off debts, in building lavish bungalows in the city outskirts or on expensive cars. The acquisition agencies seldom avoid acquiring fertile land, as locational and financial objectives override concerns of displacing food production and livelihood. Often the dominant development notion is an imminent priority for non-farm use of land. This is based on an implicit false notion that farmers' lives can be transplanted anywhere and that most farmers welcome the rare inflow of cash in bulk.

Standard of living of displaced farmers often deteriorates even after receiving reasonable compensation. The relinquished piece of land seems to have been ensuring some security (identity, food and occupation) though not much in liquid cash. In other words, money from urban expansion does not compensate farmers for what they lose along with their land—security in food, occupation, health and identity—nor offer them new material comforts.

3.3.2 Village Commons

For smallholders, access to village common lands is as important as possessing secure private land to cultivate. Village commons are used for grazing animals and collecting herbs, fruits, fuelwood, even some bush meat and makes up for the limitations of the

---

[3]http://praja.in/files/Cdurga%20DC%20Office%20Swarmed%20Shepherds%20___Press_Release_25072013.pdf.

[4]Array of amendments and objections from different States were filed in reforming the Land Acquisition Act 1894 towards the Land Acquisition, Rehabilitation and Resettlement Act, 2013.

small size of their own land. This utilitarian advantage of commons is in addition to their role in keeping natural assets and related knowledge base of the community intact while preventing complete individualisation of farmers. In addition to the direct use values, ecological functions in terms of hydrology and biodiversity performed by grasslands, hill slopes and forests are of indirect use and non-use value to all farmers.

Besides the straightforward usurping of village commons for expanding urbanisation, what is generally seen is a twin indirect impact of urbanisation on commons—(i) in de-notifying forest commons for commercial mining activities (e.g. coal mining in the Mahan forest of Madhya Pradesh, iron-ore mining in Chhattisgarh and Jharkhand, bauxite mining in Goa and Coastal Karnataka) or hydroelectric projects (Sardar sarovar and other such projects) and (ii) in using village commons as 'land banks' (Lele et al. 2013) for distribution to the landless as well as to religious and educational institutions.[5]

Acquiring excess land from large holders for distribution was the stated intention of land reform measures initiated in many States. This objective appears abandoned during the early stage of reforms itself. Instead, village commons were redistributed to the landless as well as religious and educational institutions. Short-sighted politics results in village commons being used for short-term private gains in land allotment rather than the health and livelihoods of local inhabitants. Ruling political parties in any government woo the vote banks of land-poor masses and the money sources of rich private institutions in one stroke, by distributing easily accessible commons. **How the social objective of land distribution is used to camouflage subtle subterfuge of village commons is akin to how food security concern is used for importing food; both jeopardizing food production and consumption at the bottom of the pyramid**.

Like the denotified forests and acquired grazing lands, wooded commons in the possession of large landholders (but conventionally accessible to others) like *soppinabetta*s of Karnataka's *Malenadu* (State of the Environment Report 2003) region are also getting exclusively privatised by larger plantation holdings, depriving smaller holdings of their biomass resources in the landscape. Traditional community rights to access harvested arable fields for grazing or penning animals also comes under threat from land conversion either away from agriculture itself or from arable crops to commercial plantations.

Thus traditional institutions of land use that helped spread the cost and risks of smallholders practically disappeared in most parts of India. Disappearance of commons reduces the availability of farmyard manure, adversely affecting short-term costs and long-term productivity of small farms. **Thus hike in land value in the rural–urban interface driven by urbanisation results in significant dispossession of village commons. How this dispossession coupled with acquisition and**

---

[5]Data on the extent of land allotted to religious and other private bodies in Karnataka was not available. Constructions and enclosed campuses of organizations that received common land allotted by the government make a visible presence in many peri-urban areas. There are about 35,000 institutions to which Karnataka State extends support (https://www.thehindu.com/news/national/karnataka/34229-temples-to-get-grant-of-Rs.-36000-every-year/article13978082.ece).

3.3 Exploring the Urban–Agrarian Interface

conversion of farmlands, play a role in the making of a proletariat class out of small family farms will be explored in the study sites.

3.3.3 Water

The impact of urbanisation on water availability for agriculture and household use is straightforward. Lakes in urbanising areas converted to build public utility buildings (easier than acquiring land from powerful large holders) and groundwater gets exploited by private industries. Residential layouts and theme parks directly pose challenges to the small farmer engaged in growing either rain-fed crops (requiring sufficient soil moisture) or irrigated crops (depending on tube wells or canals). Voluntary dispossession of water sources driven by farmers' helplessness is also not rare. Selling water from their farms either to a more commercial farmer neighbour or to tankers that supply water to the city (Packialakshmi and Ambujam 2017; Ruet et al. 2007) is increasingly common in peri-urban areas.

The water problem faced by the smallholder for modern irrigation and farming methods has to be contextualised within a general lack of agricultural know-how on prudent water use and an overt assumption that maximising water application can maximise food production. Should water be used for saving standing crops from wilting or should it be used to hasten production along with intensive use of other inputs? Wouldn't the latter affect soil moisture in the rain-fed lands of the resource poor? Is water balancing a prudent farming practice in conflict with food security and agricultural costs? What is the role played by urbanisation and technology in responding to this dilemma? The study explores these questions in the selected agrarian peripheries.

The race for irrigation water in private agricultural lands alongside the urban culture of wasteful consumption with an associated appetite for produce grown by intensive farming snowballs into a 'prisoner's dilemma'.[6] As farmers avail loans and strategize to compete with neighbouring farms with deeper and deeper bore wells, the common water sources of villages, in the absence of effective institutions to sustain them, await the inevitable tragedy of commons. Large-scale irrigation projects persuade small farmers, even in remote areas to adopt resource-intensive crops and compete with each other for access to water, leading to increased economic and ecological vulnerability.[7] **Wherever irrigation results in yield improvements, incommensurate storage and marketing options generally dampen the potential benefit-flow to small farmers.**

Losing the battle for water fought with huge financial burden, desperate peri-urban farmers even turn to effluents from neighbouring urban landscapes (partially

---

[6]The concepts of game theory and prisoner's dilemma have been applied to explain competitive use of groundwater by Koch and Nax (2017) and its governance by Meinzen-Dick et al. (2016).

[7]For instance, the case of vulnerability at the head end of irrigation canal in Gundal command (Purushothaman et al. 2009).

treated at best) for irrigation. Ignorance of the health impacts of using sewage for cultivation or of the food produced by the process; is instrumental in seeing it as bridging the rural–urban rift in water and soil nutrients. Wherever the problem of quantity is overcome by urban sewage water, the challenges of poor water quality surface (Jamwal et al. 2014). As seen in the case of land (Sect. 3.1 above), the water footprint of urbanisation spans across private and common resources, crucial for smallholders who are strapped for land and capital.

Field studies take cognizance of the above challenges in being a smallholder in the era of urbanisation. As the following sections show, in terms of socio-economic and political status, they share the status of society's downtrodden. Status of land, water and biomass both in the private and common domains differentiate today's smallholders from Chaynovian peasantry.

3.3.4 Crops, Animals and Ways of Farming

Urbanisation and its influence on agriculture is not a new phenomenon. Colonial cantonments and trading regions significantly influenced the choice of crops, animals and inputs in their surroundings. Cultivation of exotic crops for Bengaluru cantonment in the 1800s has been already noted in Chap. 3. Introduction of new components into a farm need not necessarily pose a problem, but it brings in new risks in farming practices and food habits. Often new farm components (new crops, animals or birds) make farmers adopt practices (culinary and cultivation practices) that may not be congenial for the long-term health of the farm and the family. It is not easy to segregate the pros and cons of new introductions. The difficulty lies in the haziness of socio-cultural boundaries in a globalised world. What is exotic and urban today becomes the local norm tomorrow. Even far away cities may be linked to remote hinterlands through their demand for various agricultural produce. Thus, what is adjudged as a problematic introduction today could be a well-accepted change tomorrow.

However, very often new crops and technologies are popularised without the necessary understanding of the consequences—ecological, social or financial. The advent of canal irrigation gave rise to the perception that more water is better for crops. While this implied higher use of other inputs too, the quality of irrigated land deteriorated due to salinity and soil erosion through years of irrigation practice, without possible local solutions. There are well-known instances of unknown risks associated with hastily introduced exotic components spelling disaster in farm households. Rise and fall of ostrich farms (Shanawany 1999), vanilla and cacao plantations (Surendranath and Suchitra 2015), of ginger kings and corpses (Munster 2015) as well as a spread of distress in BT cotton belt (Thomas and De Tevernier 2017) hold testimony to this.

3.3.5 Occupation and Migration

Assessing smallholding as a livelihood option involves looking at alternatives. Contrary to expectations, the period of intensive urbanisation does not seem to offer new employment opportunities to the rural masses. Some authors (Chandrasekhar and Sharma 2015; Basole et al. 2018) refer to the period between 2001 and 2011 as India's 'jobless growth' period. Based on an increase in short-term migration, return migration and two-way commuting of workers across rural and urban areas, this is often referred to as 'semi-proletarianisation' (Sanyal and Bhattacharya 2009; Brass and Bernstein 1992). This phenomenon demands an analysis of the following theses—(a)that agrarian society is dead in India (Lerche 2013; Bernstein 2016), (b) that agriculture has been capitalised in pockets (Yadu and Satheesha 2016); and (c) that agricultural involution is prevalent (see discussion in Chap. 1, Sect. 1.2.2).

In the time of economic growth sans agri-employment, the urban pull for rural labour to co-produce cities coincides with a push out of villages. Non-compatibility of an agrarian economy with the growing and urbanising macroeconomy thus drives migration. Yet, rural small-scale agriculture evidently persists.

Role of women in family farms though significant, remains largely unacknowledged. Following the recent discussion on feminisation in agriculture (e.g. Pattnaik et al. 2017), the book will also examine the existence of feminisation in distress and aspirational farming, as also in migration. With nearly 20% operational holdings owned by and 15% operated by women, Karnataka is close to its south Indian counterparts and some north-eastern States according to Agriculture Census (2015). Although the study does not dwell upon gender and agriculture in detail, it takes along this lens throughout the fieldwork.

With frequent and faster commutation modes and opportunities in peri-urban landscapes, households are seen diversifying their livelihood baskets with various permutations and combinations of possibilities: (a) cultivation on own or leased-in land, (b) leasing out own land, (c) seeking agricultural or non-agricultural wage labour within or outside the village and (d) petty commodity production. Such bundling of livelihood options is both a coping mechanism in times of distress and a step towards aspirational lifestyle.

This diversification again questions the conclusion about the complete disappearance of traditional peasantry (Bernstein 2003) characterised either by bondage with landlords or limited natural resources. Given the new forms of subordination in terms of adverse terms of trade, involuntary evictions as well as continued impoverishment, the study considers smallholders as the new peasantry. This approach is seen reflected in site-wise discussions on the differential impacts of urbanisation on farm livelihoods in Chaps. 6–9.

3.3.6 Markets

The most logical advantage of peri-urban farming is its proximity to different markets. The following questions are found remaining and examined in the study: does being proximate to the city help small farmers sustain their profession? Are markets closer to the city less discriminatory compared to the regulated markets in predominent production areas? What are the opportunities and challenges in the old and new informal markets—ubiquitous *santhes* (local roadside weekly markets) and new marketing initiatives in the big cities? The study approaches markets in order to understand the potential of urbanisation to sustain smallholders.

3.3.7 Institutions

Farming and local social institutions have always shared a symbiotic relationship—be it norms of synchronising operations like ploughing or sowing, working in the fields of families that lack manpower or the regressive institutions of caste and gender discrimination. While the former institutions are fast disappearing leaving a conspicuous vacuum without the emergence of alternative mechanisms, regressive institutions appear tenacious and all-pervasive. The State alone proves inadequate to institutionalise a new organic link between social, economic and technological changes with livelihoods in tandem with agro-ecology (Purushothaman et al. 2013). This institutional gap seems to aid a sweeping globalisation agenda to undermine the unique strengths of our farm sector—small, biodiverse and resilient units.

The nexus between caste and class hierarchies often determines how urbanisation plays out for certain agrarian communities compared to others (see Chap. 4 for a brief history of multiple discriminatory trends in colonial and post-colonial Mysore State). **The study bears in mind the fact that the relative force of rural–urban push-pull factors determine the changing nature of the agrarian livelihood basket amidst this caste–class dynamics.**

Communication technology appears to be the only new socio-technological infrastructure relevant to peri-urban–agrarian societies. Mobile phones play a vital role in determining the pull factors in farmer's livelihood basket. New networks around social media and communication technology can become potential levelers[8] in the above-mentioned dynamics centred around the regressive institutions of caste and class. Parts of Chaps. 6–9 will uncover the present status of this dynamics between the old and the new; formal and the informal institutions in the study sites.

---

[8] Artificial-intelligence-based mobile applications aiding farmers in reducing their dependence on traders is reported in rural areas (https://news.microsoft.com/en-in/features/ai-agriculture-icrisat-upl-india/ and https://plantix.net/en).

3.4 Research Methodology

Research process to align with the above-described conceptualisation of the urban–agrarian interface follows a *research-then-theory* strategy emphasising on qualitative processes and limited quantitative analysis.

Answering the research questions stated at the beginning of this chapter by combining qualitative and quantitative tools using primary and secondary information allows linking farm-level analysis to macroeconomic and social changes as and when needed. Blending group interactions and household interviews with survey of archives, deliberations with scholars and secondary sources of information necessitates multiple analytical approaches. Stage-wise steps involved in the study, right from conceptualisation is depicted in the process diagram (Fig. 3.3).

Visualising and designing the study

Once the broad research questions mentioned early in the chapter were identified, more literature on theoretical and empirical studies on agrarian transition in the backdrop of economic growth, urbanisation and farmers' distress in India was gathered and reviewed. The conceptualisation phase of the study based on this set of literature, apart from identifying the gaps in existing agrarian frameworks, also revealed socio-environmental changes in different peri-urban areas. This resulted in a review of peri-urban literature in Purushothaman et al. (2016). Stage 1 of the study, thus imparted clarity on possible rural–urban nexuses as well as on how to approach family farms. The framework mentioned in Sect. 3.1 is based on this understanding.

Selection of districts, taluks and villages

Having decided on the urbanisation categories to study agrarian change in their peripheries as discussed in Sects. 3.2 and 3.3, we needed to select corresponding field sites. Bengaluru was identified as the intensely urbanising neo-urban metropolitan site at the beginning of the study itself, before regional variations in urbanisation came under the scanner. The realisation from survey of literature, preliminary field visits and earlier research[9] that farmer outcomes could vary in different peri-urban areas, persuaded the inclusion of other kinds of regional urbanisms in the State.

The urbanisation process varies within the State according to planned prioritisation and policies for regional development. Karnataka has four physio-geographical regions—Coastal, Malnad, Southern Maidan and Northern Maidan. Except for Northern Maidan, the remaining three regions have a significant presence of towns with expanding secondary and tertiary sectors.

In order to align study areas with the typology of urbanisation, more than three decades of district-level data from agricultural census, economic census, economic survey, district handbooks and regulated markets was analysed.

---

[9] Project LUPIS (from 2006 to 2009) explored the impact of a policy of organic farming in Karnataka and revealed varied impacts in different agro-climatic zones (https://cordis.europa.eu/project/rcn/81388_en.html).

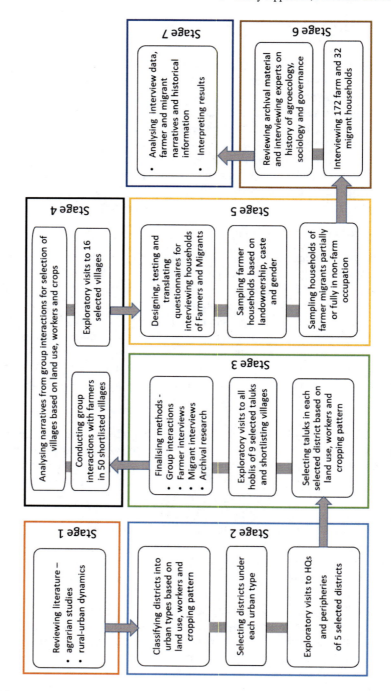

Fig. 3.3 Research process

3.4 Research Methodology

District selection followed a three-step process (see Stage 2 in Fig. 3.3). First, four districts in each category of small town, agro-urban and rural town were shortlisted after examining data on change of land use into industrial, residential and commercial use.[10] Bengaluru was already identified for an intensely urbanising megacity. This shortlisting exercise enabled us to judge the reach and extent of neoliberal drivers in different parts of the State.

Number of cultivators and labourers as well as share of agriculture in household income implied significant agricultural dependence in the study districts. Simultaneously, to confirm the relevance of family farms, the shortlisted districts were examined using data on smallholders' connect with markets and processing industries.

These parameters indicative of the importance of agriculture were used to rank the shortlisted districts within the three categories. Finally, a careful consideration of historical causation of changes in agricultural livelihoods, particularly in land use and crops grown, along with the extent and intensity of neoliberal drivers in the districts, guided the third and final step of selecting one district within each of the three urban categories.

The selection process thus far was based on district-level secondary data. This was then followed by scoping visits to verify conformity with the typology. The scoping exercise finally elicited Yadgir, Mandya and Ramanagara as the respective districts for rural, agro-urban and small-town categories. Along with Bengaluru representing the mega city site of neo-urbanism, these three completed the district selection process.

Mandya, Ramanagara and Bengaluru are situated in the erstwhile Mysore region, while the remote district of Yadgir (carved out from Gulbarga in 2009) is located in the Hyderabad–Karnataka region. The three sites in the Mysore region share a common history and agro-ecological features while Yadgir offered a contrast, with its semi-arid conditions, huge tracts of black cotton soil and a low Human Development Index. The Gulbarga region around Yadgir offered a unique interface different from the production landscapes around the mega city Bengaluru, the small town Ramanagara (carved out from Bengaluru Rural district in 2007) and the agro-processing hub of Mandya.

Selection of taluks

Once the district selection was completed, secondary data on the same set of indicators used for district shortlisting (land use, cropping pattern and dependence on agriculture, see Stage 3 in Fig. 3.3) was gathered for taluks within the selected districts. Selection of taluks followed a step-wise process similar to that of district selection including exploratory visits to each hobli (subtaluk administrative unit).

Verification of alignment of taluks with the urbanisation typology was done through conversations during village walks with individuals or small groups of farmers, women and officers from the departments of Agriculture (*Raita Samparka*

---

[10]Districts shortlisted based on population engaged in farming in addition to distance from any major city and area under agriculture for small town category—Hassan, Ramanagara, Tumkur and Belguam; agro-urban category—Mandya, Haveri, Shimoga, and Davanagere, and rural town category—Yadgir, Koppal, Gulbarga and Bagalkote.

Kendra is the department office at hobli level) and Revenue (Village Accountant—
talathi). Other consulted stakeholders included traders in the formal and informal
markets, members of dairy co-operatives, *anganwadi*[11] teachers and panchayat members.

A short checklist for these conversations was prepared in advance, covering
enquiries about farming, other occupations and urbanisation. Conversations aimed at
inferring changes in landholding and cropping pattern, social–ecological aspects of
farming, livelihood pattern, markets and agro-industries in the surroundings. Inferences drawn from these conversations informed the selection process and eight taluks
from four districts were selected for further study.

Joint explorations and group interactions

Insights on possible agrarian fallouts of urbanisation gained from exploratory visits,
literature and analysis of relevant secondary data were verified and modified, in tune
with farmers' lived experience in the study sites. That was the purpose of organising
47 group interactions[12] (referred to as just 'interactions' henceforth) in eight selected
taluks.

The interactions brought together farmers from diverse social and economic backgrounds and gathered information on the shared realities of small farmers living
with urbanisation. Participants were identified during the exploratory visits through
repeated conversations with those who had direct stakes in farming—either as cultivators on own or leased land, or as agricultural labourers. The points of discussion
included: changes in demography, farm and non-farm occupations, land ownership,
cropping pattern, infrastructure and institutions in agriculture as also challenges and
opportunities in urbanisation.

Guiding questions for the interactions were prepared and deliberated by the study
team in advance[13] and often modified to suit the group gathered. Starting with a
discussion around socio-cultural and ecological history of the village, the interactions
gradually moved to details of social groups and landholdings, followed by discussion
on tenurial, occupational and migratory patterns, concluding with individual opinions
on urbanisation.

Responses from these interactions were collated and tabulated for further analysis.
Inferences drawn from the analysis of responses helped shortlist villages that closely
represent the respective peri-urban type from each selected taluk. Attention was also
given to represent major differences in agro-ecology present in the district. In total,
16 villages were identified by this process (Table 3.1).

---

[11] *Anganwadi* is a rural daycare centre for young children and mothers run by Department of Women
and Child Welfare started in 1975 across India.

[12] Out of the 50 interactions conducted, three with the participation of five or below were excluded
from further analysis.

[13] The study team consisted of a Research Associate and two Field Assistants, apart from the authors.

3.4 Research Methodology

Table 3.1 Study villages

Urbanisation type	District	Taluk	Selected villages
Recent but heavy urbanisation	Bengaluru urban	Anekal	Siddihoskote, Dasanpura
	Bengaluru rural	Devanahalli	Vishwanathpura, Reddihalli
Small town	Ramanagara	Kanakapura	Uyambahalli, Dyavasandra
		Magadi	Maroor, Yennegere
Agro-urban region	Mandya	Pandavapura	Bevinkuppe, Shambhuvanahalli
		Nagamangala	M Kodihalli, Thoobinkere
Rural town	Yadgir	Shahpur	Khadrapur, Hurusgundige
		Shorapur	Kodekal, Mangloor

Household sampling and interviews

Following the group interactions and selection of villages, identification of suitable households for detailed interview was the next task. Selection of households for the study was done by obtaining the list of all land-owning households from the village accountant. This list also contained data on caste, religion and irrigation status of each landholding.

Households were classified according to the size of landholding. From this, a list of small farmers who own about 2 hectares of land disaggregated by gender was prepared. Given the existing social and gender composition of landholders in each village, 15 male and 8 female landowners were selected using Random Number Generation in SPSS. Thus, each village had a list of 23 farmers and 10–12 farmer migrants as potential respondents. This process of selecting households was followed for all 16 selected villages (Table 3.1).

Willingness and interest of the shortlisted farmers were the decisive factor in choosing respondents. Detailed interviews were conducted with 10–12 farm households out of the shortlisted 23 in each village. A total of 172 farmers were interviewed in 16 villages scattered in eight taluks of four districts, over a period of 16 months from mid-2015.

Small farmers who had shifted partially or fully to non-farm occupations and/or to other parts of the State formed an important constituency of this study. The names and contact information of migrated farmers who had moved to other villages, nearby towns or to Bengaluru for non-farm occupations were gathered during the initial fieldwork from group interactions, from respondents during the interviews or from other villagers we met. Altogether, we had a list of more than 50 farmer migrants resulting finally in 32 interviews in various urban areas.

Interviewing farmers and migrants

Design and testing of the questionnaires for farmers and migrants was a parallel process during the selection of sites and respondents. During this time, the field team attended a preparatory training session on how to approach the respondents for both group and individual interactions, the dos and don'ts in the field, preferred locations in the village to sit for interactions and how to manoeuver around any untoward developments like personal/political or other conflicts surfacing during interactions, and importantly how to pose each question and in what sequence. How and when to modify the planned approach and questions was also agreed upon. Thus, the process of gathering primary data was a dynamic process under constant modification from mid-2015 to end of 2016.

The finalised and tested questionnaire was converted to a Tab application so that field team could systematically enter and upload the data. The data entered from the study sites could be downloaded instantly from any location. This enabled regular checks and clarifications as required, avoiding significant data gaps and oversights.

Apart from the data collected using the questionnaire, family narratives were captured in notebooks. Selected few from these written narratives are used in Chaps. 6–9 of the book for illustrating or supporting the analysis.

Migrant interviews formed the last part of data collection. We met most migrant respondents in their new place of residence. Some of them, we met both at their village of origin and destination. Currently engaged in non-farm occupations, they could be located either in Bengaluru City, other towns or very rarely in other villages (Fig. 3.4). Having done farmer survey in their villages of origin, we could see how the life of a farmer migrant changed. Process of selecting the final respondents among migrants was similar to that followed for farmers. After a couple of group interactions in their new locations, a few farmer migrants were approached for time and willingness to sit with us in late evenings after a hard day's work. Thus, families of 172 farmers and 32 farmer migrants were identified through the process described above for detailed interviews.

Fig. 3.4 Shanties of migrant workers in Bengaluru

3.4 Research Methodology

Archival study and deliberations

While secondary data and literature on small farms and urbanisation were being analysed, it was felt necessary to understand the role of changing land-caste relations over a longer period in time. Recognising the long timespan entailed in the changing nexus between agriculture and society, an understanding of the historical linkages between farmland, ecology and society emerged crucial. The past had a visible bearing on the evolution of current practices and institutions in the two regions of Mysore Karnataka and Hyderabad–Karnataka. This evidently led to a quest into the history of the place and people from an agrarian lens (Stage 6 in Fig. 3.3) happening in parallel with household interviews.

Institutional libraries with useful resources on regional history, particularly in the cities of Bengaluru, Mysore and Dharwad were visited to access archives including travelogues of colonial officers, early gazetteers, maps and literature by local scholars from eighteenth, nineteenth and early twentieth centuries.

Archival information helped understand the temporal trajectory of both governance as well as the subaltern agrarian communities, but not with required clarity and interpretations. Hence along with archival search including digitized materials on and off the internet, we also conducted interviews with scholars on the regional history of agrarian ecology and society. Chapter four carries the analysis from this part of the study, providing a glimpse of the backdrop of site-specific discussion in subsequent parts of the book.

The last phase (Stage 7 in Fig. 3.3) in the research process involved analysis of information gathered through interviews, group interactions, archival studies as well as secondary data from the study sites and other relevant geographical scales.

3.5 Analytical Approach

Analysis of information gathered by various means as mentioned above has been a continuous process. Data from household interviews and group interactions were subjected to three processes of interpretation involving quantitative and social network analysis, along with deciphering the village narratives, in addition to the content analysis of archives and deliberations with scholars. Figure 3.5 depicts this analytical strategy in a framework.

Rectangles extending from each analytical method mentioned in circles represent data involved in the analysis. In the case of Social Network Analysis, rectangles depict the specific tools used.

Analysing primary data

The survey finally accomplished interviews with 40–45 farm households and 5–10 migrant families from each peri-urban site. Chapters 6–9 are based on the analysis of this data from farm and migrant households supplemented with secondary information as and when needed. Simple descriptive statistics separately from each study site and pooled data across the sites were worked out.

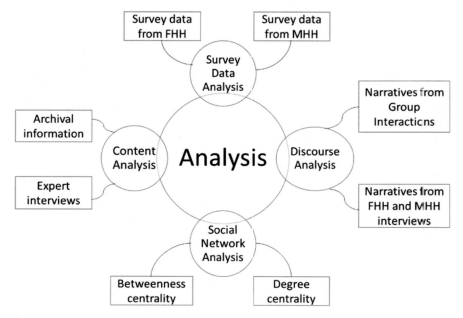

Fig. 3.5 Methods and tools.
(FHH—Farm Household; MHH—Migrant Household)

As social networks appeared to aid small farmers' continued existence, the study identifies networks and agents that connect small farmers and migrants among themselves as well as with other agents in different urbanising regions. The relative importance of and facilitating factors in specific networks were analysed using Social Network Analysis.[14] Identification of influential small farm-holders who bridge the gap between the farmer community and various networks was also accomplished.[15]

Primary data from farmer and migrant interviews was used to prepare separate matrices to depict their direct and indirect social interactions with other actors including relatives, input agents, markets, collectives, credit sources, government research and extension agencies, religious institutions, political and community leaders.

Analysing village narratives

Conversations during group interactions were recorded with due consent and were transcribed later into notes. The objective of these interactions was twofold. One was to shortlist representative villages for detailed surveys and the second was to

---

[14] 'Degree centrality' is used for identifying the most influencing actors (other than farmers) within the network by counting their direct connections with other actors. See Hermans et al. (2017) for application of social network analysis of a multi-stakeholder platform in agricultural research for development in African subcontinent.

[15] 'Betweenness centrality' is used for identifying most networked farmers. They bridge their less networked peers with other actors.

3.5 Analytical Approach

understand the urban–agrarian dynamics at a village scale. Analysing these discussions was accomplished with the tabulated information on key learning points from the transcripts. Team meetings to discuss these organised narratives resulted in the selection of most representative villages for household surveys.

During the household interviews, certain families with poignant concerns or refreshing adaptive strategies were identified and sought willingness to spend extended time with us at their convenience. These personal interactions formed thematic discourses surrounding health care, culture, customs or livelihoods or women farmers.[16] This analysis helped to connect with contemporary issues like marketing and indebtedness from a farm family perspective. Chapters 6–9 bring forth selected few of these discourses highlighting the socio-cultural linkages of farming with urbanisation and economic drivers.

Thus, thematically gleaned narratives from the study villages emerged from collective thinking and deliberations as well as from day-to-day life of individual farmer or migrant farmer. This twin-layered discourse analysis was useful given the multi-activity occupational life of respondent families and other complexities already outlined in the context of peri-urban interfaces.

Interpreting regional history

Regional history of the agrarian society and ecology was gleaned from writings of researchers (Krishna and Morrison 2010; Wilks 1810; Sastri 1940; Nanjundayya 1906; Gribble 1896; Srinivas 1976; Stein 1999), travelogues (Buchanan 1807), colonial accounts (Taylor 1920) and pre- and post-independence gazetteers on Mysore and Hyderabad–Karnataka regions (Rice 1897; Khan 1909; Husain 1940; Sathyan 1966). Comparative review of such historical literature was supplemented by interviews with scholars from the disciplinary fields of regional agrarian history and ecology. Interactions with eight scholars representing sociology, economics, history, political science, and ecology helped us clarify the somewhat blurred pictures on the past and evolution into the present, emerging from the archives.

This organised analysis of historical information from the two study regions of Mysore and Hyderabad–Karnataka helped us in interpreting the village narratives gathered during the study. Inferences drawn from the analysis of information accomplished by this dual exercise of going through archives followed by deliberations with scholars are covered in the next chapter.

References

Agriculture Census. (2015). *Department of agriculture and cooperation, Government of India*.
Balakrishnan, S. (2017). Land-based financing for infrastructure: What is new about India's land conflicts? In R. Nagraj & S. Motiram (Eds.), *Political economy of contemporary India* (pp. 260–278). Cambridge: Cambridge University Press.

---

[16]Notable stories were compiled into a blog on small farmers—*Voices from the Margins*—(https://smallfarmdynamics.blog/).

Basole, A., Jayadev, A., Srivastava, A., & Abraham, R. (2018). *State of working India 2018*. Bengaluru: Azim Premji University.

Bernstein, H. (2003). Farewells to the peasantry. *Transformation, 52,* 1–19.

Bernstein, H. (2016). JPS review symposium on Land's End. *The Journal of Peasant Studies, 43*(4), 942–962.

Brass, T., & Bernstein, H. (1992). Introduction: Proletarianisation and deproletarianisation on the colonial plantation. In E. V. Daniel, H. Bernstein, T. Brass (Eds.), *Plantations, proletarians and peasants in colonial Asia* (pp. 1–40).

Buchanan, F. (1807). *A journey from Madras throught the countries of Mysore, Canara, and Malabar*. London: East India Company.

Chandrasekhar, S., & Sharma, A. (2015). Urbanisation and spatial patterns of internal migration in India. *Spatial Demography, 3*(2), 63–89.

Gribble, J. (1896). *A history of the Deccan*. London: LUZAC and Co.

Hermans, F., Sartas, M., van Schagen, B., van Asten, P., Schut, M. (2017). Social network analysis of multi-stakeholder platforms in agricultural research for development: Opportunities and constraints for innovation and scaling. *PLoS ONE, 12*(2), e0169634. https://doi.org/10.1371/journal.pone.0169634.

Husain, M. (1940). *Hyderabad District Gazetteers Gulbarga*. Hyderabad-Deccan Government Central Press.

Jamwal, P., Thomas, B. K., Lele, S., & Srinivasan, V. (2014). Urbanising watershed: A basin-level approach to water stress in developing cities. In *Proceedings of the Resilient Cities 2014 Congress*.

Kashyap, S., & Purushothman, S. (under review). *A historical analysis of the agrarian political economy in the erstwhile Mysore region of South India*.

Khan, M. M. (1909). *Imperial Gazetteer of India. Provincial series*. Hyderabad state.

Koch, C. M., & Nax, H. H. (2017). *Groundwater usage: Game theory and empirics*. Accessed on https://pdfs.semanticscholar.org/d629/2cbd65f95a701cfb4dcdb9f8543fdd666d3f.pdf.

Krishna, K. R., & Morrison, K. D. (2010). *Histroy of South Indian agriculture and agroecosystems*. In K. R. Krishna (Ed.), *Agroecosystem of South* (pp. 1.52). Boca Raton, FL, USA: Brown Walker Press Inc.

Lele, S., Purushothaman, S., & Kashyap, S. (2013). Village commons, livelihoods and governance: An assessment of Karnataka's experience. In S. Purushothaman & R. Abraham (Eds.), *Livelihood strategies in Southern India: Conservation and poverty reduction in forest fringes* (pp. 135–156). India: Springer.

Lerche, J. (2013). The agrarian question in neoliberal India: Agrarian transition bypassed? *Journal of Agrarian Change, 13*(3), 382–404.

Meinzen-Dick, R., Chaturvedi, R., Domènech, L., Ghate, R., Janssen, M. A., Rollins, N. D., & Sandeep, K. (2016). Games for groundwater governance: Field experiments in Andhra Pradesh, India. *Ecology and Society, 21*(3), 38. http://dx.doi.org/10.5751/ES-08416-210338.

New Indian Express. (2013). *7000 villagers relocated after water level in Narmada dam crosses 130 m*, August 25, 2013.

Munster, D. (2015). "Ginger is a gamble" crop booms, rural uncertainty, and the neoliberalisation of agriculture in South India. *Journal of Global and Historical Antrhopology, 71,* 100–113.

Nanjundayya, H. (1906). *The ethnographical survey of Mysore*. Bangalore: The Government Press.

Packialakshmi, S., & Ambujam, N. K. (2017). The peri-urban to urban groundwater transfer and its societal implications in Chennai, South India—A case study. *Indian Journal of Agriculture Research, 51*(2), 135–141.

Panagaria, A. (2019). Confront the harsh reality: The only way we can really help farmers is to take most of them out of farming. *Times of India*. Retrieved on 17 Jan 2019 at https://timesofindia.indiatimes.com/blogs/toi-edit-page/confront-the-harsh-reality-the-only-way-we-can-really-help-farmers-is-to-take-most-of-them-out-of-farming/.

Pattnaik, I., Lahiri-Dutt, K., Lockie, S., & Pritchard, B. (2017). The feminisation of agriculture or the feminisation of agrarian distress? Tracking the trajectory of women in agriculture in India. *Journal of the Asia Pacific Economy*. https://doi.org/10.1080/13547860.2017.1394569.

References

Prahlad, C. K. (2012). Bottom of the pyramid as s source of breakthrough innovations. *The Journal of Product Innovation Management, 29*(1), 6–12.

Purushothaman, S., Hegde, S. S., Patil, S., & Kashyap, S. (2009). People's perception of benefits from a protected catchment: a case study of Gundal Command in Karnataka. *Indian Journal of Agricultural Economics, 64*(4), 573–584.

Purushothaman, S., Patil, S., & Lodha, S. (2016). *Social and environmental transformation in the Indian Peri-urban Interface—emerging questions.* Azim Premji University.

Purushothaman, S., Patil, S., Patil, I., Francis, I., & Nesheim, I. (2013): Policy and governance for sustaining livelihoods and natural resources in small farms—A case study in Karnataka. *Indian Journal of Agricultural Economics, 68*(2), 240–258.

Rice, B. L. (1897). *Mysore—A gazetteer compiled for government (Vol. 2).* Mysore by Districts.

Ruet, J., Gambiez, M., Lacour, E. (2007). Private appropriation of resource: Impact of peri-urban farmers selling water to Chennai metropolitan water board. *Cities,* 110–121.

Sanyal, K., & Bhattacharya, R. (2009). Beyond the factory: Globalisation, informalisation of production and the new locations of lbour. *Economic and Political Weekly, 44*(22), 35–44.

Sastri, N. (1940). *Administration and social life under Vijayanagar. Madras University Historical Series—No. 15.*

Sathyan, B. N. (1966). *Gazetteer of India, Mysore State—Gulbarga District.*

Shanawany, M. M. (1999). Ostrich production systems. *FAO Animal Production and Health Paper 144.*

Srinivas, M. (1976). *Remembered village.* Berkeley: University of California Press.

State of the Environment Report. (2003). *Land degradation* (pp. 153–166). Karnataka.

Stein, B. (1999). *Peasant state and society in medieval South India.* Delhi: Oxford University Press.

Surendranath, C., & Suchitra, M. (2015). Kerala farmers grow vanilla for profit. *Down to Earth,* July 4, 2015.

Taylor, P. M. (1920). *The story of my life.* Oxford: Oxford University Press.

Thomas, G., & De Tevernier, J. (2017). Farmer-suicide in India: Debating the role of biotechnology. *Life Sciences, Society and Policy, 13,* 8.

Varghese, P. (2016). Exploring other concepts of smart-cities within the urbanising Indian context. *Procedia Technology, 24,* 1858–1867.

Wilks, M. (1810). *Historical sketches of the South of India, in an attempt to trace History of Mysore* (Vol. 1).

Yadu, C. R., & Satheesha, B. (2016). Agrarian question in India: Indications from NSSO's 70th Round. *Economic and Political Weekly, 51*(16), 20–23.

Chapter 4
Agrarian Ecology and Society in the Study Regions: A Historical Perspective

Agriculture being spatially and temporally sandwiched between natural landscapes and urban spaces, reflects the region's nature-society dynamics at any point in time. The study sites mentioned in the previous chapter can be distinguished by their agro-ecology and socio-political history. Study villages in Bengaluru, Ramanagara and Mandya districts were part of the erstwhile kingdom of Mysore. They are located agro-climatically in the Southern and Eastern dry zones and agro-ecologically in the zone of Southern Maidan. Villages in Yadgir district lying in the semi-arid Deccan plateau of the north-eastern dry zone were part of Gulbarga in the princely State of Hyderabad (Fig. 4.1).

Just as the two regions are distinguished by different agro-ecology and socio-political history, the current urbanisation context of these regions also varies as discussed in the previous chapter. Among these differentiating factors of history, ecology, and urbanisation, we argue that it is the type of development emphasis around urbanisation and governance that determined the relative status of agrarian communities. We intend to trace the linkages between the historical characteristics of agro-ecology and society and the recent pattern in urban–agrarian nexus, discussed from Chap. 5 onwards. This chapter draws on archived historical information on the two study regions around the cities of Mysore and Gulbarga.

4.1 Emergence of Agricultural Settlements in the Study Regions

Evolving around 3000 BC, formal agricultural systems in South India emerged later compared to other regions in the subcontinent. Nevertheless, it can boast of many instances of in situ domestication of crops and animals along with the introduction of crops from other regions and adaptations in farming practices.

© Springer Nature Singapore Pte Ltd. 2019
S. Purushothaman and S. Patil, *Agrarian Change and Urbanization in Southern India*, India Studies in Business and Economics, https://doi.org/10.1007/978-981-10-8336-5_4

Fig. 4.1 Mysore and Hyderabad regions in eighteenth century AD.
Source Colbeck (1905)

4.1 Emergence of Agricultural Settlements in the Study Regions

The earliest evidence of human ancestors in South India appears around 1.2 million years ago at the Paleolithic sites in Hunsgi and Baichbal valleys in Northern Karnataka (Paddayya 1991)—part of today's Gulbarga district in the Hyderabad–Karnataka region. In addition to these open-air sites in the north-east of Karnataka, early Paleolithic tools have been recovered from the banks of Krishna and Godavari (Morrison 1999). During the middle Paleolithic period around 74,000 years ago, the first fully modern humans migrated to this part of the subcontinent, replacing the earlier populations (cross-reference Jones (2007) in Krishna and Morrison (2010)). Like their predecessors, these Middle Paleolithic inhabitants lived highly mobile lives gathering plants and hunting animals with variation in subsistence strategies across regions. Later on, as and when low-land agriculture expanded, hunter-gatherer groups moved to forested mountainous locations. ***Adivasi* communities presently engaged in marginal agriculture happen to be located mostly in and around the stretch of Western Ghats in Karnataka State, far from urban areas**.

The first surge in population that influenced the evolution of agricultural strategies in South India occurred in the Mesolithic era (Krishna and Morrison 2010). Mesolithic sites are found in most dry regions of South India except in the high elevation Western Ghats areas. But the evolution of a complex agro-pastoral economy took place only in the Neolithic period (in three phases from 2500 to 800 BC). Neolithic peoples of South India had large permanent settlements as well as extensive regional mobility. They have domesticated several plants and perhaps even animals themselves, and also adopted cultigens from elsewhere.[1] These practices were modified only in the Iron age (1000–500 BC) when new crops and strategies were adopted.

Along with the population surge, forest change and availability of wild progenitors of crop species contributed to the evolution of agricultural practices in South India. Krishna and Morrison (2010) describe how woodland openings created by human activities or open edges of natural forests might have contributed to the movement of wild species of pulses from inside the forests of the Deccan and the Western Ghats to the plains, leading to their domestication and regular cultivation.[2] This explains the persistence of pulse crops like red gram (*Cajanas cajan*, pigeon pea/*togari beLe*), making 'pulse bowls' out of the dry rain-fed areas of the subcontinent.

While red gram, black gram (*Vigna mungo, Uddin beLe*) and green gram (*Vigna radiata, Hesaru beLe*) were domesticated somewhere in South India, horse gram (*Macrotyloma uniflorum,* Hurali kaLu) was probably domesticated in the plains of North Karnataka.[3] A species of cotton and linseed are also native to North Karnataka. Different species of the same crop would have also been introduced and domesticated

---

[1] Please see Fuller et al. (2004) for evidence of domestication of pulses and millets varieties in the region.

[2] Please see Kassa et al. (2012) for domestication of *Cajanas cajan* in India.

[3] See the list of legumes cultivated in South India with their probable area of domestication (Krishna and Morrison 2010, pp. 9–10).

80

4 Agrarian Ecology and Society in the Study Regions …

in the region influencing genetic evolution of these crops to their present forms. While cowpea clearly came from West Africa and sweet peas from Southern Europe, finger millet and pigeon pea apart from domestication here, are also considered to be introduced from elsewhere, sometimes in the Neolithic period.

Though various pulse crops started being cultivated quite early, the earliest crops domesticated in South Indian savannas were small millets, black gram and horse gram. These remain part of food culture in South India even now. Krishna and Morrison (2010) mention how riverine zones, open savannas and hill slopes would have supported wild grasses and progenitors of cereals including millets. Agro-ecological history of human–nature interactions plays a crucial role in nurturing the present food and agricultural systems. While rice seems to have been introduced to South India from eastern parts of India, sorghum found in the Neolithic sites of north-eastern Karnataka is traced to Ethiopia and Mozambique. Though wheat and barley were also introduced from other parts of the subcontinent and were important in pockets of present Karnataka State, they disappeared later from most parts of South India.

While black-seeded pigeon pea and golden (yellow) rice were part of the cropping pattern in Karnataka as well as other parts of the region, hardy legumes like horse gram formed the common protein source in the dry belt. Whether food habits of early immigrants to the region influenced crop selection or early domestication facilitated their inclusion in local diet, is not clear though. However, diversity in food, farming and natural systems seem to have co-existed for long.

Tree species found in early Neolithic period included many that are commonly found now, like *Acacia, Albizia,* Mangifera, *Bauhinia, Dalbergia, Tectona, Terminalia* and *Ziziphus,* covering trees providing fruits, fodder, leafy vegetables, timber and medicinal herbs. *Piper nigrum* (black pepper) was also cultivated near upland forests in the Mysore region and traded with East Africa. Crops currently common and not found in Southern Neolithic sites include sugarcane, sesame, onion, garlic, eggplant, peanut and sunflower. Knowledge of genetic variability was used historically to suit diverse food needs according to soil status.[4]

South Indian farmers were responsible for both in situ domestication of many crops, and adapting crops introduced from other parts of Asia, Africa, China and elsewhere. There is evidence that they also abandoned some crops like wheat and barley after trying out for some time.[5] Meanwhile, crops from South India also spread to other parts of the peninsula. Thus notions of introduced and 'exotic crops',

---

[4] *'They* [ancient farmers] *demarcated them* [their areas] *based on soil fertility and cropping pattern'*—Krishna and Morrison (2009, p. 36)

[5] *"Winter crops of West Asia such as wheat and barley moved southward from northwest, while southern Neolithic crops moved northwards. However, during later periods of history, inter-se crop selection and preferences meant that, tropical crops like rice, sorghum, piegon pea and other pulses replaced winter cereals such as wheat and barley. … Agroclimate, water resources and soil nutrient status might have played crucial role in movement and establishment of new crops either way, into or outside of Southern Indian Neolithic sites. Of course, food habits and preferences, too influence cropping pattern in a location be it in Neolithic or modern times."* (Krishna and Morrison 2010, p. 12)

4.1 Emergence of Agricultural Settlements in the Study Regions   81

the pace of crop introductions, and the necessity of an external agency for genetic improvements need to be critically looked at, taking into consideration the historically adaptive entrepreneurship of farmers. **Presently popular cropping and diet patterns seem to have emerged from a long, dynamic and adaptive social–ecological process. The collective role of a mobile population, and the associated introduction, adaptation, experimentation and domestication of crops and animals have to be acknowledged in Karnataka's agricultural evolution.** More recent interventions by external and often non-agricultural agencies appear to lack logic of experimentation and local agro-ecology.

4.2 Tracing the Rural–Urban Rift and Social Differentiation

The social, ecological and historical concept of a metabolic rift describes the disruption of natural cycles as well as ruptures in human–nature relations under capitalism (Schneider and McMichael 2010). The concept emerged in the backdrop of a widening divergence between the social and ecological thoughts and practices that makes sustainability of any farming system an oxymoron. Here, we will superficially trace how such gaps started appearing in the study regions, eventually leading to their respective rural–urban dynamics in the present.

Like other parts of South Asia, agriculturalists co-existed with hunter-gatherers till recently in South India too.[6] Rock paintings and etchings reflect the regular use of domesticated and wild animals, especially chicken. Though sedentary settlements in southern coastal areas predate large-scale permanent settlements combining intensive animal husbandry with crop production, ash mounds found in parts of South India dating back to 3000 BC indicate a complex agro-pastoral economy.[7] Though reasons for such large-scale heaping and piling of highly fired cow dung found near granite hills and peaks may vary from ritualistic to economic factors and events of conflict, ash mounds of South India help us understand the culture and practice of food, cultivation and agricultural exchange. Permanent settlements without ash mounds have also been found in the alluvial plains. **Yet, archaeological evidences indicate that with penning zones adjacent to cultivated areas, closed nutrient loops characterised agricultural practices of the Neolithic period. Modern society came to flourish here from the symbiotic evolutionary relationship between plant and animal domestication, increasing human population and the agro-ecological system.**

---

[6] Archaeological records of campsites, seasonal settlements and large villages from 2300 BC indicate contemporaneous existence of South Indian agriculture with Bronze Age farming sites of Indus Valley.

[7] Fuller (2001) and Paddayya (1992).

Research on agriculture during the Iron Age period (1000 BC–1000 AD) after the Neolithic period, though inadequate, clearly points to the existence of large permanent habitations—prehistoric small and big cities. This was also the period when intensive cultivation with seasonal inundation with river water, use of iron implements and use of animals for draught as well as secondary food products began. With considerable migration, trade and conquests, this was also an age of crop introductions. Tanks or water bodies built for rituals started providing irrigation also.[8] **By now, most crops that we now see in the region were cultivated including grapes, jamun, gourds, and pumpkins. Use of spices (pepper, coriander, ginger and cumin) in food and in trade had also started in the Western Ghats region. Thus the most common food and agricultural systems of the region have been around for more than 1000 years.**

In the Medieval period from 1000 AD, cities were found in both alluvial deltas and rocky uplands, with different food-production strategies. This was the time when the elite genre of cuisine based on irrigated crops like rice, emerged in South India in contrast to the millet-based diet of the poor (Morrison 2001). Trade in spices and cotton (cotton trade moved closer to textile manufacturing units) continued to flourish, while grain crops were consumed locally rather than traded across long distance. Thus, long-distance transport of local natural resources (water, soil nutrients and biodiversity specifically) to distant geographies started through the increasing volume of trade in spices and cotton textiles.

Commercial sugarcane production arrived late and started around the city of Vijayanagara. By then, rice cultivation was already specialised and done by either *bara butta* (dry sowing), *mola butta* (broadcasting sprouted seeds), or by meticulous *natti* (transplantation) method, with most varieties taking five months or more to harvest. The varieties of cultivated rice followed specialised practices suitable for the soil and water available in the locality. Inter-cropping of millets or grain crops with legumes was common. The practice of choosing crops according to the soil and micro-climate slowly got substituted by the modern way of tweaking soil nutrients and water status according to the crop or variety demanded in the market. Sugarcane and rice are widely reported during this medieval period onwards in areas around Bengaluru, Mandya and Channapatana. Garden lands growing vegetables became a feature around Mysore, whereas in Gulbarga, these appeared much later.

Thus, while pulses and millets go back to the beginning of agriculture, rice, sugarcane and vegetables became popular much later in the agro-ecological history of the Deccan, and have since been around for centuries, and even triggered a 'food determinism' found in the present-day agriculture.[9] While irrigation led to the emergence of new water-intensive farming in any region, often consisted of the same crops or animals across regions. Together with modern distribution mechanisms, irrigated

---

[8] *"Irrigation was clearly practiced by agriculturalists in South India during the Iron Age, with well-dated examples of reservoirs (tanks) by 800 B.C."* (Bauer and Morrison 2014)

[9] Culinary culture in a neoliberal society coerced the cropping pattern and agro-ecosystems to change in certain demand driven ways rather than the other way around. We will discuss more about such tendencies in Chap. 6 on family farms around Bengaluru.

4.2 Tracing the Rural–Urban Rift and Social Differentiation

crops and intensive farming started influencing the diet pattern across the regions. The new homogenised culinary culture associated with urbanisation in turn started reinforcing a penchant for irrigated cropping pattern. **This mutual reinforcement of intensive farming and new food cultures together set in motion many changes. These include changes in the nutrient status and biodiversity of both farmlands and dietary patterns**.

Despite the emergence of such a rural–urban metabolic rift,[10] the demand–supply balance in this period of history appears to have been within what the closed nutrient loops could sustain. Vertisols and alfisols of the densely settled regions in North Karnataka developed characteristic cropping systems based on a mixture of cereal–legume–fibre crops matching the soil quality and water availability. Gravel mulching, farmyard manure production, contour bunding, water conservation structures and fallowing allowed sustained productivity in both North and South *maidan*s. **Since the Vijayanagara empire engaged in trade relations with countries far and wide, several crops like groundnut, were introduced to South India during this time (between fourteenth and seventeenth centuries). Groundnut for a long time was known as 'Mozambique nuts' in parts of South India. Irrigated areas started growing areca palms and betel vines also. With flourishing trade in spices and textiles (not raw cotton), both agricultural economy and textile manufacturing flourished**.

There seems to be enough consensus that the earliest history of agriculture in the South comes from the dry hinterlands and not from the humid coastal or upland regions. Thus, early Neolithic permanent settlements in the Northern and Eastern Karnataka are considered as the cradle of extensive farming in the region. Thus, the present impoverisation of agrarian communities in this area, compared to other regions, merits close historical examination. **Why did the cradle of agriculture in the subcontinent fade even in its agriculture, while agrarian societies that emerged later, advanced in socio-economic indicators as well as in farming? The answer to this question may point towards how to bring about a turnaround in the dry agrarian hinterlands of Karnataka**.

Alongside the expanding linkages of settled and surplus-producing agricultural communities with trade and manufacture, we see the emergence of a reciprocal relationship between agrarian systems, elite landholdings and pilgrim centres. While agricultural surplus built temples, these temples and seats of power in turn supported the construction of canals and irrigation structures. The sluice gates of the Vijayanagara period and the reservoirs built when the *nayakas*[11] financed irrigation systems were named after temples. This period also saw a considerable increase in cultivation, especially that of labour-intensive rice, displacing extensive forms of farming. Despite the extensive nature of farming, intercropping used to be practiced as an insurance against crop failures. Mix of millet crop and pulse crop was a popular combination for intercropping in north-east Karnataka (NEK). Even during such a

---

[10]Discussed in Chap. 1 Sect. 1.3 of this book. This concept is discussed in detail by Schneider and McMichael (2010) and Moore (2000).

[11]Chieftains of feudatories in Vijayanagara.

mixed cropping agriculture, farm taxes were calculated based on average long-term soil productivity, till it was made more liberal during the eighteenth century.[12]

Farming in sixteenth and seventeenth centuries in South India was a result of co-evolution of skills in rain-fed and irrigated farming to sustain long-term yield levels and land resources, as also the economy of its ruling classes. The sheer number of inscriptional records on expanding agriculture and irrigation facilities reveal the pride and prestige attached to agricultural progress. Regardless, whether this was a period in south Indian agriculture in the eighteenth and nineteenth centuries as "growth, stagnation or decline" has been a topic of debate (Guha 1992). **The one tangible feature of this period has been rapid commercialisation, which happened with the establishment of railway network. The metabolic rift that began with the nexus between consumption patterns and irrigated crops was amplified with rail transportation of agricultural produce**.

As mentioned at the beginning of this chapter, among the study sites, villages in Mandya, Bengaluru and Ramanagara districts fall in the Mysore region (part of the princely State of Mysore), and Yadgir villages in the Southern and Eastern dry zone around Gulbarga in the erstwhile Hyderabad province. Thus for this book, Mysore region is larger than the current Mysore district and smaller than the old Mysore State while Gulbarga is larger than the district of Yadgir selected for the study and smaller than the Hyderabad–Karnataka region as well as much smaller than the princely State of Hyderabad. The following section will look at the interface between agricultural and social characteristics in these two study regions. We use the terms north-east Karnataka and Hyderabad–Karnataka inter-changeably and refer specifically to 'Gulbarga' (before Yadgir district was carved out from it) if the information is very specifically about this district of colonial times.

4.3 Political Economy of Land Relations in Mysore and Gulbarga

In this section, we examine the two study regions—Mysore and Gulbarga—which are part of two different erstwhile political economic dominions, namely the princely States of Mysore and Hyderabad–Karnataka, ruled by different regimes and with contrasting agro-ecologies (Fig. 4.2).

The two regions under study showcase more differences in their socio-political history than similarities, like their agro-ecological origins. Regional dissimilarities may arise from the historical trajectory of governance. Governance in both the regions changed hands from local rulers to independent Indian federation through a series of rulers and conquerors—Vijayanagara, Marathas, Mughals, Sultanates and the British in different time periods (See Annexure 4.1 for an overview of rulers and invaders in the region). Discernible regional differences emerge from the nature of governance

---

[12]Taxing fertile soil would have been counterproductive unless farmers have incentive and requirement to sustain it and access to fertile soil is unconstrained.

4.3 Political Economy of Land Relations in Mysore and Gulbarga

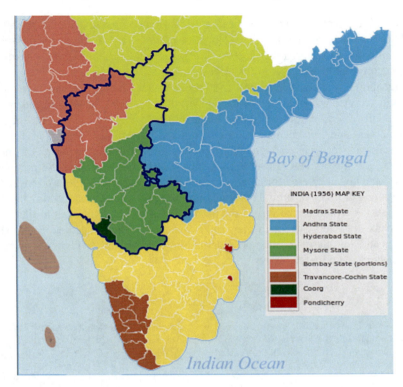

Fig. 4.2 Present Karnataka State in the map of pre-independence south India.
Source https://en.wikipedia.org/wiki/History_of_Karnataka#/media/File:Karnataka_1956_Reorg.svg

and society, alongside their geographical and ecological differences. This makes us differ from the opinion that nature significantly determines the emergence of a strong regional economy in any agrarian landscape (e.g. Pani 2017). Section below will attempt to unpack the above argument.

Gulbarga saw a faster turnover of rulers and battles than Mysore (Annexure 4.1). Most rulers of the region did not have a long-term vision for the local society. **This historical deficit of welfare orientation in local governance was instrumental in retaining the region in the margins of power and development forever. As independent India failed to turn around this history of marginality and overlooked its agro-ecological features, the socio-economic progress of this rainfed agrarian landscape stagnated, aided by inherent discriminatory tendencies along caste and class lines.**

Let us examine the above hypothesis with a closer comparative look at the history of the two study regions. While the exploitation of the villages for '*revenue farming*'[13] was common in Gulbarga region (Box 1), taxation policies were relatively mild in the Mysore region where explicit welfare schemes were implemented very early, in education, large-scale irrigation and labour wages. Tanks were maintained and irrigation service was managed by local chieftains (*Palegars*) in Mysore and tax was individually assessed by local officials at the village level *Ayagar* office. In Gulbarga, on the other hand, *Tankhwa* and *Chauth* (forms of protection money) were fixed for entire village irrespective of actual farm production. This meant ignoring the micro-climate, soil factors and household's health status in determining the production potential to be considered for taxation or protection charges. While tax waivers and concessions in times of drought were common in Mysore, it was rare in Gulbarga. At times, tax would be more than the production itself when farmers availed loans to pay tax dues so as to retain their rights over land. Thus, indebtedness of small farmers and domination of money lender landlords belonging to higher caste have a long history in Gulbarga region.

Box 1

After the eastern Deccan was annexed to the Mughal Empire with a more efficient bureaucracy, the farming of revenue collection was generally replaced by the collection through official collectors. But more strict assessment of revenue as well as the fresh imposition of capitation tax (Jiziya, abolished in 1722) at the rate of 4 per cent of assessment seems to have considerably increased the tax burden on the peasants—Fukazawa (2002, p. 196)

This does not imply that farmers were completely free from exploitation in the Mysore region. All castes/professions paid tax.[14] Heavy taxation of dryland crops (to be paid in cash compared to payment in kind from irrigated land[15]) and land concentration with the upper castes happened in both regions. Nevertheless, the method of fixing tax rates and handling defaulters were more decentralized in Mysore State compared to the *zamindari* dominated Hyderabad–Karnataka (Box 2).

---

[13]Revenue farming is the usage extensively found in historical narratives on governance in the Hyderabad–Karnataka region (southern Deccan/Gulbarga) referring to the singular approach to villages as places for the rulers to accumulate revenue.

[14]"... every professional caste pays some tax. The gollas (cow herders) pay the caretakers of gomaalas and also pay taxes to the benne or maska chavadi for the butter and ghee they produced. Golla yajamana of the locality used to fix the rent for grazing and also settle disputes on tax related issues about the grazing commons" (Buchanan 1988, pp. 5–6).

[15]Taxing drylands at higher rate than irrigated lands is a reflection of the revenue farming approach trying to extract the same revenue from unit area of land, irrespective of its relative production potential.

4.3 Political Economy of Land Relations in Mysore and Gulbarga

> **Box 2**
>
> ... the larger land holder might, as Zamīndārs or headmen or members of a favoured community, be required to pay less per unit area. The fiscal burden thus rested more heavily on the small cultivator, and must, therefore have tended to intensify the already existing differentiation among the rural population.
>
> Once the harvest was removed, the peasant felt no longer tied to the land.
>
> Habib (1995, p. 240).

Some centralisation of governance affecting autonomy given to elected representatives in Mysore State has been noted by Manor (1977). This discontinuity is noted during the time when economic activities like industries started concentrating in certain areas—beginning of urbanisation as we know now. **Generally, *Ayagar* office in the village fixed the tax rate for farmers to be paid as share of produce to all service castes. This continued till the advent of *ryotwari*[16] system by the British when non-farming professional castes began to disappear from rural areas**. Eventual migration of upper castes to jobs in the neighbouring towns, leaving agriculture in the hands of tenants from lower castes reinforced social differentiation along caste lines, with land and related benefits of infrastructural improvements like canal irrigation accruing mostly to certain social groups. Still, Mysore did not show exploitation and oppression to the scale found in a *zamindari* dominated Gulbarga region. Though Gulbarga was known for non-farm professions [like metalworks and handicrafts (Box 3)], they perhaps disappeared sooner given the history of *zamindari*, famines[17] and migration.

> **Box 3**
>
> The most remarkable form of large-scale production in the medieval Deccan as in other parts of India was the many karkhanas, established by kings at their capitals to manufacture and store arms, ammunition, robes, furniture, ornaments and so on, as well as to construct the buildings, which were all required by them and their nobles.
>
> Fukazawa (2002, p. 314).

Gulbarga, like some other prominent cities of the region, Warangal and Doulatabad (Deogiri earlier), was a capital city for a period of time. Location of Gulbaraga region at the frontiers of the kingdoms for a prolonged period also meant that the region was more or less a revenue catchment to be 'farmed' towards building power centres

---

[16]Ryots/farmers paid tax in cash (50% of the estimated value of the estimated produce) directly to the government at a rate fixed by the government. Ryotwari introduced by Thomas Munro in South India recognised private property with no responsibility towards neighbours. The system stayed for nearly three decades from 1820, and private property system got universalized.

[17]Guha (1999) quotes from Peshwa diaries on how indigenous people of Deccan agitated during a famine in 1803 as grains received by non-farming castes stopped in a new taxation regime and how Peshwa and governor managed it.

elsewhere, e.g. Pune (by Marathas), Hyderabad (by Nizams) and Agra by Mughals. Vagaries of numerous wars fought before the British era in the north-east landscape, home to the peripheral societies of Hyderabad–Karnataka region[18] were remarkably more than Mysore.

Social hierarchies were visibly prominent in both the regions. Despite Basavanna's efforts at social reforms originating in the NEK, disparity in its society appears stark compared to Mysore region where local governance had notable official presence of all castes including untouchables as long as the *Ayagar*—the village level autonomous governance system with representation of different communities—office was functional (or till *ryotwari* came into being). Similar local institutions in the northern belt—*Bara baluti*—did not seem to have comparable longevity or welfare impact. The latter had only service roles for all castes without any prescribed official responsibilities, whereas tasks such as measuring land, fixing the value of land or allocation of irrigation water, calculating the tax rates, etc., were commonly entrusted with the professional castes, including untouchables, in Mysore.

Just as village governance systems differed between the two societies, patterns of land distribution too differed. Though *inams* and *jagirs*[19] were norms than exceptions in terms of private land rights in both regions, these were much more extensive and skewed in the Hyderabad–Karnataka region. Such extensive and skewed land allotment practices ended early in Mysore. This skewness was accentuated by occupation of land by the rural elite while small holders were continously in migration.

It is, however, incorrect to presume that the entire history of Gulbarga region is one of the exploitation. Farming in the region has had its own small share of fortunes like larger landholding size and irrigation support (Box 4).

Box 4

Whether or not they held a sustained interest in the development of irrigation facilities in their respective territories, the rulers of the Deccan not only constructed the canals and tanks for royal gardens, but also, at least now and then, promoted the repair or construction of tanks, dams, and canals for agricultural purposes.—Fukazawa (2002, p. 200)

While average landholding size has been historically larger in the Gulbarga region, disparity mentioned above and heavy taxation of peasant operated dry lands ensured skewed economic power aligning with land power. Thus, land and money differentiated the resourceful and resource poor of Hyderabad–Karnataka, where indebtedness meant forfeiting land rights, and coupled with extortion and financial collapse, this

---

[18]Warfare was regular in both Mysore and Gulbarga. However, the scale and period of warfare between Moghuls and Marathas, Marathas and Nizams and the economic cost of these wars (and the plunder/pillage later on) in Hyderabad–Karnataka region were much higher in comparison with the Mysore province. See Annexure 4.1 for the sequence and turnover of rulers in both regions.

[19]Right to collect land revenue or right to cultivate a stretch of land without tax or with tax subsidies gifted for noble deeds or acts of benefits to the royalty.

4.3 Political Economy of Land Relations in Mysore and Gulbarga

translated into the inevitability of outmigration or bonded labour (Box 5). Migration was added to indebtedness and disparity as another outcome of exploitation and poor governance in the Hyderabad–Karnataka region.

> **Box 5**
>
> The great nobles not only collected the land revenue but also had police and judicial authority in their estates; besides, they held hereditary offices at court and as a result of mismanagement and embezzlement the State was constantly in debt. The land revenue was farmed out to money lenders and to Arab and Pathan soldiers who extorted as much as they could from the peasantry. The State was near financial collapse in the middle of the nineteenth century, till it was rescued by Salar Jang I, the great prime minister of Hyderabad from 1853 to 1883
>
> Dharmakumar and Desai (1982, p. 225)

Despite some inequality in landownership along and across caste lines in Mysore, education and trade (traders' guilds find frequent mention in archives on Mysore State) were favourable to the rural populace across social and gender groups (though still uneven across castes) in an environment of relatively stable governance and an inherent welfare focus beyond populist gains. Even migrant labour was treated on par for wages in Mysore region and women labourers were given food and cloth, to compensate for lower wages. Haider Ali reportedly even brought untouchable castes from Madras State and settled them as cultivators in parts of Mysore. Such notable progressive acts are rare to be found in the history of Gulbarga region (except for a short while between 1580 and 1627 when Ibrahim Adil Shah II was king of Sultanate of Bijapur) in terms of wages, irrigation measures and industrialisation.

While the land was a symbol of security and identity, possessing a plantation (*thota*/*bhagaith*) was considered to make one self-sufficient and a family was considered affluent if it owned wetland (*tari*) and dryland (*hola*) too. Security, self-sufficiency and affluence were almost an impossibility in Gulbarga region where major irrigation project was a late entrant. Most households in Gulbarga region which was synonymous with land inequality and usury were devoid of land and a secure livelihood. At best, they could be identified as owners of smallholdings. Transformation into large landholders or to a secure economic status was an almost impossible trajectory. Even in Mysore State, it was an almost impossible journey from a smallholder to an affluent farmer.[20]

While some earlier rulers of Mysore (like Purnaiah) were known to tax much more than others (including taxes for family ceremonies), it is the *palegars* (feudal lords) who were responsible for fixing tax rates on a regular basis (*Palegars* were considered extractive and distant from people or '*chieftains of the hilltop*' as referred

---

[20]Srinivas (1976) noted that for an indentured labourer (*jeethagara*) to become a tenant farmer (*genidara*), he (never a 'she' even in Mysore) needs to possess a pair of cattle and for a tenant to become a smallholder (*sanna hiduvalidara*) was the arduous requirement of being a tenant for years and owning a good pair of bullocks.

90

to in (Buchanan 1988)) who actually would have influenced Mysore's land use. In spite of such exploitations, agrarian society in Mysore fared better on account of the factors mentioned above—history of welfare orientation in governance and local dynasties allowing some space for progressive measures amidst inequalities, vested interests and battles. In both regions, agrarian transition of smallholders appears to be a non-starter for various reasons that we will unpack in Chaps. 6–9.

4.4 Agrarian Context in the Study Sites

Having traced the ecological origins and political differences, here we attempt to bring forth specific differences with respect to agriculture between the two regions of Gulbarga and Mysore. Manifestations of the differences highlighted here are elicited towards the end as emergence and/or absence of institutions and movements in the respective regions.

Agro-ecology

Both regions are blessed with major river systems (Cauvery in Mysore and Krishna in Gulbarga) though they differ in temperature and rainfall patterns. Still, the cropping calendar depends on the rainfall pattern. From the time of Vijayanagara empire (beginning early fourteenth century), seasonal classification of cropping was commonly into *mungaru beLe* in NEK or *hainu* in Mysore (kharif—rainy season crop sown in June/July) and *hingar beLe* in NEK or *caru* in Mysore (winter crop sown in November/December). In addition, a summer crop was taken wherever water was available for irrigation in Mysore or soil residual moisture permitted in Gulbarga. Soil resources were classified into *maru bhoomi* (*bayalu seeme*/ drylands), *niravari pradesha* (wet lands), *gadde* (wet paddies for ponding and puddling in Mysore), and *bagaich* or garden land. *Krishna* (black), *kempu* (red) and *maralu* (sandy) soils supported distinct crop varieties in both regions. Both regions had notable presence of milch and draught cattle (e.g. Amritmahal and Hallikar), as well as other animals domesticated by villagers. Classification of seasons, clouds, water resources, as well as weather forecast based on *panchanga* (The Hindu Almanac) was common place.

Box 6

The regar is ploughed with the large plough or nāgar, drawn by eight bullocks, only once in seven or eight years, the bakkhar or harrow is considered sufficient in the intermediate years. The Telingāna soils, being mostly sandy and finely divided, require only slight ploughing and harrowing. The land is ploughed first in one direction, and the second ploughing is done at right angles to the first.

Imperial Gazetteer 1908/1909 (p. 29)

4.4 Agrarian Context in the Study Sites

Skills for producing locally appropriate agricultural products existed in both societies (Box 6). Gulbarga soils were best suitable for jowar, bajra, safflower, pulses and cotton, and these crops continue to be grown here. Mysore region has seen vast changes in its agricultural pattern. Earlier dominated by millets, cotton, and sheep, the farming systems in the region changed first with the deindustrialisation of textile units in the colonial period and later in the early twentieth century, with the arrival of canal irrigation. While irrigation projects on river Krishna came much later than on Cauvery, open wells were a notable feature in Gulbarga region. Dug out open wells still dot the landscape unlike the tube well strewn fields of Mysore. Change in forest types and extent, irrigation (canal in riverine areas, tube wells in Mysore region after 1990 and open wells all through Gulbarga) and trade relations along with population surge and urbanisation catalysed further changes in these agro-ecosystems. Irrigation encouraged farmers to cultivate paddy, sugarcane and banana. There was an explicit bias towards irrigated crops in both regions (Box 7), and construction of irrigation infrastructure was a common welfare activity during famines.

Box 7

For the Telingāna Districts, extensive irrigation schemes have been prepared, while in Marāthwāra the protective measures include the extension and maintenance of roads and the construction of wells. In times of famine food and rations are given to those able to work, and poorhouses are established for the infirm and decrepit. Loans are advanced to the ryots to enable them to purchase cattle, and cheap grain shops are opened for the relief of others.

In Marāthwāra and in settled Telingāna Districts, remissions are not granted for 'dry' land, as assessment is very light.

Imperial Gazetteer 1908/1909 (p. 50)

Intensive irrigation rather than life-saving water (to retain minimum soil moisture) creates metabolic exchange in favour of the consumer class of urban landscapes. This is because farming areas heavily export most valuable resources like water and nutrients, rather than consuming them in situ.

Buchanan's travelogue mentions Mysore's cottage enterprises in jaggery making and weaving cotton cloth; functional irrigation networks, rice mills, use of urban waste including night soil as manure, as well as the practice of restricting to a single-irrigated crop in any given year. These indicate conscious efforts to minimise the rift between rural/farm sector and urban/non-farm sector. He also refers to small secretive units making sugar for the royalty in the region.[21] The above-mentioned efforts of the pre-independence period were followed by milk co-operatives, silk reeling units, and cocoon markets later on.

---

[21] Sugar was considered luxury and only for the royal family. "*Such miserable monopoly of good things is a favourite practice in the arbitrary governments of Hindustan*" Buchanan (1988, p. 158).

Agrarian Society

Buchanan also makes the interesting observation that most land owned by Brahmins in the Mysore region grew less labour-intensive plantation crops, except in *malenadu* (hilly terrain) where paddy was popular. Here, unlike in the plains, Brahmins used to work on their land (except for ploughing). In Nanjundayya's (1906) account of castes in Mysore, we find many caste-specific crops/trees/animals/implements as well as taboos on raising specific crops and eating specific animals. Even cultivation activities and food habits could be tagged to castes—e.g. *Holayas* for betel vine cultivation, *Vaddas* for digging wells, *Tiglars* for floriculture; castes eating termites at the beginning of monsoons; castes with taboo on raising turmeric and eating tortoise and so on. Such an intertwined history of social groups and agro-ecology is not found in the literature on NEK, except for the skewed landownership along caste lines. Also true for both regions is the fact that farmers were never non-Hindu, reflected also in the concurrence of agricultural cycles with Hindu festivals. Army, trade and handicrafts emerge as the livelihood forte of Muslims in both regions from those times. In Mysore's history, there is mention of how potters, blacksmiths and stoneworkers engaged in farming. In Gulbarga, Iyengar (p. 360) says—'*weavers are weavers first and nothing next; cultivators are cultivators first and nothing next*'. This is what has changed dramatically in the current reputation of NEK as the main origin of all migrant labour, to build various cities in the peninsula.

Given the disparate and discriminatory society, gender parity obviously was rare in the dry lands, though poorer households had more farming roles for women. Even in the Mysore region, while families trained boys in farm responsibilities at a very early age, girls were more or less confined to daily chores in the household and cowsheds. Therefore, dairying continues to be a women's forte in this region and something that women in the hinterlands do not have, since the environs of north-east Karnataka is not ideal to host large ruminants for dairying. With no other livelihoods available even after the establishment of self-help thrift groups, life and livelihoods have been dismal for women in the dry regions.

Women in both landscapes had two similarities: they were not owning any land and women of lower caste had a more active role in farming. But in terms of wages, access to dairying, and education, both lower and upper caste women appeared better off in old Mysore. It needs to be mentioned that though society was mostly patriarchal in old Mysore, emergence of dowry system (bride money) was fairly recent—coinciding with arrival of irrigation and complete commercialisation of agriculture. Urbanisation process and commercialisation of farming went hand in hand along with male domination of both the land and the family. Together they played an important role in reversing women's status *vis-a-vis* agriculture. What was 'bride price' to be paid by the groom's family turned into 'dowry' to be paid to them by the bride's family, as urbanised boys with non-farm occupations started to be considered as suitable boys compared to just land owning farmers. Land rights for women were legalised much later (1970s) even in Mysore. A surprising outcome of legalising landownership for women was the re-emergence of female foeticide.[22]

Agricultural Institutions

With the establishment of the Imperial Agricultural School in Hebbal, Bangalore (1899), the era of institutional trials (*vis-a-vis* people's experimentation and evaluation on their lands) on crop varieties and inputs began. Distancing farm science from farmers' fields diverted the flow of agricultural know–how to laboratory-to-land process instead of socio-ecologically informed in situ agricultural skilling. Though agriculture was mostly 'organic' by default till mid twentieth century, synthetic inputs and input-responsive varieties started getting popularised, coinciding with burgeoning population and soil fatigue from centuries of harvest. Lack of synchrony between agricultural science, extension and economics in the State machinery left millions of small farms at the mercy of corporate agri-business.

As all south Indian rivers were seasonal, farming continued to be mostly rain fed in both regions despite deepening water tables of tanks and scanty flows of streams connected to newly dammed rivers. Thus, massive agricultural systems centred around irrigated rice and sugarcane in Krishna and Cauvery basins co-existed with vast dryland systems struggling to grow millets and pulses in non-riverine areas with plummeting soil moisture. While rice and sugarcane were spreading in irrigated areas, the introduction of sunflower and groundnut to new areas considerably increased the oilseed production in the dry lands.

Agrarian Movements

Despite long-term deprivation of the agrarian community in the Gulbarga region and land disparity (coupled with skewed spread of irrigation) along caste lines in both Mysore and Gulbarga, major agrarian upheavals were conspicuous by their absence. Curiously, most agrarian movements in Karnataka happened in the irrigated tracts of the relatively progressive Mysore Karnataka, and that too without notable long-term consequences barring a mild favourable tilt towards land reforms. Irwin Canal movement in Mandya (1931, against the block system of cultivation suggested by the Director of Agriculture and implemented by Diwan Mirza Ismail), *Kagodu satyagraha* (during 1951 by *Deewaru* caste tenants for regulating tenancy in Sagar) and Malaprabha agitation (against price drop, during 1978 near Dharwad) took place in irrigated landscapes.

---

[22]Interview with Prof. R. Indira, Sociologist, Mysore.

Tenancy between forward caste landowners and the working class in Mysore State was noticeable. It was more prevalent in irrigated tracts where labour-intensive crops like paddy were grown. This was the genesis of agrarian movements in Mysore. Tenancy was less and holding size larger in the Gulbarga district. The highly skewed landownership (with large extent of *jagirs* and *inam* lands) along with low wages, high taxes and indebtedness of the cultivator to the landowner, created situations fertile enough to spawn potential revolts. But, perhaps the social fabric in rain-fed Gulbarga battered by long-term extractive governance was so weak that agitations could simply not be triggered. The early agitations in the Mysore State might have eventually inspired the establishment of *Karnataka Rajya Raita Sangha* in 1980.

The purpose of this brief note on potential movements is to show that even where visible deprivation is suffered by cultivators, it may not trigger mass movements potent enough to make the economic system an inclusive playing field. This makes the case for bringing out discrepancies embedded in the current economic system. It brings smallholders in diverse regions in focus whose struggles are often not manifested in political or social campaigns or protests, but whose voices need to be heard given the enormity of the crisis. This book attempts to explore and highlight this neglected issue.

4.5 Widening Divergence

So far, early history of the regions has been viewed through the prisms of native agro-ecology, society, land governance, trade links, education, commencement of large irrigation projects and agricultural research institutions. Here, we intend to highlight certain differences that persisted further or even intensified, in recent times.

Except for the great famine during 1876–78 that had gripped Mysore State as well as other parts of South India, occurrence of famines were more common in the dry regions of Deccan. The most convenient reason given for this has been deficiency of rainfall and irrigation. The role of skewed land distribution, eroded agricultural skills for dry lands, vanishing village commons and biodiversity and failure of modern institutions of governance in ensuring social welfare are rarely highlighted. Though famine-like situations in Mysore were fewer, they were conspicuous for the reasons that caused them—closure of local granaries following the arrival of railway transport to export grains (see Davis 2000 and Guha 1983 on the widespread famine in India during 1877–78). **This reveals the hidden risks associated with modern infrastructure, when functional local welfare institutions that ensure distribution of essential commodities, are absent.**

4.5 Widening Divergence

Could it have been possible to avoid extreme social–ecological distress and mass migration from the dry regions? Correcting the skewed land distribution both in terms of grazing commons and private arable lands, a soil-moisture management regime for agro-climatically suitable crops (millets, pulses, native oilseeds and cotton) if followed with dug open wells and small processing units for value addition probably could have traced a different history. Trying to emulate Krishna Raja Sagar of Mysore in Upper Krishna Project of north-east Karnataka and substituting tube wells for open wells could continue to expose Gulbarga to social crisis through ecological impacts. Imposing an incompatible agricultural system with heavily irrigated intensive crops could cause misery in near future, triggered by soil salinity and degradation.

Canal irrigation can irreversibly change not just soils but the local social fabric. Srinivas (1976) mentions homogenisation of issues and thought processes among families aligned to spread of irrigated paddy crop. Canals also encourage undue risk-taking by the selection of commercial crops that are susceptible to wide price fluctuations. It was evident by the 1940s that while superstitions were persisting and modern institutions were either insufficient or yet to emerge, traditional institutions for bridging metabolic rifts and social disparities were eroding. Blind faith in excessive irrigation stands testimony to the mismatch between the pace of adoption of new practices and the emergence of appropriate institutions. Learning from the history of irrigation is crucial for both regions while thinking of interventions, if history of inequality and/or impoverishment have to be reversed.

Flat topography and incomplete implementation of land reforms have contributed to a larger landholding size in Gulbarga region.[23] Large extents of field crops feature in the plateaus of Hyderabad–Karnataka compared to a variety of different species hosted in the relatively undulating landscapes inside smaller holdings of Mysore plateau. Being closer to the biodiversity hotspot of Western Ghats, livelihood options from natural forests and agro-forestry systems were common in the Mysore region.[24] Disruptions in these agro-ecosystems affected livelihoods in many ways. For instance, trees like sandalwood being declared as royal property by Tipu Sultan, discouraged farmers from planting or protecting such trees in or around their fields. Yet, unirrigated parts of Mysore region continue to host native trees like Ficus species (Dhanya et al. 2010).

Dryland agro-forestry systems including perinneal trees are largely missing from the current landscape of Gulbarga region, though gazetteers mention the presence of trees on bunds. The trajectory of agro-ecology and livelihoods in Mysore was determined by many policies and interventions other than canal irrigation, like taxing

---

[23]Mean holding size in Gulbarga was 2.37 and 0.96 ha for Mysore (Agricultural Census 2010).

[24]See Purushothaman and Abraham (2013) for livelihood strategies in the forest fringes of Western Ghats.

Adivasis and graziers for accessing village commons including forests, along with later interventions of popularising invasive lantana as hedge plant (around 1875, by the British). These measures meant insufficient biomass and manure for smallholders. Despite the absence of such pronounced counterproductive ecological interventions in north-east Karnataka, sheer exploitative and oppressive political environment ensured deepening rift between local ecology and livelihoods in this region.

Farming was exploited for amassing food for royalty, wealth for the treasury, waging wars and later for fueling industries in Britain. Failure of independent India's land reforms coupled with continued economic concentration in the erstwhile political economic hubs, the 'one size fits all' kind of agricultural and conservation schemes, and a history of stark inequalities together pushed Gulbarga villages to a downward spiral of distress. As we argue here, this cannot be attributed exclusively to nature. A continued lack of political will with ecological prudence is also apparent. Agriculture in the Mysore region from eighteenth to the early twentieth century, although ruled by landed upper castes, could catalyse a regional economy around the processing industries such as cotton textiles and silk.

When agriculture became just commerce, private landholdings turned out to be not large enough to be financially viable and intra-family feuds grew. The joint family system that ensured family labour for all farm operations gradually started breaking away, though drier regions have been slow in the emergence of nuclear families. Early emergence of smaller farm holdings was facilitated in Mysore region by the feasibility of lease farming in irrigated areas and employment in non-farm options like cottage industries. While the number of available hands together with the holding size in a farm family started declining, commercial interest in farming was increasing and this started determining the role of women that will be more evident in site-specific chapters.

While concluding this discussion, we must realise that historical writings on NEK (including Taylor,[25] Gribble (1896) and gazetteers) are less revealing on the socio-ecological aspects. Perhaps the overwhelming historical appeal of political upheavals in wars and battles in this region continues to overshadow the subaltern history that lies close to land and soil. Even thus compared, writings on Mysore region are more illuminating (Rice 1897; Buchanan 1988; Nanjundayya 1906; Srinivas 1976 and gazetteers). With this brief look at the historical context of the agrarian regions and communities under scrutiny, the next chapter discusses farming in Karnataka in the era of urbanisation during the first half of the twenty-first century, before delving into our specific study sites and empirical data in subsequent chapters.

---

[25]Writings on the region by Col. Meadows Taylor in the Journal of the Bombay Branch of Royal Asiatic Society, 1835, apart from his autobiography—The Story of My Life (1920).

Annexure 4.1: Rulers and Invaders of Mysore …

Annexure 4.1: Rulers and Invaders of Mysore and Hyderabad–Karnataka

Invaders (Mysore)	Rulers of Mysore Area	Rulers of Gulbarga Area	Invaders (Gulbarga)
Vakatakas,	Kadambas (300 - 400 AD) - Banavasi (Capital) in Uttara Kannada district		Vakatakas, Pallavas
Pallavas,	Western Gangas (350 - 1000 AD) - Talakad (independent empire and feudatories of Chalukyas and Rashtrakutas at various times)	Chalukyas (600 - 1200) - Badami (Bagalkot)	Kosala (Gujarat), Vengi Chalukya Cholas, Cheras Pandyas Paramaras, Pratiharas
Guptas,		Rashtrakutas (600 - 1000) - Elichpur, Kanauj and later Manyaketa (Gulbarga) in 753 AD.	
Cholas		Kalachuris of Basavakalyan (Basavanna period) Western Chalukyas (Basavakalyan in Bijapur)	
Cholas, Pandyas, Kakatiya and Seuna	Hoysalas (1000 - 1343) - Belur	Seunas or Yadavas (1200 - 1334) - Devagiri	Delhi Kakatiya
	Mallik Kafur of Allaudin Khilji destroyed Devagiri and Belur		
Bahmani, Madurai sultans, all South India	Vijayanagara empire (1336 - 1646) - Hampi	Bahmani empire (1347 - 1527) - Gulbarga, Bidar	Vijayanagara Moghuls Marathas
	Wodeyars (1565 - 1761) - Mysore and Srirangapatana	Baridshahi (Bidar) Adil Shahi (Bijapur) and Qutb Shahi (Golconda) (1527 - 1686)	
Palegars, Keladi, Ikkeri, Kodagu, Marathas and Nizam, British	Haider and Tippu (1761 - 1799) - Srirangapatana	Mughals (Aurangzeb) (1686 - 1724) - Delhi	Marathas
	Purnaiah (Diwan) - 1800 - 1811 British Commission - 1834 - 1881 Wodeyars - 1881 - Till Independence	Nizams of Hyderabad (1724 - 1954)	Marathas, Mysore

References

Agricultural Census. (2010). *Department of agriculture cooperation and farmer's welfare*. Government of India.

Bauer, A. M., & Morrison, K. D. (2014). Water management and reservoirs in India and Sri Lanka. In H. Selin (Ed.), *The encyclopedia of the history of science, technology, and medicine in Non-Western cultures* (3rd ed., pp. 2207–2214). Amherst, MA: Springer Verlag.

Buchanan, F. (1988). *A journey from Madras through the countries of Mysore, Canara, Malabar*. Delhi: Asian Educational Service.

Colbeck, C. (1905). *India, in the time of Clive, 1760*. The Public Schools Historical Atlas

Davis, M. (2000). *Late Victorian holocausts*. New York: Verso.

Dhanya, B., Viswanath, S., Purushothaman, S., & Suneeta, B. (2010). Ficus trees as components of rainfed agrarian systems in Mandya district of Karnataka. *My Forest, 46*(2), 161–165.

Dharmakumar, & Desai. (1982). *The Cambridge economic history of India* (Vol. 11). Hyderabad: Orient Longman in association with Cambridge University Press.

Fukazawa, A.-H. (2002). *The medieval Deccan: Peasants, social systems and states sixteenth to eighteenth centuries*. Delhi: Oxford University Press.

Fuller, D. (2001). Ashmounds and hilltop villages: The search for early agriculture in southern India. *Archaeology International, 4*, 43–46.

Fuller, D., Korisettar, R., Venkatsubbaiah, P. C., & Jones, M. K. (2004). Early plant domestication in southern India: Some preliminary archaeobotanical results. *Vegetation History and Archaeobotany, 13*, 115–129.

Gribble, J. (1896). *A history of the Deccan*. London: LUZAC and Co.

Guha, R. (1983). *Elementary aspects of peasant insurgency in colonial India*. Delhi: Oxford University Press.

Guha, S. (1992). *Growth, stagnation or decline? Agricultural productivity in British India*. Delhi: Oxford University Press.

Guha, R. (1999). *Elementary aspects of peasant insurgency in Colonial India*. Delhi: Oxford University Press. 1983, New edition: Duke Univ Press, 1999, ISBN 0-8223-2348-6 - a classic of Subaltern Studies.

Habib, I. (1995). *Essays in Indian history: Towards a marxist perception*. New Delhi: Tulika Publications.

Jones, S. (2007). The Toba supervolcanic eruption: Tephra-fall deposits in India and paleoanthropological implications. In M. D. Petraglia & B. Allchin (Eds.), *The evolution of history of human population in South Asia*. Dordrecht: Springer.

Kassa, M. T., Penmetsa, R. V., Carrasquilla-Garcia, N., Sarma, B. K., Datta, S., Upadhyaya, H. D., et al. (2012). Genetic patterns of domestication in pigeonpea (Cajanus cajan (L.) Millsp.) and wild Cajanus relatives. *PloS One, 7*(6), e39563. https://doi.org/10.1371/journal.pone.0039563.

Krishna, K., & Morrison, K. (2010). History of south Indian agriculture and agroecosystems. In K. Krishna (Ed.), *Agroecosystems of south India: Nutrient dynamics, ecology and productivity* (pp. 1–51). Florida, USA: BrownWalker Press.

Manor, J. (1977). *Political change in Indian state: Mysore, 1917–1955*. Manohar Publishers & Distributors.

Moore, J. (2000). Environmental crises and the metabolic rift in world-historical perspective. *Organization and Environment, 13*(2), 123–157.

Morrison, K. (1999). South Asia: Prehistory. In R. Lee & R. Daly (Eds.), *Cambridge encyclopedia of hunters and gatherers* (pp. 238–242). Cambridge: Cambridge University Press.

Morrison, K. (2001). Coercion, resistance, and hierarchy: Local processes and imperial strategies in Vijayanagara empire. In S. Alcock, T. D'Altroy, K. Morrison, & C. Sinopoli (Eds.), *Empires: Perspectives from archaeology and history* (pp. 253–278). Cambridge: Cambridge University Press.

Nanjundayya, H. (1906). *The ethnographical survey of Mysore*. Bangalore: The Government Press.

References

Paddayya, K. (1991). Acheulian cultural phase in Baichbal valley, Peninsular India. In C. Marga-bandhu, K. Ramachandrasagar, & D. Sinha (Eds.), *Indian archaeological heritage* (pp. 51–60). Delhi: Agam Kala Prakashan.

Paddayya, K. (1992). The ashmounds of south India and possible implications. *Bulletin of the Deccan Graduate College and Research Institute, 51–52,* 573–626.

Pani, N. (2017). First nature and the state—Non-emergence of regional capital in Mandya. *Economic and Political Weekly, 52*(46).

Purushothaman, S., & Abraham, R. (2013). *Livelihood strategies in southern India: Conservation and poverty reduction in forest fringes.* Springer.

Rice, B. L. (1897). Mysore–A gazetteer compiled for government. In *Mysore by districts* (Vol. 1 and 2).

Schneider, M., & McMichael, P. (2010). Deepening, and repairing, the metabolic rift. *Journal of Peasant Studies, 37*(3), 461–484.

Srinivas, M. N. (1976). *The remembered village.* University of California Press.

Chapter 5
Agriculture in the Era of Urbanisation

Having discussed the agrarian society and ecology from a historical perspective in the previous chapter, we now examine the current interface of farming and urbanisation. Chapter 1 introduced Indian peasantry at the time of urbanisation. This chapter elaborates on that introduction, focusing on the state of Karnataka.

With an increasing rate of growth, India's urban population surged to 31% in 2011. Parallel to this, we see glimpses of agricultural dynamism in terms of production and exports (Table 5.1). Yet, as indicated by the recent riots and on-going suicides,[1] the Indian smallholder—the primary stakeholder of agricultural sector—appears to be in a turmoil trying to keep pace with day-to-day challenges. While agricultural production and exports appear to be keeping pace with urbanisation, the share of agriculture in gross domestic product (GDP) dwindled and the number of farmers in distress increased. This paradox (referred to as 'agricultural oddities' by Ranganathan (2015)) demands a careful analysis of the interface between urban growth and farmers.

Does urbanisation necessarily entail anti-rural and anti-small farmer impacts? Before addressing this question by means of a village-level empirical analysis, we first engage with the above paradox by looking at the course of agrarian livelihoods in India with specific reference to Karnataka. In subsequent chapters, we go on to characterise the changes in the urban–agrarian interface of individual study sites.

---

[1] Recent reports on unabated suicides among farmers: Editorials in EPW: No panacea for Agrarian Distress (Vol. 52, Issue No. 15, 15 Apr, 2017), Unquiet fields (Vol. 52, Issue No. 24, 17 Jun, 2017); Basu et al (2016), Dandekar and Bhattacharya (2017).

See footnote 9 in Chap. 2 for a list of recent riots.

© Springer Nature Singapore Pte Ltd. 2019
S. Purushothaman and S. Patil, *Agrarian Change and Urbanization in Southern India*, India Studies in Business and Economics,
https://doi.org/10.1007/978-981-10-8336-5_5

Table 5.1 Urbanisation and agriculture in India

Average annual growth (%)	1981–1990	1991–2000	2001–2011
Urban population	10	8	12
Agricultural production index	2.04	2.94	4.21
Quantity of Agricultural exports	1.89	18.90	13.84
Share of agriculture in GDP	−15	−21	−21
Farmer suicides (average number per year)	Not available	15,210*	17,012

*Data available from 1995 onwards
Sources Census of India (1981, 1991, 2001 and 2011); Agricultural Survey (1980–2011); National Crime Record Bureau (1995–2012)

5.1 Indian Agriculture—a Journey from Food Famine to Livelihood Famine?

Structural and technological changes in Indian agriculture can be broadly divided into four phases: pregreen revolution (before 1960s), green revolution (mid-1960s to mid-1980s), post-green revolution (mid 1980s to late 1990s) and the neoliberal era that began in the second half of the post-green revolution phase and continues to date. The first three phases were individually earmarked by some significant departure from the past with respect to productivity, investment, infrastructure, intensity and expansion of agricultural area.

The pregreen revolution period in independent India till about 1960s was infamous for its abysmally insufficient food grain availability[2] despite the substantial share of agriculture in GDP (annual average of 50% during the period 1950–1960). The next 20 years—the Green Revolution period—witnessed the expansion of arable land area, rapid growth in productivity of wheat and rice, as well as the expansion of agricultural research and irrigation infrastructure. Thus, far from being 'green' in the ecological sense, the Green Revolution came as a 'surge' in the production of certain crops, opening new vistas of rural and agrarian dynamism in certain regions. The subsequent 15 years—the post-green revolution period—showcased continued growth in productivity through intensified usage of synthetic inputs and machinery alongside expanding the area under cash crops such as maize, cotton, sugarcane, and oilseeds.

---

[2] Average per person per day food grain availability was about 394 g in 1951, and 465 g in 2015, though still lower than the recommended 500 g (Recommended Dietary Allowances (2010) by Indian Council of Medical Research).

5.1 Indian Agriculture—a Journey from Food Famine to Livelihood Famine?

The fourth stage of agricultural transformation saw further diversification into crops such as fruits, vegetables, flowers as well as dairying. Regaining agricultural dynamism through a sustained sectoral growth rate of 4–5% has been emphasised by recent agricultural policies (Jaitley 2014). In this on-going phase of agricultural change, public infrastructural investment for projects such as irrigation, watershed management and scientific research declined from 4% of GDP in 1980 to 1.5% in 2000, while indirect agricultural subsidies in GDP increased from 3.1 to 10.3% (Economic Survey 2005). Investing in indirect subsidies for power, irrigation and Minimum Support Prices (MSP) now constitutes the dominant strategy (Gulati and Narayanan 2000), though it is critically revisited periodically for fertilisers.

Nonetheless, an otherwise comprehensive National Agricultural Policy (2000), based on the Green Revolution premise and focused on the well-being of Indian farmers is critiqued for the absence of implementation and action plans (Chand 2005, pp. 19–46). Moreover, as the National Agricultural Policy remains *'locked in the green revolution paradigm'* (Jha 2003), commonly prevalent, prudent and time-tested practices such as integrated management of crops, livestock, pests and diseases, crop rotations, soil mulching, on-farm preparation of inputs, seed selection, and seed exchange are disappearing. **Thus, given the ambiguities in implementation as well as erosion of commonly followed practices, the downfall of environmental, economic and social drivers of agrarian well-being is apparent, despite diversification, budgetary support and technological advancement.**[3] Meanwhile, fast-paced urbanisation redefined agrarian aspirations. Resource-intensive practices, increased unpredictability in prices and climate, stagnating yields, poor competitiveness and degradation of land and water resources cumulate into vulnerability of farm livelihoods.[4] This has resulted in the rural populace increasingly embarking on non-farm livelihood options.

Diversification of employment opportunities along with socio-economic changes in rural as well as urban areas is supposed to have helped the agricultural workforce avoid deep distress. Nearly, 50% of the manufacturing sector employment and 44% of service sector employment in the country are in non-urban areas (68th Round of National Sample Survey 2011–12). Nevertheless, about 64% of the rural workforce continues their engagement in agriculture and allied activities and nearly 83% of the total income of a typical farm family is still drawn from agriculture (NSSO 2014). Also, service and business sectors seem to contribute only 5% each in the estimated average monthly farm household income of ₹ 6426 (NSSO 2014). These numbers indicate that diversification has not helped households to move completely out of

---

[3] 'Agrarian' in this book pertains to family holdings of small and marginal agriculturists as explained in Chap. 1, Sect. 1.2.4.

[4] Growth rate of agriculture's share in India's GDP dwindled from 4.8% growth during 8th Five Year Plan (1992–1997) to 3% during 12th Five Year Plan (2012–2016). With number of people dependent on the sector not decreasing proportionately, this presents adverse terms of trade for farmers as consumers.

104   5 Agriculture in the Era of Urbanisation

farming or to raise their household income above poverty levels. About 53% of farm households were below poverty line in 2014.[5]

Agrarian change during this era of urbanisation opens up the following questions: are there reliable new livelihood options in adjacent urban areas that are accessible to smallholders, and if so, are they contributing to their long-term well-being? As discussed in Chap. 3, there are diverse ways in which urbanisation happens—this may pose further complexity in answering these questions.

5.1.1 Urbanisation and Farm Livelihoods

Urbanisation is not a new phenomenon. Urban population in India has grown from 10% at the end of nineteenth century to 31% in 2011. This growth is more rapid (Table 5.1) and clustered in recent times. The number of cities or urban agglomerations (UA) with the population of more than a million grew from 12 in 1981 to 53 in 2011.[6] Ten major cities in the country host about 25% of its entire urban population while about 70% of the urban population lives in 468 towns (out of a total of 7935 towns including Class I cities, in 2011).[7] Urban areas are classified into six with population size ranging from 5000 to more than 100,000. Based on the growth rate of population, they are categorised as towns (statutory and census towns), urban agglomerations and outgrowths.[8]

Apart from this classification, we recognise categories based on the process of urbanisation discussed in Chap. 3. This diversity of urbanisation drivers has diverse implications for the farmers surrounding them. This diversity, both in urbanisation process and its implications, gives rise to questions such as: How can non-farm opportunities arising from urbanisation translate into livelihood benefits for small farmers in the country? How do these opportunities differ across distinct types of urban growth?

While urbanisation has the potential to translate into better and assured prices for farm produce as well as non-farm livelihood opportunities for supplementing the income of smallholders, in reality, as mentioned earlier (Chap. 1, Sect. 1 1), the income-enhancing potential of urban opportunities for farmers has been meagre.

---

[5]For a rural family of five, poverty line in 2014 was a monthly consumption expenditure of ₹ 4860 (Planning Commission 2014).

[6]Urban agglomeration is the dynamics and outcome of rapid growth in the periphery compared to the core of the city (Census of India 2011).

[7]Mumbai, Delhi, Kolkata, Chennai, Bengaluru, Hyderabad, Ahmedabad, Pune, Surat and Jaipur.

[8]Census towns satisfy the criteria: (a) minimum population of 5000 (b) at least 75% of male main working population in non-agricultural pursuits and (c) minimum density of population of 400 per sq. km. (Census of India 2011).

Outgrowth is a viable unit such as a village or part of a village contiguous to a statutory town possessing urban features in infrastructure and amenities. For example, railway colonies, university campuses, port areas that may come up near a city or statutory towns but within the revenue limit of a village (Census of India 2011).

5.1 Indian Agriculture—a Journey from Food Famine to Livelihood Famine?

Below we try to unravel this impotence of current urban demand in generating livelihood spin-offs within farming.

Growth for the last two decades in sectors other than agriculture resulted in a surge in the number of middle-class consumers whose consumption levels are supposed to be income elastic. This consumer class who mostly depends on food commodities supplied from rural areas increased from 25 million in 1995–96 to 153 million in 2009–10 with the share of food in total household expenditure in rural (55%) and urban (42.5%) areas remaining high until recently (Shukla 2010).[9] Food expenditure has been steadily shifting from cereals and pulses towards vegetables, fruits, milk, egg, meat and fish. The dominant driving factors behind this persistent shift have been, among others, easy access to supply, change in relative prices, and change in taste preferences along with mechanisation and infrastructural improvements in agriculture. Subsidised supply of cereals by the Public Distribution System is also an important factor in this shift in food expenditure.

Stemming from high food expenses of poor families and changing food habits and health needs of more than a billion consumers, there are obvious concerns related to food insecurity in contemporary India. This concern is reinforced by increasing expenditure on food imports and declining per capita food grain availability.[10] Notable harvest and post-harvest loss added to these concerns (22% of food grains production was lost in 2011). **A fallout of these factors—harvest and post-harvest loss, high food imports and increasing household budget for food—has been the persisting high levels of food price inflation since 2000.**[11] **Such a demand scenario potentially implies a golden opportunity for farmer producers, though the prevailing status of agrarian communities tells a different story.**

While there has been a surge in food demand both in terms of absolute quantities and in terms of the diversity of produce demanded, this does not seem to easily translate into agrarian livelihoods. On the contrary, income growth and urban food demand seem to have by-passed the family farms that constitute 80% of the country's farmers. Vasavi (2016) points to the disparity in the growth of average income of farmers, government employees and corporate sector employees during the last 30 years. While the income of farmers increased by only 19%, the income of government and corporate staff increased by 370 and 1000%, respectively, during the last three decades. **Thus economic growth meant almost nothing to the primary sector. Food security became synonymous with imports and imports in turn became a pawn in bilateral negotiations with other countries for striking deals**

---

[9]Middle class consumer households with an annual income between ₹ 2 lakhs and ₹ 10 lakhs in 2009–10 were 153 million in nunmber. About 33.4% of them were rural. This share of rural middle class increased to 84.2% in the deprived middle class households with annual income below ₹ 90,000 (NCAER estimate, cf Table 5.2 in Shukla (2010)).

[10]Value of agricultural imports increased 90-fold between 1991 and 2011, while exports increased only 40-fold. Per capita food grain availability declined from 472 g per day in 2000 to 465 g in 2015.

[11]http://www.thehindu.com/business/Economy/article2594166.ece accessed on 28th February 2015.

for defence equipment or other trade.[12] **Food security concerns provided an easy political justification for countering inflation through imports especially since the majority of Indian farmers are small and politically unrepresented.** However, a surge in income and consequent food demand from non-farming sectors poses not just challenge but also offers new opportunities.

In order to translate the emerging demand into livelihood benefits, farmers in the rural and peri-urban settings need access to resources—natural, human and capital. Inadequacy of resources translates into many disadvantages for smallholders in the era of urbanisation. Almost 60% of agricultural land is at risk from poor cropping practices and soil nutrient deficiencies (ICAR 2010). Efficiency of irrigation water use remains low (35–40% in the case of surface water irrigation and 65–75% for groundwater irrigation) along with an increase in the proportion of irrigated land from 20% in 1981 to 35% in 2013 (GOI 2013) amidst deepening and disappearing water tables. Agro-environmental crisis looms large, threatening long-term production prospects (Das 2013) amidst short-term spikes.[13] Such a crisis in the production scene also meant a crisis in local availability of balanced nourishment and eco-culturally compatible food—both at a time when the economy has been booming in India. **These challenges in marketing, production and consumption faced by family farms along with vanishing agricultural skills snowball into distress migration, marginalization and farmer suicides.**[14]

5.2 Agriculture and Urbanisation in Karnataka

Karnataka exemplifies the paradox in the co-existence of food, ecology and agrarian livelihood concerns with increasing food demand, economic boom and urbanisation in the country. Karnataka is the fourth largest Indian State in terms of population and the seventh largest in geographical area as well as urbanisation.

With production landscapes spread across mountains, seacoasts and plateaus, Karnataka's agriculture is highly diverse. Located in south-western India, with a population of more than 61 million (Census of India 2011), Karnataka occupies about 191,000 square miles of land area. Towards the West, it is framed by a long stretch of the Western Ghats—a biodiversity hotspot, and on the central to southwestern part, it is bound by a coastal line adjoining the Arabian Sea. The rest of the state, especially the northern and eastern parts, consists of vast dry hinterlands. Karnataka has four agro-ecological regions and ten agro-climatic zones lying across

---

[12] Recent trade spat with the USA regarding the Generalised System of Preferences, forces India to incentivize import of many agricultural produces.

[13] Impacts of such spikes in output included groundwater depletion (Matson and Parton 1997), soil degradation (Giller et al. 1997; Singh 2000), loss of genetic diversity (Thrupp 2000; Tilman et al. 2002) and high pesticide residues in food products (Gupta 2004). For a wider opinion on this, see the interview in Purushothaman (2012) and for an in-depth analysis, see Patil et al. (2012)

[14] For detailed discussion of farm distress, see Vasavi (2009), Deshpande and Arora (2010) and Deshpande and Prabhu (2005). See additional references on farmer suicides in footnote 1.

5.2 Agriculture and Urbanisation in Karnataka

Table 5.2 Urbanisation and agriculture in Karnataka

Average annual growth (%)	1981–90	1991–2000	2001–10
Urban population	9.3	9.9	13.5
Agricultural production	36.61	13.78	28.87
Cultivators and farm labour	20.95	20.11	−14.90
Share of agriculture in GSDP	−23.09	−16.29	−41.20
Farmer suicides (annual average number)	Not available	2191*	2184

*Data available from 1995. *Source* Census of India (1981, 1991, 2001, 2011); Economic Survey (various years); Agricultural Census (various years); National Crime Record Bureau (various years); Agriculture Survey (various years)

its 30 districts divided into four administrative divisions consisting of 270 towns and 29,406 villages, across 6068 panchayats in 177 taluks.

According to Census of India (2011), out of 61 million people in the state, 38.6% (23.5 million) reside in urban areas. Nearly 50% of the state's population is expected to be living in urban areas by 2025. For the first time since independence, in Karnataka and for the country as a whole, the absolute increase in urban population was larger than that of the rural population between 2001 and 2011. By 2000, Karnataka overtook most other states in the decadal growth of its urban population. Among its 30 districts, the metropolis of Bangalore (also the state capital renamed Bengaluru in 2014) currently hosts 91% of the state's urban population.[15] Between 2005 and 2014, GDP in Karnataka grew by 15.7% (close to India's GDP growth of 15.04%), while more than 50% of the state's total workforce (compared to 64% for India) still depends on agricultural activities. Agricultural share in GDP decreased drastically since 1981 (Table 5.2). It declined from 28% in 1995 to 16% in 2011 (compared to 26 and 17.8% respectively for the country).

Karnataka is also notable for poor agricultural growth (Table 5.2) along with increasing urbanisation compared to the rest of the country. Agrarian distress continued with at least one farmer committing suicide every day in 2016.[16] While the state might have addressed the instability of cultivated area and crop production with green revolution and agricultural modernisation (Chand and Raju 2008), tackling farm distress and instability in yield levels remains a challenge (Deshpande 2002, Chand et al. 2011). Ironically, data on family income does not reflect this dismal story

---

[15]As per 2011 Census of India, there are 46 metropolitan cities in India (population 1 million and above) and Bengaluru was at fifth position with 8.5 million population.

[16]New Indian Express 6th January 2017—Farmer suicide doubled in state in 2015: NCRB (http://www.newindianexpress.com/cities/bengaluru/2017/jan/06/farmer-suicides-doubled-in-state-in-2015-ncrb-1556649.html).

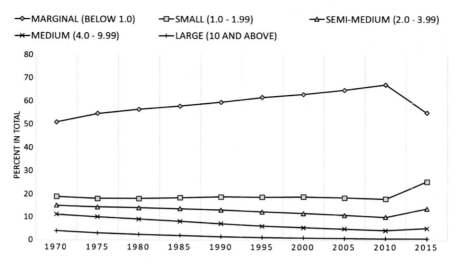

Fig. 5.1 Landholders in Karnataka (1970–2015).
Source Agricultural census, 1970–2010

of farmers in the state. We need to take a close look at the disaggregated income of these farm holdings.

NSSO 70th Round—a Situation Assessment Survey of Agricultural Households in India (NSSO 2014) estimated the total monthly income of a typical farm household in Karnataka to be ₹ 8963 (38% more than the national average) recording a growth rate of 4.5% since 2003. About 63% of this income came from farming and livestock. Service and business sector contributed 37% indicating significant engagement of farm families in non-farm activities. Nearly 42% farm households were below poverty line compared to 53% in the country in the same year. With this background, we will take a look at the changes in patterns of landholdings, land use and agriculture in the state.

Agricultural census of the state (2010–11) records 76% of its total landholdings to be small and marginal in size, cultivating 40% of the state's cropped land, with an average size of just about a hectare. Only marginal holdings have been increasing considerably in the state (Fig. 5.1). **Apart from its smaller average holding size and large number of dependent population, the agricultural economy of Karnataka is also constrained by large extent of rain-fed lands (irrigated area came to 35% of net sown area in 2010) receiving very little appropriate technology attention.**

Land use change in Karnataka shows some important trends (Fig. 5.2)—the areas under non-agricultural use and current fallows have marginally increased while permanent pasture lands decreased significantly between the mid-1960s and 2011 (Purushothaman and Kashyap (2010) highlights this trend up till 2005). Data implies a broad trend of intensification in cropping and change in the nature and emphasis on livestock keeping—from relatively larger number of free grazing local breeds to small dairy units.

5.2 Agriculture and Urbanisation in Karnataka

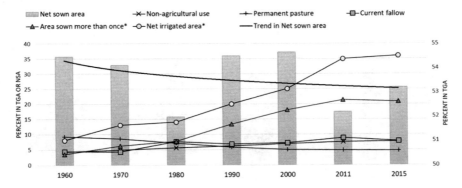

Fig. 5.2 Land use change in Karnataka (1960–2015). *Percent in net sown area.
Source Agriculture Statistics from various years from, Karnataka State Department of Agriculture

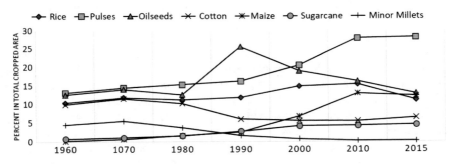

Fig. 5.3 Major crops in Karnataka (1960–2015).
Source Agriculture Statistics of various years from Karnataka State Department of Agriculture

Alongside the significant increase in irrigated area and area sown more than once, the most notable change in cropping pattern was in favour of maize, sugarcane and pulses in the period between 1960 and 2015 (Fig. 5.3). During the same period, small- and medium holders kept their share of farmland stable (Fig. 5.1), land under non-agricultural use and current fallows increased, along with a decrease in permanent pasture (Fig. 5.2).

At the same time, the area under subsistence crops, including millets (such as sorghum and pearl millet) has been trailing (Fig. 5.3 adapted from Purushothaman and Kashyap 2010). Acreage has been stable for rice but has been volatile for oilseeds and cotton (Fig. 5.3). **Such changes in cropping pattern with dwindling area under food crops has had impacts on food (nutritional) security in rural Karnataka (Suryanarayana 1997) along with an increasing share of irrigated crops and other products of intensive farming on consumers' plate**.

Though we do not have data to establish this, we can conjecture that the increasing trend of market (and PDS) dependence for food against the backdrop of disappearing common lands and water bodies that used to provide a steady (and zero cash cost) supply of wild fruits, berries and animal protein, meant nutritional imbalance in

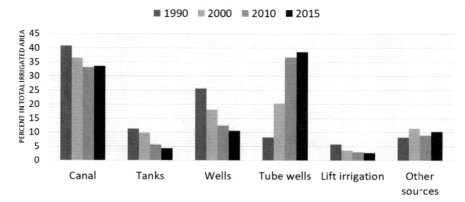

Fig. 5.4 Net irrigated area in Karnataka (1990–2015).
Source Agriculture Statistics of various years from Karnataka State Department of Agriculture

marginal holdings. In the process of generating products for the market, farm families in turn do not earn enough to purchase the required diversity and nutritional balance in their food. This eventually leads to increasing healthcare expenditure (in the backdrop of an inefficient rural public health care) from money borrowed at high interest rates.[17] **Such a cycle of commercialization of both agriculture and food in smallholdings also leads to forced migration.**

The change in Karnataka's cropping pattern reflects the pattern of irrigation and the irrigation pattern in turn implies a surge in private investment in tube wells since 1990 (Fig. 5.4). Private investment in tube wells points towards farmers' dependence on private banks for loans. This led to over 60% of farm households in Karnataka becoming indebted, a figure which has doubled since 1991 (Narayanamoorthy and Kalamkar 2005) in tandem with the spread of irrigation.

Thus, as food demand increased, agriculture transformed into input-intensive cultivation in some areas alongside fallows in other areas. Reduction in area under minor food grains translated into change in local food pattern with a larger water footprint and lesser nutritional gains. Compromising local nutritional needs and livelihoods also meant health impacts on both producer and consumer communities along with ecological damage to the production landscapes. Externally sourced market-dependent inputs meant higher operational cost and long-term debt for the sake of short-term spikes in profit and productivity.

Karnataka shows a consistent increase in the application of synthetic fertilisers per unit area (Fig. 5.5), coinciding with the surge in the number of tube wells (Fig. 5.4). However, it is interesting to note that except for food grains, crop yields do not match this surge in fertiliser application, groundwater exploitation and indebtedness.

---

[17]Jadhav et al. (2019) provide evidence for heavy indebtedness due to healthcare expenditure in rural Maharashtra. Similar stories from rural Karnataka are covered in—https://smallfarmdynamics. blog/2017/04/ and https://smallfarmdynamics.blog/2017/05/.

5.2 Agriculture and Urbanisation in Karnataka

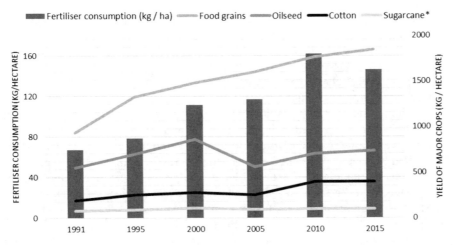

Fig. 5.5 Fertiliser consumption and yield of major crops (1991–2015). *Sugarcane yield is in tons per hectare.
Source Agriculture Statistics of various years from Karnataka State Department of Agriculture

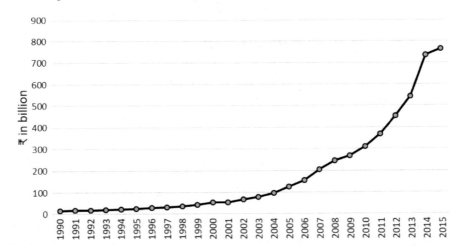

Fig. 5.6 Credit outstanding in the agricultural sector in Karnataka (1990–2015).
Source Various issues of RBI Handbook

During the period between 1991 and 2015, outstanding debt for agricultural purposes showed exponential growth. This period also shows inefficient growth in fertilizer application and area under irrigation (5.2 and 5.4%, respectively, for a 3.3% enhancement in agricultural production). In a span of 20 years between 1991 and 2010, the average annual growth in outstanding loans to agriculture was 16.3%. **This multi-fold increase in the amount of loans outstanding in agricultural sector (Fig. 5.6) is indicative of the amount of cash investment required for cultivation of commercial crops like sugarcane, maize and to some extent, cotton.**

Nearly 77% of farm households in the state have outstanding loans amounting to an average of ₹ 97,205 in 2011–12. According to Annon (2005), 44% of total outstanding loans of small and marginal holders was sourced from non-institutional sector like private lenders, traders, relatives and friends. In the case of large farmers, it was only 3%. The challenges and vulnerability of resource poor small and marginal farmers are reinforced when the share of loan repayment in total expenses increases. Accessibility and timely availability of institutional credit sources for small and marginal farmers are limited in the state as in the entire country.

So why do farmers take on risks disproportionate to their holding size and asset base? Various factors mentioned above such as shrinking land holding size. exclusive market orientation for output and inputs, and access to non-farm employment play a vital role in farmers' decision on the scale of production and engagement in agriculture. In an attempt to identify possible ways to address agrarian challenges arising out of urbanisation, this study explored the interwoven elements in land use, crops, new occupations and new constraints, using empirical observations and group interactions with farmers and other stakeholders situated in four different locations in the state chosen according to the typology of urbanisation mentioned in Chap. 3.

5.3 Study Sites—a Brief Introduction

The process of site selection (Chap. 3) was initiated by identifying agrarian peripheries located around four types of urban locations in Karnataka. Such farming peripheries were within the surroundings of a newly urbanised big city, a smaller town, an agro-processing township and a rural town.

Those parts of Bengaluru being urbanised and developed by drivers of a neoliberal economy and their agrarian peripheries are discussed in Chap. 6, while Chap. 7 examines the agrarian peripheries of a smaller town Ramanagara, lying close to Bengaluru. A recent study based on night light analysis by Gibson et al. (2017) shows that more than big cities, smaller towns were able to reduce poverty in rural India. The study recommends developing secondary towns while supporting agriculture for reducing poverty. Thus the impact of small but fast urbanised towns on smallholders may be distinctly different from that of the big cities. Chapter 8 looks at Mandya as a township around processing industries for agricultural produce, and Chap. 9 looks at the remote town of Yadgir, noted for the absence of rapid and significant urbanisation. Altogether, the study sites include two taluks each in the four agrarian peripheries (Fig. 5.7).

Pertinent socio-economic features of these sites (Tables 5.3 and 5.4) represent clear gradients in terms of distance from the nearest big city. The study sites represent a typology in terms of urbanisation process that has already been discussed in Sect. 3.1, Chap. 3.

A relatively lower share of primary sector in the local economy, fewer agricultural workers and higher Human Development Index (HDI) imply imminent livelihood shifts around the city as well as around the small towns in its proximity. Mandya, the

5.3 Study Sites—a Brief Introduction

Table 5.3 Study sites: socio-economic features

	Metropolitan city	Small town	Agro-urban	Rural town
Taluks	Anekal, Devanahalli	Kanakapura, Magadi	Pandavapura, Nagamangala	Shahpur, Shorapur
Average distance from nearest metropolitan city (km)	36	60	100	210*
Human Development Index (2014)	0.68	0.46	0.46	0.28
Sector-wise Share in NDDP (% at Constant Price, 2010–2011) — Primary	7.5	36.1	40.9	30.5
Secondary	33	16.2	20.4	29.7
Tertiary	59.5	47.8	38.9	39.8
Number of small-scale processing units for agri-produce (2011)	471	539	4133	552

*Distance to Hyderabad

Source Agriculture Census 2010–11, Karnataka Economic Survey 2013–14, Karnataka Human Development Report 2014

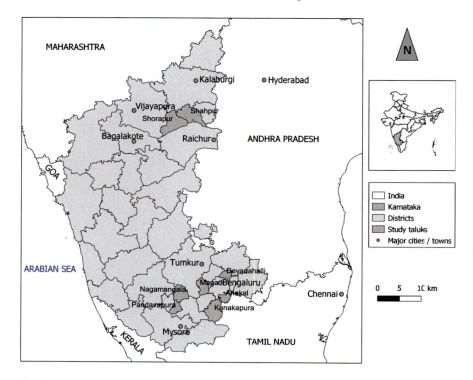

Fig. 5.7 Location of study sites

agro-processing region, where primary sector contributes the highest share (36%) to District Domestic Product (DDP), also fares well in HDI (Table 5.3). It is also the site with the highest number of landholdings and lowest proportion of large holdings. However, the noteworthy feature of Mandya is the relatively large share (28%) of local agricultural produce feeding its processing industries (Table 5.4).

5.3 Study Sites—a Brief Introduction

Table 5.4 Study sites: Demographic and land use characteristics

	Metropolitan city	Small town	Agro-urban	Rural town
Taluks	Anekal, Devanahalli	Kanakapura, Magadi	Pandavapura, Nagamangala	Shahpur, Shorapur
Total landholders (in lakhs—2010)	0.55	1.19	1.68	3.65
Large landholders (% in total landholders—2010)	3.8	3.6	4.3	5.1
Agricultural workers (% in total workers—2011)	42.2	73	80.9	80.4
Total cultivated area (% in TGA—2012 to 13)	49.2	48.4	49.3	81.1

(Total cultivated area = Net sown area + Current fallows)
Source Census of India 2011, Agriculture Census 2010–11, Karnataka Economic Survey 2013–14

Along with the above a large share of food crops indicates the importance of processing and value-adding industries in Mandya (Table 5.4). Yadgir, a remote region in north-east Karnataka reports the second-lowest economic performance (per capita NDDP of ₹ 52,527) and HDI (0.28, ranking 29th out of 30 districts in 2014). Going beyond the broad indicators listed in Table 5.4, following chapters will unpack the status of farming and farmers in the four differently urbanising locations.

References

Annon (2005) Situation Assessment Survey of Farmers. Indebtedness of Farmer Households. NSS 59th Round. Report No. 498(59/33/1)

Annon. (2011) *Employment and unemployment and household consumer expenditure.* National Sample Survey Office (NSS) 68th Round. Government of India.

Annon. (2014). *Household consumption of various goods and services in India 2011–12.* National Sample Survey Office, 68th Round. Government of India.

Annon. (2014) Key Indicators of Situation of Agricultural Households in India. National Sample Survey (NSS) 70th Round. Government of India.

Basu, D., Das, D., & Misra, K. (2016). Farmer suicides in India: Trends across major states, 1995–2011. *Economic and Political Weekly, 51*(21), 61–65.

Chand, R., & Raju, S. S. (2008). *Instability in Indian agriculture during different phases of technology and policy.* Discussion Paper NPP 01/2008.

Chand, R. (2005). India's National Agriculture Policy: A critique. In R. Chand (Ed.), *India's agricultural challenges—Reflections on policy, technology and other issues* (pp. 19–46). Centre for Trade and Development (CENTAD).

Chand, R., Raju, S. S., Garg, S., & Pandey, L. M. (2011). *Instability and regional variation in Indian agriculture*. NCAP Policy Paper 26. Retrieved on March 6, 2016 at http://www.ncap.res.in/upload_files/policy_paper/pp26.pdf.

Census of India (1981, 1991, 2001, 2011) Government of India.

Dandekar, A., & Bhattacharya, S. (2017). Lives in debt: Narratives of agrarian distress and farmer suicides. *Economic and Political Weekly, 52*(21), 77–84.

Das, A. (2013) Mapping the regional variation in potential vulnerability in India agriculture to climate change—an exercise through consturcting vulnerability index. *African Journal of Environmental Science and Technology*, 7(4): 112–121.

Deshpande, R. S. (2002). Suicides by farmers in Karnataka: Agrarian distress and possible alleviatory steps. *Economic and Political Weekly, 37*(26), 2601–2610.

Deshpande, R. S., & Prabhu, Nagesh. (2005). Farmers' distress: Proof beyond question. *Economic and Political Weekly, 40*(44–45), 4663–4665.

Deshpande, R. S., & Arora, S. (2010). *Agrarian crisis and farmer suicide* (pp. 43–69; 118–148; 374–393). Sage Publications.

Editorial. (2017). Unquiet fields. *Economic and Political Weekly, 52*(24).

Gibson, J., Dutt, G., Murgai R., & Ravallion, M. (2017) For India's rural poor, growing towns matter more than growing cities. *World Development*, 98, 413–429.

Giller, K. E., Beare, M. H., Lavelle, P., Izac, A. M. N., & Swift, M. J. (1997). Agricultural intensification, soil biodiversity and agro ecosystem function. *Applied Soil Ecology, 6*(1), 3–16.

Government of India (GOI), Twelfth Five Year Plan. (2012–2017). *Economic sectors: Vol. II. Planning commission*. New Delhi, India (2013).

Government of India (GOI). (2013). *Towards Achieving Millennium Development Goals India 2013. Social Statistics Division, Ministry of Statistics and Programme Implementation*.

Gupta, P. K. (2004). Pesticide exposure—Indian scene. *Toxicology, 198,* 83–90.

Gulati, A., & Narayanan, S. (2000). Demystifying fertliser and power subsidies in India. *Economic and Political Weekly*, 784–794.

Indian Council for Agricultural Research (ICAR). (2010). *Degraded and Wastelands of India: Status and spatial distribution, Indian Council for Agricultural Research*. New Delhi, India.

Jadhav, N., Aher, B., & Sudhindra, D. (2019) Public health system is failing the women farmers. *Economic and Political Weekly* 54(10), 17–19.

Jaitley, A. (2014). *Finance Minister presentation of 2014–2015 Budget to Parliament, Minister of Finance*. Accessed March 6, 2015. http://www.livemint.com/Politics/n2CKOUxRPwNprqgu2StUlL/Union-Budget-2014-Finance-minister-Arun-Jaitley-full-speech.html?utm_source = ref_article.

Jha, D. (2003). Policy drift in agriculture. *Economic and Political Weekly, 38*(47), 4947–4978.

Matson, P. A., & Parton, W. J. (1997). Agricultural intensification and ecosystem properties. *Science,* 577, 5325.

Narayanamoorthy, A., & Kalamkar, S. S. (2005). Indebtedness of farm households across states: Recent trends, status and determinants. *Indian Journal of Agricultural Economics* 60(3), 290–301.

National Agriculture Policy (2000) Department of Agriculture and Cooperation, Government of India.

Patil, S., Reidsma, P., Shah, P., Purushothaman, S., & Wolf, J. (2012). Comparing conventional and organic agriculture in Karnataka, India: Where and when can organic farming be susta nabile? *Land Use Policy*, https://doi.org/10.1016/j.landusepol.2012.01.006

Planning Commission (2014) *Poverty estimates*.

Purushothaman, S., & Kashyap, S. (2010). Trends in land use and crop acreages in Karnataka and their repercussions. *Karnataka Journal of Agricultural Science*, 23(2), 330–333.

References

Purushothaman, S. (2012). Evaluating the green revolution. In P. Jacquet, R. K. Pachauri, & L. Tubiana (Eds.), *A planet for life, development, the environment and food: Towards agricultural change?* (pp. 164–166). TERI Publication.

Purushothaman, S., Patil, S., Patil, I., Francis, I., & Nesheim, I. (2013). Policy and Governance for sustaining livelihoods and natural resources in small farms—A case study in Karnataka. *Indian Journal of Agricultural Economics, 68*(2), 240–258.

Ranganathan, T. C. A. (2015). Agricultural oddities. *Economic and Political Weekly, 50*(21), 16–19.

Singh, R. B. (2000). Environmental consequences of agricultural development: A case study from the Green Revolution state of Haryana, India. *Agriculture, Ecosystems and Environment, 82,* 97–103.

Shukla, R. (2010). *How India earns, spends and saves: unmasking the real India* (pp. 45–74). National Council of Applied Economic Research—Macro Consumer Research. Sage Publications, India. ISBN 978-81-321-0476-6 (HB).

Suryanarayana, M. H. (1997) Food Security in India - measures, norms and issues. *Development and Change, 28*(4), 771–789.

Thrupp, L. A. (2000). Linking agricultural biodiversity and food security: the valuable role of agrobiodiversity for sustainable agriculture. *International Affairs, 76*(2), 265–281.

Tilman, D., Cassman, K. G., Matson, P. A., Naylor, R., & Polasky, S. (2002). Agricultural sustainability and intensive production practices. *Nature, 418,* 671–677.

Vasavi, A. (2009). Suicides and the making of India's agrarian distress. *South African review of sociology, 40*(1), 94–108.

Vasavi, A. R. (2016). *The bitter reality behind the 'pro-farmer' budget. LiveMint*, March 20, 2016.

Chapter 6
The City and the Peasant—Family Farms Around Bengaluru

The great cities rest upon our broad and fertile prairies. Burn down your cities and leave our farms, and your cities will spring up again as if by magic; but destroy our farms, and grass will grow in the streets of every city in the country.
William Jennings Bryan (*Cross of Gold*, speach at the Democratic National Convention, July 9, 1896).

6.1 Mega City of the Neo-Liberal Times

In any fast-growing economy, it is common to attribute agrarian opportunities to expanding and emerging cities as described in Satterthwaite et al. (2010). Nevertheless, the opportunities arising from urbanisation come along with huge demands placed on the production landscape. If the current pattern of urban consumption continues, food production should double by 2050. Despite niche innovations in urban farming (such as vertical farms, hydroponics, aeroponics, and polymer farming), the fast depleting rural agricultural landscapes will have to meet most of this overwhelming demand. Do our urbanised societies and economies realise the extent of their dependence on agrarian landscapes for safe and healthy food? Can this dependence help sustain their farmer producers?

The previous chapter presented an overview of the tri-junction of urbanisation, economic growth and agriculture in India and in the State of Karnataka, before delving into the types of urban peripheries that this book focuses on. This chapter focuses on the interfaces encountered in the peri-urban study site around the city of Bengaluru, based on primary data collected from immediate peripheries of the city.

© Springer Nature Singapore Pte Ltd. 2019
S. Purushothaman and S. Patil, *Agrarian Change and Urbanization in Southern India*, India Studies in Business and Economics,
https://doi.org/10.1007/978-981-10-8336-5_6

Nested in an agricultural landscape, Bengaluru now symbolises India's urban aspirations.[1] Historically known for trade and manufacturing activities, it became a production and trading hub by the end of eighteenth century, hosting industries and trader guilds dealing in agricultural products such as cotton, edible oil, betel nut, silk, rice, and spices. Permanent representatives of traders from distant localities lived in the city to coordinate the trade and transport of these goods (Buchanan 1807). Later, in newly dependent India, Bengaluru became a notable hub of large-scale public sector industrial manufacturing units established along with their staff residences in large numbers.[2] In the course of its' transformation spanning five centuries, Bengaluru—a city of gardens and pensioners till about three decades ago became a technology hub noted for its traffic snarls, garbage and frothy lakes.

Though it's history as a hub of economic activities in the southern Indian peninsula is long, its transformation into a metropolis began recently, with a population increase of more than eight times in half a century from 1951 to 6.5 million in 2001 (Census of India 2001).[3] Compared to other large cities that took a couple of centuries for a continuous expansive transition, Bengaluru expanded rapidly, overtaking them in population growth by the 1980s. The city's growth relative to other big cities in south India had more to do with infilling[4] till about 2000, before it started growing laterally as well (Table 6.1). Changing and growing demands of Bengaluru then, and now, are met by agricultural landscapes surrounding the expanding frontier of the city. Ironically, the same beneficiary city plunders the land and waterscapes that supported its population over centuries, irreversibly changing the landscape along with the social fabric of the region. Seemingly in a hurry to acquire the 'megacity' status, India's Silicon Valley seems to have ignored its agrarian past and peripheries.

Alongside the growth in population, demands on land increased exponentially. What is of interest to us is not this transition per se, but how the farms and farmers around this city fared in the course of this transformation.

The periphery of a city driven by neo-liberal economic principles becomes an attractive investment target for individuals and corporate entities alike, triggering the conversion of small and large tracts of farmlands. Since the 1960s, state-driven industrial estates of private industries started occupying the cityscape. Large private residential layouts were developed in the 1990s. Farmlands in the suburbs of the

---

[1]Bengaluru ranks high globally on a city Momentum Index using socio-economic and commercial real estate indicators (https://www.jll.co.in/en/newsroom/jll-city-momentum-index-2019-bengaluru-worlds-most-dynamic-city).

[2]Immediately after independence in 1948, Indian Telephone Industries was set up in Bengaluru followed by industries like Hindustan Aeronautics Limited, Hindustan Machine Tools Limited, Bharat Earth Movers Limited, Bharat Electronics Limited and Defence Research and Development Organisation.

[3]Between 1901 and 1951, population of Bengaluru increased about five times from 0.16 to 0.78 million (Report of Bengaluru Development Committee 1954).

[4]Infilling is an increase in density of population within city limits, rather than an expansion in the physical boundaries of the city.

6.1 Mega City of the Neo-Liberal Times

Table 6.1 South Indian cities: infilling and expansion

	Population Density (Decadal change in %)			Geographical Area (Decadal change in %)		
	1981–91	1991–2001	2001–11	1981–91	1991–2001	2001–2011
Bengaluru	38.6	35.1	46.8	2.0	1.9	15.3
Hyderabad	29.5	23.9	4.7	31.7	2.8	17.5
Chennai	17.3	13.0	7.6	7.8	4.9	25.8

Source Census of India 1991, 2001 and 2011

then Bengaluru were converted into estates of private sector industries[5] set up by the Karnataka Industrial Area Development Board (KIADB) and residential layouts set up by Bengaluru Development Authority (BDA), Bruhat Bengaluru Mahanagara Palike (BBMP) and real estate developers.

In the four decades from 1971 to 2011, the geographical area of Bengaluru Metropolitan Region (includes both Bengaluru Urban and Rural districts) quadrupled to 710 km^2, cropland shrunk from 51% to a meagre 7% and mixed built-up (residential and commercial) area increased from 20 to 69%. An optimal growth scenario for 2031 in the draft Revised Master Plan (2015) envisages addition of 11.9 million people and 80 km^2 from 251 villages to the Bengaluru Metropolitan Area.

Around the city with such a growth trajectory, the physical manifestation of the rural–urban interface is reflected in the 'cusp' landscapes located about an hour's drive from the city centre in any direction towards its periphery. We reach these 'rurban' areas passing through modern residential areas, water bodies, small and medium industries, elevated expressways, metro train lines and agricultural produce markets; extending till farmlands dotted with fields and polyhouses. Figure 6.1 captures this mosaic of land use that will be used to compare with other urban peripheries illustrated and discussed in the subsequent chapters. Dotting the vast agricultural areas of peri-urban Bengaluru, we find polyhouses growing high-value flowers and vegetables, the international airport, small and medium industries, as well as residential layouts. Most enclosed residential layouts at the frontier of urbanisation lie empty, awaiting a real estate boom while denying common use for grazing or fuelwood.

Agriculture in the margins of Bengaluru

To understand the influence of the city on smallholders, we chose two taluks based on the presence of agricultural workers. Selected taluks–Anekal and Devanahalli are situated in the Southern and Northern part of the city respectively. Situated in the Bengaluru Urban and Rural districts respectively, Anekal and Devanahalli represent the closest agrarian peripheries of the city.[6] Yet, they differ in the pace and impact of

---

[5]Now these industrial estates like the ones in Peenya, Whitefield and Bidadi, lie contiguous with the centre of the city in different directions.

[6]See Chap. 3 Sect. 3.4 for the process followed in selection of taluks and a discussion on urban peripheries.

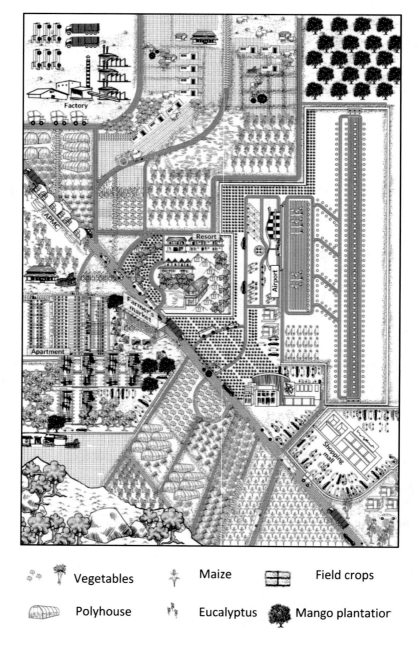

Fig. 6.1 Peri-urban Bengaluru

urbanisation. The administrative headquarters of the two taluks are located 30–40 km from Bengaluru's Central Business District, in opposite directions.

Situated on the main interstate highway with Tamil Nadu and closer to the hub of Bengaluru's information technology industry—Electronic City—Anekal has been a Town Municipal Council (TMC) since 1986 in southern Bengaluru. Devanahalli on the northern side of the city, despite being a TMC since 1959, saw significant urbanisation only after land acquisition for the new airport began in late 1990s. The two taluks also differ geographically, particularly in their groundwater endowment. Devanahalli lying upstream to the city is drier compared to Anekal lying downstream. While villages in both these taluks interact with the city in various ways, they differ in the nature of their most pertinent linkage with the society and economy of Bengaluru. This divergence gives rise to diverse patterns in the core–periphery linkages.

These taluks will continue to be different as deduced from the Revised Structural Plan 2031 of Bengaluru Metropolitan Region Development Authority (BMRDA). The proposed structural development and urban expansion for the next 15 years appear to be again geared towards Anekal. Towards Devanahalli, structural changes are proposed only around the airport, leaving the remaining agricultural zones intact.

Anekal in the south of Bengaluru is an old town founded close to AD 1603 and known for its ragi (finger millet) fields and silk weavers. The urban buzz in Anekal created by its closeness to the technological hub of Electronic City, mushrooming educational institutions, modern residential complexes and numerous stone and marble processing industries, coexists with rural features like frequent crop raids by elephants from Bannerghatta forests and a society deeply divided along caste lines.

The origin of the name 'Anekal' is said to be in *'Gajashilapura'*, interpreted as place with the elephant stone in Kannada and Tamil. The General of Bijapur granted Anekal to Chikka Thimme Gowda (of Sugatur family) after annexing his hereditary possession—Hoskote. He then erected the fort and temple and constructed a large tank. In 1760, during the reign of Dodda Thimme Gowda (grandson of Anekal's founder), Anekal was annexed by Mysore. Thimme Gowda continued as chief, by paying tribute to the King of Mysore (Imperial Gazetteer 1906).

Before the establishment of the international airport, Devanahalli's claim to fame was as the birthplace of Tipu Sultan and as a locality close to the picnic spot of Nandi hills. Resting near the hillocks here sometime in the fifteenth century, Devanadoddi got its mud fort in 1503, built by a family of refugees (to which Kempe Gowda, the founder of the city also belonged). Two centuries later, the town was conquered and ruled by Marathas, later by Wodeyars and then by Hyder Ali until the British took over in 1791.

Located in the grape growing area around Bengaluru, as a recently urbanised periphery of the mega city, Devanahalli is different in character from Anekal (Table 6.2). The emergence of infrastructural and industrial ventures, including the international airport and Hi-Tech, Defence and Aerospace parks, happened since 2000 here. Devanahalli is close to the ring road encircling the city, the Bangalore–Hyderabad highway and also to Doddaballapur—the new hub of residential constructions in North Bengaluru. Anekal is close to the interstate highway towards

Table 6.2 Anekal and Devanahalli taluks at a glance

	Anekal	Devanahalli
Total geographical area (TGA) (km^2)	530	449
Forests, pastures and tree groves (% of TGA)	14	17
Net sown area (% of TGA in 2015)	21	43
Population density (per km^2 in 2011)	972	470
Urban population (% in 2011)	32	30
Cultivators and agricultural labourers (% of total workers in 2011)	18	52
Per capita income (lakh ₹ in 2013)	2.57	1.17
Human Development Index (rank among 176 taluks of the State in 2014)	0.77 (1)	0.58 (33)

Source Human Development Report 2014; Census of India 2011 and Agriculture Census 2011

Hosur in Tamil Nadu, the Bengaluru–Mysore infrastructure corridor, the thickly populated areas of Electronic City and Bannerghatta road.

After a tour of hoblis to identify habitations that maintain active links with Bengaluru city, where influence from other cities is minimal and where farming is visibly important, group interactions were held in 12 villages—one each from all hoblis of the two taluks, mainly to assist in selecting villages for field study. Inhabited by 400–500 families on an average, each of these 12 villages reportedly hosts around 100 households working in the non-farm sector. Non-farm workers were commuting daily to the city, with only around 1–12 families completely shifting to the new location. There was general agreement on how cropping and occupational patterns changed over time.

While Anekal farmers were producing and selling more perishable crops in local markets, wholesale interstate traders were popular in Devanahalli villages. Famers in both places were buying inputs from traders and input shops and generated minimal inputs on farm. Large holdings and forward caste households were few in both taluks with more than 70% families belonging to other backward castes (OBC, mainly *vokkaliga* and *reddy*). Households of Scheduled Caste and Scheduled Tribes (SC, mainly *madiga* and ST mainly *nayaka*) were around 10–15%.

With this cursory exposure to the general situation in 12 villages of the two taluks, we selected four villages (Fig. 6.2), to represent the peripheries of a neo-urban space, following the process described in Chap. 3. Vishwanathpura and Reddihalli villages are situated in Devanahalli and Dasanapura and Siddihoskote in Anekal taluk.

From the revenue records of these villages, we identified 43 farm holdings from various social and landholding categories present in the village ensuring representation of women landowners. Following the group interactions, we chose nine additional households of farmer migrants.

6.2 Farmlands: Enduring Rapid Transformation

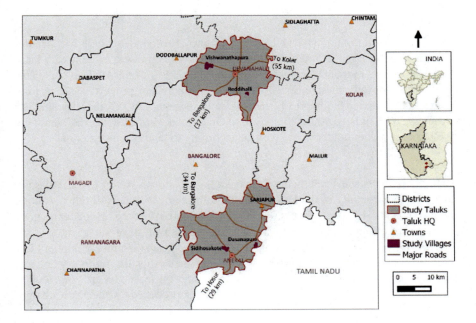

Fig. 6.2 Study villages in peri-urban Bengaluru

6.2 Farmlands: Enduring Rapid Transformation

Land has always been the pivot of accumulation by dispossession, since settled agriculture led to power divergence between the rulers (revenue/ tax accumulators) and the ruled (tax payers). This phenomenon is found both in Indian cities (Banerjee-Guha (2013), Harvey 2004) as much as in capitalist economies. Notably, this accumulation process in Indian rural–urban dynamics is complex involving alienation of ownership, access, quality and quantum of resources.

Land rights vary—ranging from individual rights to buy, sell and farm, to community ownership, State ownership, ownership by a society/ trust, and company ownership. Beginning with the *ryotwari* system in the 1830s, social disadvantage started converging with smallness of the land that one owned or operated (see Chap. 4 for history of land disparity in the study regions of Karnataka). But urbanism seemed to offer opportunities for these small landowners.

This section unpacks a major fault line in the rural–urban dynamics around Bengaluru on the issue of land. With a notable share of land under agriculture (Table 6.2) and built-up area (43 and 23%, respectively, for Anekal and Devanahalli), the study taluks represent the 'rurban' geographies implied in Gupta (2015). Yet, these two taluks differ in the land use pattern, with Anekal holding 22% lesser net sown area (NSA), and 20% more land unavailable for cultivation than Devanahalli (District at a Glance 2017).

Ownership

The average land holding size (3.15 acres) of farmer respondents here was smaller than the State average (3.8 acres).[7] Smallholder domination was evident with large holders (with more than 10 acres) comprising only 3.8% of the total holders. This smallness is despite the continued existence of undivided property held in joint ownership patrilineal families (30% respondents in Anekal and 35% in Devanahalli).[8] More than 82% of landowners[9] belonged to Other Backward Castes (OBC) and only five per cent of landholders were women according to land revenue records.

Leasing

Though leasing is restricted by the Karnataka Land Reforms Act of 1962, it was not uncommon, especially in the less populated villages of Devanahalli taluk. Among the respondents, 12% leased out 60% of their land and 9% of the respondents (none landless) were supplementing own land by leasing an average of 1.8 acres.

There were three kinds of leasing arrangements. One was among smallholders themselves. For instance, small farmers who cultivated crops like mulberry or fruits that did not provide fodder for livestock took land on lease for growing fodder. The lessor and the lessee often shared the fodder produced, while lease charges were generally paid in cash.

Another arrangement was through cash payment to farmers by a group mostly of corporate employees who leased in their land. While most such lessees cultivated vegetables and fruits, some also cultivated ragi and pulses. The group members usually took turns to visit farms periodically and appointed local farmers as caretakers.[10]

The third arrangement is closer to contract farming but without a written agreement. This involves retail commission agents who advance seeds and inputs to farmers and buy back the harvested produce at prefixed rates. This arrangement was generally followed for crops like baby corn and ladies finger.

Fallows

Fallowing productive land in this peri-urban interface is a glaring contradiction in the city-farms relationships. If the city extends a good market as also potential for leasing, how then do we explain the fallows in peri-urban farming areas? Absentee landlords may leave land uncultivated and just speculate on land value, but farmers

---

[7] Unless specified, data in these sections pertain to the city periphery combining two study taluks.

[8] Average size of joint family holdings was 2.75 acres (overall landholding size was 2.6 acres) and 4 acres (overall landholding size was 3.8 acres) in Anekal and Devanahalli, respectively, in 2015.

[9] As per Socio-economic and Caste Census (2014), about 89 and 46% of total households were landless in Anekal and Devanahalli, respectively, with large number of non-farm workers in the former.

[10] We saw such arrangements near Kanakapura road and Anekal. See also 'Farmizer'—new mobile app-based initiative for renting a remote kitchen garden around Bengaluru:—https:// www.thehindu.com/life-and-style/how-farmizen-is-helping-people-of-bengaluru-reconnect-with-farming/article22456975.ece.

leaving their lands uncultivated is unusual. Yet, 20% farmer respondents in this study site allowed their land to lie fallow for an year or more. Most of these were in Anekal (30%, compared to 10% in Devanahalli). These fallows came to an average of 40% of their farmland. About one-fourth of them reported longer fallows of more than two years. Water deficit, labour scarcity and prohibitive cost of inputs were widely cited as reasons for this scaling down in farming.

Land Conversion

Anekal town, founded very early in the seventeenth century, got modern industries from the 1980s (Attibele and Jigani industrial estates). While growth of the electronics industry and closeness to interstate highway and Tamil Nadu markets were the notable land use drivers in Anekal taluk, Devanahalli saw significant changes only from the year 2000—after the new airport brought in more population, buildings and industries.

Acquisition in this study site was driven equally by private corporate interest and the State. Public land acquisition was more commonly recognised as the determinant of land use change and of landlessness in Devanahalli. Land use change in Anekal with a history of acquisitions is now driven by voluntary transactions between private entities, apart from some state-driven acquisition still taking place.

Acquisition of around 2,000 acres of land in and around Anekal taluk happened between 1977 and 2003.[11] Fifteen per cent of sample households (all from Anekal) reported acquisition of their agricultural property either for roads or residential layouts by the State authorities like Karnataka State Housing Board. Nearly, 20% of sample households had converted their agricultural land (on an average 56% of land owned) between 2014 and 2016 either by selling it off or by using it for non-agricultural purposes. This is much higher than what has been generally reported in terms of conversion of agricultural land around the city as a whole.[12] Land was sold to meet expenses such as repayment of overdue loans, children's education or marriage costs.

6.3 Nature's Commons: Up for Acquisition and Encroachment

Having looked at how access to land for cultivation and livelihoods play out in tandem with the pattern of urbanisation in the previous section, this section deals with nature's commons in the study site. As argued elsewhere (Salman and Munir 2016;

---

[11] Anekal Local Planning Area 2031 (Zoning Regulations Provisional Approval) (2013).

[12] Using remote sensing data between 2007 and 2014, Kavitha et al. (2015) show that about 16% of agricultural land within 20 km buffer area outside the boundary of Greater Bengaluru was converted to built-up.

Fig. 6.3 Wooded grove (*Gundu thoppu*) in Devanahalli

Lele et al. 2013) land and water resources that are common property or commonly pooled are critical not just for meeting material needs, but also for sustaining the agro-ecosystems.

Common land resources used by the farming community include grazing areas, forests and sacred groves. Though small patches of grazing lands were present in all four study villages, only one village of Devanahalli taluk with an active dairy co-operative used it for livestock grazing and fodder collection. It is well known that urbanisation triggers demand for milk and milk products and hence encourages small-scale dairies (e.g. Brook et al. (2006) and Kumar and Parappurathu (2014)). This is of immense help to smallholders, especially women, but comes at the cost of having to forego multi-purpose and free grazing local breed cows, as well as grazing practice. In half the sample villages of this site, most grazing lands face conversion and/or encroachments. Between 1995 and 2005, a large portion of the land conversion through acquisition for different purposes in the Devanahalli area came from common lands and water bodies (KSIIDC 2010). As per our interactions with KIADB, of the total land acquired for Bengaluru International Airport, less than one-forth came from private landowners.[13]

As urban demand for dairy products increases, the on-farm production of draught power and manure in the farms cease to be the objectives of livestock keeping. Supply of manure and power for family farms thus came to be outsourced to the market and machines. The remaining village common lands no longer managed by local communities turn into open access no-man's land, easily available for conversion to other purposes (Mundoli et al. 2017). The cost of livestock keeping increases in the absence of rightful access to commons that have been hijacked by urban expansion. Though there are no forests in the study villages, wherever present wooded groves,[14] are still being used for worship and grazing small ruminants. Farmers in the study villages kept small ruminants, especially sheep (Fig. 6.3).[15]

---

[13] Land acquisition data from KIADB doesn't clearly differentiate between common land and private landholding. This estimation is based on village level data collected.

[14] In Devanahalli, *Gundu thoppu* (wooded grove) hosting old temples is an oasis for graziers and passers-by.

[15] About 30% respondents in Anekal and 23% in Devanahalli kept small ruminants.

6.3 Nature's Commons: Up for Acquisition and Encroachment

Rural Bengaluru also reports instances of deprived access to common lands owing to caste discrimination. **Thus, as the city creeps into the production landscapes, it seems to impart diverging impacts—offering casual employment and camouflaging social divisions while threatening economic-ecological balance and precipitating rural social divides.**

Common water bodies in the study villages used to include tanks, step wells and second-order streams. Lakes in and around Bengaluru were actually irrigation tanks built over centuries, starting from the period of Gangas, the Cholas and the Hoysalas.[16] They built tanks with high bunds to store water. In the sixteenth century, Kempegowda built more tanks for irrigation. All of them together formed a cascading system, avoiding wastage of water. Blue patches in Fig. 6.4 depict major lakes in and around the study site. Between 2001 and 2016, out of the 117 lakes in Devanahalli taluk, only one remained un-encroached. In Anekal taluk, 254 lakes have been encroached upon, of which 60% are completely converted.[17] Three among the four surveyed villages[18] had a tank or lake (*kere*), used generally for livestock and, in some parts of rural Bengaluru, for irrigation too. The lake in one study village in Anekal was functional only a few months in an year.

Maps of old Bengaluru show over a thousand open wells located within a distance of 200 m from the lakes. With the spread of tube wells, unused open/dug wells became objects of neglect. **This collective disservice meted out to large number of common water sources is seemingly another facet of the politically convenient development intervention of privatising water through tube wells and taps.**

A secondary stream (*halla*) found in Vishwanathpura in Devanahalli situated in Arkavathy basin had three check dams constructed across it in 2005 that turned defunct by 2010 due to the damaged side walls. In some streams soil was seen dumped in order to divert water into neighbouring fields. In the absence of functional community institutions to manage them, these valuable common resources end up as a tragedy of 'open access'. The tragedy of open-access water commons also in turn translates into the degeneration of social institutions. This institutional vacuum takes away the inherent collective strength of farm holdings that are individually small in size. Thus, as peri-urban farmers reel under the financial burden of failed and failing tube wells, common resources and collective institutions that could potentially ensure sustained access to natural resources vanish even from the memory of a primarily agrarian society. **Farming community here appears individualised but yet to be urbanised in terms of stable non-farm occupation or complete disengagement from farming.**

---

[16]Even now many places in Bengaluru carry names suffixed with '*sandra*' in Kannada implying the presence of a notable water body.

[17]Report of Encroachment of Lakes/Tanks in Bengaluru Urban District—http://www.newindianexpress.com/cities/bengaluru/2017/nov/23/88-lakes-vanished-in-bengaluru-in-recent-years-1708596.html.

[18]Reddihalli and Vishwanathpura in Devanahalli and Dasanpura in Anekal.

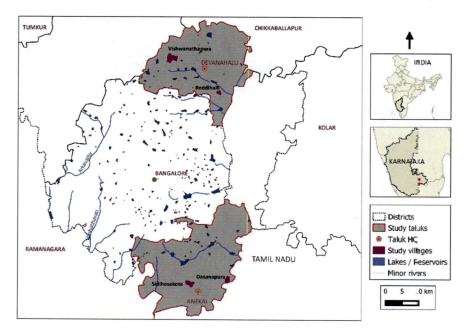

Fig. 6.4 Lakes and streams in Anekal and Devanahalli taluks

6.4 Irrigation: The Tube Well—Energy Nexus

Urbanism appears to have a strange psyche. A city that replaced water storage systems established by visionaries of yore with buildings or with dumped waste and sewage, demands products that need sumptuous water sources. With groundwater table lower than 600 ft, about one-third of the cultivated area in these taluks remains rain fed (Directorate of Economics and Statistics 2013–14). Yet, more than half of our respondents had some land with irrigation, mostly by tube wells. Thus, 28% of Net Sown Area in our sample farm holdings was being irrigated exclusively by tube wells.[19] **Shift from open wells to tube wells had many consequences. Making well digging an energy-intensive proposition as well as making the depleting levels of water invisible are examples of such impacts.**

Respondent Rajshekhar (name changed, 37 years) in Devanahalli taluk had spent almost ₹12 lakh between 2012 and 2015 for digging two new tube wells and deepening an old one, for just an acre of floriculture. Such investment intensity is not unusual, especially for high-value flowers and vegetables. Since flower crops are remunerative, this extravagance in exploiting groundwater was financially justified despite the disproportionate (to the scale of the farm and to the capital available) risks involved. The risk in dryland agriculture is no less—30% of rain-fed farms growing

---

[19]In both the study taluks, about 30% of net sown area was irrigated exclusively by tube wells in 2015 (District at a Glance 2016).

ragi reportedly lost around 70% of the crop due to deficient rainfall. Unseasonal rainfall with hailstorms is equally culpable, leaving even irrigated grape growers adversely affected.

Once again, as in the case of livestock and grazing lands, we come across a divergence in city's impact on family farms. The city offers a market for flowers and vegetables, while sucking the groundwater and surface water available in the landscape. In fact, the city not only sets precedence in water mining, but also appears uninterested in how its food and flowers are grown or how it impacts the hydrology of the region. By 2010, Bengaluru city had dug 320 tube wells per km^2 and converted 42 (out of 837) lakes covering an area of 523 ha into built-up and other encroachments.[20] **Complacency arising from a belief in the ability of water drilling technology to substitute for loss in water table and conviction in the economic power of the city to bring water from distant sources was evident.**

6.5 Farming Systems: Feeding a Mega City and Sustaining Culture

Urban demand for food, *prima facie,* offers valuable opportunities for farm families. We will now discuss some nuances underlying these opportunities and some challenges specific to the chosen villages.

Nearly, 67% of total cropped area in both the taluks was under food and related crops such as *ragi*, pulses (field bean or *avare*, horse gram or *hurali*), coconut, vegetables and fruits. The remaining was used for flowers, fodder (including fodder maize), mulberry and eucalyptus. Half of the 52 surveyed households used 40% of their land for cultivating the staple grain—ragi (Fig. 6.5). Many families growing ragi exchanged the product for other food grains with their friends or relatives. Though coconut and eucalyptus were the major perennials (other than fruit trees), eucalyptus is mono-cropped while coconut gardens generally grow mulberry or fodder grass alongside. Coconut and fodder were common in both taluks. Fodder crop (generally Napier grass) was either fed to livestock in the farm or sold to other dairy farmers. Pulses were found only in Anekal farms and maize only in Devanahalli. Mulberry was more prominent in Devanahalli.

Thus, popular crops (in decreasing order) in Anekal were ragi, vegetables, flowers and eucalyptus, while in Devanahalli it was ragi, eucalyptus, mulberry and maize. Both taluks show an increase in non-food crops and reduction in area under ragi alongside an overall reduction in net sown area from 62 to 32% of Total Geographical Area (TGA) in two decades till 2015. In both the taluks, ragi and eucalyptus reign supreme in agricultural land use, with the former decreasing in area, replaced by the

---

[20]Report of the Committee constituted by the Honourable High Court of Karnataka to examine the ground realities and prepare an action plan for preservation of lakes in the city of Bengaluru. http://static.esgindia.org/campaigns/lakes/legal/A1_HC_Lakes_Report_WP_817_2008_HC_Feb_2011.pdf.

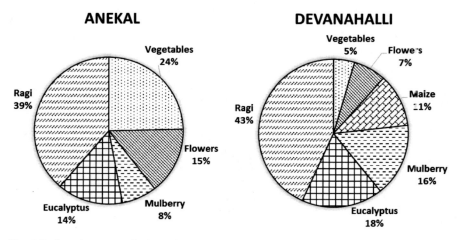

Fig. 6.5 Cropping pattern in the periphery of Benguluru (% of land cultivated by responcents). *Source* Farmer interviews, 2015

latter. This showcases the varied dependence of peri-urban farm families on their land; ranging from staple millet to purely cash-oriented land use. Between 2000 and 2010, there was a noticeable increase in the area under grape cultivation in Devanahalli and of flowers and vegetables in Anekal.

6.5.1 Flowers for and from the Garden City

Bengaluru's salubrious climate and the tag of 'Garden City' meant the presence of a well-established flower trade. Temples and florists, festivals and other functions in the city and other parts of South India demand a large volume of low-value flowers like a variety of jasmine (*kakada*), marigold, chrysanthemum (*shavante*), crossandra (*kanakambara*) grown in open fields. The low-value flower crops grown for local markets targeting temples, marriage functions, offices and residences, etc., depend on migrant labour from neighbouring States like Tamil Nadu and Andhra Pradesh.

On the other hand, high-value cut flowers like rose, gladioli, anthurium and gerbera for urbanites in and outside Bengaluru are generally grown in polyhouses. The International Flower Auction Center (IFAC) set up in 2002 gave impetus to intensive export-oriented floriculture around the city. While IFAC imparts transparency and avoids middle agents in flower marketing, it hasn't successfully addressed price fluctuation. Export-oriented polyhouse culture of cut flowers needs skilled migrant labour often arriving from far off places such as Uttar Pradesh and Bihar. Polyhouse floriculture needs full-time resident labour for timely control of temperature and humidity apart from harvesting usually done before dawn.

6.5 Farming Systems: Feeding a Mega City and Sustaining Culture

Fig. 6.6 Eucalyptus in Devanahalli and flower crops in Anekal

According to farmers, growing flowers in polyhouses over an acre of land in 2015 yielded an annual net return of ₹7–8 lakh.[21] **Farmers also understand that 5–6 years of this kind of intensive cultivation will result in depletion of soil and water. But the urge for profit embedded in city's consumerism makes farmers ignore the consequences on farming and on themselves (Fig. 6.6).**

6.5.2 Eucalyptus in Peri-urban Bengaluru

In 1952, after the successful introduction of 16 different species from Australia, eucalyptus was planted in large scale around Nandi Hills, north of Bengaluru. The tree grows easily in a wide range of soils and climate. Initially, the Forest Department planted eucalyptus trees on degraded hillsides and later on it rapidly spread to farmlands as well. From the 1980s, a World Bank aided project to generate fuelwood and timber for communities resulted in the spread of this easily cultivable tree in all directions. By 1984, taluks close to Nandi hills (Devanahalli, Doddaballapur, Chikkaballapur and Kolar) had large tracts of eucalyptus planted in private lands mainly through the social forestry programme implemented by the Forest Department. Considering the relative rapidity of decline in water table in and around eucalyptus plantations, the species was banned by amending the Karnataka Preservation of Trees Act (1976)[22] in 2011.

The spread of eucalyptus can be attributed to many reasons. Hybrid varieties of the tree start yielding returns early, within 6–7 years. Labour and water were scarce to cultivate other crops demanded by the city. Assured demand for timber, poles and

---

[21]With an initial investment of ₹10 lakhs for building the infrastructure in addition to the recurring cost of about ₹3.6 lakh per annum for inputs, labour and others.

[22]The amendment not only refrains forest department from planting eucalyptus but also urges not to encourage or support growing the species, apart from felling the existing plantations http://Bengalurumirror.indiatimes.com/Bengaluru/others/Karnataka-state-govt-bans-planting-eucalyptus-acacia-trees-owing-to-impact-on-ground-water-level/articleshow/58703790.cms.

twigs from the tree, as well as the potential to extract and sell essential oils from its leaves are further factors in favour of eucalyptus cultivation. It was mostly the choice of absentee farmers who would not need staples to be cultivated. The choice of eucalyptus also means the least amount of inputs and management while yielding some cash income. **Some farmers who did not have irrigation facility or enough family labour converted their entire farmland into eucalyptus plantation and worked as wage labour in their own village or nearby suburban areas.**

During the 1990s when nuclear families from the joint holdings in the outskirts started migrating to the city, eucalyptus was planted in their share of rain-fed family land. Whatever minimal supervision needed was done by their kin who remain in the village, doing agriculture on the rest of the land. Both migrated and resident families shared revenue or produce from both eucalyptus and agriculture. In Devanahali taluk alone, eucalyptus occupied 16% of TGA and 30% of NSA in 2010.

Every 3–5 years, the poles are harvested depending on demand. Plantations with bigger trees are contracted by paper and rayon industries through middlemen. Each ton of wood fetches anything between ₹3,000 and ₹6,000 in 2015. Medium-sized wood is usually purchased by construction contractors for scaffoldings and small-sized wood is locally sold as stakes for tomato plants and saplings of fruit trees. One hectare of 8–10-year-old eucalyptus gives a net income of ₹1.16 lakhs compared to ₹1 lakh for ragi, including the market value of the quantity consumed by the family. **As rain-fed food crops (such as ragi, pulses and oilseeds) were labour-intensive and spending available family labour on irrigated grapes, mulberry and vegetable was more important for cash income, eucalyptus was preferred for rain-fed land.** Eucalyptus though prominent in Anekal too was a later phenomenon and fewer respondents had it planted on their land.[23]

6.5.3 Animal Keeping Exclusively for Milk

Almost 80% of surveyed households kept livestock. About 78% of the livestock they kept were large ruminants (cows and buffalos), with less than 10% belonging to native breeds. Most dairying households kept Jersey, Holstein Friesian or mixed breeds with the herd size ranging from 1 to 8, though very little milk was used in the farm households themselves. Very few respondents had native species of cattle (15% in Anekal and none in Devanahalli). All Devanahalli farmers and most Anekal farmers kept high milk-yielding cows.

Thus, dairying meant fewer heads of cattle serving mostly the city's demand for milk and supplying some farmyard manure. Manure from the dairy cattle was not enough even for their keeper's own farmland. Only one respondent with eight cows could sell manure locally, after using what was needed for the four acres of land he cultivated.

---

[23]Eucalyptus plantations of respondents in Anekal were 4–5 years old while in Devanahalli they were of 15–20 years, during the survey in 2015.

6.5 Farming Systems: Feeding a Mega City and Sustaining Culture   135

On an average, two tractor loads (or two tons) of semi-dried farmyard manure from own livestock was being applied in the fields for an average size of 3.15 acres every year, compared to the generally recommended dose of 13–25 ton of dry manure per ha (Package of Practices 2016, University of Agricultural Sciences, Bengaluru), depending on the crop. We have already discussed the plight of rearing livestock exclusively for milk production in the backdrop of disappearing grazing lands of the peri-urban landscape. It was obvious that without grazing space and demand for farmyard manure, native breeds will become less popular in these villages. Most families tie their cows in or near their fields or houses.

Introduced species of dairy cattle unlike native breeds of cows are not used for draught power. The peri-urban livestock paradox (apart from keeping milch cows though they don't consume milk) is that animals are still used for ploughing by 40–50% respondent households. [24] Only a few maintained draught cattle in the villages and most others were hiring from them as needed.

Most dairying households were members of dairy co-operatives and half of them bought feed concentrates from these co-operatives. Rest of the dairy keepers either bought it from local dealers or bartered with friends who were members of the dairy society, in exchange for fresh fodder. In the year 2015, about 30% of dairying families availed an average loan of ₹57,000, either from micro-credit groups or nationalised banks, for buying cows.

6.6   Operational Expenses: Costly Outsourcing

Perpetual harvests, that too for an expanding consumerist society in the neighbour-hood, can exhaust any soil within a few decades, unless good care is taken to minimise nutrient loss and to supplement nutrients lost in harvests. This is when the metabolic rift between urban consumers and rural producers widens, trapping production practices in a vicious cycle of more inputs and more investments—a potential feedback loop that can unsettle the resilience of a production system. This concept was discussed in Chap. 1, Sect. 1.

Farms in the more urbanised Anekal taluk used a larger quantity of synthetic fertilisers per hectare of cultivated land (746 kg per ha; State average in 2016–17 was 123 kg and Devanahalli used 221 kg). **Fertiliser inputs form the third instance (after livestock products vs. commons, high-value crops vs. groundwater) where more urbanisation meant more adverse impacts on natural assets—in this case on agricultural soils, a classic case of cutting the branch one is sitting on.** This urban naivety is what William Bryan the American Democrat and Secretary of State in early twentieth century eloquently captured in his speech quoted in the beginning of this chapter.

---

[24]See photograph in the cover page of the book taken near Kengeri located at the south-west edge of Bengaluru in December 2017.

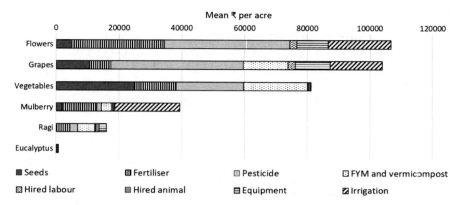

Fig. 6.7 Input costs incurred by respondent families in peri-urban Bengaluru. (Flowers included here are grown in open fields.)
Source Farmer interviews, 2015

The flow of biomass and water from production landscapes to urban consumers is rarely returned in kind. And of course, the money that is exchanged for these are incapable of bringing back the water, nutrients and species lost from the production landscapes. This ecological rift despite monetary compensation is reinforced by a loss in socio-cultural resources like agro-ecological skills. If unbridged, this cultural and ecological rift has the potential to impact food security of the society, by making farming a costly, risky and loss-making affair. Only that such an impending local impact is hidden or subdued by global transportation of cheap food that exports and postpones the visible appearance of the rural–urban rift and its consequences.

Seeds of more traditional species like ragi and pulse crops generally came from the farmers' own stock or from the agricultural extension office—*Raita Samparka Kendra* (RSK). For market-oriented flowers, vegetables, and maize, seeds were procured from local shops selling farm inputs along with fertilisers and pesticides recommended by the trader. Most input quantities and costs were not too different between the taluks selected. Hence, the cost-related data discussed below is pooled from both the taluks.

Flowers, grapes, vegetables and mulberry followed by coconut were the most expensive crops to grow (Fig. 6.7). Major overall cost heads in respondent families were labour (32%), inputs (23%), irrigation (20%) and transport (11%). In the case of grapes, flowers and vegetables (tomatoes, potatoes and beans), pesticides (36%) formed the major cost head. Expenditure on pesticides was relatively less in maize and baby corn.

Generally, cost for inputs and packaging was higher than other inputs in Anekal, while in the less urbanised Devanahalli, cost of irrigation and equipment was higher than others. Both the taluks were only marginally different in terms of cost incurred in labour and transport. Application of farmyard manure is mostly confined to vegetables, coconut and fruit crops.

Thus, in the absence of available state-of-the-art information with farmers on safe use of chemicals, on lethal dosages to be avoided, on waiting period to be observed, as also on potential occupational hazards to themselves; high-value crops are grown by generating adverse impact on the health of both producers and consumers.

Similar lack of awareness among urban consumers also contributes to unsafe production practices. Largely ignorant about farming systems and practices, consumers demand cheap and well-shaped large fruits/pods/leaves and are generally unconcerned about how these are produced. **Often the distance between the consumer and the producer in the marketing channel makes communication of information on production practices difficult and both producer and consumer become complacent about safety of food and farming.** While the discourse on minimising 'food miles' has largely focused on cost reduction (Pretty et al. 2005) of fossil fuel use, the loss of information as 'food miles' accumulate is a pertinent reason for trying to minimise distance between the farm and the plate in front of the ultimate consumer.

6.7 Labour: Competing with Other Sectors

Similar to the agricultural produce that the city demands and resultant generation of farming opportunities, urban demand for labour offers informal employment options to peripheral communities. In this section, we discuss the implications of this for sufficient and secure livelihoods.

Agricultural wages ranged from ₹150 to ₹400 per day in the study site. On an average, a farm household (with about 3.15 acres land) needed 75 hired labour days per year, in addition to family labour. Consistent requirement of labour for growing vegetables, flowers and fruits (grapes and banana) meant continuous hiring compared to mulberry that needed hired labour in bouts according to seasonal operations.

Half of all adult members in respondent families were fully engaged in cultivation alone. The remaining individuals of these families were involved in non-farm work lending their hands sparingly to farming. In a peak farming season, neighbours and friends helped each other in farm activities. Together they complete agricultural tasks on time, working on each field in a sequential fashion. **This labour-sharing practice was more prevalent in parts of rural Bengaluru (Devanahalli), especially in the cultivation of ragi and pulses. Labour sharing was generally absent in the case of crops that are more commercial in nature like vegetables, fruits (banana and grapes) and mulberry, where hiring labour was essential.** Sharing labour probably emerged as a social norm to ensure secure supply of staples within the hamlets of small scale producers. Thus, there are three ways of individual agricultural engagement—working in own farm, working as hired labour in other farms for wages and exchanging labour with kith and kin.

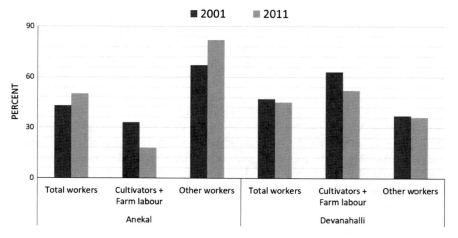

Fig. 6.8 Employment pattern in Anekal and Devanahalli taluks.
(Total workers as proportion of total population; Cultivators + Farm labour and Other workers as proportion of total workers.)
Source Census of India 2001 and 2011

Transaction of private land parcels for real estate development close to the airport (between 2000 and 2005) displaced many farms and people. A large number of farmers and farmworkers from Devanahalli moved to adjacent smaller towns like Chikkaballapur, Gouribidnur and Kolar. Although a large tract of land was acquired from 11 villages for the international airport in Devanahalli, the number of resettled families is known to be just 110.[25] Both acquisition and private land sales together are reflected in the decline in total worker population (including cultivators, farm labour and other workers Fig. 6.8). This depopulation in turn reflects insufficient generation of *in situ* jobs despite land acquisition, unlike Anekal where land acquisition from 1977 onwards generated non-farm jobs.

If depopulation characterises the peripheries of Devanahalli, with a large number of people moving out of farming, depeasantisation is seen in Anekal. Araghi's (1995) global depeasantisation analysis had confirmed the decline in Third World Peasantry between 1970s and 1990s as a result of intense industrialisation. But Devanahalli differs from China's 'void villages' (Driessen 2017), where empty village was a result of denied basic amenities and rights. Here, despite visible industrialisation, people were displaced or else they moved out by themselves.

Though part-time engagement as casual labour in farm or non-farm sectors or even in skilled salaried jobs is increasingly common in the study villages, full-time jobs in the informal sector were hard to come by. Thus while non-farm income was relatively high, farming continued in the background as the long-term low-earning option. About 25% of the respondent families had at least one member working completely

---

[25] 110 families from two villages have been relocated to a new village, as communicated by Revenue Department, Devanahalli Taluk.

6.7 Labour: Competing with Other Sectors

outside of agriculture either in a salaried job or skilled informal work—usually as technician, teacher, mobile repairer or supervisor in factories or construction sites. When more and more people move out of farming, labour scarcity (both family and hired) is a factor that determines the selection of crops or the extent of fallow lands both in the short and long term.

Women in farm households: farmers, homemakers and entrepreneurs

Women were principally engaged in activities such as seed preservation, seed preparation for sowing and cleaning of grains after harvest—activities undertaken inside the house rather than in open fields, with the exception of de-weeding a standing crop. If men in the family were completely involved in non-farm work, women took charge of all day-to-day farming activities. Thus, 25 sample households in the site were women-led farms. Whether or not owned or led by them, women took decisions on things like—how much of land to be sown with food crops and commercial crops, cultivation method (organic and synthetic inputs), sourcing food for the family (PDS or exchange with friends or private grain traders) and the kind of livestock feed to fetch.

In Anekal, the decision-making role[26] of SC women was less pronounced compared to women in dominant OBC households. The SC community consisted mostly of *Holeya* and *Madiga*, historically known for agricultural skills and leather work, respectively, in most parts of south India. Taking care of livestock and handling transactions at the dairy co-operative were done solely by women in most houses. Ferrying fresh fodder or feed concentrates once in a fortnight was generally a male domain. Sometimes, riding on their motorbikes, men also watch cattle while they grazed outside their farm and took them to village water tanks for drinking or bathing.

Women in peri-urban Bengaluru especially around its relatively more urbanised parts with garment factories and access to residential colonies of middle to high-income population, spent more number of days annually outside the farm.[27] Women in relatively rural peri-urban areas like Devanahalli still had less non-farm engagement than men. Devanahalli's textile and garment industries employed fewer women than those in and around Anekal (District at a Glance 2014–15). It is reflected in larger presence of women workforce in agriculture in Devenahalli.[28]

Non-farm self-employment for young women generally meant tailoring work, while elderly women often looked after petty shops, that also sold some fresh produce from the village.[29] There were couple of families where women also ran computer classes in addition to some engagement in farming. Women from half of the respondent families said they were active members of *Stree Shakti* groups (women's

---

[26]Questions about decision making process on various activities were posed during discussions together with family members.

[27]Days spent in non-farm jobs by women and men in Anekal were 131 and 82, respectively, and in Devanahalli it was 52 and 86.

[28]Devenahalli had 72% of women workforce engaged in farm activities compared to 58% in Anekal (Census of India 2011).

[29]About 12 out of 43 resident respondent families in this site had women who took up tailoring while five women had petty shops.

collectives supported by Women and Child Development Department of Government of Karnataka). All villages had two to four such self-help groups. These are thrift collectives of women for saving and lending money. SHGs among women, especially among disadvantaged sections seem to be totally untapped for the purpose of sharing information on crops, inputs, agricultural practices and marketing.[30] As most households and streets in these areas were supplied with tap water from local panchayat and used LPG for cooking, drudgery in household work was less.

6.8 Selling Farm Produce: Options Around the City

Studies ascribe 'forced commercialisation' [e.g. Bhaduri (1986)] to the shift from peasantry to significantly or exclusively market-oriented entities that place disproportionate risks on farmers and excessive dependence on markets. Smallholders take these risks hoping for consistent demand from markets linked to consumerist urbanism. However, it is not very clear how a consistent connection may be established between these high-risk small-scale operators in diverse produce and population of urban consumers with disposable income. This section looks at the variety of markets for agricultural produce emerging in the two study taluks around Bengaluru.

Ragi, the only staple grown here, and fodder maize are mostly for use by the farm holding, with very less marketed surplus (14%). Some portion of the grains go to farm labourers as wages or get exchanged for other grains among relatives, much like the labour exchange practice mentioned earlier. Pulses were equally important for both market and household consumption. About 50% of pulses produced was sold in the local weekly markets (*santhe*) or exchanged for food grains with other villagers. But minor crops like paddy and coconut were more for the market with only 10% of total production consumed by the family. Other commercial food crops like vegetables and fruits were fully or mostly marketed with cursory consumption in the households. Non-food crops like mulberry, eucalyptus and flowers were marketed after taking the required quantities for on-farm cocoon production, stakes for tender plants, fuelwood as well as religious and other uses, respectively.

Markets are chosen based on distance, ease of transaction and prices. Private traders were preferred for crops like flowers, fruits and eucalyptus, whereas local bazaar (*santhe*) was preferred for vegetables.[31] State-sponsored agricultural produce market was the only destination for surplus paddy and ragi (Fig. 6.9). Farmers who

---

[30] *Stree shakthi* groups in the State (2012) saved ₹11.18 billion since their inception, 1.2 lakh groups availed bank loans to the extent of ₹13.06 billion and accomplished internal lending of ₹32.16 billion for various income generating activities. Rarely were their activities based on farming and farm produce. http://dwcdkar.gov.in/index.php?option=com_content&view=article&id=260%3Astre.

[31] *Santhes* visited in and around study taluks: Tuesday market near Bannerghatta Biological Park, Friday market near Anekal bus stand, Saturday market near Chandapura bus stand, market near BWSSB office Kanakapura Road, Sunday market near Jigani industrial area, market in Banaswadi, market near railway track on Old Madras road and market near Yeshwanthpur railway station.

6.8 Selling Farm Produce: Options Around the City

Fig. 6.9 Marketing options around Bengaluru

produced perishables (including grape farmers of Devanahalli[32]) preferred private traders for on-farm/farm gate sale or local collection centres of retail chains.

Being a farmer in peri-urban Bengaluru often meant incurring additional cost to access markets. Faster routes to the city's markets involve paying toll charges. If the commission paid to a private trader is not higher than the cost in toll, transportation and handling charges put together; farmers would rather sell to the trader than manoeuver the crowded roads. If there is enough produce from many farmers from the same village or from neighbouring villages, then the produce is often pooled for joint transportation to the city. **This co-operation to reduce transportation and related costs is perhaps an instance where complete individualisation of farming is avoided despite urban push towards individualised intensification (Fig. 6.9).**

Collection centres of private retail chains for vegetables and fruits also supply seeds and other inputs against a bond as part of buy-back arrangements. Prices here generally follow the rates fixed by HOPCOMS.[33] Farmers thus get assured returns

---

[32] Grapes are sold to private traders from neighbouring States of Andhra Pradesh, Kerala and Tamil Nadu. Andhra Pradesh being the closest, traders from there bring labour for cutting and packing the bunches into crates. The variety *Bengaluru Blue* is traded further for making juice, while other seedless varieties sold to wholesale traders in cities like Hyderabad, Pune and Mumbai and also for retailing in Bengaluru city. Grapes from this area are rarely exported.

[33] Expanding the mandate of Bengaluru Grape Growers' Marketing and Processing Co-operative Society formed in 1959 to other fruits and vegetables, Horticultural Producers' Co-operative Marketing and Processing Society Ltd. or HOPCOMS has been in existence since 1965, under the State Department of Horticulture. With more than 12,000 members, HOPCOMS functions in five

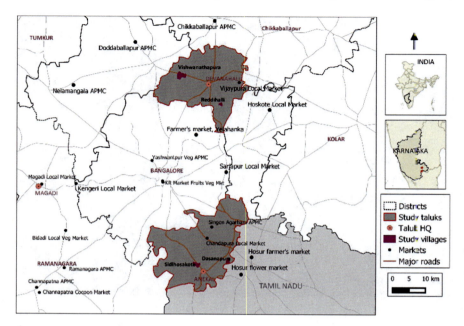

Fig. 6.10 Market locations around Bengaluru

for their produce at the cost of depriving themselves of possible windfall in price surges as well as of the freedom to choose crops and inputs. According to farmers, if they choose to be independent in all operations but carry the harvest to a collection centre run by a retail supply chain, there is 50% likelihood of being rejected based on delivery by registered growers or based on how appealing is the produce.[34] If the produce is rejected, then the farmer has to transport the produce again to a local market or to a market in the city.

HOPCOMS has recently started four collection centres in Bengaluru Urban and Rural districts, which transport the collected produce to their main branch by charging 10–20 paise per kg of produce. Anekal farmers sell leafy veggies mainly to HOPCOMS in Lalbagh or in the city market and fruits and vegetables in the Agricultural Produce Marketing Committee (APMC) in Singen Agrahara, close to Anekal. Too far from any HOPCOMS or APMCs for fresh produce, Devanahalli farmers use the farmer's market (*raita santhe*) in Yelahanka. Figure 6.10 shows the spread of different markets available for farmers in the study villages around Bengaluru.

APMCs after implementation of the amendment in 2013 are supposed to be a farmer-friendly markets, freeing them of levies and allowing retail chains also to

---

districts around Bengaluru city, with an annual turnover of ₹950 million handling 100 MT of fresh farm produce. One-fourth of our respondents were members of HOPCOMS (https://hopcoms.kar.nic.in/(S(wzsvsne2omivfyedxu4ldf55))/AboutUs.aspx).

[34] Some respondents in Devanahalli had registered with collection centres of retail chains—Reliance Fresh and Safal.

6.8 Selling Farm Produce: Options Around the City 143

procure from them.[35] **Yet, APMCs make sense only when there is some critical volume of the produce to be sold. For the small farms studied around the city peripheries, local weekly markets and collection centres are still relatively better options.**

6.9 Socio-economic Conditions: Better off with Loans?

Though 32% of TGA and 31% of population were in agriculture, the contribution of agriculture to the Gross District Domestic Product in peri-urban Bengaluru (Urban and Rural districts combined) was a meagre 7% in 2013–14 (State and District Domestic Product of Karnataka 2015–16). Secondary and tertiary sectors constitute 30 and 63% respectively of the economy of the region combining the city and its peri-urban areas.

Though the economic share of the non-farm sectors being more than 90% of the Net District Domestic Product implies a clear urban status, the region still showcases agrarian features in terms of occupation and land use, coming closer to represent 'rurban' geographies (Gupta 2015). **This feature was reflected in almost equal share of farm and non-farm sources in total family income. However, in the case of Anekal farmers, non-farm income exceeded farm income by nearly 12%, conforming to a demographically rural but occupationally urban character.**

Density of population shows that Anekal is more urbanised than Devanahalli (Table 6.2). Human Development Index-wise, Anekal was first among the taluks in Bengaluru's two districts and Devanahalli ranked towards the last (Human Development Report 2014). Anekal's primary sector was not as important to the taluk's economy as much as Devanahalli's, corroborating continuation of their historical difference mentioned at the beginning of this chapter. Small family farms generally disadvantaged in terms of land, capital and caste intuitively should be better off in the peripheries of a megacity with access to livelihood options, markets, infrastructure, education and health care. This is perhaps indicated by the absence of farmers' suicides in Anekal and a relatively few reported in Devanahalli (10, between 2003 and 2017, communication from Department of Agriculture, Government of Karnataka). We will seek clarity on some of these expectations in the following sections.

Income flow

The annual family income in Devanahalli was 35% less than in Anekal, during 2014–15. Farming was the major source of income for the respondents, accounting for 39 and 45% of total income in Anekal and Devanahalli, respectively. In terms of income-earning potential, flower crops, mulberry and vegetables had the highest returns in that order and these were more common in Anekal located towards South

---

[35] According to Karnataka Agricultural Produce Marketing (Regulation and Development) (Second Amendment) Act of 2013, no market fee is to be levied on farmers for flowers, fruits and vegetables. The marketing committee could collect user charge from buyers of the produce at such rates specified in the bylaws approved by the respective authorities.

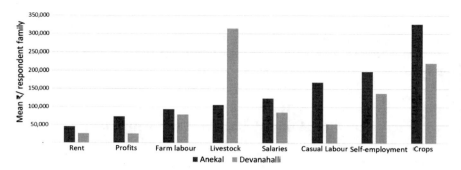

Fig. 6.11 Income sources in peri-urban Bengaluru.
(Profit came from petty shops, food carts, mobile phone repair and recharge shops. Self-employment includes contractual jobs like masonry, electrical work, plumbing, painting and driving. Livestock income includes earnings from sale of milk, manure and animal hiring.)
Source Farmer interviews, 2015

Table 6.3 Non-farm employment in Anekal and Devanahalli taluks in 2014

	Anekal	Devanahalli
Garment factories	6,818	140
Textile units	0	100
Chemical factories	9,317	0
Engineering units	13,353	300
Other manufacturing units	32,397	1,222
MSME including service sector	151,321	1,673
Total	213,206	3,435

Source Department of Factories and Boilers (2014)

of Bengaluru with better availability of groundwater. Grapes though cultivated in more than 6% of NSA in Devanahalli were not as profitable as imagined, with a net profit even lower than that of eucalyptus. Non-farm income came from varied sources of employment (Fig. 6.11).

Rental income was important for households in Anekal, thanks to migrants working in different parts of the city seeking accommodation. Apart from rent, income from self-employment formed a considerable share of non-farm income in both Anekal and Devanahalli. Industries established around 1970s in Anekal added approximately 60 times more non-farm jobs than Devanahalli (Table 6.3) where larger extent of land was acquired and villages displaced.

At least one adult member from each household in Anekal (compared to only 40% families in Devanahalli) had some non-farm skill like driving, electrical work, plumbing, masonry or tailoring.

6.9 Socio-economic Conditions: Better off with Loans?

Ratio of crop income to expenses incurred and loans availed by the families indicate profitable cultivation and reasonable credit worthiness, more so in Devanahalli.[36] But some price had to be paid for this financial performance—in terms of the cost to be incurred in buying food. The annual expense of respondent families in buying grains, pulses (red gram and green gram more than others), fruits or green vegetables needed for cooking food was much higher in Anekal villages. Thus, more commercial Anekal farms spent more on food expenses.[37] Food expenditure in Anekal villages indicates frequency of eating out or of buying packaged and processed food. High household expenses could have contributed to the relatively low financial resilience in Anekal, compared to Devanahalli, though this does not get translated into farm distress.

Farm loans

Most households (surveyed in 2015) had outstanding loans taken about five years ago from multiple sources that were overdue for repayment by at least two years. Households were shelling out an average amount of ₹6,000 annually just on interest payment. More number of farm households in Devanahalli (80%) were indebted than in Anekal (62%), but Anekal households had larger outstanding loans.[38]

Availing informal credit at an interest rate of 1% per month from relatives was common practice (60% of respondents). Such informal sources were crucial for meeting personal and agricultural exigencies. Other popular sources of credit were cooperative banks and micro-credit institutions. Although a large share of loans came from nationalised banks (Fig. 6.12), they were not too popular, especially in Anekal. Heavy indebtedness was mostly attributable to the costly enterprise of cultivating high-value flowers and vegetables in polyhouses.

Though it may not be foolproof to judge farm loans as exclusively invested or lost in agriculture, it is safe to conclude that the households that mostly cultivated commercial crops indulge in heavy borrowing.

Education, health and housing

Ninety per cent of adult family members among the respondent families had undergone formal schooling for more than five years. Respondents families in Devanahalli, given other indicators like family income and non-farm jobs, were also relatively less educated.[39] Expenses on children's education were similar in both places, at approximately ₹58,000/family/year. Likewise family expenses of around ₹50,000 annually

---

[36]Ratio of crop income to expenses incurred and to loans availed by the families: Anekal—2.1 and 1; Devanahalli—3.2 and 2.4, respectively.

[37]Cash expenses on food came to an average of ₹18,300 per head in Anekal compared to ₹11,250 in Devanahalli. It was 13% of total income and 20% of total expense in Devanahalli; while in Anekal, it was 16% of total income and 30% of total expenses. The market value of food consumed from what is grown on farm (per person/year) was ₹3,900 and ₹5,600, respectively, for Anekal and Devanahalli.

[38]Mean amount of overdue loans was ₹3.92 lakhs and ₹2.27 lakhs (for 62 and 80% respondents) in Anekal and Devanahalli, respectively.

[39]Literacy rate in Anekal—86.65% and Devanahalli—59.25% (Census of India 2011).

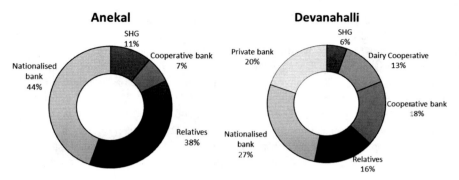

Fig. 6.12 Source-wise overdue loans (% of total loans) in peri-urban Bengaluru. (SHG—Self-help Groups for micro credit.)
Source Farmer interviews, 2015

on medical treatment did not differ much between the taluks. Apart from very common cases of viral diseases, ailments from contaminated food and water, few cases of nervous disorders and injuries from accidents were also prevalent. The latter two were costlier to treat. While the share of households with recently built multi-storeyed houses and share of families without own houses were approximately the same (10% each), a few families were living in dilapidated houses. **New multi-storeyed houses indicated a rentier economy functioning for tenant migrant families working in the city suburbs.**

6.10 Shifting to Urban Occupations

Farmer migrants are those farmers migrating to non-farm occupations either in the same village or in locations that could be rural or urban in nature. They might still be engaged in farming, albeit partially.[40] Such farmer migrants could be daily commuters or staying in the migrated location. Details of migration and migrants are generally gathered at the destinations. However, in order to study the reasons for migration, we met some of them at their village of origin as well.

Bengaluru city was obviously the most popular destination for people in these taluks for non-farm work. Almost all migrants retained a share in their ancestral land for two reasons—(1) land was not often divided or partitioned (more than one-third of the respondent holdings were undivided property), and (2) uncertainties dominated non-farm occupations. Most of our sample respondents in this site had 10 or more years of education and had migrated with their spouses when they were young. At the time of this study in 2015, most of them had completed ten years or so in their new jobs.

---

[40] Devanahalli migrants took up housekeeping or luggage handling in the airport or drove cabs/buses; migrants from Anekal worked in hospitals, factories and hotels.

6.10 Shifting to Urban Occupations

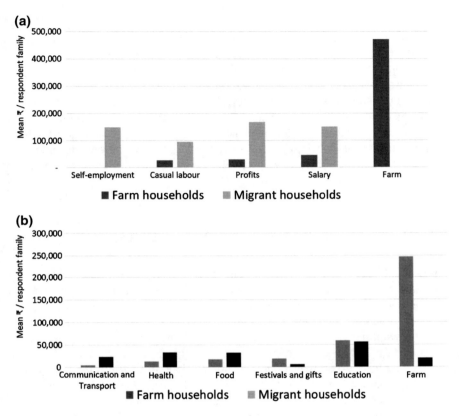

Fig. 6.13 a Income sources and **b** Expenditure in peri-urban Bengaluru.
Source Farmer and migrant household interviews, 2015

Farmer migrants may contribute to farming in their native village in the form of cash and/or labour. About 40% of migrants contributed in cash. The mean amount of annual contribution came to ₹44,000 in 2015, though increasingly these families were finding it tough to spare money for a not-so-rewarding investment. About 30% migrants laboured in their farms for more than 3 weeks divided between cropping seasons. The rest did not participate in farming at all, while still retaining their stake in the land held jointly with others in the family. The income and expenditure profiles of migrants justify this increasing reluctance (Fig. 6.13). **Migrants living in the city hesitate to invest money on farmlands, though they would like to keep their stake in family owned land as a matter of identity and belonging. Whether they contribute to farming or not, migrants seem to carry farm produce (e.g. ragi, coconuts) with them to their dwellings in the city.**

The decision to migrate is generally taken together by the whole family. Recent migrants (40% migrated within 3 years prior to the survey) reported the sole purpose as to pay off debt. For others who had migrated several years ago (60% migrated

15 years ago), the decision appeared to be driven by aspirations rather than being pushed out by indebtedness. This recent trend in distress migration even with a fast-growing urban economy in the proximity implies that all is not well in terms of agrarian opportunities offered by big cities.

Expenses on food, health care, recreation and transportation were relatively high for migrants. Migrants were availing social benefits in food distribution, school education and childcare. They were connected to private employment agencies, as their jobs were contractual and needed frequent renewals. Migration doesn't seem to have improved their plight much. Minor improvements in net income were accompanied by a larger loss in security and welfare. Thus, they seem to be farmers who had to succumb to push factors, away from farming.

6.11 Institutions: Old Norms and New Networks

With a visible array of new components and technology (e.g., exotic crops, animals or polyhouse farming) that peri-urban farms have to deal with, there is no indication of a cautious, prudent and experimental approach. Whether it is choosing the crop, seed or planting material, or choosing the method of cultivation including irrigation, this lacuna exemplifies a process of agricultural deskilling. Stone (2007) presented the problems faced by Bt cotton adopters due to absence of a skilling process that ought to occur through experimentation, evaluation, adoption and information sharing. The disappearance of collectively evolved agricultural skills useful for adapting to inevitable changes (e.g. changes in temperature, soil moisture and rainfall pattern) and for avoiding unnecessary disproportionate risks (e.g. small holder with no capital resources taking big loans for growing a high-value product for an unpredictable market) takes place alongside the disappearance of community welfare measures (community grain banks[41] or sharing mechanisms[42]). Agricultural skills and agrarian institutions in the periphery of metropolis are fading out along with *some* (not all, in fact Anekal is still known for its caste ridden society[43]) of the oppressive and discriminatory social systems.

Though individualisation has been identified as a hallmark of complete commercialisation in smallholdings, networks and institutions—both formal (like HOP-COMS, Farmer Producer Organisations or *Stree Shakti* groups) and informal (grain banks, seed sharing, transport pooling)—remain important. Farmers here are not yet informed players in the market and often follow customary norms—sharing and exchange of labour, seeds and produce, for instance. Alongside, we also see newly

---

[41] Community grain banks are being revived in some tribal areas with varying success (Rej. 2013).

[42] Vasavi (1994) explains how sharing and donating the harvest within the village was a norm in the dryland agrarian society of Bijapur.

[43] Despite the constituency being reserved for Scheduled Caste category, casteism did not vanish. See http://www.thehindu.com/news/national/karnataka/anekal-a-seething-cauldron-of-caste-dynamics/article4677689.ece.

6.11 Institutions: Old Norms and New Networks

crafted institutions such as marketing collectives,[44] thrift groups, co-operatives and producer companies. This section discusses the impact of context specific combination of customary and crafted institutions on family farms in peri-urban Bengaluru.

The kind of crops cultivated in the peri-urban farms had implications for the kind of social networks that emerge in the locality. Vegetables and flowers, being short-term crops, required farmers to be in touch with private input traders, making them (the private input traders) the most influential link. As we discussed in the previous sections, small farmers are connected with relatives for exchange of labour, draught animals, manure and small implements. Close proximity to the city and availability of non-farm employment opportunities made farmer's time a crucial element, making these exchanges a important strategy, as even women prefer non-farm work over working in fields open to the elements. Women use their own networks, e.g. SHGs, to find non-farm jobs in garment/textile factories nearby. In places where land acquisition was a concern, women found employment through friends or contractors in the sunrise sectors of institutional (offices, hospitals, restaurants and malls) housekeeping and house help.

Collectives emerged as another influential network for both farming and non-farming purposes. Marketing collectives among vegetable growers of Anekal and labour pooling arrangements among grape growers of Devanahalli show how trust and reciprocity help small farmers to generate and enhance social capital.

Information from commercials and agricultural news on television and newspaper often trigger queries that are generally posed to input dealers. Traders provide information on needed inputss and how to treat pests and diseases. Aga (2018) calls such traders of inputs in rural Maharashtra 'knowledge merchants'. Despite being untrained in agricultural science or practice, input suppliers are the main resource person for most smallholdings. We already discussed the role of contact points in local collection centres and output traders for marketing and of relatives for credit needs in Sects. 6.8 and Sect. 6.9, respectively.

In our interactions with farmers and farm families, it appeared that families with someone working in the non-farm sector take better informed decisions on input application, availing credit and marketing after consulting media (newspapers, TV and internet), input traders, output traders and even State extension agencies. Synergy between farm and non-farm sectors within a farm household thus emerges important in more than one ways. Non-farm engagement in the periphery of big city helps farming not only in advancing small capital needed for small-scale commercial agriculture but by also expanding information networks, and helping to update agricultural skills and marketing.

Some individual farmers act as mediators between fellow farmers and formal agencies. Such influential and mediating farmers generally come from not-so-small irrigated holdings. But more importantly, they possess some entrepreneurial spirit

---

[44]There are many informal farmer collectives supplying fresh farm produce to Bengaluru. Recent amendments (2004, 2013) to Companies Act urge Farmer Producer *Organisations* to be registered as Farmer Producer *Companies* in order to receive government support through Small Farmers Agribusiness Consortium and the National Bank for Agriculture and Rural Development.

and engage part time in skilled non-farm work. Such farmers tend to cultivate market-oriented crops like flower crops and mulberry and maintain active connections with input and output traders.

Although these study villages were easily accessible by any means of transport, government line agencies and academic institutions did not have major influence on most farmers, unlike agents of private input producing companies. Only 14% of respondents in both taluks consulted State research or extension agencies (*Krishi Vigyan Kendra* and *Raita Samparka Kendra*),[45] and that was mostly for choosing crop seeds and varieties for high-value floriculture. In Devanahalli where some rural features still remain intact, consulting village elders and fellow farmers was common. Communication technology, dairy cooperatives and micro-finance institutions together with media seem to partially fill the vacuum of agricultural collectives to an extent.[46] Thus, from a networking angle, closeness to the city can be perceived as a mixed bag with new institutional advantages amidst individualisation, as in the case of marketing.

6.12 Farms Around a Megacity: Give Plenty and Take Little?

Beginning with a sketch of the agrarian peripheries of Bengaluru with their often overlapping and porous boundaries with the city, the discussion above traversed most engagements and predicaments of farmers. While wages, some capital and lot of effluents flow from the city towards its peripheries, the city benefits much more than what it contributes. Depiction of key flows between the peri-urban areas and core of the city shows relative advantage to the city in terms of both outflows and inflows (Fig. 6.14). While there are more beneficial inflows to the city, even the outflows are beneficial to it. If outflow of waste is a case of good riddance for the city, outflow of money to the farms is either as urban wages in return for labour that build or maintain the city or as investment of a small portion of urban surplus in farmlands. Both these do not affect the city and are used to build and expand urbanism. Whatever capital flows into the peri-urban landscape, it takes away land from agriculture towards real estate expansion. When labour flows from the farms to the city, it partially helps production areas by decreasing dependence on land, while doing a disservice by taking away the manual labour needed for farming.

These flows within the assemblage of a mega city and its peripheries exemplify the Marxian rift in the social-ecological metabolism [from Foster (1999)] between

---

[45] Public sector marketing agency HOPCOMS seems to be better connected with farmers here than the State research or extension wings.

[46] Communication technology includes Internet and mobile phone. About 70% of respondents in Anekal were in touch with *Raitamitra* helpline (Kisan Call Center) over phone. Newspapers as medium of information, were followed by 26% in Anekal and by nearly half of the respondents of Devanahalli.

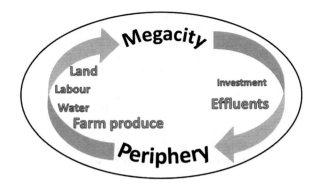

Fig. 6.14 Flows between the city and the periphery (font size indicates relative quantum of flows)

the peasant and the capitalist economy. **We ascribe accumulation, not just by dispossession [following Harvey 2004 and Banerjee-Guha 2013)], but also by diverting and weakening labour, biomass, energy and water in the family farms.**

How is it to be a farmer in the outskirts of a city like Bengaluru? On the one hand, one may feel uplifted seeing the vast colourful markets of flowers and vegetables buzzing with activities before the crack of dawn, scattered small collection centres of retail chains, the small producer companies sprouting here and there or the state-assisted networks of horticultural producers and organic farmers. On the other hand, one may be dismayed by the careless use of pesticides in the peri-urban farms or by the frothy sewage flowing into the fields south of the city and yet feel relieved about the well-oiled pillars of 'silk' (growing mulberry and rearing silk worms) and 'milk' (dairy cattle) supporting peri-urban livelihoods.

One may feel heartened by the new producers' collectives and disheartened by the tussle that small farmers have with cheap imported fruits as well as traffic-ridden roads to reach markets. While feeling anguished by the acquisition of fertile land for another highway, one may silently be hopeful of a new job for someone in a farm family. There is an irony in the fact that in this city of technologists and consumerists, the small holder still awaits the trader-lender appearing at her farm gate. This chapter revealed many paradoxes entrenched in the peasant-city relationship in the peri-urban interface. Amidst visible opportunities outside the mega city, several challenges remain in the small family farms.

References

Aga, A. (2018). Merchants of knowledge: Petty retail and differentiation without consolidation among farmers in Maharashtra, India. *Journal of Agrarian Change, 18*(3):658–676.

Banerjee-Guha, S. (2013). Accumulation and dispossession: Contradictions of growth and development in contemporary India. *South Asia: Journal of South Asian Studies, 36*(2), 165–179.

Bhaduri, A. (1986). Forced commerce and agrarian growth. *World Development, 14*(2), 267–272.

Brook, R., Bhat, P., & Nitturkar, A. (2006). Livelihoods from dairying enterprises for the landless in the peri-urban interface around Hubli-Dharwad, India. In D. McGregor, D. Simon, & D. Thompson (Eds.), *The peri-urban interface in developing areas: Approaches to sustainable natural and human resource use* (pp. 94–103). London: Earthscan.

Buchanan, F. (1807). *A Journey from Madras through the countries of Mysore, Canara, and Malabar*. London: East India Company.

Foster, J. (1999). Marx's theory of metabolic rift: Classical foundations for environmental sociology. *American Journal of Sociology, 105*(2), 366–405.

Gupta, D. (2015). The importance of being 'Rurban': Tracking changes in a traditional setting. *Economic and Political Weekly, 50*(24), 37–43.

Harvey, D. (2004).The 'New' imperialism: Accumulation by disposession. *Socialist Register*, 63–87.

Kavitha, A., Somashekar, R., & Nagaraja, B. (2015). Urban expansion and loss of agriculture land—A case of Bengaluru city. *International Journal of Geomatics and Geosciences, 5*(3), 492–498.

Kumar, A., & Parappurathu, S. (2014). Economics of dairy farming and marketing: Micro-level perspectives from three major milk producing states in India. *Indian Journal of Animal Science, 84*(2), 204–209.

Lele, S., Purushothaman, S., & Kashyap, S. (2013). Village commons, livelihoods and governance: An assessment of Karnataka's experience. In S. Purushothaman & R. Abraham (Eds.), *Livelihood strategies in Southern India: Conservation and poverty reduction in forest fringes* (pp. 135–155). New Delhi: Springer.

Mundoli, S., Manjunatha, B., & Nagendra, H. (2017). Commons that provide: The importance of Bengaluru's wooded groves for urban resilience. *International Journal of Urban Sustainable Development, 9*(2), 184–206.

Pretty, J., Ball, A., Lang, T., & Morison, J. (2005). Farm costs and food miles: An assessment of the full cost of the UK weekly food basket. *Food Policy*, https://doi.org/10.1016/j.foodpol.2005.02.001.

Reji, E. (2013). Community grain banks and food security of the tribal poor in India. *Development in Practice, 23*(7), 920–933.

Salman, M., & Munir, A. (2016). Common land resources, livelihood and sustaining the rural poor in India, a geographical analysis. *European Journal of Geography, 7*, 6–18.

Satterthwaite, D., McGranahan, G., & Tacoli, C. (2010). Urbanization and its implications for food and farming. *Philosophical Transactions of The Royal Society B, 365*, 2809–2820.

Stone, D. (2007). Agricultural deskilling and the spread of genetically modified cotton in Warangal. *Current Anthropology, 48*(1), 67–102.

Vasavi A (1994) 'Hybrid times, Hybrid people': Culture and agriculture in South India. *Man, 29*(2), 283–300.

Chapter 7
Family Farms Around Ramanagara

This is our village, Uyyamballi - 30 miles from Ramanagara town. It takes less than an hour to reach the town on a bike. And you must have noticed that now everyone has a bike here. Bengaluru is at the same distance, but we need minimum 3 hours to reach any place that we want to visit there. In Ramanagara, we get all things we need for farming and for home. Markets for our cocoons, mangoes, coconuts and vegetables are not just in the Ramanagara town, but also in Kanakapura, another 10 km from here. Many youngsters from the village work in the industries located in Harohalli and Bidadi.
So then, why should we go to Bengaluru? The smoke, the smell, traffic, all chaos. We go there only for meeting sick relatives or attending weddings.

—farmer respondent.

7.1 Small-Town Urbanism

Cities are known for disparity in income, in contrast to disparity based on caste and land in rural villages. Disparity in any two or all the three axes (class-caste-land) may converge or combine with other axes of power and agency (political, educational or the environmental). Small towns are supposed to be less unequal spaces than big cities or rural villages and even better performing in terms of poverty reduction (Behrens and Robert-Nicoud 2014; Gibson et al 2017). However, small towns are varied in their character. Appearing non-descript, these administratively 'urban' areas could be formed around specific industries, educational or religious institutions.

In terms of urban typology, most small towns in India fall under the category of census towns,[1] with a population ranging between 0.05 and 0.1 million. Popular focus on major cities as hubs of urbanisation ignores the fact that a notable share

---

[1] From an administrative point of view, census towns are rural areas governed by a village committee, but they are considered urban by Census of India as they fulfil the three criteria that define an urban settlement (see Footnote 8 in Chap. 5).

© Springer Nature Singapore Pte Ltd. 2019
S. Purushothaman and S. Patil, *Agrarian Change and Urbanization in Southern India*, India Studies in Business and Economics,
https://doi.org/10.1007/978-981-10-8336-5_7

of urbanisation in India has been around census towns [30% of the urbanisation process in India between 2001 and 2011 (Denis et al. 2012)]. Harriss-White (2016) identifies the non-metro urban world of 7438 small towns (mofussil towns other than the provincial capital cities) experiencing low end, bottom up, indigenously evolved urbanisation as middle India. Such spaces and processes that form the vibrant new middle India may be termed subaltern urbanisation (Denis et al. 2012).

Referring to the increasing share of small towns in urban India, Sen (2014) points out that though the corporate engine of urban development is able to propel GDP in the initial years, as economic growth continues, this engine tends to weaken. Harriss-White (2016) attributes this shift in the locus of urbanisation to a growing presence of informal unorganised economy in small towns. Dominated by the informal sector, middle Indian economy appears blurred and complex (Gupta 2006; Harriss-White 2016), comprising of an intricate web of connections (Thompson et al. 2015).

Basu (2014) (cf. Harriss-White 2016) paints another picture of such small-town urbanism. According to Basu, a string of small towns will come up wherever land is cheaper than in the big towns or cities, and these will absorb labour and provide services to the global economy. According to him, the government only needs to provide infrastructure like roads, electricity and a legal system for effective land and labour markets and the rest will emerge organically from the enterprise of the people where land and labour are adequate.

Economists seldom consider the economic potential of such sectors with serious regard. That middle India's informal economy can fuel growth using the agency of people without major interventions from the state or corporate sectors is an uneasy paradigm for policy makers and economists. Despite being the new fulcrum of demand for consumer goods and economic growth, popular discourse is still enamoured by the rural versus mega city imagery. Small towns are overlooked in the outlay of public expenses (e.g. National Urban Renewal Mission) for infrastructure and sanitation. And, as Harriss-White (2016) points out, these 'forgotten cities' (Datta 2013) are often socio-politically volatile and vulnerable to communal riots.

It is also true that traditional rural activities like farming crops, trees, animals, fish or birds are better adapted and practised by small town peripheries than intensively urbanising areas. With disproportionate attention being given to the 'big city', research on the functional as well as structural role of small towns in the dynamics hovering around natural resources, labour, industries and agriculture was scanty until the turn of twentieth century. Denis and Zerah (2017) have emphasised the need to study small towns as sites of an urbanising economy and social transformation and for their unique rural–urban linkages.

Typical south Indian small towns with population of around a lakh and with notable agrarian peripheries can be visualised as secondary urban areas. Usually, a major highway passes through such a town with its arterial roads leading to interior taluks. These roads are lined with commercial establishments (stationery and hardware stores, eateries, lodges, petrol bunks, agricultural input traders, etc.), some residential areas, government offices, banks, bus stands and cab stands for about a kilometre or so. Small towns also host regulated markets for non-perishable farm products that the region is known for, apart from more generic weekly bazaars for the

7.1 Small-Town Urbanism

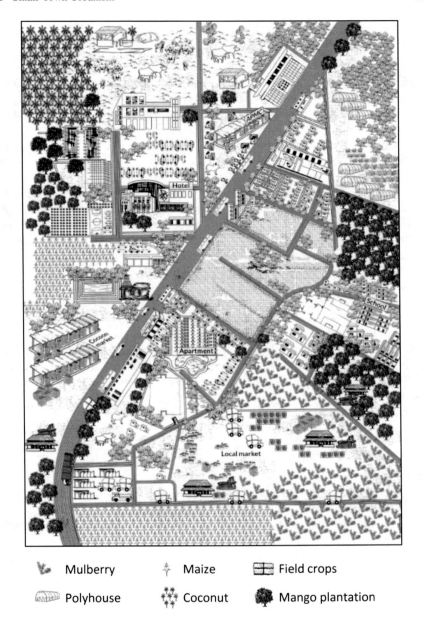

🌿 Mulberry	🌱 Maize	▦ Field crops
🏠 Polyhouse	🌴 Coconut	🌳 Mango plantation

Fig. 7.1 Small-town periphery

local populace. The landscape at the periphery of these towns changes abruptly with contiguous stretches of field crops. Figure 7.1 depicts such a small-town periphery.

Ramanagara—the small-town study site

Much like the Tamil town of Arni portrayed in Harriss-White (2016), Ramanagara along with others[2] of its kind forms the 'middle India'. Ramanagara lying en-route to Mysore from Bengaluru is a Class II town (with population of 95,167 in 2011). While the district headquarters is not too far from the metropolitan city of Bengaluru (53 km by road), it displays features of subaltern urbanism (Denis et al. 2012) in its own economic vibrancy originating in autonomous economic drivers. The rate of economic growth was accelerated recently in Ramanagara (GDP grew at 33% in 2015 compared to 12% in 2009), while it decelerated in Bengaluru (from 42 to 34%, Karnataka Economic Survey 2016).

Ramanagara derived its nomenclature after the hillocks where Lord Rama was supposed to have stayed during his exile in the forests. It was known as Shamserabad during Tipu Sultan's time and then as Closepet (after the British Officer Sir Barry Close, 1756–1813). In 1884 Closepet sub-division was formed with Chanrapatna, Kanakanahalli and Magadi taluks. Ramanagara with vast farmlands and distinct rock formations is a popular location for movie shooting, adventure sports and tourism. The soft brownish stone formation is also known as Closepet granite. Even now granite mining is rampant in many parts of the district. Present district of Ramanagara was formed in 2007 adding Ramanagara taluk to the three taluks of erstwhile Closepet. Ramanagara is a major silk cluster in Karnataka and contributes about half of mulberry silk produced in India. Ramanagara district has three regulated markets trading in silk cocoons and the headquarters proclaims itself as 'silk city'. In this study, Ramanagara comes out as a small town with rural farm and non-farm sectors, linking production landscapes with the town, through specialised produce markets for cocoons, coconuts and mango, as well as wooden handicrafts.

Many small towns have such unique trajectories of growth, or they host specialised livelihood clusters. Though the district is known for silk, peripheries of Ramanagara showcase diverse activities—cultivating staples (e.g. ragi), crafts (wooden toys and crafts), granite mining and manufacturing industries.

Taluks in Ramanagara district were sorted (just the way districts in Karnataka were) according to number of cultivators. Kanakapura and Magadi taluks with the largest number of cultivators were chosen for detailed study. The headquarters of these selected taluks are located at 55 and 51 km, respectively, from Bengaluru City and are nested in vast agricultural landscapes, even though some parts of the taluks overlap with peri-urban Bengaluru. Rather than choosing other less agrarian taluks of the district to avoid this overlap, we retained these two, with the added intention of examining whether the impact of big city Bengaluru cascades from its immediate peripheries to smallholders located further away.

King Kempe Gowda I, founder of Bengaluru, built a mud fort in Magadi in 1537. Kempe Gowda kings were known as founders of the 'farmers' empire', 'traitor's nightmare' and as humble kings who established village-level governance systems.

---

[2]A sorting of the districts of Karnataka according to proportion of cultivators (data from population Census of 2011) elicited Ramanagara and Hassan as candidates for the small-town category, apart from Mandya that was already chosen as an agro-urban town. We chose Ramanagara over Hassan as a typical middle Indian town with considerable urban population (25%).

Kempe Gowda's popularity and the power and prosperity of the 'Yelahankanadu' they ruled were instrumental in strengthening the Vijayanagara Empire. Magadi was known historically for its thick forests.[3] Magadi was the seat of power for almost a century—from 1638 when Kempe Gowda lost Bengaluru to the Sultan of Bijapur in 1728, it was captured by the army of Mysore. Buchanan (1807, Vol. 2) mentions that Hyder Ali of Mysore strategically settled some tribes near Magadi for mobilising an army at short notice (Fig. 7.2).

Both taluks have significant population engaged in farming (Table 7.1). Of the two, Magadi, which is smaller in size and population, has a relatively better Human Development Index, despite a larger share of cultivated area (53% NSA in TGA during 2015) and comparable number of workers in farming. Relative to its size and population, Magadi has lesser area under forests and larger urban population.

With notable area covered by forest and with the Arkavathy River flowing through it, Kanakapura is a popular tourist destination. The National Highway No. 209, from Bengaluru to Dindigul passing through Kanakapura town, makes it familiar to travellers between Bengaluru to parts of Tamil Nadu and Kerala. While the entire Ramanagara district in general lives up to the 'silk city' tag, among the two taluks considered here, Kanakapura hosts the main silk cluster.

Following exploratory visits to all 11 hoblis of the two taluks, we chose ten villages to conduct group interactions to discuss the extent and role of agricultural activities. Based on these group interactions, we narrowed down to four villages which had extensive agriculture along with prevalence of non-farm engagement (Fig. 7.3).

Fig. 7.2 S*anthe* in the backdrop of remnants of Magadi fort built by Kempe Gowda; tomb of Kempe Gowda near Magadi

---

[3] Anderson (1929)'s '*Old Munnusamy and the man-eater of Magadi*' is said to be based on a true story.

Table 7.1 Kanakapura and Magadi taluks at a glance

	Kanakapura	Magadi
Total geographical area (TGA) (km^2)	160	80
Forests, pastures and tree groves (% of TGA)	36	22
Net sown area (% of TGA—2015)	38	53
Population density (population per km^2—2011)	220	251
Urban population (%—2011)	15	18
Cultivators and farm labour (% of total workers—2011)	67	64
Human Development Index (rank among 176 taluks of Karnataka—2014)	0.44 (95)	0.48 (75)

Source Human Development Report (2014), Census of India (2011) and Agricultural Census (2011)

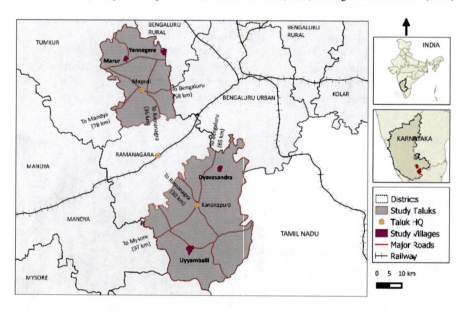

Fig. 7.3 Study villages in Ramanagara

After multiple visits to the selected villages and perusal of revenue records, we identified respondent farmers and farmer migrants. Selection of 43 farm families representing diversity in caste, gender and landholding size, and 10 migrant families followed the same process as in other sites (refer to Chap. 3, Sect. 3.4 for household sampling process).

7.2 Farmlands: Persisting Smallholdings

Average holding size of the farmer respondents in the two taluks was around 3.18 acres, after a decline of more than 40% over a period of 15 years from 1995. Nearly 93% of all agricultural holdings were owned by Other Backward Caste (*Vokkaliga and kuruba*) and 7% by Scheduled Caste communities (*madiga*). Women owned about 16% of holdings and about 2% of the population were landless.[4]

Ninety per cent of the farms in both the taluks are below 5 acres. Non-declining number of smallholders for the past 15 years or so coexists with increasing number of marginal holdings and decrease in large holdings.[5]

Leasing and fallowing

Over the last 15 years, Kanakapura has witnessed co-existence of mutually divergent trends—increasing temporary fallows (5%), increasing net sown area (6%) and high incidence of land leasing (24% of respondents and 23% of landholding).[6] In the periphery of Ramanagara, urbanites from Bengaluru often buy farmlands but engage the previous landowners as lessees. Thus, farming continues though ownership changes hands and the farmer who formerly owned land now becomes a lessee. Leasing takes place by oral arrangements but is largely non-exploitative, unlike the post-colonial tenancy between lower caste tenants and upper caste landowners who moved to cities for jobs during the first wave of urbanisation in Mysore State (Kashyap and Purushothaman, forthcoming). Urban farmers' entry into city peripheries can have different repercussions. For instance, aboriginal communities of Northern Mali discontinued farming altogether as urban farmers entered the peri-urban areas (Bah 2006). But here, farmer lessees of absentee landlords who live in the cities continued farming with ragi in rainfed lands and mulberry in irrigated lands.

The terms of lease in Kanakapura varied. In the case of ragi, the produce was equally shared between the owner and the cultivator. For mulberry, leasing was on payment of cash—about ₹20,000–30,000 per acre per year. Leasing practice in the mango and sapota orchards of Magadi was different. Landowners who moved into non-farm jobs planted fruit trees on their ragi fields and leased it to traders. The traders took care of the trees and shared the proceeds in accordance with the terms of the lease. Thus, land-owning farmers working in non-farm informal sectors as well as absentee landlords lease out their lands.

Though there are considerable non-farm occupations and leasing practices in both Kanakapura and Magadi, land fallowing is not much (13.5%) though it is slowly increasing. Scarcity of labour and water is the commonly cited reason for fallowing.

---

[4]Information gathered from 10 group interactions in two taluks.

[5]Between 1995 and 2010, while marginal holdings increased by 19% (with 15% increase in area) and medium to large holdings decreased by 3% (reducing 17% in area), smallholdings (1–2 ha) did not change much (7% decrease in numbers without any reduction in area).

[6]About 20 and 24% of the respondents leased-in land in addition to own farmland and leased-out part of their own farmland, respectively.

Land conversion

Currently, Ramanagara district has two industrial areas and four industrial estates. In 2010, two new industrial parks were proposed and an area of 5527 ha of land was identified for the same.[7] In 2012, 4880 ha were notified and acquired for another industrial park and 50 ha were earmarked for an integrated textile park. Ramanagara district is proposed as the garment hub of the state and also to host Asia's biggest cocoon market. According to the Industrial Profile of the district (2012), companies have shown interest in setting-up processing units of ragi and mango in the district.

Land acquisition for industries has been relatively high in Kanakapura taluk. Nearly 1700 ha were acquired between 1997 and 2013 in this taluk as against just 25 ha in Magadi (Industrial Profile, Ramanagara District 2012). In the study villages, conversion of farmlands occurred when families sold their land, rather than by way of acquisition by the state. A few respondents reported land acquisition for railway line. About 10% of respondent families reported selling farmland to meet expenses related to house construction and medical exigencies.

7.3 Nature's Commons: Forests, Grazing Lands and Water Bodies

Ramanagara's surroundings have a characteristic rough terrain, with undulating surfaces forming valleys and ridges of gentle slope. Forests, village commons and rivers have a noticeable presence in both the study taluks. These are generally used for livestock feeding, washing and grazing. Erstwhile sacred groves, wherever they existed, had just a few trees around the temples.

The extended area of common lands converted in Kanakapura up to 2010 was three times more than the area of private lands acquired for industries. This is significant and can be attributed to granite mining and institutional holdings.[8] No estimate was found about *gomaala* conversion, but a tour of villages in the taluk showed that

---

[7] Industrial area is a zone usually within the city boundaries for setting up private small-scale industries. Private industries purchase land from the government and invest in industrial infrastructure. Road, water and electricity supply and drainage will be provided by the local government.

Industrial estate is a place where the required facilities and factory buildings are provided by the government to entrepreneurs to establish industries who lease or rent premises inside the estate, from the government.

Industrial park is an area zoned for industrial development, like special economic zones. Industries here are of specialised commodities (like manufacturing industries in food processing, textile or apparel and automobiles) or in the service sector (like telecommunication, information technology and financial services). Individual industries buy land from government at a subsidised rate. They get tax benefits prescribed in the Industrial Park Scheme 2008.

[8] By 2010, 3716 ha out of 5885 ha of forests and *gomaala* were encroached near the buffer zone of Bannerghatta National Park in Kanakapura taluk.

http://wgbis.ces.iisc.ernet.in/biodiversity/sahyadri_enews/newsletter/issue54/article1/encroachment.html.

7.3 Nature's Commons: Forests, Grazing Lands and Water Bodies

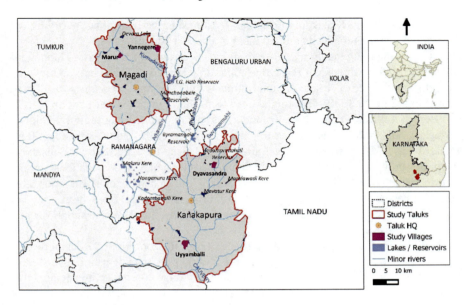

Fig. 7.4 Lakes and streams in and around Magadi and Kanakapura

almost all hillsides and tops now had multi-storied buildings of various institutions. Kanakapura lost 9306 ha or 42% of permanent pastures over a span of 15 years since 1998 while Magadi lost 655 ha (7%).

Situated in the main Cauvery River basin, the district has two major rivers—Arkavathy and Shimsha. The Kumadavati, Suvarnamukhi and Vrishabhavati streams meet Arkavathy at various points on its course before its final confluence with Cauvery near Kanakapura.

Most of Magadi and Kanakapura taluks are encompassed by six watersheds of the River Arkavathy. Small streams originate in these watersheds and empty into lakes scattered across the entire region (see Fig. 7.4). The topography helps the natural flow of water from a relatively higher altitude in the eastern and northern parts through storm water drains (*raja kaluve*). Over the past 10 years, the eastern side of Magadi adjoining Bengaluru South taluk saw extensive levelling of land for residential layouts. This has resulted in reduced flow of water in *raja kaluves*, leaving the soils dry and devoid of moisture.

Other water commons such as step wells and lakes were degraded, and grazing areas either converted or encroached. Lakes in this region were part of a cascading system. Water overflowing from one lake would get collected in another lake downstream along the slope, ensuring some amount of water throughout the year in most lakes that are part of the system. This interconnected system of lakes was disrupted when vast tracts of land were levelled for residential layouts, industrial areas and road building, in addition to stone quarrying in their catchments, resulting in complete drying up of interconnected lakes. Between 2000 and 2010, as many as 288 lakes in

Magadi and 592 in Kanakapura dried up.[9] Alongside the lakes that are drying up, water table in the tube wells around them is also fast depleting.

It is worth noting that Bengaluru's drinking water supply comes from Thippagondanahalli's Chamarajanagar reservoir (commonly known as T. G. Halli dam) which is at the confluence of Arkavathy and Kumudavathi. This man-made reservoir started functioning in the 1930s diverting about 148 million litres of water per day (MLD) to Bengaluru in what otherwise would have flown into parts of agricultural fields in Magadi. Till 2001, T. G. Halli used to supply 110 MLD (13% of total demand) to Bengaluru City. With consistently declining storage since then, currently the reservoir supplies only 30 MLD (4% of total demand) to the municipal corporations around. Further south of T.G Halli is another reservoir at Manchanabele on River Arkavathy. Manchanabele dam, commissioned in the 1950s, receives water from the eastern part of Arkavathy catchment. In addition to irrigating fields, this dam also supplies water to Magadi town.

Villages in Kanakapura and Magadi taluks bear the footprint of Bengaluru City that is more than 50 km away. Whether it is flooding by sewage water, diversion of river water, dumping solid waste or encroaching village commons, it is evident that the mega city's sources (of land, water, labour and farm products) and dumps (for wastewater and solid waste) extend beyond its immediate peripheries. Looking at the state of commons in these rural taluks, it appears that they are exploited rather than benefited by Bengaluru. When it comes to agricultural and livelihood spin-offs, we will see if villagers who eke out a living around the small town Ramanagara lying not far from Bengaluru City are benefitted.

7.4 Irrigation: Tanks, Sewage and Streams

As with forests, Kanakapura is better endowed in terms of water too. Nearly 24% of the net sown area (NSA) is irrigated in Kanakapura, compared to 11% in Magadi (District at a glance 2015–16). Two medium-sized irrigation projects—Byramangala reservoir (in Ramanagara taluk) on Vrishabhavati River and Manchanabele reservoir (in Magadi taluk) on Arkavathy River—along with another small dam at Medamaranahalli (in Kanakapura taluk) on Suvarnamukhi River, irrigate agricultural fields in this study site.

Though Arkavathy flows through Magadi, canal irrigation here is limited to 17% of the net irrigated area in contrast to 34% in Kanakapura from Vrishabhavati and Suvarnamukhi streams, all part of the Cauvery basin.

In recent times, while canal irrigation is increasing, tube well irrigation has been showing a decline (see Fig. 7.5). Tube wells are deeper in Magadi between 300 and 1000 ft. compared to 300–400 ft. in Kanakapura (Central Groundwater Board 2012).

---

[9]Report on drying up of lakes due to drought, delayed monsoon and heat wave in 2015–16—http://www.thehindu.com/news/national/karnataka/1234-lakes-in-ramanagaram-159-in-mandya-run-dry/article8531007.ece.

7.4 Irrigation: Tanks, Sewage and Streams

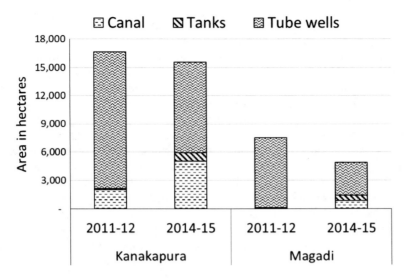

Fig. 7.5 Source-wise irrigation in Kanakapura and Magadi taluks.
Source District at a Glance, 2015

Nevertheless, with a density of one tube well for approximately a hectare of land, they still dominate the irrigation scene, supplying water to about 60–70% of the irrigated area in Kanakapura and Magadi.

Since the establishment of dams (Manchanabele in Magadi, Byramangala and Medamaranahalli in Kanakapura) between the 1940s and 1950s, water user associations have been managing irrigation in their area, while the Department of Minor Irrigation has been responsible for administration and maintenance of canals.

Prior to the construction of Manchanabele dam, Arkavathy River used to irrigate the region around Magadi in a field-by-field design. Group interactions suggest that narrow earthen channels running along the field bunds used to carry water for long distances. Farmers whose lands were adjacent to channels and those who had land away from channels had mutual understanding on planning farming activities (land preparation, sowing, weeding and intermittent watering) based on pre-decided water sharing schedule.

Earthen channels that ran at the same level as fields used to maintain soil moisture levels in the adjacent fields. With the advent of the Manchanabele dam, shorter, wider and stone-walled canals were introduced at an elevation lower than the adjacent fields. This new canal system resulted in new inequalities in water sharing (apart from the usual conflicts between farmers at the head and tail ends). As a result, top soil began drying up faster than usual after the rains. Conflicts started emerging among farmers raising vegetables, mulberry and paddy at the tail end of Byramangala canal.

As mentioned above, villages in Kanakapura enjoy better access to irrigation water due to its convenient slope and scattered presence of storage tanks connected by a canal system. Despite this water endowment, drastic conversion of land and depletion of water quality are major issues in Kanakapura. Deep pits created by stone quarrying are being used for dumping solid waste from nearby urban and industrial areas including Bengaluru, resulting in air and water pollution. Byramangala reservoir across Vrishabhavati that originates in Bengaluru and flows through industrial, commercial and residential areas receives the city's effluents and transforms itself into a sewer before reaching the fields as irrigation water.

Ironically, Bengaluru not only pumps and lifts Cauvery water all the way for about 100–150 km, but also empties its wastewater into Vrishabhavati—a tributary of Arkavathy that joins Cauvery. Thus, the huge amount of sewage water in this belt contaminated with heavy metals can be used only for specific crops such as fodder grass, baby corn and coconut. It is pertinent to note that these were lands where earlier paddy, vegetables and floriculture flourished not so long ago. As in the case of land discussed in the previous section in this chapter, Kanakapura pays the price for being downstream of a big city, in terms of its water access too.

At the same time, the continuous supply of sewage water allows for a good amount of soil moisture as well as groundwater availability, even in fields outside the command area of Byramangala dam. Benefiting from such groundwater recharge, comparatively shallow tube wells have been extensively dug, especially for irrigating mulberry. Mulberry growers in such villages were also making use of financial assistance for drip irrigation from the government scheme such as *Krishi Sinchayi Yojana*.

River Suvarnamukhi, that originates in the protected areas of Bannerghatta National Park, is a seasonal river used for irrigation through the canals from Medamaranahalli dam. The river meets Vrishabhavati 10 km further down from the Byramangala reservoir and is relatively free from sewage influx.

Limited canal irrigation in Magadi is due to functional length of the canal from Manchanabele dam being shorter than what was originally planned.[10] With limited water sources (both ground and surface), compared to Kanakapura, farming here suffers as its sparse surface water gets diverted to Bengaluru for domestic and industrial use as mentioned before. Despite a declining trend in groundwater in Magadi, some farmers risk their investment in planting crops such as paddy (2% of NSA) and areca nut (4% of NSA) relying on uncertain supply from deep tube wells.

Water: axis of rural–urban conflict

According to Krishnan (2014), who uses narratives around irrigation schemes involving tanks in the neighbouring watershed of Tungabhadra in Tumkur district, lack of involvement of beneficiary communities and political interference in the functioning of engineers undermine the very purpose of the irrigation project. This, she mentions, has led to conflict between villages located at the head and tail ends of the distribution canal. Varied conflicts even within the tail and head ends of Mandya's canal system were exposed in another study by Folke (2001). Folke identified interference from

---

[10]Original design of Manchanabele canals probably miscalculated the inflow; hence the actual length had to be shortened than what was stipulated (Gayathri et al. 2015).

politicians and elite farmers as key factors leading to unequal access to irrigation water and conflicts.

Yet another study—Shah (2003)—of three tank irrigation systems in Northern Karnataka points out that irrigation technology and design are conducive for conflicts and contestations. Elite farmers, according to Shah, influence the design of the project as well as its operational processes. They try or manage to get state funds to implement the project but seldom seek skills in actual implementation and management of the projects.

All three studies quoted above point towards the fact that **both a strong state machinery and collectivisation across various beneficiary groups are essential to prevent elite capture of the benefits of irrigation and conflicts in sharing irrigation water. The State machinery together with inclusive local water user groups of the Arkavathy basin should have deliberated the water debt that the city owes to the fields of Ramanagara**. Such efforts and local concerns on the unequal urban–rural exchanges in provision of fresh water and dumping sewage are conspicuous by absence.

7.5 Notable Farming Systems

If shiny green patches of mulberry between rows of coconut trees characterised Kanakapura's agriculture, increasing number of mango trees on ragi fields was striking in Magadi. Ragi (finger millet) is the most common crop in Kanakapura and Magadi, occupying about 45% of the net sown area in the respondent farms (Fig. 7.6).

Growing mulberry for rearing silkworms turn out to be time tested and popular enterprise in Kanakapura. Crop cultivation in the study villages around the small town Ramanagara consists of two major commercialisation trends—the old enterprise of

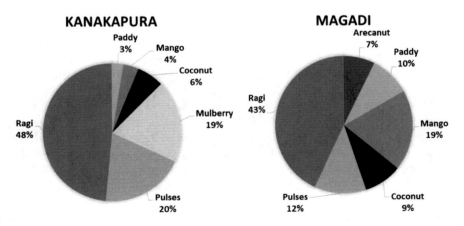

Fig. 7.6 Cropping pattern in the periphery of Ramanagara (% of land cultivated by respondents). *Source* Farmer interviews, 2015

mulberry cultivation spreading further in tube well-irrigated parts of Kanakapura and a more recent trend since the 1980s of spreading Mango trees in ragi fields in water and labour scarce Magadi. Coconut, areca nut and mango in Magadi; Coconut, mulberry and paddy in Kanakapura are the top cash earners, though areca nut and paddy are not significant in acreage.

In both the sites, we see some access to irrigation and a combination of commercial and food crops sustaining family farms, despite the urbanisation push (demand and impact on land and water for instance) and pull (availability of non-farm jobs). **These agricultural areas around small towns are perhaps instances of urbanisation sustaining small-scale farming in multiple ways. These beneficial outcomes are in contrast to drastic commercialisation for instance in polyhouse cultivation and eucalyptus around Bengaluru, fuelled by hijacking land, water and labour.**

We now take a closer look at the diversifications in family farms around small town Ramanagara.

7.5.1 Silky Shine in Kanakapura

Mulberry silk is produced by the larvae of *Bombyx mori* L. after feeding on the tender leaves of mulberry plant. The bulk of mulberry silk in India comes from Karnataka, specifically from parts of the erstwhile princely state of Mysore. Mechanised production of Mysore Silk started in 1912, with the establishment of imported looms by the then King of Mysore. The origins of this important livelihood can be traced back to 1785, when the first cocoons were imported by Tipu Sultan from China. Ramanagara, a district headquarters and part of old Mysore, pronounces itself as silk city.

Till about five decades ago, mulberry used to be a backyard plant raised using wastewater from the kitchen. Getting a few eggs of the silk worm from Bengaluru, farmers used to grow very small quantities of cocoons. Arrival of irrigation and the cocoon market in the region was a game changer. Acres were earmarked for mulberry cultivation, and regular cash income became a reality for smallholders in this belt.

Raw silk production happens in four phases undertaken in four different places, by different communities—seed production, hatching caterpillars, rearing the worms into cocoons and then reeling silk from the cocoons into yarn. Only the third phase (longest among the four, of about 20–25 days) is taken up by mulberry farmers. Some farmers in Magadi produce (as also others elsewhere in Mysore, Hassan and Kolar) seeds of silk worm from the female moth (the male moth is generally brought from Anekal) and sell them too. Leaves of mulberry are strewn over a cloth that is stretched and fitted onto wooden frames, where the worms are placed (Fig. 7.7).

Once mature, the worms are mounted on bamboo frames with concentric grooves (*chandrike* Figs. 7.7b and 7.9) where they start pupating into cocoons. Fully formed cocoons are extracted from the chandrike (Fig. 7.8) and sold in regulated markets from where reelers buy them.

7.5 Notable Farming Systems

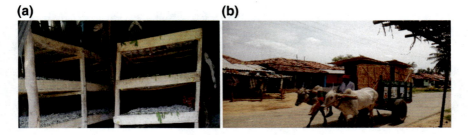

Fig. 7.7 **a** Trays with silkworms and mulberry leaves, **b** transporting *chandrike*

Fig. 7.8 Extracting cocoons from *chandrike*

Reelers treat cocoons in boiling water before extracting long individual fibres for spinning. Silk reeling skill has been mostly confined to specific communities[11], who do not take up mulberry cultivation or worm rearing. Communities engaged in seed production, hatching and rearing belong to the dominant castes—generally *Vokkaligas and Reddys*. Silk weaving is done at a larger scale by capitalist entrepreneurs, hiring local skilled labour.

Once planted, mulberry crop can be maintained for years together by pruning once in three months for regular supply of leaves to feed the worms. With three months required to grow the plant and one month for rearing worms and cocoons, farms usually receive quarterly income. If the land is managed efficiently by rotational pruning in patches of mulberry, income flow could even be in monthly cycle. Such enterprising mulberry growers are locally referred to as '*sambaLa gaLasuva rayataru*' (salaried farmers). In the study villages, one acre of mulberry was yielding an annual profit of ₹1–2 lakhs, depending on the quality of management and price of cocoon.

Mulberry silk is thus a result of regional integration of effort by hatchers, chandrike makers, farmers, reelers and weavers, with renewable local resources and inherited farm skills. Apart from being used to make fabric, this silk yarn is

---

[11] Among the silk reeling communities in Ramanagara, 61% were muslims, 22% SC and ST and remaining 17% were others (Ahmed 1997).

168   7 Family Farms Around Ramanagara

also used for making tyres of automobiles, ropes and fishing nets, thus generating constant domestic demand.

Despite some volatility caused by the import of cheaper Chinese silk, sericulture continues to ensure a well-paying land-based occupation for farm families. However, similar to many such commercial crops, the spread of mulberry in the place of food crops appears to have individualised and insulated agricultural families. Similar concerns were noted in Bidar where fields with jowar and pulses changed to hybrid varieties of paddy, wheat and sugarcane in a big way (Vasavi 1999, 2009).

7.5.2 Spread of Mango in Magadi

If mulberry replaced staple millets and pulses in Kanakapura, in Magadi it was the spread of mango trees over the past two decades or so.

Since early 2000, most young women started opting to work in garment factories and young men in other industries nearby. This contributed to declining interest in farming in Magadi compared to Kanakapura.[12] Thus, crunch in labour availability along with groundwater depletion and lack of price incentives for field crops led to the spread of mango plantations in Magadi. Mango needs irrigation only during the initial establishment phase. This crop has consistent demand from processing industries as well as consumers in Bengaluru and abroad. *Raspuri* and *totapuri* mangoes grown in Magadi are taken to the APMC yards at Ramanagara or Channapatna. Sometimes standing crop is auctioned off on the trees themselves before harvest to private contractors as mentioned in Sect. 7.2. A large portion of these fruits eventually reach the fruit pulp makers in Bengaluru or in the neighbouring state of Tamil Nadu. On an average, after deducting the cost of farmyard manure and transport, farmers were getting a net profit of about ₹1600 from a 6–8 years old mango tree.

Patches of land between the rows of mango trees are still used for intercropping with ragi and pulses during the monsoon season (*mungaru*—between June and November), keeping local culinary cultures intact (Fig. 7.9). Though Karnataka state has implemented National Horticulture Mission in Ramanagara too, farmers deny any significant role played by the horticultural department in the spread of mango. According to them, the department started working on mango only after large-scale mango planting was already popularised by farmers.

Recently, however, an indifference has already crept in maintaining mango orchards. Fluctuations in rainfall, dwindling groundwater[13] and incomplete irrigation projects together with primate menace affected the marketable surplus of mango. Further, being closer to the Bangalore Metropolitan Region, land value escalation

---

[12]Between 2001 and 2011, number of cultivators was stagnant in Magadi (grew only 1.7%), while in Kanakapura it increased significantly (10.5%).

[13]Groundwater table fell from 0.4 to 2 m between 2002 and 2011 (Central Groundwater Board 2012).

7.5 Notable Farming Systems

Fig. 7.9 Ragi fields with rows of mango trees in Magadi

makes it a lucrative option to sell the land. In recent years, there has been no fresh land coming under mango cultivation and many existing orchards are ready to be sold to real estate agencies. This indifference takes Magadi's agrarian society one step closer to depeasantisation.

7.5.3 *Livestock—For Milk, Draught and Meat*

Two-third of the sample households kept livestock, and 60% of them kept large ruminants. Among the large ruminants, 30% were local breed cattle used for ploughing, transport, farmyard manure and to meet partial requirement of milk by the family. Local breed animals were found mostly in Kanakapura. Despite the lack of grazing commons, Magadi had large heads of cattle and earned more than Kanakapura from dairying and selling manure (₹1 lakh annually compared to ₹58,000 in Kanakapura). Goats and sheep were more common in the forested parts of Kanakapura. *Gomaala* wherever available and uncultivated fallows were used for grazing and to supplement stall feeding of cattle. Livestock keepers used common water bodies for washing animals. While the households of Kanakapura tended to consume more farm produced crops, Magadi farmers consumed more of livestock products.[14]

---

[14] Value of crop produce consumed by families came up to ₹16,000 and ₹20,000 in Magadi and Kanakapura respectively, while corresponding consumption of animal produce was worth ₹16,000 and ₹10,000.

7.6 Running Cost: Labour for Ragi and Small Capital for Silk

With significant area under ragi - the staple food crop, fertiliser application in Ramanagara villages was less than the state average (97 kg/ha against 123 kg/ha for Karnataka in 2016). Ragi needs farmyard manure (FYM) and labour as major inputs apart from seeds that are generally kept from previous year's production. In addition, it may require some life-saving irrigation. But the highest quantity of FYM was applied to plantation crops—areca nut, coconut and mango. The cost of fertiliser input per unit area was lower in Magadi attributable to a relatively more visible presence of livestock.

Mulberry and areca nut were the costliest and most profitable, though the area under areca nut was not significant. The highest expense in sericulture was for buying hatchlings (150–200 layings to be fed by an acre of mulberry plants in a rearing cycle of about a month) followed by FYM (annually 3–4 tonnes for an acre). Preventive use of organophosphate pesticides was common, and this continues to be applied till 10 days before the leaves are fed to worms. Disinfectants for the rearing room (*reshme mane*) and NPK fertilisers are other operational costs. Sericulture depends heavily on family labour preventing them from availing any regular employment outside the farm.[15]

Land preparation was mostly done by tractor, though some farmers of Kanakapura were using draught animals. Maintaining draught animals was not easy for smallholders with very little common lands left in the village. Still, farmers usually prefer bullocks despite government incentives for buying tractors.[16]

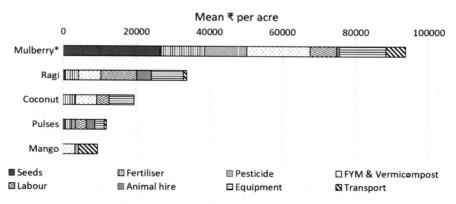

Fig. 7.10 Input costs incurred by respondent families in the periphery of Ramanagara. (*Seeds for Mulberry include silk worm hatchlings.)
Source Farmer interviews, 2015

---

[15] Only 8% of total cost in sericulture was spent on hired labour.

[16] See the story about pushing bank loans to farmers for purchasing tractors in North Karnataka (https://smallfarmdynamics.blog/2018/02/).

How it Goes on—A Family Farm in the Small-town Periphery

Kapil who studied till 10th standard is living with his brother (with a B.A. degree) and parents, near Kanakapura. They cultivate four acres of ancestral land. In the two acres of land irrigated by a tube well, they grow paddy and mulberry. This contributed 85% of their annual income of ₹2 lakhs in 2015. Five years ago, Kapil's family availed a loan of ₹1.8 lakhs from a co-operative bank to supplement their own savings for digging a tube well. ₹40,000 of this loan is still outstanding.

On the two acres of rainfed land, a mixed crop of ragi, horse gram and groundnut are raised during kharif. Keeping nearly half the harvest of ragi and horse gram for home use, they sell the rest either in APMC or *santhe*. That year (2015), they had lost 70% of the groundnut crop to wild boars from the forest nearby. Kapil did not bother to claim compensation money from the state Forest Department dreading a complex procedure.

They keep 17 local breed cows mainly for manure and milk for the household, and a pair of local breed bull for ploughing. Sometimes they lend the bullocks to other farmers. The cattle yield more than 8 tons of farmyard manure annually, minimising their expenses on fertilizers.

With two acres of irrigated and rainfed land and a large herd of local cattle, this family of four adults seem to be doing well without a huge loan to pay back.

Farmers buy synthetic inputs from local dealers and farmyard manure from peer farmers who keep cattle. They sought information on inputs from television, newspapers and Kisan Call Center (a dedicated toll-free helpline for farmers), apart from input traders who always introduced them to new synthetic inputs. Relatives were important for sharing inputs such as seeds, animals, equipment and labour. Figure 7.10 compares the cost break up for various inputs across major crops.

7.7 Labour: Balancing Farm and Non-farm Work

Employment in Kanakapura and Magadi may be characterised as largely agrarian with almost two-third of the total workers engaged in cultivation and farm labour (Fig. 7.11). However, with meagre availability of off-farm and non-farm employment in Magadi, farmers are forced to commute outside their village to supplement their income, taking away their time from farming. As Census of India data 2001 and 2011 shows (Fig. 7.11), this points to a tendency to depeasantise—beginning of what is seen in the immediate peripheries of Bengaluru (Chap. 6, Sect. 6.7). **Close proximity to industries in the neighbouring taluk of Bengaluru Rural district and a shift in the cropping pattern from a combination of ragi and pulses to Mango in the late 1990s have made this occupational change possible in Magadi. On the**

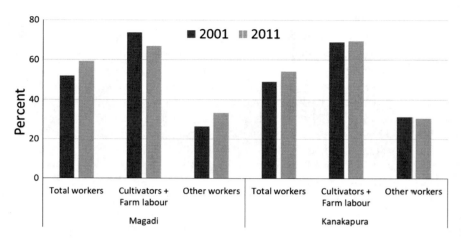

Fig. 7.11 Employment pattern in Kanakapura and Magadi taluks.
(Total workers as proportion of total population. Cultivators + farm labour and other workers as share in total workers.)
Source Census of India 2001 and 2011

contrary, in Kanakapura, due to the presence of lucrative commodities such as silk and milk, involvement in farming is getting intensified and reinforced.

According to farmer respondents here around Ramanagara, hiring labour for farm work was not very common about 15–20 years ago. There was enough family members to work on the farm through all crop seasons. This scenario has changed with new non-farm occupations available in the surrounding areas, even though size of holding has decreased over time.[17]

Staples like ragi, pulses and paddy and more recently, mulberry were the most labour-intensive farming options. Both men and women from the surveyed farm families spent almost equal number of days in farm labour. In about 10% of the respondent families in both the taluks, the women also worked as wage labour in other farmlands for nearly 240 days in a year. Men generally did not engage in farm wage labour as they were able to commute every day seeking better paying non-farm jobs.

Women in family farms: tending silkworms and dairy cattle

Men dominated the market place—the agricultural frontage visible to the economy, while women supported agriculture uptill the harvest is taken out from the farm. This is reflected in high proportion of women workers in farming (83%), more so with crops like pulses, mango, areca nut and vegetables. Mulberry demanded women labour constantly—for feeding silkworms, cleaning bamboo frames and trays, spreading worms on *chandrike* and periodically changing the position of *chandrike* so as to face direct sunlight, cleaning and sorting of cocoons, storing the cocoons

---

[17] In 20 years' time, average land size in this site reduced by 40–45% (see Sect. 7.2).

7.7 Labour: Balancing Farm and Non-farm Work

till they are sold, applying manure and fertilizer and de-weeding mulberry fields. Women also took care of livestock, cow sheds, farm house, the elderly as well as children.

With Public Distribution System supplying rice at subsidised rate, families consumed less of smaller grains like millets that need effort to clean, de-husk and process—all manual work for women. But the nutritional impact of such a shift to a less diverse diet on women was not really acknowledged by the families we interviewed, except for an increasing inability to toil on hard soil or pound grains in a grinding stone. It was surprising to see that no small and appropriate machinery was so far available for this common task undertaken in most farms, despite the visible presence of research institutions in agricultural science.

Conversations with middle-aged and older women did not reveal any aspiration to work outside their farms. They seemed content in household activities like taking care of silkworms and cows. Having a large number of native cattle, grazing was full-time work for at least one member of the family. Along with farm work, some younger women also run enterprises like computer training centre, tailoring class, beauty parlour and petty shop.

Women took care of feeding and milking the cows and also delivering milk to the dairy society in the village. In Kanakapura taluk, there are dairy co-operatives operated exclusively by women, like the Kaggalahalli Dairy Co-operative Society.

Women in half the families we interacted with were active members of self-help groups. Some of them organised trainings in making incense sticks and candles with support from National Rural Livelihood Mission. Apart from engaging in wage labour on other farms, very few women worked outside their farm.[18] Though violence against women was not common, there were incidences of alcohol-induced domestic violence reported from Magadi usually by men working as part-time drivers.

7.8 Selling Farm Produce: Private Traders and Regulated Markets

Regulated markets for silk cocoons and coconut have been long established (since 1962) in Ramanagara town. Other smaller local markets are also scattered all over the region (Fig. 7.12).

Coconuts, like mangoes and areca nuts, are often sold on the tree to traders who come scouting for contractual arrangements. Among the food crops, pulses recorded considerable marketable surplus (45%) and were generally sold to private traders who in turn sold them to wholesale dealers in nearby towns.

Mature mango fruits, depending on the variety, are transported to wholesale—mainly to APMCs—or retail markets around Bengaluru. During the mango harvest season, APMC sets up temporary sheds for traders to cater to mango farmers from

---

[18]Only 2 families had women working outside—one a teacher and the other a community health worker in a village nearby.

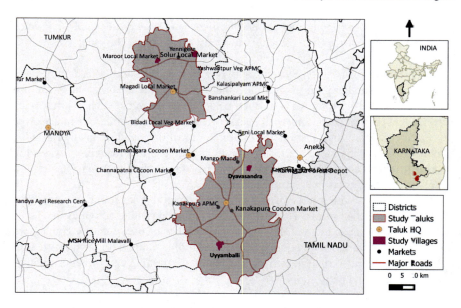

Fig. 7.12 Markets for agricultural produce in Ramanagara

nearby areas. Prices vary with the variety of the fruit as also with the trader in such temporary markets, though the commission to be paid to APMC is incurred by the trader. Home-based pickle making units in Magadi also procure small amounts of suitable raw mangoes. The state government has plans to set up mango processing units in the industrial estates located in Kanakapura (State Industrial Profile 2014).

Integration of farming with local processing units appears to benefit farmers engaged in certain activities like sericulture. But medium-scale ragi and pulse mills that exist in the locality often struggle to get enough produce. They cannot afford to import raw grains from other states like Andhra Pradesh as is usually done by bigger mills. **Small-scale value adding and processing units for ragi, pulses, mango and coconuts are of clear advantage to the rural economy in the peripheries of Ramanagara. Drying facility for copra will benefit small producers who do not have drying and storage facility. The challenge in bringing in processing units is the inadequacy of aggregators (not extractive middle-men) in order to link the smaller quantities of milled, value added or raw produce to the wider market. Mulberry and silk worm rearing with a high-value non-food final product seem to be channelised well, and this easily takes away land from food production, as most agricultural produce seem to lack well-knit vertical and/or horizontal integration.**

7.9 Socio-economic Conditions: High Farm Income and High Indebtedness

Ramanagara has established itself as a small but growing town.[19] With HDI of 0.533, it is ranked 13th among the 30 districts of the state, in terms of human development.[20] Ramanagara's economy received less than 20% of its GDP from the primary sector engaging 66% of its workers.[21] Until 2009–10, the primary sector contributed more than the secondary sector to the district economy and then started declining as the economy accelerated, fuelled by tertiary and secondary sectors.

Though the secondary sector overtook the primary sector in the economy of this small town, farm households have a different story to tell. Income from the farmland is still crucial and exceeds their income from non-farm occupations. Farming contributes 58% of the total family income.

The net financial surplus of farm families—considering all costs and liabilities in an year—in Kanakapura was almost double that of Magadi, though the share of non-farm income was relatively more in Magadi households. With ratios of family income to expenditure and to outstanding loan at 2.1 and 2.8, respectively, farm families appear to have a relatively strong financial status. This perhaps is reflected in lesser number of farmers' suicides in the study taluks of Ramanagara, at least till 2014. This seems to have changed in the subsequent years.

Income flow: farm and non-farm

Most families (64%) we interacted with had some member(s) working in the non-farm sector, while 35% of our primary contacts (heads of the families) were themselves partially engaged in some non-farm occupation. Despite this, as mentioned above, farming (crops and livestock together) provides crucial family earnings, especially in Kanakapura, *vis-a-vis* other occupations currently available (Fig. 7.13).

Among the major crops, the most profitable was areca nut followed by mulberry and then coconut (the latter two are grown in Kanakapura). Areca nut, locally known as 'lazy man's crop' (*somaari beLe*), which is cultivated in some parts of Magadi incurs much less cost and effort than other high earning crops which are more common in Kanakapura.

In terms of supplementary sources of income, self-employment as electricians and mechanics was popular in Magadi. In Kanakapura, tailoring and computer training classes run by women and petty shops were noticeable. Remittances from family members in non-farm employment outside the village also contributed to the family kitty. In Magadi, industries in the neighbouring taluk of Nelamangala, about 20 km away, have been offering non-farm jobs to farmers since around 1970.

---

[19]Urban population in the district grew from 17% in 1991 to 25% in 2011.

[20]Study taluks—Kanakapura and Magadi—had lower indices of HDI than the district—0.444 and 0.478, respectively.

[21]The state GDP received 15% from primary sector in 2012–13 (Economic Survey of Karnataka 2013).

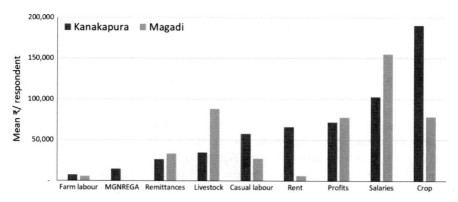

Fig. 7.13 Income sources in the periphery of Ramanagara.
(Casual wages includes only wages for farm labour.)
Source Farmer interviews, 2015

Salary income in Kanakapura was mainly from contract employment in factories in the industrial areas developed recently by Karnataka State Industrial Area Development Board (KIADB). Though more than 30% of workers were engaged in non-farm jobs, just above six per cent of these were in regular factory jobs. Women worked in textile, garment, confectionery or bakery units, while men worked in mechanical and automobile assembly or manufacturing units. Salaries in Magadi came from relatively skilled work in the technical and engineering domains. Casual wages in both the taluks came from farm work. The existing employment sources do not seem to be enough to meet their household expenditure and farmers in both taluks availed loans from various sources.

Farm loans

Availing loans from different sources and defaulting the repayment schedule were prevalent in the study villages. More than 80% of respondents availed loans of an average amount to the tune of ₹3 lakhs and had an average outstanding amount close to ₹2 lakhs beyond the repayment period. Figure 7.14 shows overdue loans from various sources.

According to the special committee appointed to evaluate cases of farmer suicides. About 83% of the total number of farmers' suicides in Kanakapura over the last 3 years were due to indebtedness. Mulberry farmers had the highest amount of loans availed from nationalised banks as well as the highest overdue. Although returns are high in sericulture, the risk involved due to climatic factors and price fluctuation is also high.[22] The inability of small farmers to cope with such risks manifested in mounting unpaid loans and extreme distress.

Micro-credit institutions were the major source of credit generally availed by women and for purchasing livestock or for setting up their own enterprise such as a

---

[22]Price crash pushed sericulture farmers towards suicide—https://www.thehindubusinessline.com/economy/agri-business/price-crash-pushes-sericulture-farmers-towards-suicide/article7496120.ece.

7.9 Socio-economic Conditions: High Farm Income and High Indebtedness

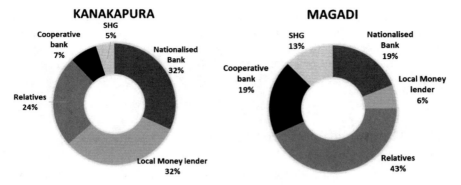

Fig. 7.14 Source-wise overdue loans (% of total loans) in the periphery of Ramanagara. (SHG—Self-help Group for micro-credit.)
Source Farmer interviews, 2015

computer training centre or tailoring institute. Loans from relatives dominated in both the taluks, especially for non-farm expenses—house renovation, marriage and other ceremonies. Almost 75 and 50% of indebted households in Kanakapura and Magadi respectively had outstanding loans from relatives, most of which were availed five years ago with an understanding that they would be repaid within two to three years.

Education, health and housing

Although Kanakapura has a lower HDI rank than Magadi, better access to Bengaluru City (through NH 209) and the presence of institutions in higher education and spiritual organisations make it a frequently visited destination by the city populace. However, sewage discharge and industrial waste from Bengaluru polluting the land and water bodies have a negative impact on human as well as animal health. Instances of skin diseases were reported by households, in addition to heavy mosquito menace. The literacy rate in Kanakapura was lowest compared to other taluks Ramanagara district. Nevertheless, comparatively higher per capita income assured better housing condition.

Socio-economically, Magadi displays several contradictions. Alongside larger urban population (18%) and comparatively better literacy, health status and Human Development Index,[23] the houses here are in a dilapidated condition, compared to Kanakapura. In the year 2015, the share of agricultural income in total family income was relatively less in Magadi[24] and non-farm expenses per household were more (80%) than in Kanakapura (69%). Expenditure on celebrations—festival and family functions—in Magadi[25] was more than double compared to their counterparts in Kanakapura, while expenditure on food—including both for the kitchen and for buying food from eateries—was lower.[26] Though Magadi seems to be casting off its

---

[23] Refer to Table 7.1 for relevant indicators.
[24] 50% in Magadi *vis-a-vis* 65% in Kanakapura of family income was from agriculture.
[25] ₹27,000 in Magadi compared to ₹13,000 in Kanakapura in 2015.
[26] ₹47,000 in Kanakapura and ₹39,000 in Magadi in the year 2015.

rural mantle with respect to parameters such as non-farm workers (40% against 25% in Kanakapura), better literacy, higher population density, lower share of farm income and less food for the family coming from agriculture,[27] its rural appearance persists with relatively large net sown area (53% of TGA, compared to 38% in Kanakapura) and 60% workers in farming.

7.10 Migration from Farming: Recent and Unappealing

Farmers leaving agriculture appears to be a recent phenomenon in this small-town periphery. Despite industrial growth since 1970s in parts of Ramanagara adjacent to Bangalore Rural district, farmers seeking non-farm employment was notable since early 2000s. We found them still apprehensive about entering new occupations.[28]

According to the migrant respondents in this site, their decision to leave farming was more often motivated by land acquisition or water scarcity. In Magadi where the number of non-farm workers is high, most of them were commuting every day from their village. However, except for one migrant respondent who worked once a week on his family's land, not many contributed cash or labour to farming.

Migrants appeared to be worse off in terms of net income compared to those who remain in farming. They spent less on food, health care and festivals (Fig. 7.15) and did not indulge in extravagances such as modern houses, new cars, bikes, mobile phones, grand wedding parties or religious ceremonies.

Many farmer migrants ran automobile mechanic shops, mobile repair and currency shops, general petty shops or were engaged in driving. A few had government or private sector jobs as lecturers, engineers in factories, managers in private companies, etc. Widows of farmers were found to claim their husband's share of land, sell it partially or fully and set up very small enterprises—usually beauty parlours, petty shops and small eateries. These women and their children moved out of their family (deceased husband's) home.

On the whole, instances of both distress and aspirational migration were found in the study villages of Kanakapura and Magadi, though migration from farming or their village did not seem to improve their socio-economic situation.

7.11 Institutions and Integration

Since the shift in occupation from farm to non-farm was not so lucrative and agricultural transformation in crops and practices happened fast and on a large scale in this

---

[27] In Kanakapura, 65% of food crops produced from their farms were consumed as compared to 56% in Magadi in the year 2015.

[28] Group interactions revealed that only 14% of households in the study villages stopped farming, though Bengaluru City was not too far.

7.11 Institutions and Integration

region, smallholders maintained a good balance between tradition and modernity in both lifestyles and farming. As mentioned earlier, though the small-town periphery is located close to a megacity, its rural character remains intact and is seen in the extent of land under farming, local millet and pulse crops standing alongside exotic vegetables and fruits, local breed and hybrid cows grazing around and traditional festivities with incursion of modernity in them.

Social norms and obligations are still considered important. **Although farming is fast becoming individualised, other social formations like SHGs, youth collectives and farmers' groups keep the intra-village relationships alive.** Farmers seem to be highly adaptive to the changing environmental and social factors driven by the megacity close to Ramanagara. This includes switching to crops suitable for sewage irrigation, labour scarcity, urban demand and to new ways of internet-based marketing. But such adaptation demands specific social networks and institutional linkages, and farmers here seem to be cautious in adopting new technology. Instead, they rely on input traders for crop choice or managing a pest or soil condition.

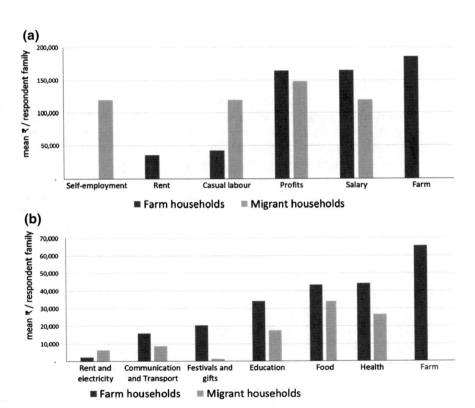

Fig. 7.15 Income sources (a) and expenditure (b) in the periphery of Ramanagara. *Source* Farmer and migrant household interviews, 2015

Private silkworm rearing centres or authorised dealers for disease free layings and traders of sericulture essentials (*chandrike* and protective nets for the worms and fly traps for mulberry) had active links with farmers. Similarly, in small-scale dairying, forward and backward linkages with feed concentrate dealers, animal insurers, veterinary doctors and co-operatives (for milk collection and processing) have come to stay.

The role played by kith and kin remained significant—for sharing draught animals, farm equipment and manure, and also in availing loans, as seen earlier. Sharing labour, crop produce and seeds was not too common here—this can be attributed to the significant spread of commercial farming and shrinking acreage under staple crops.

Youth and women's collectives were more active compared to farmers' collectives. Women's groups were more than just thrift groups and were also engaged in organising training sessions in self-employment skills. Youth collectives referred to as 'friends' group' (*geLeyara gumpu*) organised sports events, medical camps, blood donation camps, leisure trips, etc. Though we are aware that these groups may mirror local social divides across caste and gender, we have not delved into this aspect and confine ourselves to discussing the impact of urbanisation on farming and farmers in general.

Farmers from the dominant landholding community of *Vokkaligas* are the ones who bridge the gap between their less networked peers and the State, including banks. Such link-farmers were not too different from others in formal education, but their holdings were comparatively larger and they cultivated mango or coconut. Given the high propensity for fraud by traders (there was repeated mention of traders duping farmers), it was important to bring reliable private traders for mango and coconut to the villages. Link-farmers, being part of larger social networks, were expected to bring reliable traders to the village.

As farmers move out from farming and get involved in non-farm occupations, their social networks also take different forms. Other institutions or individuals, mostly unconnected with agriculture, become more influential. Most farmer migrants we interacted with were in close touch with friends and relatives in their villages. They kept in touch with local employment agencies and officials (fair price shop dealers, school teachers, corporator or panchayat members) in the migrated towns. Links with relatives blurred as farmer migrants gradually moved completely out of their native places.

7.12 Urbanisation with Smaller Agrarian Footprint

Small towns with bustling economies, at the confluence of urban demand and rural produce, of urban culture and rural ways of life, as well as of farm engagements and non-farm, form the dynamic middle India of the twenty-first century. They are also the melting pots of new livelihood trends across sectors. Middle India hosts clusters of commercial agricultural products, industrial manufacturing, technology companies and real estate agencies.

7.12 Urbanisation with Smaller Agrarian Footprint

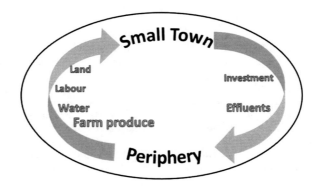

Fig. 7.16 Flows between small town and its periphery (font size indicates relative quantum of flows)

The hustle and bustle in Ramanagara's markets originate in the production landscapes that we saw in the peripheries of Kanakapura and Magadi taluks. But they are impacted adversely by the extended function of being a source (of good water) and sink (of sewage and solid waste) to the megacity Bengaluru, just 60–65 km away. Despite bearing the brunt of these externalities, the cherished possession of formal or informal urban occupations in the big city appears hard to come by, except for the few who drift sufficiently and successfully away from farming. Even such migration does not seem to really take them anywhere close to the average income of a city dweller. Annual per capita income of a resident Banglurean worker in 2015–16 was twice that of a farmer migrant to Bengaluru.[29]

The core–periphery dynamics between the small town and its surrounding agrarian landscape is depicted in Fig. 7.16. Water, land, farm produce and labour flow from peri-urban farms to the small town, in moderate quantities. Water, though mostly in the common or open access domain and perceived as a private resource by farmers who invest in tube wells, remains influenced by (and influence) other ecosystem functions in these peripheries. Apart from competing for water resources, industrial expansion converts farmlands and uses them for dumping effluents. Land in the diagram below could be in the public or common domain, apart from those that are privately owned.

The only two outflows from small towns towards the farms outside the town are small capital and waste from consumption and production activities in the small town. While flow of small capital may help in buffering agricultural risks of farm families, urban effluents (both in solid and in liquid forms) impact agro-ecology and farmers adversely, though it appears less threatening than the effluents from Bengaluru.

We notice that most families in the production landscape around Ramanagara stay back in farming, holding onto their small piece of land and small flows of income from both the small town and the mega city in the neighbourhood, through farm and non-farm engagements.

---

[29] Annual per capita income of a resident of Bengaluru was ₹2.7 lakhs versus that of a farmer migrant from study taluks of ₹1.3 lakhs (Economic Survey 2016 and Farmer interviews in 2015).

References

Ahmed, M. K. (1997). *Economics of Silk reeling with reference to production and marketing in Karnataka*. Doctoral Thesis. Institute of Social and Economic Change.

Anderson, K. (1929). Old Munuswamy and the Panther of Magadi. In *The Black Panther of Sivanipalli and other adventure of the Indian Jungle* (pp. 65–83). UK: Rand McNally and Company.

Bah, et al. (2006). Changing rural-urban linkages in Mali, Nigeria and Tanzania. In C. Tacoli (Ed.), *The Earthscan reader in rural-urban linkages*. UK: Earthscan.

Basu, K. (2014). http://www.bbc.co.uk/news/world-asia-india-25742983 [cf. Harriss-White, B. (2016, p. 276)].

Behrens, K., & Robert-Nicoud, F. (2014). Survival of the fittest in cities: Urbanisation and inequality. *The Economic Journal, 124*(581), 1371–1400.

Buchanan, F. (1807). *Journey from Madras through Mysore, Canara ad Malabar* (Vol. 2)

Central Ground Water Board. (2012). Brief Industrial Profile of Ramanagara District. MSME-Development Institute, Ministry of MSME, Government of India.

Datta, A. (2013). *City forgotten*. (https://www.opendemocracy.net/en/opensecurity/city-forgotten/).

Denis, E., Mukhopadhyay, P., & Zerah, M. H. (2012). Subaltern urbanisation in India. *Economic and Political Weekly, 47*(30), 52–62.

Denis, E., & Zerah, M.-H. (Eds.). (2017). *Subaltern urbanisation in India: An introduction to the dynamics of ordinary towns*. Springer Asia Series.

Folke, S. (2001). Conflicts over canal water for irrigation in Mandya District, South India. *Journal of Social and Economic Development, 3*(1), 106–120.

Gayathri, S., Latha, N., & Ramachandra Mohan, M. (2015). Water quality status of Manchanabele Reservoir: Bangalore West Region, Karnataka, India. *International Journal of Innovative Science, Engineering and Technology, 2*(12), 364–372.

Gibson, J., Dutt, G., Murgai, R., & Ravallion, M. (2017). For India's rural poor, growing towns matter more than growing cities. *World Development, 98,* 413–429.

Gupta, A. (2006). Blurred boundaries: The discourse of corruption, the culture of politics and the imagined State. In A. Sharma & A. Gupta (Eds.), *The anthropology of the state*. Oxford: Blackwell.

Harriss-White, B. (Ed.). (2016). *Middle India and urban-rural development: Four decades of change*. Springer Asia Series.

Industrial Profile of Ramanagara District. (2012). Ground Water Information Booklet, Ramanagara District, Karnataka. Central Ground Water Board. Accessed at http://cgwb.gov.in/District_Profile/karnataka/2012/Ramanagaram-2012.pdf

Kashyap & Purushothaman (forthcoming). *A historical analysis of the agrarian political economy in the erstwhile Mysore region of South India.*

Krishnan, C. (2014). The state and drought- villagers' experiences. Knowledge in Civil Society. Accessed at http://www.kicsforum.net/kics/State-Drought.pdf

Sen, K. (2014). The Indian economy in the post-reform period: Growth without structural transformation. In D. Devin & B. Harriss-White (Eds.), *China-India: Pathways of economic and social development* (pp. 47–62).

Thompson, E., Bunnell T., & D. Parthasarathy. (2013). Introduction: Place, society and politics across rural and urban Asia. In E. Thompson, T. Bunnell, & D. Parthasarathy (Eds.), *Cleavage, connection and conflict in rural, urban and contemporary Asia* (pp. 1–14) Springer Asia Series.

Shah, I. (2003). *Social designs: tank irrigation technology and agrarian transformation in Karnataka, South India* (p. 64). Orient Longman.

Vasavi, A. R. (1999). Agrarian distress in Bidar: Market, state and suicides. *Economic and Political Weekly, 34*(32), 2263–2268.

Chapter 8
Agricultural Urbanism—Family Farms Around Mandya

"India became impoverished when our cities became foreign markets and began to drain the villages dry by dumping cheap and shoddy goods from foreign lands."

The above quote from Mahatma Gandhi (1937)[1] implies the potential of villages to drive urbanisation and development. Agrarian urbanism is intuitively comprised of economic and demographic dynamism around marketing as well as processing of agricultural products farmed in the vicinity. This dynamism caters to a stable intertwined rural–urban relationship.

8.1 Agriculture as a Driver of Urbanisation

Agrarian urbanism here refers to a multi-activity, multi-product economy originating in the family farms of the region. Such towns of course will also be driven by the economic drivers of the twenty-first century, though their agrarian character continues to be discernible. Food grains, local fruits, plantation crops or farm animals could trigger slow and steady urbanism in the neighbourhood, depending on the scale of farming, transactions and turnover. Specific commodity markets can drive urbanisation in the vicinity—such as paddy in Arni, tea in Dibrugarh and spices in Kochi, as cited in Chap. 3, Sect. 3.2.

Imagine a town driven by small-scale agriculture in its surroundings resulting in a landscape as in Fig. 8.1. It shows the potential fusion of rural and urban characters—formal markets (*mandi*) and weekly bazaars (*santhe*); farm machinery and draught animals; processing units of varying scale and so on.

Using this image of an agro-urban region, we sifted through the districts of Karnataka using data on farming patterns, agricultural trade, processing industries and urbanisation. In the process, we identified Mandya to represent the subaltern

---

[1] India of My Dreams, Chap. 23—Back to the Village, pp. 92–95 (cf. Harijan, 27-2-1937).

© Springer Nature Singapore Pte Ltd. 2019
S. Purushothaman and S. Patil, *Agrarian Change and Urbanization in Southern India*, India Studies in Business and Economics,
https://doi.org/10.1007/978-981-10-8336-5_8

184   8 Agricultural Urbanism—Family Farms Around Mandya

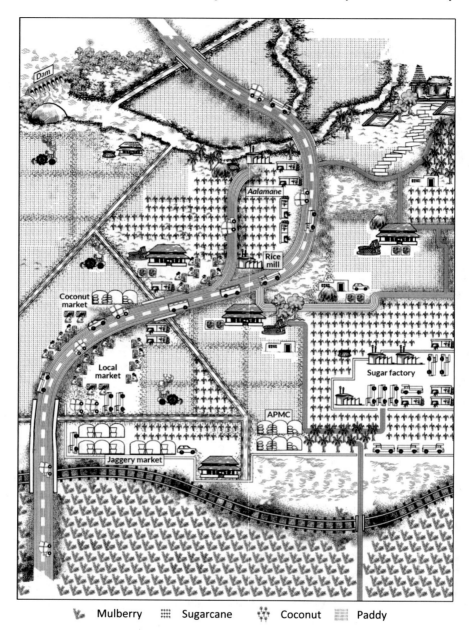

Mulberry   Sugarcane   Coconut   Paddy

Fig. 8.1 Periphery of agro-processing town

8.1 Agriculture as a Driver of Urbanisation

force of agrarian urbanism. The process described in Chap. 3, Sect. 3.4 was followed to select study taluks and villages within Mandya district.

Mandya: Karnataka's Model of Agricultural Urbanism

Mandya is one of the well-studied agrarian regions of Karnataka. M. N. Srinivas' eye for 'messiness' through a structural functionalistic lens disentangles the accounts of a village in Mandya.[2] Epstein's ethnography of wet and dry villages of Mandya in the mid-twentieth century provided another well-known narrative. It was difficult to resist the temptation to undertake a similar village study in Mandya. But, keeping in mind the primary purpose—looking for a pattern in the differential impacts of urbanisation on smallholders—we had to take a call on the study approach (elaborated in Chap. 3, Sect. 3.1). In the process, a complete village studies was inevitably compromised. Studies that informed our perception of Mandya include Srinivas (1957, 1976), Epstein (1962), Folke (2001), Ramachandran and Swaminathan (2002) and Swaminathan and Baksi (2017), among others.

Any mention of Mandya conjures up images of farmers' agitations, sugar mills and networks of canals traversing green fields of paddy and sugarcane. Recent incidences of farmers' suicides (Manjunath and Ramappa 2017; Sheth 2015) suggest that the beauty and lushness around the landscape may be deceptive.[3] The headquarters of the district, lying on the highway between Bengaluru and Mysore (100 and 50 km from the two cities, respectively), is a bustling municipal corporation with 364 residents per km^2.[4] Urban Mandya, which houses 18% of the district's population and dotted with agro-processing units, reflects the largely agrarian character of the district. This chapter unpacks what Mandya stands for—a medley of agrarian urbanism in a region where globalised economy thrives (Fig. 8.2).

Mandya was part of Mysore district in the princely State of Mysore till 1939. It was carved out as a new district with the purpose of improving administrative

Fig. 8.2 National highway through Mandya town

---

[2] Beteille in p. XV and p. 2 of Srinivas (1976).

[3] Mandya reported suicides of 56 farmers between April and October 2015. The number was highest among all districts of the State in that period (https://www.thenewsminute.com/article/map-shows-farmer-has-committed-suicide-every-district-karnataka-year-34917).

[4] All population figures are taken from Census of India 2011.

efficiency of the vast canal system in the region. Taluks of Mandya can be identified with specific agricultural features. We chose Pandavapura and Nagamangala taluks to represent the irrigated and rain-fed areas of Mandya and reflect the crop diversity that caters to the agro-processing units in and around Mandya. Nagamangala is the largest among the seven taluks of Mandya district, with a lower population density (182 persons per km^2) than Pandavapura (347 persons per km^2). The two taluks are similar in terms of representation of different castes in the population and share of rural/urban population. While rural population itself has been declining since the 1980s in both the taluks, the rate of growth of urban population has also been showing signs of decline.

Pandavapura taluk with 12% urban population is notable for its sugar mills and water bodies,[5] and has a rich cultural history. Irrigated fields of paddy and sugarcane criss-crossed by roads, railway lines, canals and dotted with jaggery making units (*alaamanes*) alongside sugar mills and rice mills describe Pandavapura in a nutshell (Fig. 8.3). Named after the five Pandava princes in the epic Mahabharata, its archaeological history talks of Ramanujacharya, the saint social reformer, making Melukote in Pandavapura taluk, a seat of higher learning. This eventually led to the establishment of the Academy of Sanskrit Research in Melukote about three decades ago. In the year 1798, the French Army is known to have camped here while helping Tipu Sultan in his fights with the British.

Nagamangala (*'blessed with snakes'*), the land of beautiful ancient temples and coconut palms, was also a seat of religious studies (*agraharas*). People and agriculture in Nagamangala bore the brunt of many aggressions involving Marathas, Tipu and the British (Buchanan 1807, p. 66; Wilks 1817, p. 52; Rao 1943, vol. 2, p. 83; Rice 1897, vol. 2, p. 286). A sparsely populated taluk town, Nagamangala, was known for its artisanship in metalworks especially in bronze cast, till about early twentieth century. The skills and artistry of the people of Nagamangala appear to be legendary as seen in the temples and irrigation structures. Currently almost everyone in the taluk struggles to continue rain-fed farming and livestock keeping, which are the only remaining local occupations.

Fig. 8.3 Glimpses of Pandavapura

---

[5]Not just the rivers Shimsha, Cauvery, Hemavati, Lokapavani and Veervaishnavi, but also tanks like the ancient and enchanting Tonnnur kere.

8.1 Agriculture as a Driver of Urbanisation

Fig. 8.4 Glimpses of Nagamangala

Opportunities to acquire new life skills to enable participation in the urbanising world have been sporadic and ad hoc, at best (Fig. 8.4).

Nagamangala town, located around the beautiful *Saumya Keshava* temple built in the twelfth century, has the look of a 'big village' (as in Harriss-White 2016) compared to the 'small-town' look of Pandavapura. A handful of small oil mills (mainly grinding copra, castor or sesamum), an expansive market yard for trading all agricultural produce, a separate mandi for coconuts, along with the usual commercial and official establishments of a taluk headquarters, make up the town of Nagamangala.

Although parts of the same district, the two taluks have different agro-ecologies and showcase different socio-economic features (Table 8.1). While both have similar history in terms of rulers and wars, Pandavapura after the onset of canal irrigation and sugar processing mills, hosts a vibrant agricultural society compared to a drier Nagamangala.

Following two or three exploratory visits to all hoblis of the two taluks, we held group interactions in nine hoblis. These interactions were around land distribution across caste and holding sizes and changes in the pattern of crops, livestock, livelihoods and village commons over time. These interactions helped in two ways—to confirm the rural–urban linkages that we were looking for in this particular site and to select villages for detailed enquiries. Following a series of visits and interactions,

Table 8.1 Nagamangala and Pandavpura taluks at a glance

	Nagamangala	Pandavapura
Total geographical area (TGA) (km^2)	103	52
Forests, pastures and tree groves (% of TGA—2014)	3	12
Net sown area (2015) (% of TGA)	29	42
Population density (per km^2—2011)	182	347
Urban population (%—2011)	9	11
Cultivators and farm labour (% in total workers—2011)	79	76
Human Development Index (rank out of 176 taluks—2014)	0.453 (87)	0.481 (73)

Source Human Development Report 2014; Census of India 2011 and Agricultural Census 2011

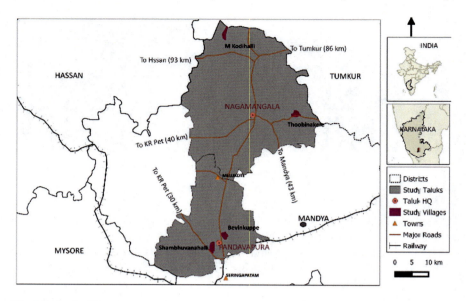

Fig. 8.5 Study villages in Mandya

we selected four villages (Fig. 8.5) from both the taluks—Bevinkuppe and Shambhuvanahalli in Pandavapura and M. Kodihalli and Tubinakere in Nagamangala.

Below we try to show the urban-agricultural interface manifested in these taluks through changes in land, water, farm practices, occupations and institutions, from both secondary sources and our fieldwork. Unless there is considerable distinction between the two taluks selected, the description below pertains to the agrarian periphery of Mandya in general.

8.2 Farmlands: With Dominant Communities

Historical changes in the Mysore State from a locally controlled land governance regime to the *ryotwari* system of the British seem to have sidelined the lower caste smallholders.[6] Unlike the irrigated belts of Tamil Nadu and Andhra Pradesh, big agricultural capital did not emerge from Mandya. Pani (2017) argues that this lack of successful transition among both small as well as relatively large holders of this region was the combined effect of (i) large tracts of cultivable area available in the eighteenth century, making land-based dominance infeasible and (ii) poor soil quality that allowed only limited capital accumulation. Looking at the governance during this period, we find a history of welfare orientation of rulers and inclusive institutions. Thus, Mandya seems to have escaped a deeply intertwined land, caste

---

[6] See the transition to *ryotwari* explained in Kashyap and Purushothaman (forthcoming).

8.2 Farmlands: With Dominant Communities

and class inequality found in some other districts, keeping large-scale exploitative tenancy at bay, even with the land tenure system introduced by the British.

Ownership and Leasing

Mandya's agrarian urbanism, mentioned at the beginning of this chapter, was built on canal irrigated agriculture and is reflected in its extensive cultivated lands (56% of total geographical area), population in farming (77% of total workforce) and share of urban population (18%). About 66% of land was less than 5 acres, 24% was between 5 and 10 acres, and only 10% was larger than 10 acres. One-sixth of the total landholders were women. In the study taluks, marginal holdings have been decreasing, while smallholdings increased from 2005 onwards. Nagamangala, historically known for large holdings, shows reduction in their average size in the same period.

Vokkaliga has been the dominant landholding caste in both the study taluks. Joint families in the irrigated belts started disintegrating into smaller nuclear holdings faster than other areas. This was mostly driven by the statutory requirement to own the farmland so as to avail subsidies and State procurement.[7] Generally, leasing is not too common in Mandya and confined to less irrigated villages in Nagamangala.

Land Fallowing and Conversion

Nagamangala farmers mentioned water and labour scarcity as well as land disputes as reasons for fallowing their ragi fields. Unlike what is reported in the Agricultural Census (2011), we did not find huge extents of fallows in Nagamangala. Unreliable water supply and lack of sufficient capital needed for the cost-intensive crops were responsible for the large extent of fallows in the farms studied in Pandavapura. Irrigated land was often left fallow if sufficient family labour was not available for farming. While indebtedness was the major reason in both places to sell off agricultural land, expenditure in medical exingencies and house construction figured prominently in Pandavapura. Land acquisition has evaded the study taluks in Mandya, giving them the benefit of combining some non-farm employment with continued access to land.

8.3 Nature's Commons: Lakes and Rivers

Mandya has meagre forests and grazing lands, but the district is endowed with lakes, open wells and rivers that fuel the agricultural economy. Lakes have a long history in this landscape and date back to the legendary courtesan lakes (*soole keres*). These lakes were established or supported by the concubines of the then rulers[8] (Imperial

---

[7]Details about how procurement of sugarcane by sugar mills in this area came to be divisive is discussed in Sect. 8.5.1.

[8]*Soole keres* were common in other parts too—e.g. Channagiri, Maddur and Arsikere taluks.

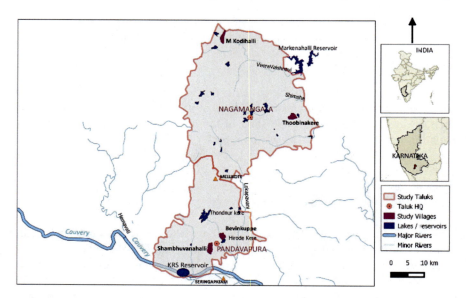

Fig. 8.6 Lakes and streams in and around Nagamangala and Pandavapura

Gazetteer 1908.) Currently, the district hosts 630 lakes and tanks that contribute to irrigation (District at a Glance 2015–16).

Many streams and rivers flow through Mandya (Fig. 8.6). Most of them flow towards river Cauvery traversing the study taluks.

The drainage system of Mandya is spread across three basins: Cauvery, Shimsha and Lokapavani. The pereinnial rivers Hemavati, Shimsha and Lokpavani, and Veervaishnavi—a seasonal river flowing through Mandya district, join the major pennunsila river Cauvery. Lokapavani flows in the north–south direction through study taluks and meets Cauvery near Srirangapatna, before Hemavati joins it. Veervaishnavi flows from west to east through Nagamangala and leaves the district before joining Shimsha that joins Cauvery at Chamarajanagar.

8.4 Irrigation: Confluence of Old and New Ingenuity

Tanks are the oldest irrigation system in this region. Villagers constructed small tanks across streams to store water for farming. There were hundreds of such minor and major tanks spread across the district. British historian Rice (1897) described these tanks as below:

An interesting account of *soole kere* in Nagamangala is portrayed by Chandran (2016)—https://www.livemint.com/Sundayapp/MV1aSAEZsc6IFMbf6SbvBO/Of-legends-and-lakes-built-by-courtesans.html.

8.4 Irrigation: Confluence of Old and New Ingenuity

> "... the streams which gather from the hillsides and fertilise the valleys are, at every favorable point, embanked in such a manner as to form series or chains of reservoirs, called tanks, the outflow from one at a higher level supplying the next lower, and so on all down the course of the stream at a few miles apart. These tanks, varying in size from small ponds to extensive lakes, are dispersed throughout the country to the number of 38,080; and to such an extent has this principle of storing water been followed that it would now require some ingenuity to discover a site suitable for a new one without interfering with the supply of those already in existence. The largest of these tanks is the Sulekere, 40 miles in circumference. Other large ones are Ayyankere, Madaga-kere, Masur-Madaga-kere, Vyasa samudra, Ramasagara, Moti Talab, etc."

Moti talab, the tank mentioned in Rice's account, popularly known as Thondnur kere (or Thirumalasagara) and situated in Pandavapura taluk, is one of the oldest dams in the world. Constructed under the leadership of saint Ramanujacharya across the Yadava nadi in twelfth century AD during the Hoysala dynasty, this water body has been faithfully irrigating farmlands of more than ten villages downstream, since then. According to researchers at the Academy of Sanskrit Research in Melukote, the dam was built in order to make this region self-sufficient in food production.

Thondnur was a major centre of Hoysala kingdom inhabited by religious learners and their families. The command area of the tank mainly cultivated paddy. This vast and beautiful water body continues to irrigate thousands of acres despite being regulated by Gorur dam built in 1975 across Hemavati River. There are smaller water bodies in the surroundings of Thondnur mainly used for irrigating paddy fields, for example, Markenahalli near Devalapur in Nagamangala, Kadalegere and Huligere tanks near Melukote in Pandavapura among several others (Fig. 8.7).

The most conspicuous modern intervention in Mandya is the dam across Cauvery. Krishna Raja Sagara (popular as KRS), the hydroelectric project built in Kannambadi between 1911 and 1931 at an expense of ₹13.4 million then, promised to irrigate 79,352 ha. Heavy investment in this project was justified on the basis of a stipulated hike in agricultural income. Enhancing agricultural income needed large-scale shift in the cropping pattern. This in turn triggered socio-cultural changes in the region. Changes in cropping pattern meant new farming techniques, and these invariably faced varying levels of acceptance. The Japanese technique of intensive transplantation of paddy spread despite resistance from women planter groups and a few sugar mills replaced many jaggery units.

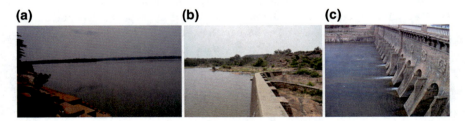

Fig. 8.7 Barrages in Mandya district—**a** Thondnur and **b** Kadalegere near Melukote and **c** KRS in Kannambadi

Apart from these changes in cultivation practices and processing, the new canal irrigation also meant loss of conventional precautions in water use. The logical link between crops grown and the available source of water as well as the traditions of water sharing also faded away. **In the absence of strong non-farm sectors and social security schemes along with the failure of new agricultural institutions (e.g. water user groups), economic aspirations set in motion by big State funded projects accelerated the erosion of traditional irrigation norms.**

Though canal irrigation is best used for intensive farming of sugarcane and paddy, the following questions remain unanswered—to what extent should traditional crops be displaced? How much irrigation should be provided to the new crops? **Water prudence suggests that tank irrigation is appropriate to be used for crops requiring moderate irrigation like millets, pulses and oilseeds. Tube wells from groundwater aquifers should be used for life-saving irrigation of high-input-intensive crops like mulberry and areca nut.**

With a mismatch between the introduction of new and highly impactful interventions in irrigation, crop production and processing and the evolution of social institutions, conflicts between upstream and downstream communities around the canal became the norm. Violent conflicts between social groups even within the upstream and downstream communities itself are also now common in a region that boasts of long established water regulating and sharing systems.

In study villages, though caste was not a factor in accessing irrigation, the beneficiaries of canal water in Nagamangala predominantly belonged to the dominant castes. Perhaps, we need a context specific relook at Epstein's (1962) reference to how the restricted differentiation in canal irrigated holdings of Maddur was limited to intra-peasant caste (*Vokkaligas* and *Reddys*) and intra-Scheduled caste. Folke (2001) elucidates the differential prosperity brought to farmers in Mandya by the canal irrigation scheme—'... *No doubt, canal irrigation has brought prosperity to Mandya, particularly to the farmers with substantial lands and easy access to water for irrigation. But as demonstrated in this article it has also created divisions and conflicts between those who are favoured—by landownership, location, caste affiliation and political backing—and those who are not'.*

When KRS was designed and planned, Madras presidency, through which a major portion of the river flows (416 km in Tamil Nadu and 320 km in Karnataka), had raised many objections. **Every year in summer, KRS is invariably in the news for conflicts and politics over sharing the dwindling flow of Cauvery. On the contrary, neither conflicts nor drying-up of canals are reported around Thondnur and smaller anicuts.** Barrages have been existing for centuries across Cauvery, Hemavati, Shimsha, Lokapavani, Veervaishnavi rivers for serving local agriculture. Three of the six anicuts in Mandya district were in the study taluks, two across Lokapavani (one each in Pandavapura and Nagamangala) and one across Veervaishnavi (in Nagamangala). **Now, after almost a century in blind pursuit of big dams, the realisation that smaller anicuts may be better suited to ensure environmental flow in the rivers (see Silva et al. 2014)and for sustaining water yield is slowly emerging.**

8.4 Irrigation: Confluence of Old and New Ingenuity

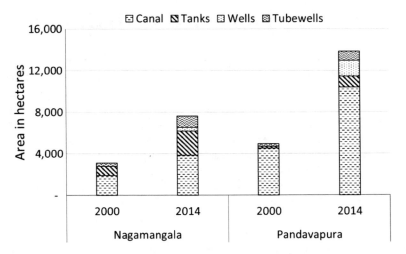

Fig. 8.8 Source-wise irrigation in Nagamangala and Pandavapura taluks.
Source Agricultural statistics of Karnataka, 2001 and 2015

As KRS—one of the famed 'temples' of modern India—started falling short of its promises, newer technologies to extract another source—groundwater—came to be relied upon. Tube wells with submersible pumps became popular even in the command area of a large irrigation project like KRS. Density of tube wells in the canal irrigated taluk of Mandya seems to be relatively high compated to other command areas with one tube well for every 15 ha. Groundwater seems to be available at shallow tables (170–450 ft) in both the taluks (Central Groundwater Board 2014). Although rainfall pattern since 2004 did not show much variation in either of the study taluks, Pandavapura generally receives more rainfall (700 mm) than Nagamangala (608 mm).

Thus, currently three major sources of irrigation coexist in the study taluks of Mandya—canal, tube wells and tanks in decreasing order of the area covered (Fig. 8.8). Dominance of canals in Pandavapura and canals and tanks in Nagamangala is noteworthy.[9]

In 15 years since 2000, tube well and canal irrigation in both the taluks declined, while there was an increase in irrigated area under tanks and open wells (Agricultural Statistics 2014). **On an average, irrigated farmlands have a larger holding size. The presence of irrigation, irrespective of its source, is aligned with a larger holding size.**

---

[9] Among the respondents, 37% in Pandavapura and 4% in Nagamangala use both canals and tube wells irrespective of the smallness of their holding.

8.5 Farming: Canal Irrigated and Rain-fed Systems

Buchanan (1807, vol. 2), a Scottish traveller in colonial India, describes Mandya as a poor village. He says half the region was covered with rocks, looked barren and impoverished, where locusts of unusual size used to destroy the fields of sorghum. History of modern agriculture in Mandya starts with the appointment of its first Director of Agriculture in the State of Mysore—Dr. L. C. Coleman. A Canadian entomologist, Coleman was responsible for modernising the irrigation system around the Visvesvaraya Canal (earlier Irwin Canal and now popular as VC canal) and setting up the sprawling 600 acres experimental farm in Mandya, known as VC farm.

Now, Mandya is distinctive with its vast paddy lands, sugarcane and coconut. Ragi and mulberry are the two other crops grown. While almost 40% of the total land in Mandya is sown at least once an year, 35% of that is sown more than once. Net sown area is comparatively low in Nagamangala where rain-fed system of coconut and ragi has been prevailing for more than two centuries (Buchanan 1807, p. 66). Though the currently popular cropping pattern of sugarcane and paddy in Pandavapura is less than a century old since the inception of KRS, reduction in net sown area is already conspicuous.

While area under ragi came down in both the taluks over the last 15 years, area under pulses and coconut increased. Figure 8.9 shows the current cropping pattern in the farms we studied.

Crop diversity in individual farms was higher in Nagamangala, with at least three crops in every holding—ragi, coconut and pulses. Sugarcane, though occupying larger share of area in Nagamangala, continues to be in the command areas of Markenahalli and other smaller dams. Ragi–coconut was the most popular pattern seen in drier Nagamangala. In Pandavapura, while sugarcane dominated in terms of area covered, paddy was comparatively more popular. In the subsections below, we trace

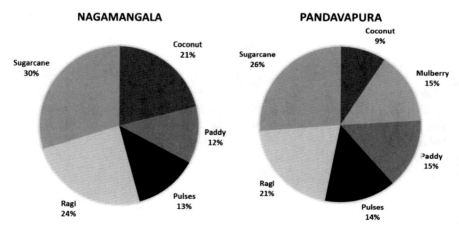

Fig. 8.9 Cropping pattern in the periphery of Mandya (% of land cultivated by respondents). *Source* Farmer interviews, 2015

8.5 Farming: Canal Irrigated and Rain-fed Systems

the growth of sugarcane—the hallmark of irrigated Pandavapura, and coconut—the perennial crop of Nagamangala, in detail.

8.5.1 From Small Town to 'Sugar City'—Journey of Irrigated Mandya

The making of and maintaining a sugar economy in Mandya is the story of replacing a slow and mostly dryland economy into an irrigated commercial production system geared for a processing industry catering to the global market. Travelling anywhere in Mandya, it is difficult to avoid the imprints of the legacy of M. Visvesvaraya—the Diwan of Mysore during 1912–1918. More than his photograph that is invariably displayed in houses, shops and offices, his legacy is seen in the river intervention projects strewn across the landscape. Sir MV's strategy for young India's development was 'State supported development based on local capital' (Hettne 1978).

Following the construction of Irwin Canal, later known as Visvesvaraya Canal, fed by KRS, the total irrigated area which was 12% of arable land in 1933 jumped to 75% in 1939. Among the many changes brought in by canal irrigation, the most important was the spread of sugarcane cultivation and sugar manufacture. Sugarcane takes 18 months to mature. Family farms require State support to tide over the 18–20 months period between sowing and selling of the new long duration crop. It became necessary to invest in iron ploughs, sturdier bullocks and fertilisers. In the initial years of canal irrigation, many smallholders sold part of their land to raise the capital needed for switching to sugarcane cultivation. Though the crop was not entirely new, as there used to be small patches of tank irrigated sugarcane, the varieties suitable for canal irrigation and extracting sugar (rather than jaggery) were new to the farmers here.[10]

State support for sugar mills and cane growers, State procurement of cane and the spreading of cane varieties suitable for sugar production meant that jaggery units were ignored since the spread of canal irrigation, inspite of a sugar glut in the market. Many jaggery units in Mandya survived partly because of the demand from north Indian confectionery makers for light coloured jaggery that necessitated addition of chemicals that are unsafe for human consumption.

Jaggery production uses bagasse, the residue after crushing, as its fuel source and generally molasses is not separated from cane juice. Factory-scale sugar production that uses electricity does not require bagasse—the vegetative residue. Sugar factories also filter out molasses while making white sugar. As the sugar market is mostly in a glut, sugar factories need to use by-products like bagasse and molasses in order to break even. For this purpose, ancillary industries like distilleries and chemical factories were set up in Mandya, Mysore and Srirangapatna to extract spirit and alcohol from molasses. A paper factory was set up in Mandya and Srirangapatna that

---

[10]Sugarcane varieties Co 7219, Co 0212 and Co 86032 were considered suitable for sugar production.

used sugarcane bagasse. Sugar mills along with their ancillaries discharge wastewater into the rivers in Mandya, polluting the fresh water resources of the region.[1]

The natural source of jaggery used to vary in different agro-ecologies—date palms in Bengal, palmyra (ice apples) in Tamil Nadu and coconut palms in Kerala, Lakshadweep and coastal Karnataka. Unlike the water-hungry sugarcane, palms grew on scrub land and did not need much investment or care. Gandhian economist Kumarappa's calculations showed that these rain-fed perennials could amply address the demand for sweeteners by the then Indian population (Govindu 2017). Buchanan (1807, vol. 2) also narrates how locals used to brew liquor from the numerous date palms found in the areas around Mysore. The expansion of area under sugarcane cultivation is the outcome of a classic case of supply driving demand (Epstein 1962). Unfortunately, the democratic State played a major role in this entire process of destabilising a regional economy dependent on a resilient social–ecological system.

As Govindu (2017) says: '*In 1947, some two-thirds of Indian sugar production was still in the form of jaggery and India's democratic government set about transforming this situation. In the early days of independence, under the influence of Indian capital, a rash of government orders were passed by administrative fiat effectively banning the age-old traditional manufacture of jaggery in many regions. Left with no choices, the farmer was slowly but surely delivered into the hands of the many mills that sprouted across the country*'.

Sugar mills with huge support from the government manage to offer better prices than jaggery units despite the glut in the sugar market. For example, the Central Government recently announced ₹83 billion to bail out sugar mills with advance payments to farmers.[12] Recent fluctuations in sugar price and delay in payments for cane growers together with urban health concerns in consuming processed sugar have rekindled some interest in the *alaamanes* of Mandya.[13] Consistency in payments made to cane producers makes the cottage production of jaggery more reliable than the higher but fluctuating and deferred payments by the sugar mills.

The differential scales of operation of sugar mills and jaggery units, the State support and academic attention in favor of sugar all managed to hijack a potential economy of permanence towards farming for industries propped up by the State.

Sugar factories used to maintain sample farms to show peasants how to grow sugarcane, homogenising the cultivation practices. Transforming to a sugar economy entailed impacts beyond cropping practices. Srinivas's *Remembered Village* (1976) tells us how the sugar factory formally divided the joint land owners, as it took sugarcane from owner cultivators.

---

[11] Sugar mills discharge effluents into the river—http://www.thehindu.com/news/national/karnataka/sugar-mill-warned-against-discharging-wastewater-into-river/article7672535.ece.

[12] Bera (2018) Government set to announce ₹83 billion plan to bail out sugarcane farmers—https://www.livemint.com/Politics/djWk1pzFbnoFMOpEoH1Z5J/Govt-set-to-announce-Rs8000-crore-plan-to-bail-out-sugarcan.html—bail out for sugar mills projected as is to benefit farmers.

[13] On *alaamanes* of Mandya: http://www.ourstories.org.in/2015/december-2015/reviving-alaamanes-the-jaggery-industry-of-mandya/. On reviving jaggery units in UP: http://www.iisr.nic.in/download/publications/PolicyPaper_Gangwar.pdf.

8.5 Farming: Canal Irrigated and Rain-fed Systems

Cash flow in the new sugar economy brought in other social changes including in-migration and commercialisation of fairs, festivals and customs (such as dowry). Exchanging gifts that include sweets bought from the market became more popular than the rituals and food made in the farm households. Prosperity was visible in modern houses and automobiles. But the other side of this euphoria is little known. With water stagnating in the sugarcane fields, malaria came back with a vengeance and air and water pollution from factories became common place.[14] To make matters worse, the new money spinner of the canal irrigated production system became prone to 'irrigation drought' as canals began to go dry often.

The political economic lobby around cane sugar thus overpowered concerns about health of consumers and the production system while creating path dependency in consumption of subsidised sugar through Public Distribution System. The journey of predominantly rain-fed Mandya into an externally controlled sugar economy recently marred with extreme distress in family farms,[15] pre-empted the possibility for a vibrant subaltern urbanism of the agrarian kind.

8.5.2 Coconut, Ragi and Livestock—A Long-Standing System in Rain-fed Areas

Most parts of Nagamangala feature tall coconut palms and ventilated storage spaces for drying whole coconuts either in the attic or in separate structures close to the house. Some coconut orchards also have patches of ragi between the rows of palms. This landscape, unlike the vast irrigated fields of paddy and sugarcane in Pandavapura, appears quieter with tall trees, scattered water bodies and native cows, buffaloes as well as goats and sheep roaming around.

The coconut–ragi system of Nagamangala is at least three centuries old. The destruction of 150,000 palms in the 1790s by the Marathas finds mention in Buchanan's travelogue and in the Mysore Gazetteer (1906). Loss of coconut palms during wars, together with famine and epidemic between 1790 and 1800, led to inhabitants fleeing the landscape towards nearby hills and woods. For more than a decade the area remained deserted. However, the coconut-based socio-economic system seemed to have revived in due course.

This centuries-old, mostly rain-fed, seasonal-perennial system of millet, oilseed and pulses, along with native livestock has not been too demanding in terms of inputs and time. Each standing tree yields nuts for about a century and easily sees three generations around it (Epstein 1962). Although far removed from major technological innovations, this long-standing agrarian economy provides a staple millet diet

---

[14]Malaria and irrigated agriculture: http://health21initiative.org/wp-content/uploads/2017/08/2002-IWMI-Malaria-in-Irrigated-Agriculture.pdf.

[15]Gopal (2018) 'Why Farmer suicides have spiked in Karnataka's sugar belt'—https://www.hindustantimes.com/india-news/why-farmer-suicides-have-spiked-in-karnataka-s-sugar-belt/story-pFKoo2Ey1Zof2qURhBUaZN.html.

and reasonable farm income. More importantly, with low investment in terms of labour and capital, it spares time and money needed to pursue higher education and non-farm occupations. Thus, it is not surprising that Nagamangala fares better than Pandavapura in terms of literacy and non-farm income.

Mysore Gazetteer (1906) mentions presence of hundreds of small wooden oil mills in this taluk. Even today, Nagamangala trades coconuts and copra. Each dehusked nut sold to traders at the farm gate fetches ₹13–15. An adult palm of coconut (about 10 years, depending on the variety) can produce about 75–100 nuts every year. Thus, against a total expense (including family labour) of ₹400 per palm, returns are threefold.

Rather than copying the unviable irrigated models with the accompanying volatility in farm earnings, Nagamangala continues to cultivate less water-intensive crops of millets, pulses and oilseeds. What is missing from the landscape is the presence of small processing units that could ensure consistent demand and savings in the cost of transportation.

Dry and irrigated parts of Mandya differ from each other not just in the crops grown but also in the animals kept. Nagamangala is known for its small ruminants—goats and sheep. Canal irrigated Pandavapura stocks much less animals and prefers exotic dairy cattle. While VC farm is a well-known institutional presence in Mandya's irrigated cropping scene, the sheep breeding institute in Nagamangala is known for research on small ruminants especially for conservation breeding of the much demanded *Bandur* goat.

In terms of income from livestock in the study sites, the survey again shows that the drier taluk of Nagamangala is better endowed than Pandavapura. The small ruminants they keep are sold for meat. Although farm families in Pandavapura kept hybrid cows, income accruing from animals, including manure (for sale and for use in farm) and hiring out animals for ploughing, was more common in Nagamangala. Sale of animals including both small and large ruminants, generated nearly 50% of farm income in Nagamangala (as against 22% in Pandavapura). The relative importance of livestock in Nagamangala is reflected in lower cost incurred in application of manures and fertilisers.[16]

8.6   The Cost of Farming: Capital and Family Labour

The most expensive crops in Mandya were mulberry, sugarcane and paddy in decreasing order. Input cost was found to be negatively correlated with livestock numbers and positively correlated with the extent of irrigated land and use of hired labour. Though Nagamangala's crops are not as lucrative compared to the canal irrigated crops of Pandavapura, they are also not cost heavy.

---

[16]Cost of manure was ₹6000 and ₹1000 per unit area, while fertiliser cost came to ₹17,000 and ₹12,000 per unit area, respectively, for Pandavapura and Nagamangala.

8.6 The Cost of Farming: Capital and Family Labour

Fig. 8.10 Input costs incurred by respondent families in the periphery of Mandya. (Seed cost in mulberry includes purchase of hatchlings.)
Source Farmer interviews, 2015

While fertiliser and labour for mulberry and sugarcane formed equally important cost heads, for ragi and coconut the most (more than 50%) important input was fertilisers (Fig. 8.10).

Farm Labour

Both Nagamangala and Pandavapura show an unchanging occupational pattern since 2001 (Fig. 8.11). Almost 75% of the total workers are engaged in farming as cultivators and farm labour. Pandavapura had a relatively higher percentage of farm labour and Nagamangala had more cultivators (Census of India 2011). While Pandavapura's paddy–sugarcane growers are slowly moving to the worker category, Nagamangala's coconut–ragi farmers continue as cultivators.

Farm families we studied used both family and hired labour. Wherever requirement of hired labour was high, the cost of other inputs was also high. Family members who were engaged in full-time farming worked for 210 days on a hectare of their land and hired 40 days of labour annually.

Sugarcane and mulberry were not only water intensive, but labour intensive as well. Wherever a perennial component is part of a farming system, as is usually the case with rain-fed agriculture, labour input is much less. Thus, the average wage rate in less irrigated Nagamangala was ₹175 per day compared to ₹400 per day paid to migrant labour brought in by the sugar mills for harvesting cane in Pandavapura.[17]

---

[17] The minimum agricultural wage rate in Karnataka was fixed at ₹303 for the three years between 2013 and 2016 (Karnataka Labour Journal 2016).

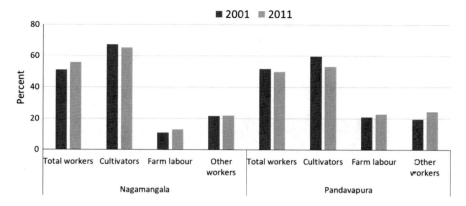

Fig. 8.11 Employment pattern in Nagamangala and Pandavapura taluks.
Total workers as percentage of total population. Cultivators, farm labour and other workers as percentage in total workers.
Source Census of India 2001 and 2011

Farmers' individual engagements involved cultivating own land (210 days), farm wage labour (56 days) and non-farm work (54 days). Family members engaged in skilled jobs also work in the fields when required. A typical farm family in Mandya with two working adults thus finds around 640 days of employment.

8.7 Selling Farm Produce: Processing Units and Regulated Markets

Despite several marketing options, a considerable portion of the produce is kept aside for family consumption in the case of crops like ragi, pulses, paddy and coconut. About 75% of the study farms grew paddy, ragi and pulses and consumed 80% of the produce on an average. Some portion of the produce is also offered to local temples. Mutual exchange of different pulses and oilseeds among families was common. Needless to say, commercial commodities like sugarcane and silk cocoons were completely marketed. Ragi, which occupies 35% of the net sown area in the study taluks (relatively more in Nagamangala), is mostly for consumption (87% of production) and gets value added on farm.

Small quantities of marketable products are generally taken to local bazaars (*santhes*) in the taluk headquarters that deal in all agricultural produce including perishables like vegetables, fruits and flowers. Farmers reach the bazaar around four a.m. with their produce and stay on till their harvest is sold by around 11 a.m. Thereafter, traders with semi-permanent stalls buy the remaining unsold produce from the farmers and supplement it with what they have bought already from other markets.

8.7 Selling Farm Produce: Processing Units and Regulated Markets

If not in the *santhe*, farmers sell their produce to private traders who dispatch agents to farm gates and processing units. State operated Agricultural Produce Marketing Committees (APMCs) mainly deal with ragi, paddy, coconut and cocoons. Apart from these, there are weekly markets at designated places for specific commodities where farmers congregate. Some of these special markets are set up by APMC, e.g. the coconut *mandi* in Pandavapura or jaggery market in Mandya. These markets send produce from Mandya to Delhi, Mumbai and other cities. Market reforms such as internet auction and electronic trading of jaggery, which were introduced in 2009–10, are yet to be well-established, with traders citing many concerns including perishability (Fig. 8.12).[18]

According to the Industrial Profile of Mandya, in 2012 the district had 250 rice mills, 5 sugar factories, 532 jaggery making units and a few oil mills. Figure 8.13 shows the locations of sugar mills, APMCs and *santhe* around the study taluks.

Most oil mills, rice mills and jaggery units are owned by dominant communities in this region—*Vokkaliga Gowda* or *Reddy*. Sugar mills are established by capitalists except for a co-operative mill in Pandavapura. Mysore Gazetteer (1897) mentions the presence of 1295 wooden oil mills in the then Mysore district, processing mostly sesamum and castor seeds. A handful of small mills extracting oil from coconut, castor and sesamum were seen in Pandavapura and Nagamangala towns, supplying oil for domestic needs in the locality.

The rice mills we visited were struggling to function. As paddy production declined over the last 4–5 years (reportedly due to insufficient rainfall and canal water), even small-scale units were laying off workers. Relatively larger mills procured paddy from North Karnataka to keep their units running. A rice mill owner mentioned how Food Corporation of India (FCI) used to call for tenders for paddy milling when APMC's own mills were overloaded. But, for the last 4–5 years such tenders were not called for because of a dip in paddy procurement. Between 2009 and 2012, the area under paddy seems to have declined at an annual rate of 13.3%, reflected in the increase in temporary fallows (Agricultural Statistics 2009–2012).

Fig. 8.12 Markets in Mandya Nagamangala and Pandavapua

---

[18]Recommendations of the State Committee for Agricultural Marketing Reforms including Comprehensive Electronic Auction System was adopted by Karnataka Agricultural Marketing Policy (KAMP) in 2013 (https://darpg.gov.in/sites/default/files/68.%20Electronic%20Tender%20System%20of%20Sale%20in%20Agircultural%20Produce%20Market%20Committees.pdf). Upon the success of such system on a pilot basis for jaggery in Mandya market, it was introduced in 18 APMCs in 2008–09 and 24 APMCs in 2009–10.

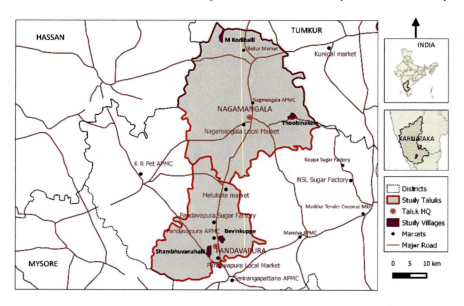

Fig. 8.13 Markets and sugar factories around Mandya

Nonetheless, 2017 was a good year for about 9000 registered paddy growers in terms of paddy yield. There were efforts by the State Department of Agriculture to help farmers to get Minimum Support Price (MSP) and mill owners to get enough supply of grains. As the implementation of the scheme faced opposition from millers, even an year with good monsoon turned out to be stressful for paddy farmers.[19]

This leads us to question the proclaimed benefits of factory-scale processing *vis-a-vis* small cottage industries. **Locally processing of sugarcane for sugar or jaggery *vis-a-vis* large- and small-scale units for oil extraction and milling rice have differential viability and impact on smallholders. Year-long supply of raw material (be it cane, paddy, copra or pulses) to large processing units cannot be ensured given the small size of individual farms and the large numbers of such units managed by families with varied endowments.** Also, it is easier and affordable for smallholdings to transport produce to small but nearby units for value addition or processing.

---

[19]Rice mill owners not willing to procure paddy under MSP scheme—https://www.thehindu.com/news/national/karnataka/mill-owners-shy-away-from-procuring-paddy-owing-to-govt-conditions/article25987220.ece.

8.8 Socio-economic Situation: Deceptive Prosperity

The overall observation about Mandya's economy corroborates the secondary data on the continued economic relevance of agricultural sector in the district. Compared with the State economy of Karnataka, Mandya's economy was earning more from farming—contributing 17.4% to Gross District Domestic Product as against 11.8% at the State level in 2014 (DES 2016).

Apart from the contribution of agriculture to district GDP, declining inequality of Mandya is also noteworthy. Purushothaman and Patil (2017) compare the regional economy of Mandya with the neoliberal economic drivers of Bengaluru for distributional outcomes. Historically, the society of erstwhile Mysore region has been notably less regressive. Mandya's contemporary society is notably less unequal than the other urbanised study districts of Bengaluru Urban and Rural.

Between 1990 and 2011, the Gini coefficient for rural Mandya declined from 0.28 to 0.23.[20] In terms of land distribution also Mandya seems to be less unequal. In the study villages, 66% of the operated land was with holdings less than 5 acres irrespective of caste. Development status also improved in the same period, with HDI increasing from 0.33 in 1981 to 0.66 in 2014. Despite a relatively benign history as an agrarian society and as a vibrant agricultural economy, Mandya came to be known for farmers' suicides since 2000. The highest number of farmers committing suicides reported in Mandya was in the year 2015.

Financial surplus of households was negative in the irrigated taluk of Pandavapura. Although the ratio of family income to expense was similar in both taluks, the ratio of income to loans was more comfortable in Nagamangala. Larger and frequent loans taken for irrigated cultivation have evidently not been translated into real and lasting prosperity. The dynamism visible in the meandering canals, green fields and sugar factories thus appears deceptive. We take a closer look at other sides of the green countryside of Mandya.

Income Flow

In terms of official statistics on per capita income, Human Development Index and Gross District Domestic Product, Mandya ranks high in the State of Karnataka. The one commonality between the study taluks is the similar share (about 77%) of agriculture in family income. Among the major crops here, the most profitable was mulberry followed by sugarcane and then coconut. Mulberry and sugarcane were mostly cultivated in Pandavapura, while coconut was prominent in Nagamangala.

As indicated above, farm income was important for households in the two different agro-ecologies of Mandya. It is interesting to note the differences in what constitutes the flow of on-farm and off-farm incomes. Firstly, the ratio of income from crop to livestock in the drier agricultural system of Nagamangala was lesser

---

[20]In 2011, Mandya's Gini coefficient, together for urban and rural areas calculated based on per capita expenses, was 0.26 compared to 0.30 for Bengaluru and 0.25 for the State as a whole.

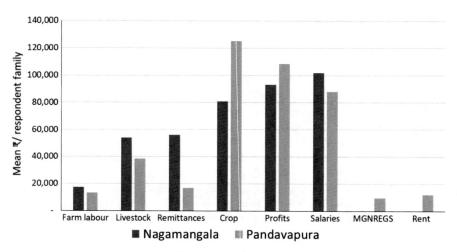

Fig. 8.14 Income sources in the periphery of Mandya.
Source Farmer interviews, 2015

than Pandavapura (0.77 and 1.64 respectively). Secondly, Nagamangala's non-farm income, unlike Pandavapura's, was more from formal employment (Fig. 8.14).[21]

The third major difference is in the financial vulnerability of farm families that we will discuss below.

Farm Loans

Growing sugarcane and rearing silkworms are costly ventures for which farmers rely on credit. Additionally, delay in payment for cane delivered to sugar mills and advances required for cocoon production or any exigencies in the family force them to avail further loans without repaying already outstanding loans.

While Regional Rural Banks (like Kaveri Grameena Bank, Visveswaraya Grameena Bank) and co-operative banks (Canara Co-operative Society, Mandya Co-operative Society) are common in the landscape, respondents predominantly availed loans from non-institutional sources. In the less irrigated Nagamangala, almost no one borrowed from nationalised banks. Relatives formed the single major source of credit in farm households around Mandya, especially in the drier belts (Fig. 8.15). Distressed farmers in the sugar belt of Mandya,[22] especially in Pandavapura, availed loans from money lenders and other informal sources. But according to the data available, half of the total 57 suicides reported in Pandavapura taluk in 15 years since 2003 could be attributed to the burden of formal loans. **In Nagamangala, farmer suicides**

---

[21] Formal sources of non-farm income included salaried jobs. There were teachers, factory supervisors and government employees in Nagamangala. Other sources of income included small businesses and petty shops.

[22] Debt laden farmers committed suicide in Mandya—https://www.thenewsminute.com/article/debt-and-despair-nine-farmers-karnataka-have-committed-suicide-8-days-31821.

8.8 Socio-economic Situation: Deceptive Prosperity

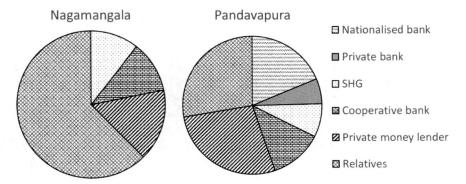

Fig. 8.15 Source-wise overdue loans (% of total loans) in the periphery of Mandya. (SHG—Self-help group for micro credit.)
Source Farmer interviews, 2015

reported in the same period were one-third of what was reported in Pandavapura, questioning the notion that distress is entirely attributable to informal sources of credit as well as lack of irrigation.

About 88 and 77% of respondents from Pandavapura and Nagamangala taluks respectively, had outstanding loans, with an average outstanding amount of ₹2.5 lakhs and ₹1.1 lakhs per family in Pandavapura and Nagamangala respectively. **Though it may not be fully correct to conclude that all overdue loans were availed for investment in agriculture, it is safe to say that farmers in canal irrigated Pandavapura indulged in heavy credit from multiple sources with higher outstanding amounts**.

Education, Health and Housing

Pandavapura has a rich educational history in Vedic studies. Scions of the royal family of Mysore used to stay in Melukote for lessons in philosophy, spirituality and governance. In Nagamangala, *agraharas* set up by the rulers enabled knowledge exchange in many spheres. Although a drier Nagamangala was ranked lower than the irrigated Pandavapura with respect to education infrastructure (District Human Development Report 2014), the farm families studied in Nagamangala were better off in terms of higher education. Similar to other drier landscapes like Magadi growing perennial crops, Nagamangala displays better literacy and non-farm engagement than the irrigated landscapes.

Despite lagging behind in terms of living standards, Nagamangala ranked higher than Pandavapura in terms of health status. Higher expenditure on health care along with other expenses in Pandavapura taluk might be contributing to a dip in financial surplus.

Women in Family Farms

Although, only 16% of total landholdings were legally owned by women, 83% of women workforce was engaged in farm activities (Census of India 2011). Irrespective of a low stake in land ownership, women were the decision makers in 40% of households apart from their engagement in agricultural activities. Women of 20% of households in these taluks worked as farm labour for wages. Though women spent more days in their own farm than men, they also spent a similar number of days in non-farm jobs. Among the respondents, only four to five per cent of the households had women working in the formal sector. Women of irrigated Pandavapura were comparatively more visible in both farm and non-farm activities. Women's collectives were more prominent in Pandavapura than in Nagamangala owing to the presence of active dairy co-operatives and thrift groups. Women in at least 10% of the respondent families were stressed out due to disputes related to land sharing and alcoholism of men in the family. Irrigated Pandavapura taluk recorded relatively more number of crimes against women.[23]

8.9 Migration: Stress and Aspirations

Searching in Mandya town or Bengaluru city, it was difficult to locate farmers migrated from the study villages in Pandavapura and Nagamangala taluks. Out of the eight identified and contacted families who moved out from the villages, five agreed to be interviewed. They had migrated about three years prior to the study. Farm families in Mandya encouraged skilled members to secure a job in the urban formal sector. Migrants generally take their spouse and children along, leaving the extended family and the land behind them.

It is useful to differentiate family members in farm households engaged in non-farm work from farmer migrants. The latter own land in their source villages but live outside and rarely engage in farm operations or share the expenses. They generally receive some produce from their land and in turn extend help to relatives by hosting them for education, hospital visits or job search in the city [resembling Thai families of 'mutual convenience' (Rigg et al. 2018)]. Usually, the share of land owned by the migrant continues to be cultivated by the extended family. On the other hand, non-farm workers who continue to live in their family farms occasionally participate in farm operations and share the expenses regularly.

Outstanding loans and water scarcity were the Stated push factors for migration. Despite seeking a livelihood elsewhere, migrants were worse off in terms of family income (₹62,000 for migrant families compared to ₹2.3 lakhs for farm families). Migrants appeared to be spending less on festivals, transportation and alcohol consumption than farmers (Fig. 8.16). Farmer migrants from this site work as drivers, hospital ward boys, factory helpers in Mandya town or Bengaluru City.

---

[23]While Pandavapura had 306 cases of violence against women, Nagamangala reported 245 such cases between 2009 and 2012 (District Human Development Report 2014).

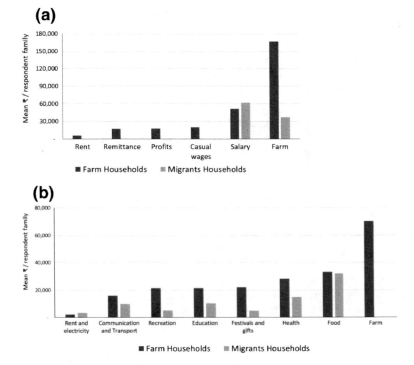

Fig. 8.16 **a** Income sources and **b** expenditure in the periphery of Mandya. *Source* Farmer interviews, 2015

8.10 Agrarian Norms and Institutions

The history of institutions in agrarian Mandya in the last century has been full of dynamic changes. From what used to be a belt of natural and manually constructed tanks and *anicuts* that enshrined co-operation among farmers, an individualised and deskilled agrarian society came to exist alongside some accumulation of capital and many conflicts.

Beneficiaries of very old small-scale tank irrigation projects particularly in Pandavapura taluk meet their irrigation needs without much conflict, even in the absence of formal institutions in water sharing (like water user groups formed by command area authorities). For instance, the Kadalegere lake has an *anicut* built during the late 1950s which is just 30 ft high with one channel of 1 foot by 2 feet running for 10–12 km. This perennial lake irrigates 150 acres downstream belonging to both dominant and marginalised communities. These farmers have an agreement on the frequency and timing of water release to the fields located at the head and tail ends of the channel. Farmers at the head end grow two crops of paddy, while tail-end farmers grow paddy in one season followed by vegetables.

With the major hydroelectric project of KRS coming up in Kannambadi, interState conflicts over Cauvery water became the norm. Furthermore, Mandya saw various social movements. The Irwin Canal agitation of 1932 was against the heavy tax imposed on the irrigated farms for recovering the construction cost of the dam [24] Also, there were movements against seed companies, illegal mining and State policies. These generated sufficient momentum leading to the formation of the Karnataka Rajya Raita Sangha (KRRS) in the 1980s. But KRRS could not sustain the momentum and various splinter factions emerged from it in the due course.

Remnants of old informal social institutions can be found in sharing water. labour, seeds and crop produce. Cultural norms like contributing the first harvest to the local deity followed by a village feast are still in vogue. This custom is observed in different temples run by different castes. Some established norms make penetration of new technology difficult as was the case with Japanese technology for rice cultivation. Women's labour groups (*mahileya kuli Thanda*) who were operating collectively were instrumental in evolving mechanisms to systematically complete paddy transplantation in the whole village in a time-bound fashion. As the technology spread, women's labour collectives disappeared along with folk art forms like songs sung during transplantation and harvest. New social institutions though taking time to emerge effectively, are showing signs of promise. For instance, the new collectives that are being formed (e.g. those under the banners Sahaja Samrudha and Mandya Organics) in making and using organic inputs and aggregating produce from sustainable agriculture.

Groups of villagers regularly but informally gathering to share general information were common in the villages of Mandya. Though these gatherings are not specifically for farming issues, sharing of agricultural information also happens in smaller groups. While input traders were important for both sugarcane and paddy, output traders and processing units were equally significant in Mandya. Traders, especially output traders, are usually migrants from other places who settled in Mandya for trading jaggery, oil, cocoons, etc. Srinivas (1976) gives a brief account of the *Banajiga* traders settled in Mandya. Most traders we interacted with were originally from other States. This invokes continuation of the same phenomenon of cultural diffusion that appears in Srinivas's (1976) Rampura.

The farmers who bridge the gap between their less networked peers and relevant establishments were relatively younger. They were not from any specific caste or community but were found to be holding larger land parcels. These link-farmers were instrumental in helping smaller holders in marketing their farm produce, especially sugarcane.

Social connectedness of migrant farmers at their destinations seems to be less prominent compared to those who stayed back. The few connections that migrants nurtured were generally with labour contracting individuals and agencies as well as panchayat officials. Some migrants from Mandya were in touch with voluntary

---

[24] An old tree standing in the Silver Jubilee Park of Mandya town became the hub of such movements from Irwin Canal agitation onwards and continues to host protests and speeches around inter-State Cauvery dispute.

agencies for upgrading skills necessary for informal sector employment.[25] They tend to shift from one job to another, depriving themselves of leisure and entertainment in daily life, which is reflected in low expenditure incurred on gifts, travel, etc. Accentuated individualisation and reduction in quality of life was thus evident in the life of a farmer migrant.

8.11 Family Farms in a Struggling Agricultural Economy

Mandya town is comparable to any other intermediate or middle town in India. Among the study sites, Mandya is unique in many aspects—it has a long history of canal irrigation, various agro-processing units and pre-independence history of good governance. **Nevertheless, today's agrarian Mandya manifests the ironic coexistence of its notable contribution to the district economy alongside agrarian distress.**

Given the dominance of small family farms in India and the diversity of crops and animals raised in these farms; the logical development strategy should consist of diverse mechanisms for decentralised value addition and processing. This strategy was in discussion during 1930s when Mahatma Gandhi started popularising *Charkha*—the spinning wheel. However, until the heyday of green revolution in Punjab and Haryana, regional economic strategies did not get any serious impetus in most parts of India. What mechanised high-yield farming brought to rural Punjab was only rice and wheat mills—all of which were medium to large scale in their operational capacity. The capacity of modern rice mills in Punjab is about 10 MT/h (Singha 2013). **Even the average capacity of rice mills in Mandya of about 2.5–5 ton/h turn out to be unviable given the uncertain and small-scale cultivation of canal dependent paddy.**

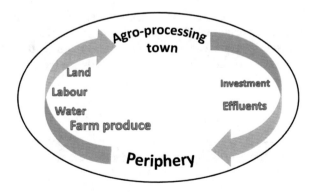

Fig. 8.17 Flows between the agro-processing town and its periphery (Font size indicates relative quantum of flows)

---

[25]For instance, institutions like Janatha Vidya Samsthe, Siri Institute for Rural Development and Sanjeevini Trust in Mandya.

Subsequent waves of agro-processing around the country included sugar mills, milk processing plants, solvent extraction units for oil seeds and pulse mills. In recent times, fruit processing seems to be getting some policy traction.[26] Yet, agricultural inputs and machinery manufacturing units outnumber those that process agricultural produce.[27] This reveals lack of thoughtful developmental action amidst political indifference towards rural well-being in general and specifically to the cause of small farmers and nation's long-term food self-reliance.

We need to critically and carefully look at agricultural dynamism found in Mandya. The core–periphery relations between the agro-processing town of Mandya and family farms around it constitute a regional agricultural economy depicted in Fig. 8.17. The coexistence of various processing units in the region should be potentially capable of sustaining farm income by generating relatively stable demand. Local processing of ragi, paddy and sugarcane seem to fetch relatively stable prices.

Since local consumption and processing of farm produce is relatively high in Mandya, nutrient loss from the agro-ecosystem may not be too high, unlike the agrarian landscapes that completely export their produce. Small capital from such processing towns flows towards their peripheries in the form of investment in farming, small-scale industries or educational institutions. The negative externalities flowing from the town of Mandya to the peripheries are also minimal. Thus, the core and periphery relationship here is non-extractive and fosters forward market linkages. Nevertheless, trapped in intensive farming of paddy and sugarcane, any fluctuation in water availability or prices—rampant in the time of global warming and economic globalisation—hits small farmers very hard, triggering extreme distress.

Comparing the flows between the core and peripheries of Mandya with other regions reveals the varied pattern of inequality across differently urbanising regions. Despite the skewed attention given to unviable intensity of cultivation and scale of processing units, this landscape retains its farmers in their profession in a much more politically empowering fashion than other urban–agrarian interfaces.

Family farms need both output processing units and input suppliers. However, identifying the nature of such forward and backward linkages that will sustain the interest of both producers and consumers in the long run is generally overlooked. Pitching consumer against the producer and the political misuse of concerns around population and food security may backfire because most producers are net consumers themselves.

---

[26]In June 2016, the federal government announced plans to set up 250 clusters of small agro-processing units for perishables at an estimated cost of over ₹50 billion (https://economictimes.indiatimes.com/news/economy/agriculture/government-to-establish-250-agro-processing-clusters-all-over-india/articleshow/52553625.cms).

[27]In Karnataka there were 850 manufacturers of machinery and another 300 farm input manufacturing units compared to around 700 agricultural and food processing units registered in 2015 (Directorate of Economics and Statistics, 2017).

References

Bera, S. (2018). Government set to announce ₹ 83 billion plan to bail out sugarcane farmers. *Livemint.* https://www.livemint.com/Politics/djWk1pzFbnoFMOpEoH1Z5J/Govt-set-to-announce-Rs8000-crore-plan-to-bail-out-sugarcan.html.

Buchanan, F. (1807). *Journey from Madras through Mysore, Canara and Malabar* (Vol. 2, p. 66).

Chandran, R. (2016). Of legends and lakes built by courtesans. *Livemint.* https://www.livemint.com/Sundayapp/MV1aSAEZsc6IFMbf6SbvBO/Of-legends-and-lakes-built-by-courtesans.html.

Epstein, S. T. (1962). *Economic development and social change in South India.* Manchester: Manchester United Press.

Folke, S. (2001). Conflicts over canal water for irrigation in Mandya district, South India. *Journal of Social and Economic Development, 3*(1), 106–120.

Gopal (2018). "Why Farmer suicides have spiked in Karnataka's sugar belt" Hindustan Times. https://www.hindustantimes.com/india-news/why-farmer-suicides-have-spiked-in-karnataka-s-sugar-belt/story-pFKoo2Ey1Zof2qURhBUaZN.html

Govindu, V. M. (2017). 100 years of Champaran and a forgotten figure. *Economic and Political Weekly, 52*(14). Web Exclusive.

Harriss-White, B. (Ed.). (2016). *Middle India and Urban-Rural Development: Four Decades of Change.* Springer Asia Series.

Hettne, B. (1978). *The political economy of indirect rule: Mysore 1881–1947.* London: Curzon Press.

Kashyap, S. & Purushothaman s. (forthcoming). A historical analysis of the agrarian political economy in the erstwhile Mysore region of South India.

Manjunath, A. V., & Ramappa, K. B. (2017). *Farmer suicide in Karnataka.* Bangalore: Institute for Social and Economic Change.

Pani, N. (2017). First nature and the State: Non-emergence of regional capital in Mandya. *Economic and Political Weekly, 52*(46), 73–77.

Purushothaman, S., & Patil, S. (2017). Regional economies and small farmers in Karnataka. *Economic and Political Weekly, 52*(46), 78–84.

Ramachandran, V. K., & Swaminathan, M. (2002). *Agrarian studies.* Manohar Publishers and Distributors.

Rao, C. H. (1943). *History of Mysore (1399–1799 AD)* (Vol. 2, p. 83). Bangalore: The Government Press.

Rice, B. L. (1897). Mysore—A gazetteer compiled for government. In *Mysore by districts* (Vol. 2, p. 286).

Rigg, J., Salamanca, A., Phongsiri, M., & Sripun, M. (2018). More farmers, less farming? Understanding the truncated agrarian transition in Thailand. *World Development, 107,* 327–337.

Sheth, A. (2015). A map that a farmer has committed suicide in every district of Karnataka this year. *The News Minute.*

Silva, E. I. L., Manthrithilake, H., Pitigala, D., Silva, E. N. S. (2014). Environmental flow in Sri Lanka: ancient anicuts versus modern dams. *Sri Lanka Journal of Aquatic Sciences, 19*:3–14.

Singha, K. (2013). *Hulling and milling ratio of major paddy growing States: All India consolidated report.* Bangalore: Institute for Social and Economic Change.

Srinivas, M. N. (1957). Caste in modern India. *The Journal of Asian Studies, 16*(4), 529–548.

Srinivas, M. N. (1976). *The remembered village.* University of California Press.

Swaminathan, M., & Baksi, S. (Eds.). (2017). *How do small farmers fare? Evidence from village studies in India* (p. 355). New Delhi: Tulika Books.

Wilks, M. (1817). *Historical sketches of the south of India in an attempt to trace history of Mysoor* (p. 52). London: Longman.

Chapter 9
Family Farms in Yadgir District

> *"...The modern industrial and social ideal is to suck out everything that is best from the village into the city... Rural life has no separate existence of its own, its existence is for the city. ....It has made our middle class helplessly subservient to employment and service, and has also killed the independence of our peasant proprietor. It has jeopardized food supply, and is fraught with the gravest peril not only to handicrafts but also to our national industry, agriculture.....India will tend to establish a solidarity between the village and the city, the labourer and the employer, the specialist and the layman, the multitude and the genius, the brain worker and the manual labourer."*
>
> Mukerjee (1916)

9.1 Rural Agrarian Towns

With reasonably accessible transportation, infrastructure and communication networks, hardly any area or community remains totally disconnected from the globalised urbanised world. However, regions distant from the centre of political and commercial power continue to be countrysides, unlike the immediate peripheries of metropolitan cities or intermediate towns. With few non-farm employment options and weak development indicators, towns in remote rural locations retain more of their rural nature and culture. They house small buildings that host mostly government agencies (panchayat office, hospital, post office, train and bus stations and market yards) and a few shops selling consumer goods and services like mobile phones or home appliances, apart from a few local markets for perishables, agricultural inputs and equipment. People and produce from the surrounding areas regularly pass through these nondescript towns.

The regions surrounding these minimally urbanised towns usually practise rainfed agriculture in a single farming season. Unlike what Mukerjee (1916—as in the quotation above) expected of cities and villages of India to be, small farmers and the landless in these regions head to big cities for the rest of the year. These are hubs of poverty that attract regular political promises of development like manufacturing

© Springer Nature Singapore Pte Ltd. 2019
S. Purushothaman and S. Patil, *Agrarian Change and Urbanization in Southern India*, India Studies in Business and Economics,
https://doi.org/10.1007/978-981-10-8336-5_9

industries. Yet, functional sources of non-farm employment are conspicuous by their absence. Historically situated in the margins of capital flows, these vast agrarian landscapes (Fig. 9.1) encircle very small statutory towns like the headquarters of economically meek districts or taluks.

The district of Yadgir in North-East Karnataka (NEK) provides us with such an assemblage of a remote town and a rural backdrop, with a different story on the impacts of urbanisation and economic growth, from what Chaps. 6 to 8 revealed.

Yadgir: a rural agrarian landscape

The Kannada speaking areas of the Nizam's Hyderabad province till 1956 form the six districts of present NEK.[1] These six districts that form the poorest and driest parts of the State together with the seven districts of neighbouring Bombay Karnataka region showcase different urbanisation trends and associated agrarian changes. They are distinct from the southern parts of the State (subject of Chaps. 6–8), in the dialect and vocabulary of Kannada, history, cuisine and culture. Many of them are characteristically semi-arid, with low socio-economic indicators. In our typology of urbanising regions, Yadgir qualifies as a rural town. Historically located in the war zone between the Moghuls and the empires south of the Deccan, these were more war ravaged than most parts of erstwhile Mysore State in the south.[2] Agrarian changes around the remote rural town of Yadgir stand apart, with different strengths and different challenges.

The entire area, inclusive of all the three taluks of the present district, was under the kingdom of Shorapur until 1863, when the British annexed and made it into Shorapur district with nine taluks including Gulbarga. In 1873, Gulbarga, under the rule of Nizam, became a separate district with seven taluks. With the reorganisation of the States in 1956, Gulbarga became a Divisional Headquarter in Karnataka State. Later in 2009, Yadgir district was formed with three taluks carved out from Gulbarga district.[3]

Agro-ecologically being in a hot semi-arid region, Yadgir's mean annual temperature soars to 45 °C in summers. Receiving less than 650 mm of mean annual rainfall in a span of 40–50 days from July to September, this region constitutes a distinct agro-ecology in terms of cropping pattern and agricultural cycles. Persisting pastoral tendencies are more visible here than in irrigated production systems. Along with pastoralism, the deep black calcareous and medium red clayey soils makes Yadgir district highly vulnerable to drought (Karnataka Meteorological and Disaster Monitoring Center 2017).

Among the three taluks of the district, though Yadgir hosts more urban population than the other two—Shahpur and Shorapur, it has a similar share of cultivators in total worker population. Since we were looking for remote agrarian locations, we chose Shahpur and Shorapur taluks for detailed study. With a population of over 50,000

---

[1]The six districts of North-East Karnataka are—Bellary, Bidar, Kalaburagi, Yadgir, Raichur and Koppal.

[2]Comparative history of both the regions has been discussed in Chap. 4.

[3]Recently, renamed as Kalaburagi implying stony land.

9.1 Rural Agrarian Towns

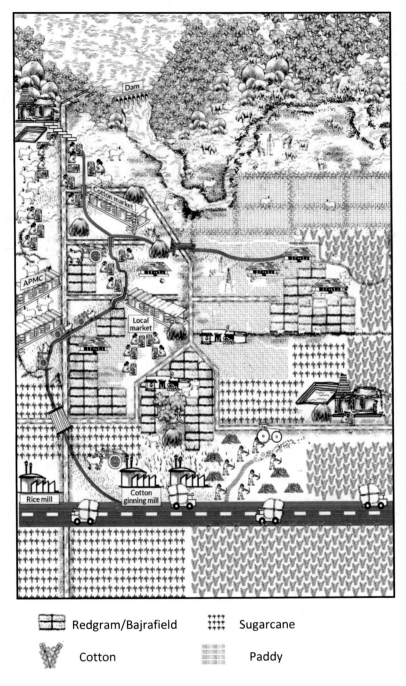

Fig. 9.1 Rural agrarian region

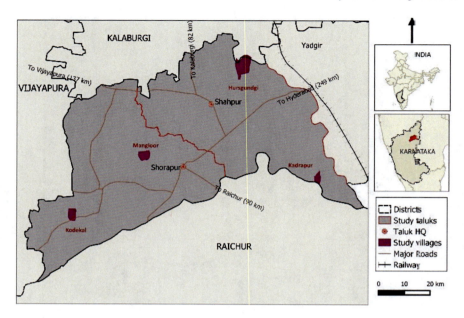

Fig. 9.2 Study villages in Yadgir

in 2011, the headquarters of both these taluks are Class II towns. As discussed in Chap. 3, the process of village selection was based on group interactions conducted in ten villages and covering all eight hoblis in the two taluks. Based on the prevalence of farming as a livelihood option, four villages were selected (Fig. 9.2)—Hurusgundige and Kadrapur from Shahpur taluk and, Kodekal and Mangloor from Shorapur taluk.

In mythology and historical texts, Shahpur, lying in the area between Krishna and Bhima rivers, was known as Sagar or 'Sagara Nadu' and ruled by the Sagara King of Vijayanagara dynasty. Later on under Islamic rulers, it also got the name Nusratabad. Shahpur town, 32 and 82 km away from the district towns of Yadgir and Gulbarga respectively, was formed in 1954 as a Town Municipal Corporation and later upgraded to City Municipal Council in 2015.

Among the well-known places in this taluk is Bendegumbali village known for its houses built without using modern tools and the small village—Sannati, where inscriptions of Emperor Ashoka are found. The cliff resembling sleeping Buddha is a prominent feature of this taluk. The bullock festival lasting for about 10 days hosted annually in Chara Basaveshwara temple conducts cattle trading with thousands of bullocks congregating from surrounding areas (Fig. 9.3).

The hilly terrain of Shahpur hosts a hydropower station—the Bhoruka Power Corporation Ltd.—commissioned in 1997–98 across the Krishna canal in Narayanpur, generating 6.6 MW of electricity annually. The hills of Shahpur are contiguous till Shorapur.

9.1 Rural Agrarian Towns

Fig. 9.3 Stone pulling competition during Chara Basaveshwara *jatre* in Shahpur

Shorapur is a sleepy Town Municipal Corporation located 54 and 108 km from Yadgir and Gulbarga, respectively. Formerly known as Surpur, this hill-locked town is the place where Prince Venkatappa Nayaka fought against the British in 1857.[4] Shorapur kingdom was founded in 1636 by Gaddipida Nayak. From 1703 the *Bedar* (stands for tribal, Bhil, Nayaka, Valmiki communities) kingdom rose and ruled Shorapur up to 1858, with the last king being Nalvadi Venkatappa Nayak. History states that the King, Venkatappa Nayak, was instrumental in constructing tanks and bunds, wells and water stations. Mandakini lake situated inside the Shorapur fort and the lotus lake (*Tavare kere*) beside the fort are the two prominent water bodies of that time. The King also encouraged afforestation as well as initiated measures for soil and land conservation.

Venkatappa Nayak aligned the Southern kings against the British in 1857. After King Venkatappa Nayak was found dead under mysterious circumstances,[5] the British annexed Shorapur in 1858 and British soldiers looted Shorapur homes. The

---

[4] Chiefs of Valmiki community are called Nayaka (Taylor 1920; Khan 1909).

[5] Governor-General Dalhousie asked young Raja Venkatappa Naik of Shorapur to appoint a British officer at his court. The Raja refused and began strengthening his army. The British sent a force under Captain Newberry to capture Shorapur. On 7 February 1858, the *Bedar* army with support from other Principalities retreated to the Wagingera Fort (on the outskirts of Yadgir town surrounded by rocky hills) and waged a fierce battle. On 8 February 1858, the British army with fresh reinforcements besieged the fort at Shorapur. Raja Venkatappa Nayaka fled to Hyderabad where he was summoned by the Military Commission and was sentenced to death. Upon request from Meadows Taylor, the commission reduced punishment to four years to be housed at Kurnool. When he was being escorted to the prison, it is reported that Raja picked up the commander's revolver and shot himself dead.

Table 9.1 Shahpur and Shorapur taluks at a glance

	Shahpur	Shorapur
Total geographical area (TGA in km^2)	1706	1840
Forests, pastures and tree groves (% of TGA)	5.3	6
Net sown area (% of TGA—2015)	70	57
Population density (per km^2—2011)	213	224
Urban population (%—2011)	19	12
Cultivators and farm labour (% of total workers—2011)	74	74
Human Development Index (rank among 176 taluks of Karnataka—2014)	0.303 (161)	0.249 (175)

Source Human Development Report (2014), Census of India (2011) and Agricultural Census (2011)

British declared some of those warring castes as criminal tribes by the Criminal Tribes Act, 1871. Col. Philip Meadows Taylor,[6] appointed by the British as a political agent, questions this pronouncement in his autobiography—*The Story of My Life*. He gives an account of how the *Bedars* were proud of their righteousness and were even reluctant to touch date palms—a common source of intoxicating brew in those times. To quote Taylor on the notification of *Bedars* as criminals:

> '*As a body, the Shorapoor Beydurs had been free from crime. They were not dishonest, and there was no petty thieving or roguery among them; they used to say they were too proud for that sort of thing.*' (Taylor 1920, p. 282)

The history of wars and discrimination against this landscape and people along with the history of lacklustre welfare orientation in governance (for a comparative account of the history of the regions of old Gulbarga and Mysore, see Chap. 4) provides the necessary backdrop to a discussion of the region's current agrarian status seen in the present district of Yadgir. Table 9.1 reflects characteristic features of the two selected taluks.

---

[6]In 1841 upon the demise of Raja Krishnappa Nayak, Philip Meadows Taylor was appointed by the Nizam of Hyderabad as their political agent at Surpur (present Shorapur), as prince Venkatappa Nayaka was just seven years old. Taylor returned to Hyderabad when Raja turned 19. Taylor Manzil, the unique and beautiful bungalow on a rocky hill just outside Surpur town, was built during Taylor's 12 year posting here.

9.2 Farmlands: Larger Parcels and Diverse Communities

Ownership

A distinct feature of landownership pattern in the study villages of Yadgir is the visible presence of lower caste landholders, in accordance with their relative share in the population of these taluks. The share of agricultural land owned by the Scheduled Caste (SC) and Scheduled Tribe (ST) communities was 21 and 25% in Shahpur and Shorapur taluks respectively, with the ST communities holding more land in Shorapur taluk. The dominant communities of *Lingayats*, *Kururbas* and *Reddys* together formed only 40% of landholders with about 70% of farmlands in these taluks. The mean holding size in the two taluks was around a comfortable 2.2 ha, varying from 1.7 ha among SC/ST farmers to 4 ha among farmers from dominant communities of OBC. In terms of number of holdings of the less dominant communities, the major presence in the study villages was of SC (*Maadigas* and *Vaddars* formed 28%) followed by Muslims, General Hindu (about 10% each) and ST (4% *Bedars* and *Lambani*). Most landholders among the less dominant communities in the study villages belonged to SC (Maadigas and Vaddars) followed by Muslims, General Hindu and ST (Bedars and Lambani).

This distribution of land across social groups should be read in the backdrop of a failed land reform agenda in the region. While only 10% of tenancy applications[7] were accepted from Shorapur, in the case of Shahpur it was closer to 20%, which was the average for the then Gulbarga district that these taluks were a part of (Deshpande and Torgal 1994). In the whole district of Gulbarga, only 0.6% of the total declared area for ceiling was distributed, despite a high land inequality during the 1970s with just 4.8% of land held by small and marginal holders who constituted 26% of all landowners. Land distribution improved by 2010, with small and marginal holders constituting 54% of landholders owning around 25% of agricultural land.

Leasing

Land leasing and sharecropping were a common practice in irrigated lands belonging to the respondent farmers in both taluks. During the field survey in 2015, we noticed that while the terms of sharecropping generally followed in cotton varied with the proportion of share in inputs borne by the individuals involved, leasing norms for paddy ranged between ₹2000 and ₹4200 per acre. Leasing generally happens when the family cannot cultivate the entire stretch of land by themselves, a trend found in holdings of about 2 ha held by SC and ST communities. About 61% of all land holdings of the respondents in both taluks were under such arrangements.

Fallowing

District Agricultural statistics in 2014 recorded that about 30% of the net sown area (NSA) in these taluks were left fallow. Large rocks found strewn around pose a

---

[7]Implementation of land reforms in Karnataka State involved receiving applications from tenants claiming ownership rights over the land they cultivated.

major deterrence to cultivation. We found a significantly high incidence of fallowing in the relatively less irrigated Shahpur taluk. Thus, apart from the issues of land distribution and acquisition for non-farming purposes, productivity of farmlands was also a concern. This is where village commons are supposed to prove useful by providing supplementary sources of water, fodder, fuelwood, fruits and other bio-resources for human and animal use.

Land conversion

Land acquisition started happening since the 1990s, though it was minimal. Agricultural lands in the study taluks have been acquired by the Upper Krishna Project (UKP).[8] Nearly 123 ha of land in Shahpur were acquired for canals of UKP Phase II in 1992. About 470 ha in 2005 in Shahpur and 1200 ha of farmlands in Shorapur were acquired for UKP Phase III. Yadgir taluk also reports on-going acquisition of more than 3000 acres for an industrial park[9] and other manufacturing establishments, expected to generate more than 12,000 jobs. In 2016, it was estimated that about 1000 acres would be used for a textile park and 500 acres for pharmaceutical industries. So far the employment generation in the industrial sector has been negligible.[10]

9.3 Nature's Commons: Limestone Deposits and Deep Black Soils of Shorapur Doab

The predominant hill ranges of Yadgir district are in Shahpur and Shorapur taluks. The meagre forest cover in the district of about 6% of the total geographical area, is mostly of the mixed firewood type. Shorapur is rich in pastures and groves. Barren uncultivable land in Shorapur, despite its vast irrigated area, is about four times more than that in Shahpur. While limestone deposites are found in both the taluks, uranium has been discoverd in Shahpur and building stone (*Shahabad*) are abundent in Shorapur. Generally, the presence of lime content in acidic black soil is known to be good for its fertility, but lime embedded in the stones forms a hindrance to crop cultivation. Soil with limestone is suitable only for dryland crops such as groundnut,

---

[8]The Upper Krishna Project consists of two dams constructed across the river Krishna and a network of canals. The main storage is at Alamatti Dam, a few kilometres downstream of the confluence of Ghataprabha and Krishna rivers. A lower dam, Basava Sagara dam, situated at Narayanpur a few kilometres downstream of the confluence of Malaprabha and Krishna rivers, serves as a diversion dam. The Project was planned to be implemented in different Stages and Phases. Stage-I of the project utilised 119 TMC of water to irrigate 4.25 lakh hectares and in Stage-II, 54 TMC of water is utilised to irrigate 1.97 lakh hectares. Thus, the command areas in the drought-prone districts of Northern Karnataka viz. Gulbarga, Yadgir, Raichur, Bijapur and Bagalkot are irrigated under UKP Stage-I and II with total utilisation of 173 TMC water.

[9]Yadgir Industrial Park was promoted in 2016 encouraging investors to move away from Bengaluru—https://www.thehindubusinessline.com/news/national/yadgir-industrial-hub-attracts-13500crore-investments/article8140895.ece.

[10]In 2012, only 1200 workers were employed with 290 registered industrial units—http://dcmsme. gov.in/dips/DIP-%20Yadgir.pdf.

9.3 Nature's Commons: Limestone Deposits and Deep Black Soils ...

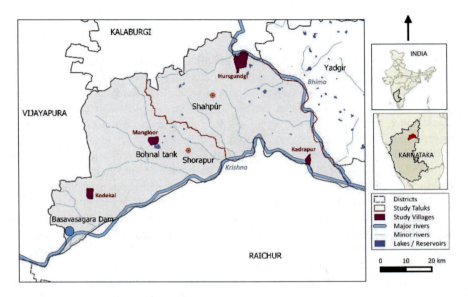

Fig. 9.4 Lakes and streams in Shahpur and Shorapur

safflower and red gram. But limestone deposites supply raw material for cement factories in and around Yadgir and Gulbarga, or for building construction. Though the region has very little forest and grazing lands, it has abundant water resources. Bhima flows along the eastern boundary between Shahpur and Yadgir taluks and Krishna to the south of Shorapur and Shahpur taluks (Fig. 9.4). Referred to as 'Shorapur Doab', the beak-shaped land with black cotton soils of more than 1 m depth lying between the two rivers is known for its fertility and suitability for crops such as millets, groundnut and cotton (Paddayya 1977).

During the fifteenth and sixteenth centuries, rulers of Bahmani kingdom built water tanks to store rainwater in the erstwhile Gulbarga region of which study taluks were part of. Major tanks near Shorapur like the Bohnal tank were built by Adil Shah and minor tanks by local *zamindars*.[11]

Other water bodies include many lakes and, more commonly, open wells.[12] Various water resources including rivers and tanks provided irrigation in about 64% of NSA in the two taluks in 2014 (District at a Glance 2015), 87% of which has been double cropped from 2000 onwards. Thus, while grazing continues to be dependent on village commons, extraction of limestone and criss-crossing irrigation canals are shrinking the natural resource base under the collective use of communities around.

---

[11] Bohnal tank was renovated by Surpur King Nayaka in the seventeenth century, later expanded by Meadows Taylor and converted to a bird sanctuary in 2010.

[12] District at a Glance (2015) reports 50 lakes and 1200 open wells in Shahpur and 26 lakes and 1147 open wells in Shorapur. Wells in these parts of the State are bigger and used historically for irrigation. According to State Agricultural Statistics (2015), mean area irrigated by each well was 2.96 ha, compared to 1.02 ha per well in the State as a whole, in 2014–15.

9.4 Irrigation: Favouring Intensive Crops

With shallow water tables, irrigation in old Gulbarga region was notable for its use of dug wells and tanks. With the ground water table at 30–50 ft, Shahpur has shallow wells of 20 ft depth yielding yearlong supply of water. In the early twentieth century, nearly 56% of the total irrigated area of 38,000 acres in the district of Gulbarga was using water from open dug wells and 40% from tanks (Khan 1909). Based on information from other Gazetteers (Husain 1940; Sathyan 1966), the following is the irrigation history of the two study taluks part of old Gulbarga district.

In 1939, Shahpur's 2148 acres of irrigated lands were dependent exclusively from tanks. In the next three decades, wells took over 22% of irrigation in Shahpur. By the 1960s, irrigation by wells increased in Shahpur and tank commands reduced.

Shorapur was devoid of irrigation sources till the advent of Upper Krishna Project (UKP) in the 1990s. Canal irrigation first came to Shorapur taluk through Basava Sagara dam as part of UKP (Narayanpur Left Bank Canal) during 1992 and spread to Shahpur in 1995 by which time the canals had become the largest mode of irrigation in both the taluks (Fig. 9.5). Canals of about 76 km length came up in Shorapur and Shahpur on land acquired from private farm holdings, forest and other government lands.

Presently the two study taluks in Yadgir are no longer using tanks and wells and are embracing extensive irrigation by canals (Fig. 9.6).

By 2014, out of the overall irrigated area (55% of NSA) of Yadgir district, 79% was under canal irrigation. Shorapur taluk is relatively wetter in terms of the extent of irrigated land and in terms of the share of irrigated land in net sown area. Currently, 64% of NSA in both study taluks is under irrigation. It was only 9.3% till 1981 (Gulbarga District Gazetteer 1995). In three and a half decades, the share of irrigated area increased close to seven-fold.

The spread of canal irrigation in this region happened amidst concerns over its suitability for the soils of the area—deep black calcareous and medium deep red

Fig. 9.5 Basava Sagara dam in Shorapur taluk

9.4 Irrigation: Favouring Intensive Crops

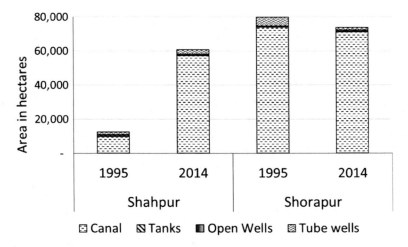

Fig. 9.6 Source wise irrigation in Shahpur and Shorapur.
Source District at a Glance (1995, 2015)

clay. With swelling and shrinking habits in wet and dry conditions, the soils here call for careful irrigation practices.[13] Spread of canal irrigation discouraged people from using water judiciously (Wallach 1985). Since 1995, the entire region adopted paddy as its major crop. When farmers at the tail end of the canal command faced 'canal or irrigation drought', open wells came to the rescue. Over 35,000 acres of land were affected by salinity in the command area of UKP due to indiscriminate use of water for cultivating paddy.

We now focus on the major agricultural transformation happening in the region triggered by paddy, the sign of 'prosperity' in conventional agricultural parlance.

9.5 Farming Systems: Declining Jowar and Disappearing Groundnut

A rocky terrain scattered with shrub wood commons, clayey soil, scanty rainfall and shallow water tables together used to determine the kind of crops and animals farmed in this landscape. Paleontological evidence from Kodekal region of Shorapur taluk suggests domestication, introduction and spread of ragi, jowar and green gram in Shorapur doab during Neolithic times (Paddayya 1977). Present cropping and culinary pattern continue to have jowar and green gram, but ragi seems to have disappeared from the land and foodscape of the region. Jowar still forms an essential part of food and farming though the crop is losing acreage. Rice is increasing its

---

[13] https://www.thehindu.com/todays-paper/tp-national/tp-karnataka/Change-in-cropping-pattern-threatens-fertility-of-soil/article15278929.ece.

presence on farmland and in culinary habits. Jowar had completely disappeared from the Shorapur farms we surveyed, similar to how the groundnut disappeared from villages of Shahpur. This corroborates the agricultural census data presented in Fig. 9.7.

Data for the year 1939 (Husain 1940) shows that jowar, cotton and red gram dominated Yadgir's agriculture, when paddy was only 0.55% of sown area and irrigation was mostly from tanks. Net sown area of the district increased from 1939 till 1995 and then it began to decline. Hence, the increase in irrigation and change in crops that happened later was more about substitution of crops (Fig. 9.7) than about additional area under cultivation or about increase in crop yield. Extensive area under paddy largely came from jowar, while it also displaced bajra and groundnut.

Currently, cotton is the first major crop in Shahpur followed by paddy and vice versa in Shorapur, where canal irrigation is more widespread. Thus, from a jowar-cotton landscape it became a paddy or cotton dominated system. Red gram, jowar and ground nut formed the third tier of the cultivated area, in that order of prominence.

Prominent annual crop cycle in the irrigated lands of Shorapur appears to be two crops of paddy, while in Shahpur it is mainly cotton all through the year (Fig. 9.8). The rainfed cropping cycle is the same in both taluks with a short summer crop of green gram or sunflower followed by bajra or red gram in the kharif season and jowar, groundnut or bajra in the rabi season.

The current cropping pattern in the study villages largely matches with the pattern seen in the taluk as a whole in 2014 (Fig. 9.7), except that the actual extent of paddy is not reflected in farmholdings that we studied. This is because paddy was being cultivated on land leased by farmers from Andhra. This practice was more prevalent in Shorapur where land parcels were larger in size and irrigated (Fig. 9.9).

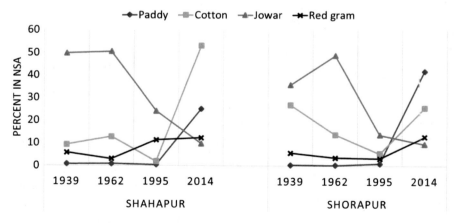

Fig. 9.7 Shift in major crops in Shahpur and Shorapur.
(Green gram, ragi and groundnut are negligible at present.)
Source Agriculture Census (1995, 2011) and District at a Glance (2015)

9.5 Farming Systems: Declining Jowar and Disappearing Groundnut

Fig. 9.8 Cropping season in Yadgir—**a** irrigated paddy, **b** rainfed sorghum

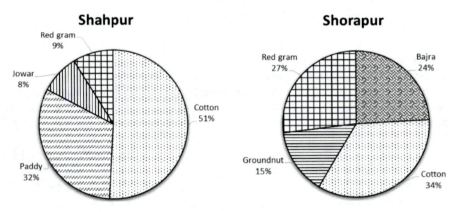

Fig. 9.9 Cropping pattern in the periphery of Yadgir (% of land cultivated by respondents).
Source Farmer interviews (2015)
(The year 2015 was declared as drought year, reducing paddy area considerably from previous years.)

According to the Gulbarga District Gazetteer (2004, p. 155), paddy was not included in the recommendations by the University of Agricultural Sciences, Dharwad and the Department of Agriculture for this region based on the soil pattern. With the spread of canal irrigation, a package of practices for paddy is now being recommended for the region by the farm varsities.

9.5.1 Spread of Paddy in Semi-arid Yadgir

Till the late 1990s, paddy was almost non-existent in the region comprising today's Yadgir district. After the Alamatti irrigation project across Krishna River, it began to spread at a rapid pace in all three taluks of the district. By 2014, Shorapur taluk located at the head end of Basava Sagara dam that was established in 1982 at Narayanpur had 68% of net sown area (NSA) under paddy. What did this spectacular shift in farming pattern within a span of a decade mean to the local communities?

Paddy—a sign of prosperity in conventional agricultural parlance—was a new crop for the soils and for the farmers who were engaged in rainfed farming. The farmers lacked skills and resources to cultivate this demanding crop. In what appeared to be a fortunate circumstance, enterprising Reddys experienced in cultivating irrigated paddy started moving in from neighbouring districts. Reddys started buying land or engaging in oral land leasing in the command area of Alamatti and Basava Sagara dam. Local rainfed farmers found it easier to migrate in search of other occupations which although unfamiliar, would not demand capital investment. Some of them also tried their hands at this lucrative crop with borrowed money. Thus, loans and out-migration became hallmarks of this region, reaching a peak during the period from 2005 to 2015.[14] While seasonal out-migration was an old phenomenon, indebtedness from irrigated commercial farming was a new push factor. Still, migration from here was mostly seasonal confined to the lean season for wage labour as paddy is taken only in one season annually.

Thus irrigation-induced social differentiation had an unexpected pattern here. The commoditisation of head end farms along with the influx of resourceful farmer migrants from Andhra co-existed with increased circular migration of land-owning farmers at the tail end of canals. Mollinga's (1998) study in the Bhadra commands of Raichur draws a similar conclusion on migration of smallholders but stops short of attributing a push factor to the supposedly 'progressive' measure of canal irrigation.

More than a decade later, locals now feel confident to cultivate paddy. This is reversing the sociology of holdings—Reddy camps are moving to more recently irrigated areas of the neighbouring district of Bijapur or back to their native places. What is of interest here is not just the sociology of paddy growing in Yadgir, but the ecological and cultural repercussions of this watershed development in the recent agricultural history of Yadgir.

Twists and turns in the purpose of irrigation and dams

The historical purpose of dams here was to provide lifesaving irrigation in times of drought for the vast expanse of rainfed crops. After severe famines and disease outbreaks in the mid-nineteenth century, the British proposed many minor and major irrigation projects in the Krishna basin to support traditional food crops like jowar, bajra and pulses. Planning for large irrigation projects in the sub-basin of Bhima started in the late 1800s with a continued thrust on dry-land crops. Wallach (1985) speaks of how the huge investment in big dams and the consequent expectation of revenue in all seasons made the practice of light irrigation by tanks and open wells redundant. **Since jowar and bajra did not require irrigation when rainfall is normal, the dam authorities had to incentivise farmers to cultivate water-**

---

[14]Information from interactions with farmers and local researchers.

9.5 Farming Systems: Declining Jowar and Disappearing Groundnut

intensive crops like paddy and sugarcane for revenue generation throughout the year. This proved to be an irreversible pattern, even in times of drought.

Irrigated black cotton soils are difficult to work on. Yet, farmers at the head end persisted (or had no other choice) in growing irrigated paddy, leaving the tail end farms as dry as ever. As Wallach noted, the revenue generation objective of dams that tied the irrigation management tightly with water-guzzling crops defied the primary objective of dams. Mollinga (1998) reaffirmed this complexity, pointing to the socio-geographical dimensions of agrarian differentiation as a constraint for management reform in irrigation.

Citing research findings and discussions, Wallach (1985) and Mollinga (1998) also bring out the need for judicious irrigation on deep black cotton soils to avoid salinity and yield reduction through protective rather than productive irrigation.[15] These precautions were totally absent in farmers' fields where the study took place. There is anecdotal evidence on reduced productive capacity of the soil as a result of continuous flooding and intensive fertiliser use for a decade in the deep clayey soils of Yadgir, along with loss of biodiversity (Attri and Nautiyal 2016). However, there is no serious academic discussion regarding this.

The dominance of low-value rainfed crops in NEK was more a sign of agro-ecological prudence than that of resource scarcity. Dug open wells were abundant in Hyderabad–Karnataka that enabled lifesaving irrigation for dry crops without jeopardising long-term productivity of soil, culinary habits or household finances. The jowar-bajra-pulses culinary culture in the semi-arid landscape of Yadgir has been changing drastically, along with the spread of irrigation and paddy. Most paddy farmers are from the dominant Lingayat and Reddy castes.

Irrigation schemes in independent India have had an obvious welfare thrust and this is again seen in its trysts with green revolution measures. Canal irrigation came late to Yadgir, in an apparent vacuum of ecological and historical stock-taking. It could well be suspected that the consequences of rapid expansion in flood irrigation and the consequent spread of paddy were far from what is expected in terms of agrarian outcomes—not just in distribution of benefits but also in the revenue generation aspect. **Shorapur in the nineteenth century was not known for its poverty when it was growing mostly rainfed millets and pulses . By the late twentieth century, the district was declared as one of the poorest taluks in the State of Karnataka (District Gazetteer 1984).**

Changing nature of irrigation and related policies with disastrous consequences is not new to the region. Comments made by the colonial administrators in the region on East India Company's mismanagement of land taxes and irrigation systems reinforce this fact. To quote Taylor (1920), '… *whole villages which once yielded handsome*

---

[15]Protective irrigation refers to supplementary source of water applied as per requirement. It covers maximum possible area and protects crops against soil moisture deficiency. Productive irrigation with higher water input per unit area aims at achieving high productivity.

revenues are little better than heaps of rubbish'. Such observations were available on other areas in the region along the Kurnool-Cuddapah canal.[16]

In order to avoid such huge failures, the Irrigation Commission (1900–03) and the Royal Commission on Agriculture (1927) advised the British Indian Government to consult the prospective beneficiaries. Yet, commissions and policies post-1947 did not consult dryland farmers in any reasonable fashion. **The saga of good intentions, like avoidance of famines and increasing farmers' income leading to unintended consequences like loss in soil fertility and indebtedness, continues. This is even more of a threat now, in the backdrop of a widespread disabling of critical thinking about the popular mode of productive irrigation.**

The ecological, financial and culinary changes that came with paddy in Yadgir may have a silver lining. The relatively better income from paddy compared to millets has probably improved school enrolment rates (Jacob et al. 2015).[17] But, for how long will this costly experiment continue to yield a slightly better cash flow? Experience from other irrigated black cotton soils is not too promising.[18]

9.5.2 Land of Cattle Fairs and Festivals

Yadgir farmers, like in most places of NEK, keep large herds of native breed cattle along with a few heads of exotic and high yielding milch animals. A typical herd possessed by households in the study villages consisted of six large ruminants of indigenous variety and around 20 small ruminants. With harsh climate and soil conditions, the region is not considered suitable for high yielding milch cattle. Hence, dairy societies were absent in the villages studied. Livestock Census (2012) also shows the dominance of native stock of cattle and sheep in Yadgir. Thus, the purpose of keeping livestock was either for draught power or for liquid cash in times of need. Some households rent out their draught animals earning almost 27% of farm income from it with the daily rent ranging from ₹700 to ₹1200 for a pair of bullocks. Shahpur hosts more large animals (cows and bulls) as well as small ruminants like goats and sheep compared to Shorapur taluk.

The cattle market facilitated by APMC in Hunsagi village of Shorapur taluk is particularly noteworthy. Every week close to 10,000 animals are traded in this market including Hallikar cows, bullocks, buffaloes, goats and sheep. Another big fair of local cattle is organised once in three years during the famous *Allamprabha jatre* near Kadrapur village. Along with the annual bullock festival in Chara Basaveshwara temple, the above two cattle markets make Yadgir buzzing with activities around livestock (Fig. 9.10).

---

[16]Questioned by the irrigation commission (1903) on the benefits to farmer in growing rice, Deputy Collector in charge of Kurnool-Cuddapah canal replied '... *their dry crops pay them better'*.

[17], In our study taluks rainfed areas show better literacy rate.

[18]See Mollinga (1998) and Singh (2005, pp. 209–212) for experience from irrigating black cotton soils in command areas of Tungbhadra, Krishna and Godavari.

9.5 Farming Systems: Declining Jowar and Disappearing Groundnut

Fig. 9.10 Cattle fair near Kadrapur

Having discussed the larger context of land, water and farming, we now get into the operational aspects of Yadgir's agriculture—inputs, labour and marketing.

9.6 Running Cost: Increasing with Irrigation

Among the major reigning crops, cotton and paddy were the costliest to grow (Fig. 9.11). Fertiliser and pesticide usage were highest for cotton. Cotton farmers among the respondents applied 320 and 470 kg of complex fertilisers for an acre of dry and irrigated cotton respectively, while the recommended package is only 80 and 120 kg respectively. Paddy received 250 kg of fertiliser per acre (against the recommended 66 kg). This high level of fertiliser application has an impact on the water quality of the region. Groundwater in Shorapur tested for pollution (2010) reveals high levels of nitrate.[19]

Inputs required for cotton and paddy are usually procured in bulk from local private dealers. On the other hand, inputs for food crops like red gram, jowar and bajra were usually bought from *Raita Samparka Kendra* (RSK). Many a time the input dealer himself doubles up as the output dealer too. He would give the required inputs on credit, with a buyback condition at a price decided by him during the early stages of cultivation.

Unlike what was recommended by the University of Agricultural Sciences, application of farmyard manure was negligible and confined to irrigated cotton and red

---

[19] Study taluks with 273 kg of fertiliser use per ha of net sown area as well as the whole district of Yadgir with 204 kg/ha rank high in the State. Water quality impact of this high level of application has been reported. https://www.thehindu.com/todays-paper/tp-national/tp-karnataka/Alarming-chemical-content-in-Surpur-water/article16528900.ece.

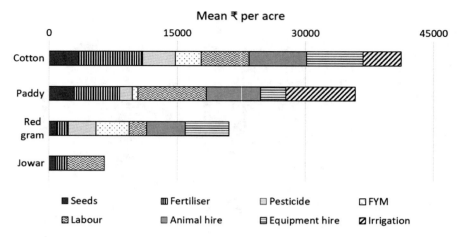

Fig. 9.11 Input costs incurred by respondent families in Yadgir.
Source Farmer interviews (2015)

gram in rainfed fields. This could be linked to the shift from rainfed agricultural systems that depended on residual soil moisture, requiring little input. In the new irrigated systems, use of farmyard manure and vegetative biomass are meagre. Free grazing native breeds that dominate these systems make collection of dung and farmyard manure difficult. When such intrinsically low-input systems with sufficient seasonal fallow periods for soil replenishment, change into input intensive irrigated systems with high cropping intensity,[20] nutrient imbalance is a fallout. Study areas with relatively low extent of forest and dedicated pastures depend on seasonal fallows for free-grazing local breed livestock. Cattle grazing on seasonal fallows in-turn used to ensure soil fertilisation needed for the rainfed crops.

9.7 Labour: Seasonal Circulation Between Farm and Non-farm Work

Almost a third of the working population in both the taluks together was engaged in agriculture (Fig. 9.12). While the number of people dependent on agriculture increased in the decade since 2001, their share in total workers has marginally declined. Interestingly, more number of people were engaged in non-farm work at least for few months every year, in Shorapur than in Shahpur. Working members of a typical farm family in Yadgir spend about 105–140 days on their own farm, 90–140 days as farm labour and about 80 days in non-farm work. While on-farm engagement in own farm was high in the study villages of Shahpur, engagement in off-farm wage labour was high in Shorapur.

---

[20]Cropping intensity is high when the same land is cultivated multiple times in an year.

9.7 Labour: Seasonal Circulation Between Farm and Non-farm Work

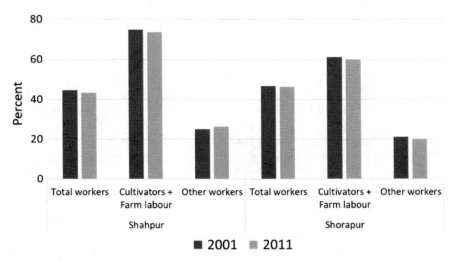

Fig. 9.12 Employment pattern in Shahpur and Shorapur taluks.
(Total workers as proportion of total population. Cultivators + Farm labour and Other workers as proportion in Total workers.)
Source Census of India (2001, 2011)

Most respondents we interviewed were engaged either in casual jobs or farm labour. Each family has at least two members, usually a man and woman, engaged fully in taking care of their farmland. Thus, a typical farm family needed only 30 days of hired farm labour. Around 40% of the respondent families had members engaged in off-farm labour inside or outside the village. The wage labourers usually came from Dalit and tribal families with smaller land holdings. About 70% of the households interviewed had at least one member seasonally migrating to cities like Pune or Bengaluru for construction work. These trends were similar across Shahpur and Shorapur.

The two major commercial crops—paddy and cotton—need more hired labour than other crops such as jowar, red gram, bajra and groundnut. Paddy was generally grown in the larger holdings of OBC communities whereas cotton was grown by all communities. While irrigated farms paid higher wages than rainfed farms, the gender gap remained, with women's wages being three times lower than that of men in both irrigated and rainfed farms. The trends, drivers and fallouts of the well-known existence of migration from this region will be examined later in this chapter.

9.8 Women in Farm Households: Burdened and Discriminated

Nearly 85% of the female workforce in study taluks was in agricultural sector according to Census 2011. However, only about 16% of total landholdings covering 15% of area were wholly owned by women in the study taluks irrespective of caste (Agricultural Census 2015).

In terms of literacy status, Yadgir district is ranked lowest in Karnataka. Out of all the interviewed households, around 57% of women and 42% of men were illiterate. Irrespective of caste, average formal education was three and six years respectively, for women and men. Maximum education among women members in the families we interviewed was class 10 and it was undergraduate degree among men.

Marrying off under-aged girls was common especially in areas from where out-migration was high.[21] In the year 2016, the highest number of child marriages in the State was from Yadgir.[22] Domestic violence and alcoholism were common and polygamy was not rare in certain communities in this study site. However, women were reluctant to talk about these and alcohol was held culprit. *Stree Shakti Sanghas* were more active in Dalit and Adivasi communities, though their activities confined to savings and credit.

Women in the less irrigated belts worked for considerably more number of days on their land. For the remaining part of the year, women engage in wage labour mostly in farm work in the village. Women in skilled or salaried jobs and small enterprises were very rare in this site. Open grazing of local cattle remains a predominantly male domain in and around Yadgir as is marketing the farm produce.

9.9 Regulated Markets: Dominating the Agricultural Marketing Scene

Being a semi-arid agrarian region producing grains, pulses and cotton, perishable products are minimal in Yadgir, thereby diminishing the role of weekly *santhe*. Regulated markets are the prominent marketing spaces in the district (Fig. 9.13). Except for rice mills and some ginning units, processing enterprises are non-existent. About 15–20 small and large rice mills and four cotton ginning units established since the year 2000 are currently functional in the district. Marketable surplus with respondent farmers for paddy, red gram and jowar was about 90, 50 and 45% of the production respectively. Bajra was mostly for consumption, whereas cotton was only for commerce.

---

[21] Report about crushing poverty in six districts of NEK forcing under-aged girls into early marriage and motherhood—https://www.thehindu.com/todays-paper/tp-opinion/Reluctant-mothers/article17286108.ece.

[22] Karnataka accounted for 23% of child marriages reported in India (Karnataka State Commission for Protection of Child Rights).

9.9 Regulated Markets: Dominating the Agricultural Marketing Scene

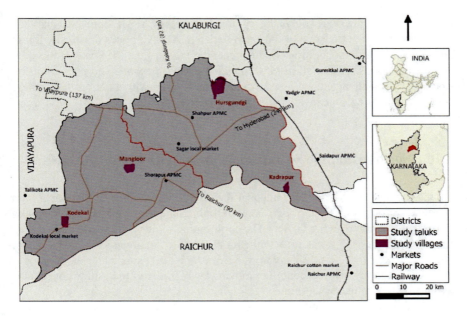

Fig. 9.13 Regulated markets in and around Yadgir

Fig. 9.14 Roadside marketing of cotton and a ginning unit around Yadgir

With increasing spread of irrigation from Krishna, markets in Shorapur started gearing up for paddy transactions.[23] Paddy and cotton were traded in APMCs, but transported directly to and billed at the rice mills and ginning units, respectively. Most often, mill owners would send trucks and porters equipped with gunny bags and other transporting material directly to farms. So farmers avoid transportation charges but loses out on the best possible price that a process of bidding by the traders could fetch. Private trader doubled up as money lender (*savukar*) for cotton and paddy and often fixed prices at the initial stage of crop itself, pretty much like input dealers (Fig. 9.14).

---

[23]President of Shorapur APMC: '… around the year 2000, we had hardly 100 traders and commission agents. Now there are more than 600 commission agents and around 300 traders for paddy in Shorapur market alone'.

Red gram and jowar are sold in the regulated markets of APMC or in local markets, as well as to private traders. For red gram traded in APMC, prices drastically fell in 2017 despite drought conditions in the preceding years as the MSP was reduced by 50%. The reasons for the fall in MSP included a ban on exports and restrictions on stocking by private agencies. This left red gram growers with a net profit of barely ₹600 per quintal even in an year of bumper crop.[24]

9.10 Socio-economic Situation: Mounting Debt and Distress

Yadgir society seems to be less unequal than the State as a whole, but has a high incidence of poverty.[25] Yet, Yadgir is close to the State average in terms of growth in per capita income and in GDP.[26] The contribution of agriculture and animal husbandry to Yadgir's GDP was 15%, while for the State it was about 9% in 2015 About 70% of respondents' family income was from farming. Thus, while the State was more influenced by district economies moving away from farming, study households remained predominantly agrarian.

The study villages are among the poorest in terms of housing, distance to schools, school enrolment as well as rate of school drop-out. These parameters varied between villages, especially between irrigated and rainfed areas. In terms of income, education and health indices (child and maternal mortality rate), Shahpur with a relatively larger urban population performed better than the tribal populated Shorapur. Also, though Shorapur is better irrigated than Shahpur, it has water quality issues.

Pockets in the districts were home to weaver communities of *Neikars*. Weaving occupation is in duress mainly due the negligent attitude of the State and society towards the handloom sector. The proposed industrial park of more than 3000 acres with about 1000 acres earmarked for textile industries is expected to '... *improve the condition of cotton growers and weavers, besides generating employment for a large number of people*'.[27] Skilled in weaving cotton on handloom, the *Neikars* have been reluctant to take up the not so lucrative option of farming. Some *Neikar* households

---

[24]Report explains how an increase in production did not compensate fall in price of red gram—https://www.financialexpress.com/opinion/deal-with-dal-how-processors-jack-up-prices-during-lean-seasons/528481/.

Farmers failed to take informed decisions based on the likely future price and not based on previous year's market price. More details at https://www.business-standard.com/article/economy-policy/drop-in-pulse-prices-despite-good-rains-reveals-india-s-flawed-agri-policy-117041200154_1.html.

[25]Gini coefficients calculated based on per capita expenses in 2012 was 0.199 in Yadgir compared to 0.254 for the State. Human Development Index for Yadgir was 0.28, while for the State it was 0.519 in 2014.

[26]Since 2009 when Yadgir came to exist as a separate district, per capita income increased at an annual rate of about 21.5% and GDP grew by 18.5% for both Yadgir and the State till 2015.

[27]https://www.thehindubusinessline.com/news/national/yadgir-industrial-hub-attracts-13500crore-investments/article8140895.ece.

9.10 Socio-economic Situation: Mounting Debt and Distress

continue to weave cloth under the State governments' *Khadi Gram Udyog* initiative encouraged by a local voluntary agency—Sarvodaya.[28]

Surprisingly, Yadgir's poor human and social development indicators did not result in farmers' distress and suicide till 2015. However, between 2015 and 2017, the district witnessed 171 farmer suicides. In the following sections, we take a further look at the varied angles of distress in Yadgir, starting from the precariousness of small farming. Thereafter we examine migration that makes little contribution to the economy of family farms.

Income flow

Families with higher dependence on farming appeared better off in terms of income (Fig. 9.15). The share of farm income (crops and livestock) in total income was 87 and 53% in Shahpur and Shorapur, respectively, and the total household income of farmers in Shahpur taluk was 30% higher.

Compared to the paddy dominated Shorapur villages, villages in Shahpur, with significant area under rainfed cotton were better off in terms of education and health indicators as well as total family income and farm income. Among the respondent farms, the net income from an acre of rainfed cotton was about 15% higher than that from paddy. In the context of Shorapur's lacklustre farm economy, farm households earned from petty trading including mechanic and electrical shops, livestock trading and farm wages. This diversity in the livelihood basket perhaps points towards lower levels of extreme farm distress in Shorapur.

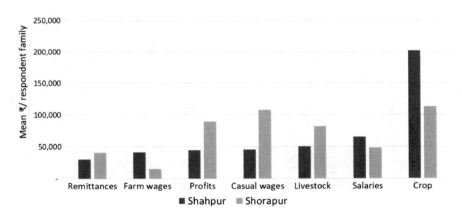

Fig. 9.15 Income sources in Yadgir.
Source Farmer interviews (2015)

---

[28] Any employment generation scheme that does not revive and strengthen diverse skilled occupations in rural India generally remains ad hoc and patchy in impact. For instance, even the ambitious and widely implemented scheme like MGNREGS (Narayanan et al. 2014; Breitkreuz et al. 2017). Joblessness for the masses, intrinsic to the neo-liberal economic model that displaces these livelihood options is well-known now (Sanyal 2007, pp. 245–247; State of Working India 2018).

Expenditures were highest for farming followed by medical treatment. Expenditure on mobile phones was relatively high in Yadgir villages on account of out-migrant members. Reportedly, mobile usage in Yadgir is second highest in the State after Bengaluru.[29] Much like migrants, pastoralists also find mobile phones very useful.

From the discussions so far, we find negative financial surplus prevailing among households in both the taluks, with incidence of extreme distress occurring more in the cotton dominated Shahpur.

Farm loans

Respondent farm families had outstanding loans of ₹1.4 lakhs on an average, taken for various purposes from multiple sources. Though incomes were higher in Shahpur, there was not much difference between the two taluks in terms of the outstanding amount and sources of loan. Outstanding crop loans from formal sources such as nationalised banks and SHGs were universal. But relatives emerge as the first major credit source, followed by private money lenders, SHGs and co-operative banks (Fig. 9.16).

Loans taken for farm and non-farm purposes not only push migration but also emerge as the major cause of farmers' distress. Almost 85% of reported farmers' suicides in last three years from both taluks were attributed to indebtedness.[30] Among the loans taken for non-farm purposes (18 out of 41), most were for wedding ceremonies in the family, and the remaining for house construction, medical expenditure

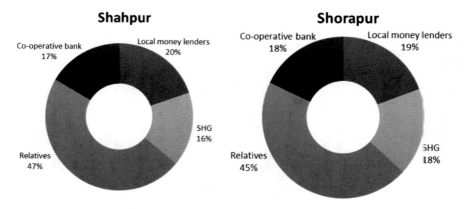

Fig. 9.16 Source-wise overdue loans (% of total loans) in Yadgir. *Source* Farmer interviews (2015)

---

[29] More than 86% people of rural Yadgir owned a mobile phone, second only to Bengaluru with 91%—https://www.huffingtonpost.in/open-magazine/a-call-to-action_2_b_8120574.html.

[30] Out of 81 and 40 reported cases of farmer suicides from Shahpur and Shorapur, respectively, 58 and 34 were attributed to indebtedness (communication from Department of Agriculture, Government of Karnataka).

and household maintenance. About 23 out of the 41 respondents took loans for buying tractor, laying irrigation pipes and removing large stones from their land.

Between the two study taluks, higher farm income coincides with higher incidence of distress without noticeable difference in credit pattern. In the hope of clarifying some of the complexities behind distress, we move on to look at the status of those who migrate from this landscape.

9.11 Farmer Migrants as Construction Workers in Cities

Seasonal migration from the north-eastern districts of Karnataka is not a new phenomenon. Plantations and mines in Goa and Maharashtra used to attract labour from this region since nineteenth century (Sharma 2004). While jobs at migration destinations changed to construction and other urban informal sectors, Goa and Bombay are still preferred destinations, in addition to Bengaluru. Such intra-state migration appears to play a more dominant role than inter-state migration in the development process of the State (Chandrasekhar and Sharma 2015).

Two members each (usually, a husband–wife couple) from 39% of respondent households migrate to Bengaluru, Pune or other cities for about 5 months every year.[31] Most migrants from Yadgir prefer Bengaluru for various reasons including familiarity with language and food as well as for the presence of already migrated relatives. A single migrant typically earned about ₹9000 per month (2015) and sent half of it back home. During weekends, it is common to see migrant workers queuing up at bank ATM kiosks in Bengaluru to send money home, soon after receiving their weekly wages.

Living in makeshift shanties without basic facilities such as electricity, toilets and drinking water, migrant families appeared to be servicing their debts at least partially, though asset generation is extremely rare. Except for food, expenses in the migration destination were low. Most work as construction workers, and others as gardeners, housekeepers or watchmen at garment industries, hotels, hospitals, educational institutions and residential complexes.

Many long-term circular migrants owned rainfed land in their native village. On an average, each migrant family brings 200 kg of jowar every year from their family farm and 150 kg of rice either bought from neighbouring irrigated farms or from PDS. Seven out of the nine migrant households from Yadgir we interviewed, go home for two to three months every year for partaking in land preparation and sowing. Additionally, most migrants make homeward trips for family functions and festivals though each round trip costs them at least ₹1000 per person.

According to migrant families, even if farm wage work is available with large landholdings in their source villages, the wages are low and discriminatory practices prevail. **Building the city thus provides an escape from social humiliation while**

---

[31]Categorised as seasonal migrants, members of 16 out of 41 farmer families we interviewed were engaged in non-farm work outside their villages for almost six months every year.

fetching better rewards for their labour. While unavailability of rural non-farm employment and difficulties in farming along with a larger family size provided the push factors, growing urbanisation provided the expected pull for farmer migrants from Northern Karnataka.

Migrant couples mostly were in the age group of 25–30 years. Their parents and children generally stayed back, and sow the rabi crop (generally groundnut or pulses) or take up agricultural wage work whenever available. **Thus, seasonal circular migration is not aspirational; rather, it is a coping strategy for the survival of families in off seasons. The remittances are generally used to repay loans or for household maintenance and rarely for meeting farm expenses.** Migrant respondents' financial situation appeared worse off compared to their fellow villagers who stayed back farming (Fig. 9.17).

Similarly, the migrant families from NEK in Bengaluru were more indebted than the farmers we met in Yadgir. Each migrant family had outstanding loan ranging from ₹56,000 to ₹2.5 lakhs taken from private money lenders at a rate of interest of two to three per cent per month.

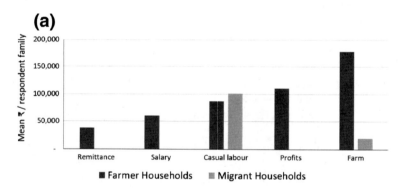

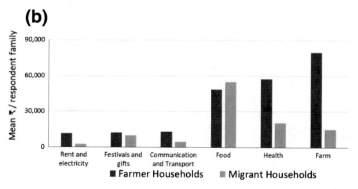

Fig. 9.17 a Income sources and **b** expenditure in Yadgir.
Source Farmer and migrant household interviews (2015)

Similar to Pattenden's (2012) findings on migration from Raichur, the migrant respondents from Yadgir we encountered were also mostly from Dalit communities. High out-migration of families with relatively small and unproductive landholdings from Yadgir is the outcome of agrarian differentiation. This resonates with the discussions we had in Chap. 4 (Sect. 4.3) on the missing focus of local welfare in the governance history of Hyderabad–Karnataka. This was further followed by failure of land re-distribution including the quality of land that was distributed. In parallel, as we discussed earlier in this chapter, entry of lucrative paddy crop along with temporary camps set up by enterprising Reddy farmers in the aftermath of a supposedly progressive measure of canal irrigation, also seems to have triggered out-migration of those with less resources.

During summer, availability of canal water determines the prospects of cultivation in more than half the sown area. In any case, landowners in rainfed area can sow only during one cropping season (kharif). Thus, as expressed by both farmers and farmer migrants, non-farm engagement by a couple of members in each family was a necessity. The younger generation in the villages were undergoing industrial training to get employment in factories in Bengaluru or Mumbai. **Thus, geriatrisation and not feminisation of peasantry is visible in Yadgir taluks where younger population opt to migrate.**

Women from migrant households of Yadgir, especially those from Dalit communities, were happy to be in the city. Back in the villages, even if they managed to find work, it paid much less than a city job. The responsibility of household chores was also less cumbersome in cities. Unlike in villages, where men roamed around the village with friends and played cards, here in an urban landscape they went to work every day and did some household errands. Wage differential in the cities is not as stark as it is in the villages. As a construction labourer, a woman gets ₹350 per day while men get ₹450 per day. This difference is less in jobs like housekeeping, cooking, gardening, etc. Once the labour contract ends, some of them find work on their own as housemaids. As our respondents said, most urban employers do not seem to have any issue with their caste. Yadgir women in the city are happy that their children attended school regularly. Migrant women working as domestic help keenly watched working women in their employer families and in the neighbourhood and used to get some support for children's education.

Nevertheless, migration pattern is witnessing some change especially since the urban real estate sector was yet to pick up after demonetisation of Indian currency in November 2017. Whether the expansion of irrigation in the villages, and the exit of Reddy camps [32] translate into reduced circular migration confining to aspirational drivers has to be confirmed by further studies. The surge in voters' turn-out in Yad-

---

[32] When the peak yield levels start dipping, immigrant workers from Andhra put up in camps around the head end of irrigation canals leased by Reddys were relocated either back to their source villages or to newly leased-in land in other command areas. Thus, local lessors who worked in the Reddy farms trained themselves in paddy cultivation to take on the mantle of rice farming.

gir for recent elections in 2018 probably is an indication of reduced migration in some seasons.[33]

9.12 Social Institutions: Bound to Customs

Yadgir continues to showcase institutionalised inequalities on caste, land and gender lines as discussed in Chap. 4. Unaccomplished land reform measures and persisting social negativities, disparity with more urbanised parts of the State and lack of political representation, may have acerbated the situation. The notable absence of mass movements may have reinforced inequality and governance failure in the region.

Nayakas, belonging to the hunter tribe of the *Bedars*, were dominant in Yadgir till recent history. Higher caste Hindus were not visibly dominant till colonial times when zamindari systems ended the prominence of the non-farming tribe of *Bedars*. Taylor's writings (1920, p. 232) draw a conclusion similar to that. He quotes others on a well-governed Shorapur under *Bedars*. Mixed portrayal of *Bedars* as being both righteous and aggressively combative is seen in Taylor's records during his tenure as Shorapur's administrator. His writings capture skewed distribution of land and tax in Shorapur after *Bedars*—'... *So it was in every village; the powerful paid no rent in comparison with the poor, and thus the revenue had been diminishing year by year*' Taylor (1920).

While land inequality continues to be stark and village institutions appear to have a path dependency in perpetuating inequality, it is important to also look at the modern institutions of irrigation and input intensive commercial farming in Yadgir. After the introduction of Upper Krishna project, irrigation institutions failed to adhere to their objective of supporting 'irrigated dry crops'. Thus, semi-arid Yadgir with deep clayey soils started emulating intensive cultivation of irrigated paddy in extensive areas. This new venture was undertaken by the relatively resourceful farmers from other canal irrigated areas.

An influential dominant entity—the Reddy camps—entered Yadgir with the arrival of canal irrigation and changed the look of a laid-back semi-arid landscape. Difficult lands were brought under the plough and hard enterprise, in an otherwise placid farm life in Yadgir. Their interactions with local farmers resulted in a gradual change in attitude among the local farming community towards a more market-oriented farming. According to our farmer respondents, Reddys had informed them the potential pitfalls in continuously cultivating heavily irrigated paddy. With Reddy camps and the changes in cropping pattern they brought in, other players like input dealers, output traders and money lenders also became active. Sleepy APMC yards used to dealing with a few occasional trucks loaded with pulses, started constantly buzzing with rice trading activities.

---

[33] Between 2013 and 2018, 4 constituencies of Yadgir district recorded 20% increase in voters' count—https://timesofindia.indiatimes.com/india/voter-count-surges-in-north-karnataka-districts/articleshow/63840450.cms.

9.12 Social Institutions: Bound to Customs

Thus output traders, input sharing among kith and kin as a traditional norm, and nationalised banks became the most important networks for respondent farmers in the villages of Yadgir. Farmers bridging the gap between the agrarian community and other institutions belonged to dominant castes (*lingayat* and *kuruba*) owning relatively larger holdings, which were mostly irrigated and cultivating commercial crops like paddy and cotton. Though not highly educated, they were active in local politics.

Thus, agrarian Yadgir came to be a dynamic landscape with irrigation and paddy. It looked forward to more jobs in the locality with the proposed industries that are supposedly based on raw material sourced from local agriculture. **Less talked about is the relevance of small or individual enterprises using agro-ecologically suitable raw materials—cotton, jowar, pulses and oilseeds—in transitioning and strengthening the local socio-economic fabric.** Existing cultural institutions can play a role in this rural transformation by reviving the positives of the non-agrarian occupation of its past. Our fieldwork in this landscape was full of interesting encounters with folk artistes, joint families and huge cattle fairs.[34]

9.13 Small Holdings in the Hinterlands: Rainfed Systems, Intensification and Persisting Migration

Yadgir district, with a reasonable net sown area per cultivator (1.9 ha against 1.5 ha for the State) and second lowest share of (8.5%) urban population, typifies a remote agrarian landscape around a small town. With urbanisation taking place at a very slow pace, Yadgir town acts mostly as the administrative headquarter and a gateway for people who commute between the villages and economic hubs like Bengaluru.

The region was known as Shorapur Samsthan from the late seventeenth century under the Nayaka kings of *Bedar* community till it was annexed to Hyderabad province by the British in 1857. **The rural and agrarian differentiation began at this point in time and continues through modern agricultural interventions like canal irrigation. Diverging from a past ruled by the hunter tribes, the region is a hotbed of discrimination, disparities and quiet discontent.**

Irrigation was uncommon in this semi-arid landscape bounded by the rivers Krishna and Bheema. With meagre forests and abundant livestock, cultivation—the major occupation of the populace—was confined to winter season, making use of residual moisture in the soils after a scanty 600–650 mm rain received during September–October. Though Nayakas as well as the British built tanks, it was only by the late 1990s that irrigation became a common practice in Shorapur. **Today's Yadgir presents the contradictory coexistence of a notable area under canal irrigation as well as rainfed farming with large extent of fallows and high incidence of out-migration.**

---

[34]Read about the study team's narratives as folk artists and traditional festivals at https://smallfarmdynamics.blog/2017/06/.

Though Yadgir continues to host relatively large holdings and diverse cultivator communities as compared to the State of Karnataka as a whole, farming is characterised by skewed ownership of fertile land and extensive leasing practice, owing partly to failed land reforms. Herding and keeping local breeds of cattle and sheep relying on seasonal fallows are still widespread. Spreading irrigation might popularise dairy as an enterprise, at least in pockets, in just the same way it brought paddy to this semi-arid landscape of millets, pulses, cotton and oilseeds. Shift from a cycle of jowar or bajra followed by pulses along with small extent of cotton, to intensive monocrops of either cotton or paddy has increased cash flow in the families—but there is a corresponding rise in both expense and income. Cost escalations alongside yield and price fluctuations as well as other non-farm expenses are managed through credit networks among kin.

While the new intensive cash crop economy does not appear to have reduced out-migration of the small holders, the impact of flood irrigation on the deep clayey soil is yet to be acknowledged. Adequate attention is needed to safeguard the local agro-ecology, so that vulnerabilities and agrarian differentiation are not concurrently reinforced.

Though seasonal migration is not new to the single cropping farmlands here, discriminatory social customs and resource requirement in newly irrigated areas further intensified out-migration from Yadgir. People from Dalit communities who own low-quality land or have leased out their irrigated land tend to avail the opportunities offered by the construction sector in Bengaluru and other cities. Such outflow largely happens to be circular, undertaken to service debts and tide over drought situations. Among the migrants we met, there were a few aspirational outcomes of such ventures. Communication technology is a boon to these families, helping in both finding and changing jobs as well as in connecting with kith and kin back home. Though these low caste migrants are far from being urbane in their attitude, lifestyle or duration of their residence in the city, they are the primary workforce in building the city. When their villages receive normal rainfall, they choose to return home for farm work.

The relatively weak flows (Fig. 9.18) between a rural town and its peripheral agrarian landscape implies significant outflows from this coupled core–periphery loop to other more dynamic urban cores (see Figs. 6.14, 7.16 and 8.17) in the form of labour and agricultural produce.

While the rural town does not take over much of the land surrounding it, it also fails to generate enough investment to secure farm and/or non-farm livelihoods. This points towards the need to create in situ opportunities for adding value to human and farm resources. Expectations of new farm-driven non-farm jobs are high with the proposed textile parks. Policies of crop insurance and market linkage also kindle some hope. Adding a fillip to this buzz is the political attention to the region in the wake of a socio-political movement for a separate *Lingayat* religion and demand by some political outfits for a separate State in North Karnataka.

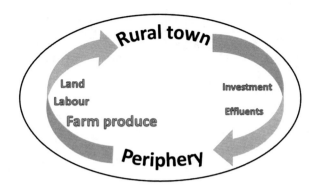

Fig. 9.18 Flows between rural town and its periphery (font size indicates relative quantum of flows)

References

Attri, S., & Nautiyal, S. (2016). *Vulnerability assessment of the agricultural sector in Yadgir district, Karnataka: A socio-economic survey approach* (Working Paper 295). Institute of Social and Economic Change.

Breitkreuz, R., Stanton, C.-J., Brady, N., Pattison-Williams, J., King, E. D., Mishra, C., et al. (2017). The Mahatma Gandhi National Rural Employment Guarantee Scheme: A policy solution to rural poverty in India? *Development Policy Review, 35*(3), 397–417.

Chandrasekhar, S., & Sharma, A. (2015). Urbanisation and spatial patterns of internal migration in India. *Spatial Demography, 3*(2), 63–89.

Deshpande, S. V., & Torgal, V. (1994). Administering land reforms in Karnataka. *Economic and Political Weekly, 29*(33), 2132–2134.

Gulbarga District Gazetteer. (1995). Government of Karnataka.

Gulbarga District Gazetteer. (2004). Government of Karnataka.

Husain, M. (1940). *Hyderabad District Gazetteers Gulbarga*. Hyderabad: Deccan Government Central Press.

Jacob, S., Natarajan, B., & Patil, I. (2015). Explaining village-level development trajectories through schooling in Karnataka. *Economic and Political Weekly, 50*(52), 54–64.

Jefferson, T. (1785). *Equality: Thomas Jefferson to James Madison* (Vol. 1, Chap. 15, Doc. 32. Papers 8, pp. 681–682). The Founders' Constitution.

Khan, M. M. (1909). *Imperial Gazetteer of India. Provincial series. Hyderabad state*.

Mollinga, P. P. (1998). *On the waterfront: Water distribution, technology and agrarian change in a South Indian canal irrigation system*. Wageningen: Ponsen en Looijen.

Mukerjee, R. (1916). *The foundations of Indian Economics*. Longman: Green and Co. London.

Narayanan, S., Ranaware, K., Das, U., & Kulkarni, A. (2014). *MGNREGA works and their impacts: A rapid assessment in Maharashtra* (IGIDR Working Paper 2014-042).

Paddayya, K. (1977). The Acheulian Culture of the Hunsgi Valley (Shorapur Doab), Peninsular India. *Proceedings of the American Philosophical Society, 121,* 383–406.

Pattenden, J. (2012). Migrating between rural Raichur and boomtown Bangalore: Class relations and the circulation of labour in South India. *Global Labour Journal, 3*(1), 163–190.

Sanyal, K. (2007). *Rethinking capitalist development: Primitive accumulation, governmentality and post-colonial capitalism*. New Delhi: Routledge India.

Sathyan, B. N. (1966). *Gazetteer of India, Mysore State—Gulbarga District*.

Sharma, R. (2004, December). *A history of migration*. Frontline.

Singh, N. T. (2005). *Irrigation and soil salinity in the Indian subcontinent—Past and present* (pp. 209–212). Lehigh University Press.

State of Working India. (2018). *Center for sustainable employment*. Bengaluru: Azim Premji University.

Taylor, P. M. (1920). *The story of my life*. Oxford University Press.

Wallach, B. (1985). British irrigation works in India's Krishna Basin. *Journal of Historical Geography, 11*(2), 155–173.

Chapter 10
Withering Family Farms

10.1 The Study

Small and marginal farmers seem to be trapped in a precarious persistence between the city slums and empty villages. The study began by placing the precariousness of a smallholder family farm at the centre and considering various schools of thoughts on peasants, family farms and agriculturists, before using these terms interchangeably.[1] Their precariousness resonates with the need economy of Sanyal (2007). Marx's peasant (Shanin 1971) appears to converge with the small farmers of today, forming an economic 'class' rather than a political or social entity, while being closer to nature than other economic actors. They emerge as the lowest strata of the society (similar to Marx and Engels' (1848) characterisation of peasants), but still could often be differentiated into poor and middle peasants, adapting Lenin's (1903) typology of peasant classes.

At times, today's smallholder also conforms to the petit bourgeois mass (Kritsman 1984), although he/she can be distinguished from the provincial propertied class (Balagopal 1987a), while being a 'part culture' community—midway between the tribal and the industrial urban society (Kroeber1953; Foster1965). With rural–urban, consumer–producer and farm-nonfarm dichotomies converging in an entity whose life and livelihood are inseparable (Naik 1989), it is obvious that applying a productivity approach that is centred around maximising farm size, income or production to any one of the partial identities becomes meaningless.

There is no dearth of studies and reports on smallholders of the global South (e.g. FAO 2012; Fan and Chan-Kang 2005; Negi 2014). The need to have a contextual analysis of the multiple ways of experiencing agrarian distress is well espoused

---

[1] Though used interchangeably, in literal sense, 'farmers' imply more commerce; 'family farms' and 'agriculturists' have a cultural connotation, while 'peasant' sounds a little closer to being a 'proletarian class'.

© Springer Nature Singapore Pte Ltd. 2019
S. Purushothaman and S. Patil, *Agrarian Change and Urbanization in Southern India*, India Studies in Business and Economics,
https://doi.org/10.1007/978-981-10-8336-5_10

(Jodhka 2018). Possible ways of agrarian adaptation and transition also deserve a context-specific analysis.

This study steers away both from a rural productivity approach looking at the efficiency and scalability of smallholdings, as much as from an ethnographic narration of distress. It argues the need to find ways to sustain smallholders in an era of urbanisation. In that process, it illuminates why a socio-economic constituency with widespread presence and multiple nomenclature is invisible to the society. The motivation behind carrying out the study was the felt need to reverse an apparent invisibilisation of the smallholder constituency. In this effort, the study brings together the history of governance and agro-ecology, and the political-economic and socio-institutional angles associated with livelihood and distributional perspectives, using empirical observations from Karnataka State.

Why, where and how of the study are detailed in the first five chapters of the book, before presenting the site-specific features of the urban–agrarian dynamics in Chaps. 6–9. This final chapter synthesises and highlights the essence of all previous chapters, though not in any sequential order of study sites.

10.1.1 Invisibility of Small Family Farms

Urban versus rural, the same discursive binary as 'developed versus underdeveloped' that we unquestioningly inherited from colonial times (Himanshu 2018), leads to an invisibilisation of the interlinkages between the food security and farm livelihood, between rural poor and the urban poor and between food producer and consumer. This invisibilisation is reflected in the lack of legitimate agency assigned to small farmers who stay back in the rural setting without seeking urban employment or after having returned from a short stint in the city.

Though rurality is not entirely agrarian in nature, agrarian features continue to dominate as the major occupational identity in rural Karnataka. The next widely identified occupation is that of a migrant, who mostly engages with the urban informal sector. Even while enjoying easy access to a variety of cheap farm produce, a typical urbanite is oblivious to the impact s/he causes to the producers or the fact that the cab driver, security guard, house help or the construction worker s/he happens to meet, could be a farmer.

Are small farmers the left behind or the perseverant? While trying to unravel the scattered constituency of the invisible millions (125 million farmers in India having two hectares and less (Agricultural Census 2015)), the challenge is multi-fold. They negotiate between identities (migrant, off- and/or non-farm worker, farmer), which in turn straddle different geographical zones and economic sectors. The study looks at the agrarian presence in diverse rural–urban interfaces and focuses on the South Indian State of Karnataka, known on one hand for its economic vibrancy and on the other for agrarian distress in some parts.

10.1.2 Contexts and Regions in Focus

The historical emergence of the relationship between agrarian peripheries and various urban geographies that form the hub of larger economic forces were traced in Chap. 4. It is now well known (Vasavi 2016; Vakulabharanam 2005; Jodhka 2018; Colatei and Harriss-White 2004) that this rural–urban dynamics continues to be reinforced as the basis of differentiation, rather than modified/levelled by State policies and neo-liberal political economic structure. Hence, bearing in mind the politics and economics of the rural–urban social currents, we explored the physical flows between the urban core and agrarian peripheries in four different core–periphery (or urban–agrarian) assemblages. Dynamics within any single core–periphery assemblage (Fig. 3.2 in Chap. 3) entails physical flows of farm produce, labour, natural resources or capital for instance, along with other flows like cultural exchanges (not discussed here).

These exchanges or flows also happen between any two urban centres (or economic hubs, Fig. 10.1). Presumably, these flows between any two urban centres or those between any urban centre and a distant agrarian landscape (dotted lines in Fig. 10.1) are relatively subdued compared to the flows within closely coupled urban–agrarian assemblages (within each ellipse), except when the urban area under scrutiny is a mega city (solid lines between ellipses).

Capturing the intra- and inter-exchanges in urban–agrarian assemblages, Chaps. 6–9 unpack the status of farming and farmers in villages located around a megacity, a small town, an agro-processing town and a remote rural town. The representative districts of these locations identified were Bengaluru, Ramanagara, Mandya and Yadgir, respectively. Each of these four sites has varying levels of economic development, with Bengaluru being highly developed, Ramanagara developed, Mandya backward, and Yadgir highly backward according to the Economic Survey of Karnataka (2015).

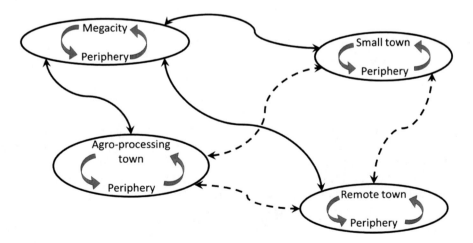

Fig. 10.1 Exchanges within and between core–periphery assemblages

Each site with its urban centre and agrarian peripheries implies an unique exchange dynamism (Sects. 6.14, 7.14, 8.13, 9.14). In terms of the extent and impact, the flow of labour, water and farm produce from the periphery was most visible in peri-urban Bengaluru. Effluent flow from the core to periphery was equally high from the urban core of Bengaluru and Ramanagara, while the impact was significantly higher in former. Labour flow to the core was least from Mandya's villages. Capital flow from core to periphery also increased in a gradient of urbanisation.

Mega cities often nurture linkages with agrarian landscapes far-off from it. Bengaluru City for instance, uses smallholdings in Yadgir as construction labour or for the supply of millets and pulses and Ramanagara villages as a sink for its sewage. Drivers, such as import policies, can impact all landscapes, except for the city peripheries that mainly cater to the urban demand for perishable products. For instance, import of pulses, cotton and silk yarn impacts farmers in Yadgir and Ramanagara, while farmers in Bengaluru's peripheral areas deal mostly with perishables for the city and are almost unaffected by volatility in international trade.

If land distribution was most skewed in Yadgir, it was income and expenses in peri-urban Bengaluru, while Mandya appeared relatively less skewed in both land and income. However, the rural–urban disparity in the study districts was uniformly higher than rural disparity. It appears that neither the heavy urbanisation in Bengaluru nor the rurality of Yadgir has helped farmers in their surroundings evenly. Vasavi's (2018) 'rural middle class' consists of communities who gained from commercial farming in the late twentieth century and moved to other sectors. This rural middle class is notably present in all study sites, and the opposite extreme—'marginalized majority' has a visible presence in Yadgir.

Prior to summarising the specific aspects of the rural–urban interface introduced in Chap. 3 and covered in detail in Chaps. 6–9, here we briefly compare the two larger regions which comprise the studied agrarian peripheries.

10.2 Trajectories of Regional Divergence: Nature or Governance?

Agro-climate wise, four of the eight study taluks fall in the eastern dry zone and two each in the southern and north-eastern dry zones. In terms of the history of governance, they fall in two regions: two taluks of the north-east dry zone were part of Nizam's Hyderabad region and the remaining six situated in the dry zones of east and south were part of the erstwhile Mysore State. Regional differences in the history and agro-ecology of the two regions were explored in Chaps. 4 and 5. This section touches upon the divergence of the study contexts so as to critique a blanket copying of mainstream farm policies. The basic drivers of social differentiation play out differently in different landscapes in interaction with the forces of urbanisation and demands arising from that.

10.2 Trajectories of Regional Divergence: Nature or Governance? 249

Across and within the four study sites, agrarian communities were not uniformly distressed or developed and varied in terms of peasant differentiation. That is where we found the core–periphery (or urban–agrarian) interactions playing a crucial role. The history of dynamics between social structure, power around land and regional politics as well as governance is found to be the genesis of the current social differentiation based on access to quality natural resources in private and common domains—soil fertility and soil moisture; diverse forms of biomass for green manure, mulching, fodder, as well as for the family's nutritional supplements in berries, fruits, leaves and tubers.

Sections below briefly look at how governance in general and particularly measures and mechanisms that impacted the distribution of natural resources became an important determinant of agrarian status both in history and the present.

10.2.1 Agriculture and Development

Looking at the current plight of agrarian Yadgir in the north-eastern part of the State known as the Hyderabad Karnataka region, it seems incongruous that settled agriculture in South India originated in these dry plains. Unfortunately, the long history of cultivation and pastoralism from the Neolithic times did not blossom into a thriving farm economy unlike the production landscapes in Mysore Karnataka where farming appeared much later in the history of human settlements (Krishna and Morrison 2010). Pastoralism and rain-fed agriculture in the two regions prevailed and evolved over time with diverse agrarian outcomes—one vibrant and less unequal; the other, distressed and visibly unequal. The reason behind this divergence could partly be found in the differential history of governance—including wars, disparities and welfare orientation—as explained in chapters four and five.

The diverse history of institutions and governance prior to privatisation of land rights can be deduced with reasonable confidence, even indespite the absence of concrete and dedicated studies, from scattered mentions in colonial memoirs and imperial gazetteers (Wilks 1810, pp. 73; Sastri 1940, pp. 217–220; Rice 1897, pp. 575–599). The variance in pre-colonial structure and functioning of village-level governance institutions (e.g. *Ayagar* system in Mysore Karnataka and *Bara Balutedar* system in Hyderabad Karnataka) with representation of various service castes of the respective regions is noteworthy.

Although both regions have had a history of famines, they were markedly different in their outcomes. From the writings of Rice and Taylor and the Imperial Gazetteer authored by Khan, it becomes apparent that in terms of the number of people impacted, crop loss and expenses in relief work, Hyderabad Karnataka region was more severely affected than Mysore in the South.[2] Much like the case of famines,

---

[2]Hyderabad Karnataka (of which Gulbarga was a part) had three major famines in eighteenth century and 11 in the nineteenth century (Khan 1909, pp. 48). Last famine in Gulbarga (Yadgir was part of Gulbarga district till 2009) was as recent as 1980, after similar occurrences in 1972 (Gulbarga

caste hierarchy was common to both regions. Heavy taxation, exploitative tenancy and land-credit nexus added to the woes of Hyderabad region. Taylor's memoir offers glimpses of a heavily discriminatory society in the Shorapur State of colonial times to which current district of Yadgir belonged (Taylor 1920). A comparison of the two regions—Mysore region versus Hyderabad Karnataka—(see Buchanan 1807; Srinivas 1976; Jai Prabhakar 2010) reveals stark inequality in Hyderabad Karnataka.

The well-known 'Mysore model' of pre-independent India built on good governance along with early progressive steps in education, health care, technology and decentralisation (see Kadekodi et al. (2007) for an account of the model and comparison) paved a 'bubbling up' development path. This was in contrast to the use of Hyderabad region as a frontier for revenue farming to feed distant power centres. Even in independent India, distance from the seats of power reinforced a path dependency of inequality and impoverishment in Hyderabad Karnataka.

Policy discussions and literature have attributed this divergence in developmental outcomes to the difference in ecology and extent of irrigation. Attribution of underdevelopment to differences in the 'first nature' (Pani (2017) following Croncn 1991 on the Great West of eighteenth-century Chicago) reflected in the availability of large extent of arable land and occurance of fragmentation appears illogical after the above comparison of the regional history of agricultural economies.

The common trend seems to hold agro-ecological variation responsible for regional variance in distress, but at the same time recommend uniform interventions irrespective of agro-ecological features. The above historical analysis reveals a pre-occupation with water-intensive agriculture and societal apathy towards the culture and science of dry lands from mid-twentieth century onwards. This preoccupation of a populist welfare State (akin to the 'politics of rescue' in Vasavi (2018)) or a casual 'one-size-fits-all' attitude in agricultural interventions ignores the ecological differences in the soil type (clayey vs. red loamy), water resources (open wells vs. tanks) and forest type (dry scrub vs. moist deciduous).

The indifference to finding regionally suitable models of agricultural interventions resulted not only in lack of attention to the semi-arid agro-ecology, but also in a casual 'copy-pasting' of canal irrigated paddy to deep black cotton soils, straight from the populist water-intensive and external input models. Populist policies also gloss over the agitations, conflicts and even suicides in the flagship agricultural areas of Mandya, where farmers, sugar industry as well as the irrigation project are fully reliant on the exchequer for financial viability.

To add to the agony of the Hyderabad Karnataka region, traditional non-farm enterprises like large factories of jewellery, and furniture (see Fukazawa 2002, pp. 314) also diminished considerably, along with a non-blooming agrarian economy.

District Gazetteer 1995), 1960, and 1943 (Hyderabad District Gazetteer by Satyan 1966). Last major famine in Mysore Karnataka occurred in 1976 after five sporadic famines in the nineteenth century (Imperial Gazetteer of Mysore and Coorg 1908, pp. 74).

10.2.2 Agrarian Movements

Such historical differences between the two regions even extend to the nature of agrarian movements and mobilisation (see Sect. 2.4 in Chap. 2). Though Dalit movements in Gulbarga are more visible than the conflicts in Mysore (see Assadi and Rajendran (2000) as well as Pinto (1994)), farmer agitations have been reported only in the latter. However, these agitations were mostly politically mobilised among the landed farmers typically for more water from Cauvery or for payments for sugarcane supplied to the factory.

In the remote agrarian landscapes, community's potential to protest against inequalities and discrimination is weak because they tend to spend half the year elsewhere as migrants. Trapped in a weak and dual existence as farmer and migrant worker in two or more places, finding the time and energy to think, collectivise, garner support from the society and make their voice heard is almost impossible. Despite continued polarisation by means of land and caste on all development indicators, social mobilisation of smallholders in Hyderabad Karnataka is not foreseeable in the near future.

In recent times, the demand for a separate religion and statehood has forced the political-economic powers to take a serious look at the Hyderabad Karnataka region. Whether the recently announced industrial investment in textiles and the entry of cement manufacture using limestone deposits of the region will add any significant employment to local communities is to be seen.

10.2.3 Farming Systems

Extensive fields of food grains dominate Northern and Central Karnataka and Mandya in the South (Fig. 10.2). But as mentioned in the previous section, historically, paddy—the all-pervasive food crop of the present times—was not a major cultivated crop or part of the cuisine in the north-eastern part of the State. Imperial Gazetteer (Khan 1909) mentions millets and pulses as the only staple food. Taylor talks about how he enjoyed food made with jowar, bajra and pulses, cooked by the locals (*The Story of My Life* 1920).

Irrigated by Upper Krishna Project (UKP) since 1992, paddy dominates a significant part of Yadgir in Kharif and Rabi seasons, at present. Wherever irrigation canal does not reach, cotton crop stays for two to three years, before the stubble is removed for a new crop of cotton or others. Farm families here keep livestock—mostly goats, sheep and local cows, significantly more than other study sites. Millets had a negligible and declining presence in the cropping system of Yadgir, compared to study sites located in the south of Karnataka.

If two contrasting cropping patterns in tune with the status of irrigation constitute the remote agrarian landscape, farming systems in the study villages of an agriculturally dynamic Mandya reveal this contrast differently. The agro-urbanism of the present Mandya town is both driven by and drives the surrounding agricultural systems. Here, the long-established presence of sugar and paddy mills in the command areas of Krishna Raja Sagar (KRS) dam over Cauvery has ensured cultivation of sugarcane and paddy for about half a century, though there are plenty of signs of soil and socio-economic wearing out. Villages that cannot access KRS water host centuries' old mixed dry farming systems, generally with coconut and ragi integrated with small ruminants as signature farming system. Providing copra to the oil mills around while ensuring nutritional security in farm families, these rain-fed systems also facilitated and allowed time for education and non-farm employment. Others, with very old small tank irrigation systems, continue to grow paddy for centuries.

The small-town landscape of Ramanagara district is nurtured by different production systems—either tube well-irrigated mulberry or rain-fed ragi integrated with cattle or a rain-fed combination of mango and ragi. The latter, as in the case of integrated rain-fed systems of Mandya, combines commercial perennials and staple grains, thus supporting non-farm engagements along with nutritional security. Along with industrial estates in the locality and closeness to Bengaluru-Mysore highway, these farming systems make Ramanagara a lively and growing small town.

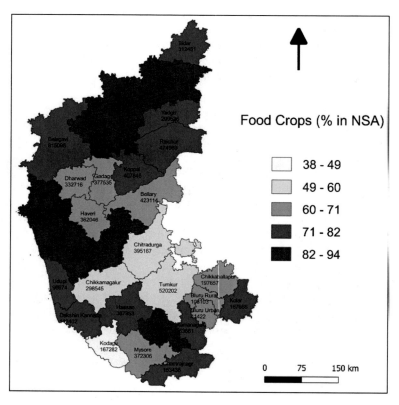

Fig. 10.2 Area under food crops in Karnataka State (2016).
Map based on Karnataka State Agriculture Profile, 2016; number inside the districts indicates net sown area in hectares

10.2 Trajectories of Regional Divergence: Nature or Governance?

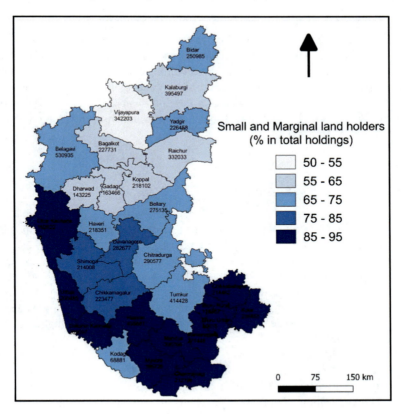

Fig. 10.3 Small and marginal landholders (2011).
Map based on Agricultural Census 2011; numbers inside each district indicate total landholdings

The agricultural peripheries of Bengaluru city form a hub of vegetables, flowers and fruits irrigated entirely by tube wells. Rain-fed areas in these peripheries mostly grow ragi or eucalyptus. In the outskirts of this city of neo-liberal times, culinary culture of the place and lack of irrigation together translate into growing staples like ragi.

10.3 Farmlands—Equity, Management and Conversion

Coastal and southern parts of Karnataka have smaller holdings than others. They also form the belt where vast areas are under non-food crops (Fig. 10.2) and land inequality is less, but economic inequality is high. The map in Fig. 10.3 depicts the proportion of small and marginal landholders in all 30 districts in the State of Karnataka.

254   10 Withering Family Farms

There are some striking features about farmland ownership in the study sites. First among these is the fact that Mandya's farm income is high despite its small average holding size which is even smaller than some parts of peri-urban Bengaluru. This apparent dynamism in Mandya's smallholdings, which can be attributed to its irrigated paddy and sugarcane, has to consider the sociology of ownership. Most agricultural land in Mandya is owned by the dominant OBC castes. The striking feature of Yadgir is the coexistence of social diversity and disparity along with larger holding size (5–10 acres).

10.3.1 Land Distribution

Wherever the size of holdings or annual income of the families is high, inequality exists. While Yadgir with relatively larger holdings has the highest land inequality among the study sites, its income inequality was not high.[3] Mandya appears to have better distributional outcomes in terms of landownership and household income. Among the study sites, it had the least share of agricultural landholdings with SC/ST communities, but had the highest landownership among women (28%). Yadgir had both in the reverse order—least share of holdings with women and highest share of holdings with SC/ST.

Women landholders were fewer (9–12%) in the most and least urbanised sites. Overall, women's landownership in the study villages was found to be around 16%. High expenses incurred in girls' marriages emerged as the reason for not giving them a share of the family land. Mandya, where proof of landownership is essential to register with regulated markets or processing industries, granting legal land rights to women often created conflicts. **Lavish weddings, dominant caste male ownership of land and dowry system acted together as a mutually reinforcing cycle to deny ownership to women, despite legal interventions.**

Inamdars of Mysore Karnataka—mostly high caste Hindus—had dominant *Vokkaligas* and *Lingayats* as tenants, who started wielding political and economic powers. Decades after Devaraj Urs's government in Karnataka abolished tenancy, dominant agricultural castes repeated the same phenomena of exploitation in other ways (Thimmaiah 1997). Pani (1997) also corroborates the fact that reforms like 'land to the tenant' did not change the agrarian structure in the maidan districts of old Mysore. Since lessors and lessees belonged to all castes and size classes, beneficiaries and affected categories of land reforms also included all castes and land-owning classes.

Administration lapses and lack of pressure from the bottom are cited as reasons for the failure of land reforms in Gulbarga (Deshpande and Torgal 1994).[4] In many

---

[3]Gini coefficient for landownership in study villages was 0.44 in Yadgir, 0.40 in Ramanagara, 0.35 in Bengaluru and 0.32 in Mandya. For household income, it was 0.48 in Bengaluru, 0.46 in Ramanagara, 0.45 in Yadgir and 0.41 in Mandya.

[4]While land reforms in the State during 1961 (Mysore Land Reforms Act) made no difference (large owners got sufficient time to prepare for reforms through tenant evictions), marginal impact

10.3 Farmlands—Equity, Management and Conversion

parts, and especially in Mysore, the smallness of land size was cited as one of the reasons for ineffective land ceiling measures (see Chap. 4, Box 5). Historically, the menial castes in Hyderabad Karnataka were not allowed to own land and formed a class of forced labour or '*begars*'. The number of agricultural labourers is still very high in Yadgir, with 33% agricultural labourers in its worker population compared to 12–13% in other sites.

Land ceiling and distribution are inevitable for the State to address inequality between farmers and non-farming communities. However, since this is politically unappealing even in democracies like India, policy discussions centre around the need for farmers to completely shift to other occupations, citing unviability of smallholdings. Land reforms, wherever it addressed inequity in ownership between social categories to some extent, did not address the issue of agricultural livelihoods. An important reason for this failure is the fact that collective elements integral to farming operations were ignored. Navigating the smallness of millions of holdings envisages sustainability of nature's commons and culinary cultures and they in turn rely on social commons.

However, the persistent skewness in land distribution did not trigger mass movements in Gulbarga. The actual control of power over agrarian communities in many parts continues to be around money lending, or when land power is clubbed with money power. This power is slowly fading way due to changes such as irrigation, affirmative action by the State and industrial employment, along with formal credit sources. What reforms could not do in terms of shrinking the larger holdings, population increase has been doing to some extent.[5] According to records of various agricultural census, average size of holdings in Yadgir reduced to the current 4 acres (from what was 10 acres in 1970) and n Mandya to 1.9 acres (from 5 acres in 1970).

How feasible is it to correct land inequality as a means to make small farms viable? It might need land distribution and/or collectivisation in different parts, depending on the existing landholding size. The prescribed minimum land size of 2 ha of irrigated land per family (Dorin et al. 2013[6]) can potentially avoid a poverty trap. But, the historical perspective of land rights in the study regions presented in Chap. 4 points to the fact that agrarian reforms do not seem to facilitate control and rights over quality natural resources for small-scale farming.

---

was felt during the second attempt between 1974 and 1984 with comprehensive amendments to the act (Karnataka Land Reforms Act) when some claims were settled (Aziz and Krishna 1997). Land ceiling declarations received by the government (in 1961) under the land reform laws as well as tenancy applications were quite high in Gulbarga (of which Yadgir was a part till 2009). Yet, guaranteed occupancy rights as proportion of applications was only 18% (compared to 55.7% in Mandya) making the overall distributional impact in Gulbarga, feeble (Rajan 1997, pp. 83–84).

[5] Average size of each landholding declined among all social categories between 1990 and 2015 in the State. In the case of SC and ST holders, the decline was 29 and 37%, respectively, while for others it was 36%.

[6] Dorin's analysis shows the need for a minimum of 5 acres irrigated land for a family, if Lewis trap of poverty has to be avoided. His comparative assessment was based on income convergence between farm and non-farm workers as well as the relationship between growth of labour productivity and of the agricultural sector.

Ambedkar (1918) was of the opinion that neither consolidation of holdings nor expansion of holdings was feasible due to the conversion of joint families to nuclear ones and the population pressure on land. He found 'State socialism' appealing—State taking charge of all agricultural land, dividing it equally into groups of working population for collective farming akin to, yet different from both Gandhiji's Gram Swaraj and people's farming communes in China and Russia. Far from going anywhere close to those radical but possible corrective measures, independent India attempted half-hearted land reforms that failed to make any noticeable correction, perpetuating land inequality.

10.3.2 Leasing, Sharecropping and Contract Farming

Agronomic features (topography, soil, crops and rainfall) of semi-arid Yadgir necessitates larger fields to grow rain-fed pulses, cotton and oilseeds, compared to the high-value farming of perishable commodities in more urbanised landscapes. However, as we discussed earlier, distribution of land in Yadgir has proven to be a challenge despite some efforts at land reforms. Hence, leasing is an important practice for cultivators here. Tenancy abolition of 1974 makes leasing illegal in the State of Karnataka.[7] But leasing and sharecropping are widely practised among farmers with landholdings of similar size and shared social status. Both leasing and sharecropping happen on oral agreements with clear terms on sharing inputs, cash and harvested produce.

Leasing here entails cultivating land owned by someone else and paying lease charges in cash and/or produce. Leasing and sharecropping are generally observed in irrigated or irrigable land where the owner is unable to cultivate his/her land partially or fully due to various reasons. Even land without its own source of water may be leased if water can be fetched from a tube well in the adjacent field, as is often seen in peri-urban Bengaluru.

Leasing practices are more popular in Yadgir, Ramanagara and Mandya than in Bengaluru. While Yadgir and Mandya are canal irrigated, Ramanagara is largely rain-fed. But Yadgir and Ramanagara share one common reason for leasing—engagement in non-farm jobs that are driven by a variety of factors. Members of farm families from the dry lands of Ramanagara opt to work in industries nearby, leasing out their mango plantations to contractors.

Yadgir farmers, whose average holding size is larger than the other sites, lease out larger pieces of land (3.1 acres on an average) from their holdings for two reasons. One set of lessors are forced to migrate out due to indebtedness. They lease their land

---

[7]Section 10.5 of the Karnataka Land Reforms Act 1961 prohibits leasing of land except by soldiers and seamen. State is trying to bring in Model Agricultural Land Leasing Act (2016) to legalise leasing so as to promote efficiency, equity and poverty reduction; along with security of ownership right for landowners and security of tenure for tenants.

to relatives or neighbours at cheap rates. The second set of lessors are in areas where canal irrigation reached recently, introducing paddy as the only sowing option. Paddy cultivation, perceived by most farmers as a sign of prosperity, requires large amount of water, capital and know-how. For the hitherto rain-fed smallholders for whom both capital and irrigation were alien, leasing out to enterprising Reddy migrants from Andhra was more convenient. Some of them, as our conversations in the villages of Yadgir revealed, just lived off the lease amount and some other lessees worked as hired labour on their land given on lease.

In Mandya, non-farm engagements of family members often prompt owners to lease their land to farmers who have enough family labour available to cultivate more land than what they own. Thus, reasons for leasing were different within the irrigated landscapes of Yadgir and between Yadgir, Mandya and Ramanagara.

Apart from leasing and sharecropping, there are subtle forms of contract farming. Formal regulations on this are yet to be enacted in line with related provisions in the Model APMC Act (2003). Though contract farming is prevalent in the State [8], our study sites were free of such formal contractual arrangements. Some farmers in peri-urban Bengaluru enter into written agreements with processing companies or retail chains for cultivating high-value crops for urban consumption.

10.3.3 When Is Farmland Left Uncultivated?

Information from farmlands left uncultivated for a period of two to three years prior to the survey indicates that fallowing is high in Yadgir (35% of NSA, and larger share of holdings) and Mandya (25% of NSA).

The survey period—2015–16—was declared a drought year in four study taluks (Shahpur, Shorapur, Nagamangala and Kanakapura). Drought might have resulted in larger than usual extent of fallows, more so in rain-fed areas and lands close to the tail end of canals. But, secondary data from earlier years[9] corroborates the spatial pattern of fallows found during the study period, with fallows in Yadgir way above the State average of 16% (Fig. 10.4).

Most fallowed lands around Bengaluru had dysfunctional irrigation facilities. High-value perishable crops grown here need a lot of water and labour and this was often difficult to meet even with tube wells deeper than 1000 ft. Cultivable fallows in Yadgir on the other hand were stony and difficult to work. Most such fallow lands in Yadgir have been allotted to the landless by the government at various points in time (read this along with the earlier discussion on land ceiling for redistribution to the

---

[8](Mostly in areas close to Bengaluru, Tumkur, Kolar and Hassan for crops such as potatoes, gherkin, baby corn, herbs, fruits and vegetables (Erappa 2006)).

[9]District-level Agricultural Census (2011) data on proportion of NSA under current fallows.

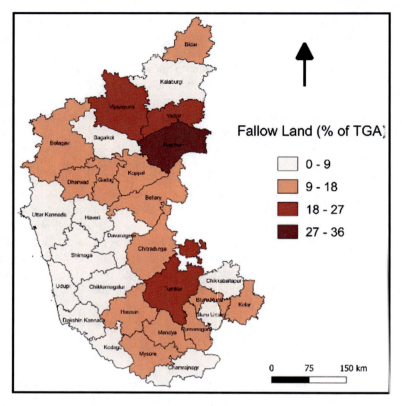

Fig. 10.4 Fallow lands in Karnataka (2016).
Map based on Karnataka State Agriculture Profile, 2016

landless). Without any support to remove the stones, such land grants to the landless are no more than a political gimmick. One possible solution is to use MGNREGS to support cleaning farmlands of stones following the guidelines for implementing the scheme on private land.

Even in the irrigated lands of Yadgir, given the nature of soil and declining number of farm animals, biomass regeneration for green manure is urgently needed to improve and maintain soil fertility and reduce fallowing. As synthetic fertilisers cannot be of much use without irrigation, rain-fed lands need vegetative biomass and farmyard manure. Biomass regeneration in the farms and in the biodiversity commons are crucial in reducing fallows apart from supplementing fodder from crops, improving retention of soil moisture and meeting the nutritional-cultural needs of families.

10.3.4 Women in Smallholdings

It is not common to see women who own land. Land-owning women were around 15–16% of the landholders in the study sites, slightly higher than the national average of 13.5%. Also, lands owned by women are smaller in size. Of the 19% of holdings owned by women in Karnataka State, 58% were marginal and 25% were small in 2011. Irrespective of landownership, women's involvement in farming is universal, highest in dairying and then in sericulture. Ramanagara had the largest share of women (17%) engaged in sericulture and dairying. Bengaluru with exotic vegetable and flower had the least number of women holders (5%).

Women in family farms engaged in non-farm work were mostly found around Bengaluru and then around Ramanagara, with garment factories and urban informal sectors as their leading employers. Yadgir villages with their high incidence of seasonal migration fail to show signs of feminization of agriculture. Labour contractors look for couples who are willing to migrate as the construction industry needs both men and women labour and hiring them as couples is the only way to get women labour come to the city.

Women migrants generally like to stay on in cities. Ease of work, better mobility, and the very different experience from rural life are all welcome changes for them. However, most migrant women accompany their spouses to the village during the agricultural seasons and often stay back to take care of the elderly or the farm. Very few women from remote areas manage to stay on permanently in the city. They work as housekeeping staff in residential and commercial complexes and as domestic help.

Women self-help groups (*stree shakti sanghas*) are now almost universal in rural Karnataka and engage exclusively in savings and micro-credit activities. They do not seem to engage in collective action or take up issues related to land or farming. This lacuna is supposed to be addressed by a recently formed national forum—*Mahila Kisan Adhikar Manch* (MAKAAM), by working on issues of women's land rights and wages, in fishing, livestock rearing and forest-based livelihoods.[10]

10.3.5 Change in Agricultural Land Use—Transactions and Acquisitions

Farmlands are acquired by the government for various purposes—establishing industrial estates, irrigation projects, roads and railways, with acquisition for industrial purposes ranking first. Nearly, 8000 ha of land was acquired by Bengaluru Development Authority for roads and neighborhood parks between 1960 and 2010. Around 60,000 ha of land was acquired for industrial area development (both public and private) in Karnataka between 1970 and 2015. Acquisition of about 4000 ha in just one year during 2012–13 for public institutions (Defence Research and Development

---

[10]More details about the forum are at http://makaam.in/about/.

Organisation, Bhabha Atomic Research Centre, Indian Space Research Organisation and Indian Institute of Science) had generated protest and public debate.[11]

Alienation of land in the city peripheries begins much before de facto conversion. This is reflected in the 'empty enclosure' phenomenon common in the peripheries of Bengaluru. Stretches of land that have already been sold by farmers to real estate developers or industries lie vacant but enclosed for long periods of time, denying even common uses for grazing and fuelwood.[12] Given the uncertainties in non-farm employment in general and the relatively large size of holdings in remote agrarian landscapes, it might be prudent to avoid complete displacement (voluntary or otherwise) of large number of farming families.

Conversion of agricultural land outside of acquisition depends on urban expansion. While urbanisation precedes involuntary conversion through acquisition, voluntary conversion through land transactions follows it. While there is no dispute about the fact that farm households in the hinterlands are in need of more rural non/off-farm employment, the question of whether this should be built on local small-scale agricultural production or by displacing it, is not raised or discussed.

10.4 Ecological Commons—Forests, Village Lands and Water Resources

As discussed in the site-specific Chaps. (6–9), village commons include land and water resources. Providing green manure for soils and fodder for cattle, land commons help reduce input cost while functioning as a habitat for variety of pollinators and natural predators of pests. Water commons also support livestock and ensure soil moisture in the fields, apart from the more visible use of rivers and large tanks for irrigating commercial crops. The economic process of seeking ecological rent through converting commons was touched upon in Sect. 2.2 in Chap. 2.

As political priorities tilted towards privatisation of commons, a large number of diverse multi-purpose livestock were replaced with fewer milch cattle. With this, the most important functionality of cattle in maintaining soil fertility was impacted adversely. Livestock wealth that was a function of agricultural needs and of access to grazing lands became exclusively driven by the city's demand for milk and milk products, though none of the villages we studied reported any significant use of milk or milk products.

Figure 10.5a and b shows how pastures and forests are aligned in their presence. Southern Karnataka fares better in terms of land commons. But this does not seem to indicate the presence of livestock, as one would have expected. Among the study sites, Yadgir and Mandya possess less forests as well as grazing commons though

---

[11] Saldhana (2013) and Gowda (2016).

[12] Hoffman et al. (2017) examine the case of 'empty layouts' awaiting construction activities along with other changes in the rural-urban interface of Bengaluru.

10.4 Ecological Commons—Forests, Village Lands and Water Resources

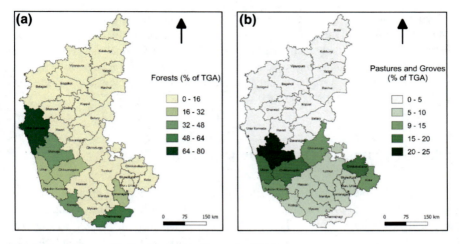

Fig. 10.5 a Forest and b Grazing land in Karnataka (2016).
Maps based on Karnataka State Agriculture Profile, 2016

they host good number of cattle. On an average, Yadgir farmers in our study villages kept five heads of local breed cows per household, while in Mandya it was three per household and mostly cross-bred cattle.

As was the case with land re-distribution, the interplay of social-ecological systems including land and water commons with agricultural occupation is overlooked in prescriptions for raising farm incomes. This realisation has to emerge across institutions in agricultural research, agricultural extension as well as in local governance including grass-roots institutions such as collectives and self-help groups. If any short-term increase in the income of small family farm has to be sustained for a longer time, village commons need to be revived and protected.

Village commons used to be the norm around small towns as in the production areas spread around Ramanagara town. At present, exclusive conservation of forests is generally prioritized over preservation of village commons in Ramanagara. Forest area has not undergone much change in the study taluks, while pastures declined in peri-urban Bengaluru (71%) and Ramanagara (42%).[13]

Though being in the neighbourhood of Bengaluru provides the outskirts of Ramanagara some marketing advantages, it does this at the cost of land, soil fertility, and water. In addition, clean water from the watersheds of Ramanagara is diverted to Bengaluru and wastewater from Bengaluru city is dumped in parts of this district. Thus, the geographical reach of the peripheries of a mega city, both in terms of sourcing raw materials and labour as well as dumping effluents extends much beyond the city boundaries (see arrows from the mega city in Fig. 10.1).

---

[13] Highest decline in pastures to the tune of 74% happened in Devanahalli taluk (acquisition for airport and allied purposes), followed by Anekal (68%) and Kanakapura (42%), between 1998 and 2015.

Mandya and Yadgir were two study sites rich in tanks and irrigation wells. Though Mandya had more of these water sources in terms of numbers, in terms of area under command, Yadgir's tanks and wells performed better individually.[14] Yet, the most visible agricultural commons in use were rivers. The harnessing of rivers for irrigation while increasing the overall external dependence for farming in these two study sites is dealt with in the next section.

10.5 Irrigation: A Dangerous Treadmill

Irrigation is a misunderstood and often mismanaged agronomic practice. Conventionally, the agricultural purpose of irrigation was to save crops from drying in order to ensure local food security. This purpose later changed to that of increasing crop yield and then to maximising production. The impetus to maximise production came to prevail and the purpose shifted from avoiding local famines to increasing global trade. This trajectory of irrigation perspective meant ignoring optimum soil moisture status at different stages of plant life as also the water-holding capacity of soils. Enhanced application of water also implied intensified application of soil amendments.

Changing Role, Impact and Political Economy of Irrigation

Irrigation is now perceived not just as more water is better, but as legitimate right of a farmer. If low-lying areas awaited ever-flowing canal water from dammed rivers, garden lands started usurping groundwater with more and deeper tube wells. Intensive irrigated cultivation with total dependence on external inputs thus came to stay as 'progressive farming'.

Canal irrigation meant a cropping pattern that can tolerate flooding (paddy or sugarcane mostly) while tube well irrigation popularised high-value horticultural crops (fruits, vegetables). Together these water-augmenting measures not only made smallholders ignore rain-fed farming but also to borrow and invest in new crops and practices in a volatile agricultural market. Thus, heavily irrigated systems have locked themselves with certain crops and practices. Never taken into account are the problems in economic efficacy[15] and social-ecological cost of public (mostly in canal irrigation) and private (in tube wells mostly) expenditure alongside longevity of irrigation projects.

---

[14]In 2014, the study taluks of Yadgir had 2345 open wells irrigating 1379 ha, while Mandya had 4000 open wells that irrigated 1508 ha. During the same period, there were only 76 tanks in Yadgir and 184 in Mandya, though on an average, command area of tanks in Yadgir was larger in size (District at a Glance 2014).

[15]Even after spending about ₹560 crores, objectives of *Cauvery Neeravari Nigam* of filling up 81 tanks, providing drinking water to 310 villages and irrigating 3200 acres of water deficit command area; and efforts to restore and rejuvenate Arkavathy, remain unaddressed (Upadhyaya 2019) https://sandrp.in/2019/01/28/will-cag-reports-of-irrigation-sector-in-2018-help-improve-performance/.

10.5 Irrigation: A Dangerous Treadmill

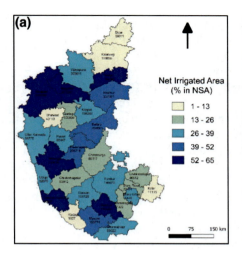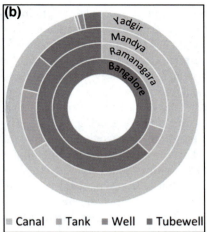

Fig. 10.6 **a** Net irrigated area in the districts of Karnataka (2016) and **b** Source-wise irrigation in study sites (2014).
Map based on Karnataka State Agriculture Profile, 2016; District at a glance, 2014

Little or no discussion takes place about how best to maintain soil moisture in different terrains hosting various soil types in a watershed. Location-specific soil mulching techniques and amendments that are irrigation neutral became knowledge of the past. Adverse impacts of continuous flooding on different types of soils are neither understood nor recognised adequately.

With the changing role of irrigation from a mechanism to avoid wilting of crops to one of maximising production, it became the generator of 'modern hydraulic societies'. Hydraulic society stands for a social order in arid settings, where differentiation is attributable to intensive use of technology to control water (see Worster (1985), on how irrigation curtailed freedom of people of colour in the history of American West). While it is now known across developing and developed economies that large-scale dams for irrigation have accentuated existing inequalities (see Singh (1997), Beinart and Hughs (2007) for detailed account from India and Egypt), the above-mentioned widely prevalent notion on the purpose of irrigation continues to be reinforced by vote bank politics in the agrarian belts inhabited by middle peasants.

It is useful to remember that regional differentiation among agrarian communities in the green revolution era has been aligned with canal irrigation and later in line with the spread of tube wells (see Shah (2011) and Mukherji et al. (2013)). The pattern of the spread of tube wells seems to follow urbanisation (see Fig. 10.6b). It is worth noting that tube wells are now spreading in the canal commands where canal water fails to reach in expected frequency or duration.

Copying an Obsolete Model

Yadgir and Mandya are the two canal irrigated production areas among the study sites. It appears that bringing canal irrigation to semi-arid Yadgir was politically easier than sustaining rain-fed smallholders in the long term through land distribution. Upper Krishna Project started irrigating parts of Yadgir from the 1990s. By then, some taluks of Mandya had been irrigated for almost half a century.[16]

Since commissioning Upper Krishna Project (UKP), paddy crop is more prominent in Yadgir than even Mandya. Studies by Mollinga (1998) and Wallach (1985) in the Krishna basin caution against the practice of flood irrigation in this belt. Without access to biomass or farmyard manure to balance soil nutrient status, and without reliable marketing and/or processing options, canals in semiarid regions could prove ecologically and economically risky in the medium to long term. Chapter 9 dealt in detail with this drastic shift with the arrival and spread of flood irrigation in the black cotton soils of semi-arid Yadgir.

Yadgir's experiment with canal irrigation is reinforcing land and caste disparities in the short term, alongside an impending productivity crisis in the medium-long term. Irrigation-induced differentiation within Mandya (Epstein 1973) is now seen reflected in Yadgir. Differentiation was already visible within Yadgir after the arrival of UKP—the differentiation between the landed, irrigated and market-oriented holdings of the dominant caste and the mostly rain-fed holdings located either at the canal ends or in stony unproductive areas with both dominant and lower castes.[17] **Given the already existing land-caste polarisation, this irrigation-driven differentiation in Yadgir is starker than the vertical differentiation across agrarian castes noted in Mandya with canal irrigation (Epstein** 1973) **and in the aftermath of land reforms (Pani** 1997). Irrigation-induced differentiation in the context of failed land reforms in Yadgir could be closer to the divergence between peasantry and the provincial propertied class in Andhra (see Balagopal 1987b).

The key message here is to caution that efforts to emulate the Mandya model in Yadgir could have the same (loss of productivity, indebtedness, distress and agitations), if not worse, consequences given the remoteness of Yadgir villages from urbanised areas for alternate livelihoods.[18]

We need agro-ecologically and hydrologically informed conversations (ideally watershed based) among farmers and agencies that work in the agrarian landscapes, geared towards evolving a contextual logic. This local social-ecological-economic logic can tease out suitable irrigation options including maintenance and replication of other functional models found in some pockets. Centuries old and still fully functional tank irrigation near Mandya and large open wells scattered in Gulbarga, with their low public and private costs both under capital and operational heads, stand testimony to this.

---

[16]In 1974, the share of canal irrigation in net irrigated area was 2.2% in Gulbarga (when Yadgir was part of Gulbarga) whereas in Mandya it was already 32%. By 2014, irrigation by canals was 70% and by open wells it was 14% of net irrigated area in Yadgir district. In Mandya, it was 72% by canal and 12% each by tube wells and tanks during the same year.

[17]Village revenue records (2014) shows that the mean size of holdings owned by OBCs and others was 8.4 acres, while SCs and STs had a mean holding size of 5.1 acres.

[18]Mean annual non-farm income in 2015 of sample households in Mandya was ₹1.12 lakhs, while in Yadgir it was ₹61,000.

10.5 Irrigation: A Dangerous Treadmill

Unexpected Fallouts

In a sense, the second wave of organised farmers' movements in independent India in the 1980s, after the spread of green revolution, is a reflection of the unmet aspirations of agrarian communities who had invested all their resources in irrigated intensive agriculture when market reliability and soil quality were dwindling. This could also be the force behind recent farmers' marches in Mumbai and Delhi in 2018 or the Patidar, Maratha and Gujjar agitations in 2015 and 2016.

The apparent agrarian angst lies in the potential realisation of two kinds of 'treadmills' that are set in motion—(a) farmers' dependence on technology and market and (b) farmers' dependence on public investment. Apart from the investment-heavy projects of dam and canal irrigation, modern drip irrigation also makes farmers mount the first treadmill of technology and market. As against traditional drip irrigation (pot and wick or channels with hollow bamboo poles), modern drip irrigation systems and precision farming techniques aim at water use efficiency.[19] However, these modern systems demand complete surrender to market by farmers apart from adverse impact on the soil in terms of use and wastage of non-degradable materials and chemicals.

The cycle of high public investment in irrigation, shifting of the cropping pattern, setting up of associated industries to generate demand for the new crops, followed eventually by heavy dependence on financial ventilators extended by the State is clearly socially, ecologically and economically illogical. Perhaps, irrigation as a means of sustainable intensification needs more information on best practices for obtaining a non-declining output without accumulating monetary or ecological debt. This argument was espoused in Chap. 8 (Sect. 8.4) on Mandya.

Yet another risk in creating a hydraulic society in semiarid Yadgir is the loss of increasingly rare adaptation skills embedded in rain-fed agriculture, which are sorely needed to survive on a planet with changing climate. Shifting from a diverse food culture to one that is rice dominated also poses an unforeseen risk to the health and nutrition status in the centuries old pulse bowl of peninsular India.

The route to stable and reliable farm livelihoods in Yadgir can be found in its agricultural systems consisting of sorghum, cotton, red gram and groundnut along with hardy livestock. This is where the health conscious consumer should play a role in demanding rain-fed grains, oilseeds and pulses. Right now, agroecology is being tweaked to suit market demand and capital-intensive technology—to feed consumers and markets that transcend ecological and political-economic boundaries. This reverse logic, deceptively progressive in the short term could be disastrous to farmers in the medium to long run, as demonstrated in many case studies.

Introduction of new crops, animals or practices to any agro-ecological region is not a new phenomenon. If the introduction is a hasty response to new urban demand and accompanied by financial burden, it could result in ecological and human distress in smallholdings. There is ample evidence of this elsewhere—ginger (Munster 2015), vanilla (Sethi 2017), cardamom (Ducourtieux et al. 2006) and high yielding milch animals (Groot and Van't Hooft 2016).

---

[19]For details of precision farming, see Ladha et al. (2000).

10.6 *Mandis*, *Santhes* and the Urban Niche Markets

Mandis under the Agricultural Produce Marketing Committee (APMC) dominates the marketing scene in the study sites, except in the case of perishable commodities mainly grown around Bengaluru city. *Mandis*, the most common regulated market, established in 1936 is now present in 163 taluks (out of 227) of Karnataka.[20] Regulated markets are of different types. Some are commodity specific and others deal in multiple commodities. Farmers' markets (*raita santhe*) form the third not so common, quasi-regulated market in Karnataka. APMCs are designed to provide a level playing field for all types of growers and traders.

About one-fourth of the 80 lakh farmers in the State are registered with APMCs and around 36% of marketable surplus reaches APMC yards.[21] But, of the 68 lakh small and marginal farmers in Karnataka, only around 1.5–2 lakh are registered with APMCs—this is only 15–20% of the 20 lakh farmers registered with APMCs. Nearly, 29% of the respondent farmers used to access APMCs on a regular basis. Apart from the regular APMCs for paddy, most of them were also accessing specialised regulated markets for copra (Tiptur), tender coconuts (Maddur), jaggery (Mandya), silkworm cocoons (Ramanagara), vegetables and fruits (Singen Agrahara near Anekal) or the cotton market in Raichur.

Thus, access to fair price, accurate weighing, and storage, supposedly the strengths of APMC, seemed to benefit very few small farmers. More than the limited accessibility for smallholders, *Mandi* is also reflective of the discriminatory tendencies in rural society centred around caste, land and politics (see Krishnamurthy (2012) and Aggarwal et al. (2016) for a critical look at *mandis*). Several States are in various stages of dismantling the monopoly of APMCs and trader lobbies, in the process of ensuring the stipulated accessibility to fair price, accurate weighing and needed storage.[22] Karnataka is also working towards strengthening APMCs within the purview of the Model APMC Act (2003). Karnataka's Agricultural Prices Commission adopts scientific calculation of support price.[23] Yet, trader cartels remain powerful in the State for many produces.

---

[20]First regulated market in Karnataka came up in Belgaum district, under the Royal Commission on Agriculture in Bombay presidency, followed by a market in Tiptur in 1948 followed by many other districts. In 1966, legislature of the unified Karnataka State enacted the Karnataka Agricultural Produce Marketing (Regulation and Development) Act, which was enforced it in 1968.

[21]Source: Presentation by Dr T N Prakash Kammardi, Chairman of Karnataka Agricultural Prices Commission in the workshop on Urbanisation and Family Farms in Karnataka organised by Azim Premji University on 26th June 2018 in Bengaluru.

[22]Maharashtra amended APMC Act in August 2018 making it illegal for private traders to purchase any agricultural produce below MSP. The amendment later had to be withdrawn in Oct 2018, under pressure from traders (https://indianexpress.com/article/cities/pune/msp-agrarian-crisis-farmers-amendment-to-apmc-act-as-traders-continue-to-protest-govt-says-no-resolution-issued-so-far-5336731/).

[23]Scientific price is the sum of many components with different weightages. The components include production cost (input, daily wages, bullock/machinery and family labour), rental value of the land, managerial cost, risk premium and interest on working capital. Scientific price is usually above the MSP announced by the Central Agricultural Costs and Prices commission and often,

10.6 *Mandis*, *Santhes* and the Urban Niche Markets

Markets for perishables are concentrated around urban areas. These could again be in the form of *mandis*, weekly *bazaars* or *raita santhes*. *Raita santhe* or farmers' market facilitated by the State government under APMC act was supposed to be established in the outskirts of all cities and towns, but just one farmers' market close to the city of Bengaluru is fully functional. *Raita santhe is* supposed to offer space to registered farmers to sell their produce at prices higher than wholesale prices. *Mandis*, on the other hand, offers space and facilities to traders.

All produces, including perishables, often find their place in the weekly neighbourhood bazaars or *santhes*. These are ubiquitous trading spaces, generally set up on the roadside or in common spaces in the taluks. Apart from the three types of markets discussed so far—*mandis, raita santhe* and weekly *bazaars*—private traders going from farm to farm are also welcomed by small farmers especially those growing fruit crops and coconut.

Other unique marketing options found in peri-urban Bengaluru are suitable for the crops grown here. Collection centres of retail chains, farmers' marketing collectives,[24] NGO mobilised producer organizations,[25] and contractual arrangements with corporate and private vendors for exotic/high-value commodities such as baby corn, sweet corn, gherkin and grapes, are most important among these. New marketing initiatives are also found in other study sites, though rare, like the co-operative society of organic farmers in Mandya.

Villages in Yadgir still depend on the two extreme marketing spaces of large *mandis* (mainly catering to relatively larger holdings and durable commodities) and smaller scattered *santhes*. The question of how new models prevailing around the city can be adapted to the hinterlands and to the commodities grown there, deserves serious consideration. When processing industries are locally established, markets become redundant, especially if commodities are outside the purview of APMC act. Among the study sites, only Mandya had visible access to processing units—both medium-scale industries like sugar factories along with smaller ones like jaggery units, rice mills, oil mills and silk reeling units. A few small-scale value addition enterprises were found in Ramanagara.

If processing units of farm produces are more prevalent around green revolution belts like Mandya, other manufacturing industries are mostly concentrated around Bengaluru, making augmentation of both farm and non-farm incomes impossible in

---

when there is a market boom, involves bonus payment for specific produces over and above the scientific price declared (Perspective Report, Karnataka Agricultural Price Commission, 2017).

[24] Shivaganga in Nelmangala and Honneru in Bengaluru are examples of such collectives.

[25] Like Sahaja Samrudha and Buffalo Back in the outskirts of Bengaluru.

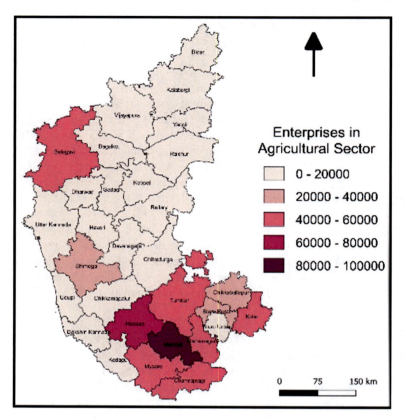

Fig. 10.7 Enterprises in agriculture in Karnataka (2015).
Map based on Karnataka Economic Survey, 2015

remote landscapes. This pattern is visible in Fig. 10.7 which shows the concentration of value addition units, processing units and trading services in south Karnataka.

Contract farming modalities that are under discussion suggest that companies have to work out contracts with groups of farmers. The Model Contract Farming Act (2018) encourages setting up of facilitation groups at village or panchayat levels. Farmer Producer Organisations (FPOs) are instrumental in mobilising these groups of farmers. There are around 120 FPOs (Small Farmers' Agribusiness Consortium 2018) collectivizing about 1.2 lakh producers in the State. During the study period, there were five FPOs in Yadgir and one in Mandya. The threat of political interference and power dynamics around caste and capital are challenges that insidiously creep into such set-ups.

10.7 Fragile Balance—Wages, Farm Income and Loans

As mentioned in the beginning of this chapter, agrarian communities did not seem to be uniformly distressed or progressed and varied in terms of peasant differentiation across and within the four study sites, reflective of the core–periphery dynamics. Here we present the varied pattern of persistence found among family farms in the study sites. Despite the varied pattern, farmer respondents were largely surviving on a fragile financial surplus,[26] though net income and loans repaid during 2015 varied among the smallholders we studied.[27] Financial surplus with small farm holdings was highest in Bengaluru with ₹1.81 lakhs and lowest in Yadgir with ₹−91,600.

Among the study sites, positive surplus was found in the farms around Bengaluru, followed by the villages around Ramanagara. Yadgir followed by Mandya show negative surplus. Financial precariousness seemed to vary depending on the expenses incurred, loans taken and non-farm incomes. **Significantly high non-farm and farm incomes and earnings from dairying combined with high expenses and loans characterised the financially better-off farm holdings around Bengaluru. High medical expenses and low share of food produced on farm were the features of the most precarious farms in Yadgir.** Of the 172 farm households surveyed (excluding the 32 farmer migrants), 135 had outstanding loans, more or less equally distributed across sites. Farms without loans were found mostly in Mandya (41%) and least (4%) in Yadgir.

Negative financial outcomes in Mandya's farms were more due to depressed incomes from both farm and non-farm options rather than high expenses. This phenomenon of negative surplus and depressed incomes in a green revolution region known for agrarian activism occurs in spite of the long-term public investment in irrigation and processing. **The major commodities grown and processed in Mandya—sugarcane and paddy—are subject to State policies on procurement, distribution and external trade.**

On the other hand, crops grown around Bengaluru and Ramanagara find local, diverse and less uncertain markets. Despite incurring high expenses and loans in these two production landscapes, local marketing options pay better. But the high-value perishable crops grown here are resource depleting intensive ventures targeting urban demand in the neighbourhood and hence unsuitable elsewhere.

The study points to the absence of agrarian differentiation among small farmers, on account of significantly varying capital accumulation from farming.[28] The existing income differential generally found in the peri-urban sites of Ben-

---

[26]Financial surplus is the annual amount available to farm families after deducting the sum of total expenses and loan repayment from their total income.

[27]During 2015, mean annual net income per family was ₹57,000 (excluding the loan repayment), while loans repaid came to ₹1.28 lakhs.

[28]Net agricultural income per family ranged from ₹70,000 in Yadgir to ₹190,000 in Bengaluru in 2015. Net farm income per acre of farmland was ₹20,000 in Yadgir and ₹102,000 in peri-urban Bengaluru. This calculation excludes repayment of loans as it was difficult to segregate loans availed and used exclusively for agricultural purposes.

Table 10.1 Irrigation and vulnerability in family farms (2015)

Districts	Taluks	Net irrigated area (% in net sown area)	Financial surplus (₹/family/annum)	Non-farm income (% in total family income)	Ratio of total income to total expense	Number of suicides reported (2003–17)
Irrigated taluks (>50% of NSA)						
Mandya	Pandavapura	52	−43,814	23	0.8	57
Yadgir	Shahpur	54	−78,561	38	0.7	81
	Shorapur	57	−106,408	34	0.6	40
Mean		54	−76,261	32	0.7	59
Rain-fed taluks						
Bengaluru	Anekal	24	207,542	61	1.7	0
	Devanahalli	20	154,647	55	1.5	10
Ramanagara	Kanakapura	26	70,286	35	1.2	32
	Magadi	17	32,498	50	1.2	10
Mandya	Nagamangala	35	8178	24	1.0	17
Mean		24	94,630	45	1.3	14

galuru was attributable to proximity to the city. Interestingly, financial status including farm and non-farm income and expenses of the family and distress resulting from it was found to be correlated with the extent of irrigation in the study taluks. Families with negative financial surplus and higher incidence of suicides due to indebtedness were found more in taluks (Pandavapura, Shorapur and Shahpur) with about 50% of net sown area irrigated. Yadgir's suicide phenomenon is more recent as is its irrigation. Table 10.1 shows how irrigated smallholdings and vulnerability go hand in hand.

In irrigated taluks just as the presence of livestock was comparatively less than in rain-fed taluks, value of livestock produce consumed and marketed were also low.[29] In these taluks, while engagement as farm labour was relatively high, non-farm work and income accrued from it was relatively low compared to rain-fed taluks.[30] Evidently, lack of engagement with livestock as well as with non-farm work adds to fragility in irrigated taluks.

Many farm families we talked to were linking family health, food consumed, farming and soil quality in their land. Yet, in the absence of non-farm jobs and in the hope of generating better cash incomes, they tend to grow crops exclusively for markets. This trade-off is also influenced by the proximity to public health care

---

[29]Mean value of livestock produce consumed by family was about ₹3200 in irrigated taluks, while it was about ₹11,000 in rain-fed taluks. Mean annual livestock income per family was ₹32,000 in irrigated taluks and ₹131,000 in rain-fed taluks.

[30]Each working member of the family in irrigated taluks found farm labour work for 87 days in a year, whereas in rainfed taluks it was available for 40 days only.

and food distribution systems that generate (a deceptive) feeling of availability of potentially sufficient, accessible and affordable services as and when needed. This leads to a complacency with respect to the food and health needs of the family leading to a casual bypassing of the food production aspect of agriculture. Rather, they embrace intensive commercial farming and in the process take undue financial risks in volatile markets and informal credit sources, thereby compromising their nutritional needs and environmental safety.

If distributional aspects are integral to the discussion on fragility of family farms, it is to be noted that income and land inequalities are found in mutually opposite directions. Farmers around Bengaluru were rich in terms of income, while their counterparts in Yadgir held larger parcels land. Nonetheless, rural inequality in Bengaluru in terms of income Gini coefficient was high in villages where financial surpluses were high. In the financially precarious households of Yadgir, land inequality was conspicuous. Thus, land inequality may not be substantially contributing to income inequality given the fact that agricultural lands were not adding much towards financial surplus in the current scenario.

Avoiding precariousness thus would mean many things for farm families. It involves a context-specific combination of reliable non-farm occupations, culturally suitable and nutritionally adequate food distribution, functional and accessible public health care, along with production planning to balance profit with unmet nutritional needs. This combination would limit debts to the risk-taking ability of a farm household; while meeting basic healthcare needs. In the most financially vulnerable areas of Yadgir, the largest loans were taken for medical treatment and observing social customs. A shift in focus from spreading irrigation to fine-tuning farming and markets to suit local agro-ecology, combined with access to reliable and affordable medical service, can curb the debt burden and thereby out-migration too.

10.8 To Farm or to Migrate?—The Dilemma

There are many dilemmas that today's smallholder grapples with while trying to combine food production and income from land. What to grow and how to grow are more common among them. A more recent, but widely felt dilemma is—when should one stop farming and pursue an alternate occupation, and for how long should one keep away from farming? Also, if not cultivating, then what does one do with the land without parting with it for good? These are the real-life manifestations of the dilemma of transition discussed in Chap. 2.

However, it must be mentioned that among the farmers studied, no one wanted to abandon farming altogether. This reluctance was more a case of lack of other skills, options, and a matter of being resigned to one's fate and saying, '*this is our past and destiny*'. Farming by choice is confined to high-value production in the outskirts of Bengaluru. Here, there also exists the option of selling part of the land and using the proceeds to construct multi-storied buildings to rent out rooms to migrant workers

272   10 Withering Family Farms

or students. Moving from farming to be a landlord who manages rented property is not rare in the periphery of Bengaluru,[31] but hardly found in other study villages.

Family land continues to be farmed in Ramanagara and Mandya as long as at least one adult person is available to do farming. We found it difficult to identify farmer migrants from Mandya for the study. Apparently, the agro-urbanism of Mandya has the potential to secure a subaltern economy of the agrarian kind. This could be well achieved only if land-based production of the region is not undermined (even if not supported) by public policies with a known penchant for sacrificing agrarian social-ecology for short-term economic growth.

With limited options available, the waxing and waning pattern of agricultural livelihoods observed in the gradient of urbanisation complements the pattern in the production potential of land. Remote dry lands sustained farm livelihoods in relatively larger holdings that grow pulses, oilseeds and cotton. In the peripheries of Bengaluru the households that are sustaining in farming are either into farming high value produce or catering to the demand for fresh organic produce.

Thus, the nature of persistence varies among smallholders, though accumulation from farming does not. Farm holdings sustaining for years on eucalyptus and mango fields are indicative of a step taken closer towards full time non-farm jobs and depeasantisation. In contrast, flower crops (local flowers for the local market) and mulberry have sustained families in farming for long on their land. Where landowners are farmers themselves, they choose commercial crops in such a way as not to completely replace ragi and pulses which are part of the culinary culture. Locked in the closed chain of agro-processing and canal irrigation, farmers in Mandya remained farmers albeit meagre financial surplus.

Agrarian dynamism that emerged from the peri-urban villages of Mandya, reflected even in its political and voluntary social movements,[32] co-exist with a high Human Development Index, large number of farm holdings, high contribution of the primary sector to the district's gross domestic product[33] and the gradual emergence of Bengaluru-Mysore corridor as an urban agglomeration.

Livelihood Dilemma When Options Vary

The dilemma of choosing between farming and other occupations differs between sites. Farmers around Bengaluru who benefit from the real estate market have the option to choose between farming (as a high income—high-cost occupation) and non-farming lives. In villages of Mandya where cropping options are limited by

---

[31] Sampat (2016) relates to this rentier economy phenomenon. In the case of Dholera Special Investment Region in Gujarat, she finds the rentier economy brought together by combination of speculative markets, real estate and other urban infrastructure investments at global and domestic scales, private consultants and developers and landowners willing and able to benefit from rentiering.

[32] Prominent political outfits of farmers, like the *Karnataka Rajya Raita Sangha* (KRRS) and other voluntary organizations like *Raita Teerpu, Hasiru Sene, Krushi Koolikarara Sangha* have notable presence in Mandya.

[33] Primary sector contribution in GDDP in 2014 was high in Mandya (₹32 billion—17% of GDDP) compared to peri-urban parts of Bengaluru (₹16 billion—6.3% of GDDP) 14, Yadgir (₹14 billion—20% of GDDP) and Ramanagara (₹18 billion—15% of GDDP) as well as State average (₹825 billion—12% of GDP).

10.8 To Farm or to Migrate?—The Dilemma

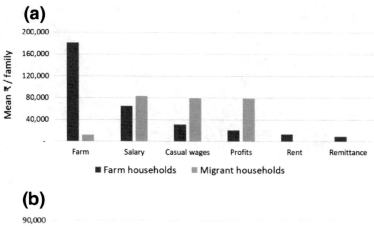

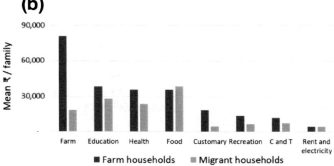

Fig. 10.8 **a** Income and **b** Expenses of farmers and migrants.
'C and T' stands for Communication and Transport.
Source Interviews with farmers and farmer migrants, 2015–16

canal irrigation, the choice is limited to a few reliable non-farm occupations. In Yadgir, the dilemma of whether to leave farming or not is of a different kind. Land and manual labour are the only assets these smallholders possess. Smallholders of Yadgir choose to migrate for different time spans depending on their attachment to land. Reasons for this could be either unproductive lands, recently arrived canal irrigation that allows only an unfamiliar capital-intensive crop, or high indebtedness.

During our initial exploratory visits and group interactions, it was clear that seasonal and circular out-migration was most prevalent in the agrarian landscapes of Yadgir. Entire families of about 15% of households in the village were engaged in circular migration. It was common to see nuclear families that are part of joint family holdings taking turns to go to Bengaluru, while the rest of the extended family continued in farming and rural wage labour. These families are part of active networks that include labour and transport contractors,[34] and already migrated relatives in Bengaluru.

---

[34]Trips to Bengaluru could be door to door transport service provided by a local vehicle owner, unless the village is easily connected to the State capital by public transport.

Fig. 10.9 Living environment of farmers and migrants

In Yadgir, caste discrimination emerged as a reason for migration of SC farmers though most migrants belonged to dominant OBC castes. Farmer migrants from the immediate peripheries of Bengaluru were in salaried jobs or had their own business in the heart of the city, while those from Yadgir were engaged in construction labour, staying in different labour camps. Those from the villages in Ramanagara and Mandya (remember that farmer migration was least from Mandya) were working mostly in skilled jobs like cab driving or electrical work.

Farmer migrants were also seen working closer to their village of origin, in the towns of Ramanagara, Mandya and Bijapur. When we compare the options that small landholders could choose from, their social and economic precariousness becomes clear. Figure 10.8 presents a comparison of the household economy of a farmer and a farmer migrant.

Apart from the evident difference in the financial status of farm and migrant households, the difference in the living and social conditions was also noteworthy (Fig. 10.9). Most migrants felt discriminated against while others didn't either feel safe or like the job. Despite this, only a quarter of all migrants we studied expressed unhappiness in their new assignments. Though not unhappy with their stint in the city, about the same proportion of migrants also felt that their living environment was unhealthy.

Contrary to our expectation, only 20% of women from migrant families felt benefitted by an exposure to life outside the village, felt confident to move around by themselves and to communicate with others in the society. Most of the 32 migrants we interviewed were missing the seasonal festivals and the rustic environment of their village.

If one strikes up a conversation with cab drivers, security guards, housemaids or construction workers in Bengaluru City, irrespective of whether they are from Bihar, Odisha, Assam, West Bengal or North Karnataka, most of them turn nostalgic and talk about their ancestral land, parents and children left behind back home. Most of them tend to go back home during the peak farming season and festivals. They also tend to help others in their extended families to connect to the city or with labour contractors.

10.8 To Farm or to Migrate?—The Dilemma

The Other Side of Migration

The to-and-fro migration of rural people between their villages and urban parts of India is generating a phenomenal subaltern cultural exchange within the country[35] apart from supporting regional economies. Jam-packed trains leaving south Indian railway stations during festival seasons to Bihar, Jharkhand, Odisha, Assam and West Bengal; cinema halls in North Bengaluru buzzing with Bhojpuri, Assamese or Bengali conversations on Saturday nights; States enacting regulations to protect the living conditions of migrants[36] and migrants adopting new lifestyle and skills (e.g. cooking different cusines and region-specific farming operations) all showcase the new '*rurban*' character of both Indian cities and villages. **Our interest in this phenomenon of subaltern cultural infusion is to bring out the mixed bag of experiences and to understand the push factors that make footloose labour out of small landowners and the role this circular movement plays in the life of agrarian communities.**

Even as we argue the need to proactively avoid jeopardising agrarian livelihoods through the dominant development path, it is also possible to see some less negative aspects of out-migration. The positive side of migration experience is the possibility it offers to strengthen farm holdings to tide over risks in both farm and non-farm aspects of livelihood through financial and other means, offering new paths for their future. Living in close proximity to the urban society, according to migrants exposed them to new social positives learning in children's education; caste and gender relations, and even financial prudence. Yet, in the small towns amidst agrarian landscapes, we met cab drivers and hotel workers who had returned from their stint in bigger cities in order to settle down closer home, despite lesser earnings.

According to the migrants we interviewed, reasons to migrate out from peri-urban agriculture around Bengaluru were mainly water scarcity, job aspirations and loans. In Ramanagara, the reasons were land acquisition and water problems, and for rural Mandya it was mostly water woes. Indebtedness was stated as the primary push factor in Yadgir, where accumulated household loans were about 80% of the total household income. Evidently, unlike the other study sites, there was distress migration from Yadgir. In Yadgir, loans were availed mainly from local money lenders for medical emergencies and for ceremonies during marriages or death in the family. Thus Yadgir, where land disparity and indebtedness were high and non-farm engagement low, became a hub of forced centrifugal migration to build our cities.

Taking into account the revealing stories of both the farmer and the migrant, it is apparent that it is not just access to quality natural resources like soil, water and biodiversity that limits sustainability of agrarian livelihoods. Shortcomings in public delivery systems of education, health care and marketing have impacted farm livelihoods the most. It is unfair to state that reasons behind migration lie exclusively in unviable farming. It is of course a matter of concern

---

[35]This is in contrast to the cultural globalisation happening among the elite Indian families travelling worldwide for studies, work and leisure.

[36]Karnataka enacted The Building and Other Construction Workers (Regulation of Employment and Conditions of Service) act in 1996.

that farming currently does not provide for contemporary social needs. Significant push for taking loans has its genesis in the failure of public healthcare and capitalisation of rural customs with pervasive urbanism.

Providing irrigation or setting up agro-processing units will not sustain agriculture as a self-reliant livelihood. Rather, volatility in marketing needs to be addressed while maintaining the agro-ecology. If meagre financial surplus, lack of employment options, degraded land and water resources and indebtedness were the primary cause of migration, gaps in decentralized formal and informal institutions too add to distress in farm holdings. We discuss that in the next section.

10.9 Local Institutions and Mobilisation for Adaptive Skilling

The ecological and institutional blind spots in analysing small-scale farms identified in Chap. 2 were further elaborated upon in subsequent chapters, showing the impact of alienation of village commons, biodiversity and soil moisture on smallholdings. Addressing this blind spot which is reflected in governance and policy-making too needs a political-economic perspective on development moulded in a social-ecological systems framework. Shifting from policy programmes with a saddled vision of development as solely economic growth, demands change at both grass-roots and also in macroeconomic policies.

At the local scale, we need agro-ecologically informed deliberations by local government agencies to facilitate adaptive skilling of agrarian communities. This in turn can prepare smallholders with well-informed trade-offs entailed in any change in agriculture. Local government bodies should deliberate on trade-offs involved in linking local production and consumption with that of the outside world. Making this stipulated role of local governments (as per 73rd and 74th amendments on Panchayati Raj Institutions (PRI)) functional in reality is a prerequisite to continue farming by choice and not just by destiny. Such informed perspective on development and deliberative processes in PRIs can potentially fuel a much-needed paradigm shift in macroeconomic policies.[37]

Farming communities need adaptive skilling for experimentation and social evaluation of any proposed change at an agro-ecological scale. There is sufficient literature about agrarian deskilling (e.g. Stone 2007; Flachs and Stone 2018) as a consequence of introducing new technologies or crops without a process of experimentation and evaluation by local smallholders. Information and science at the local agro-ecological scale can stimulate and set inmotion a continuous process of adaptive skilling among agrarian communities. The Zero Budget Natural Farming (ZBNF) movement in Kar-

---

[37]Recognising this potential of local governance, Azim Premji University offers a short-term training program on the links between agro-ecology and rural livelihoods for panchayat members and functionaries in the interior districts of Karnataka. (https://azimpremjiuniversity.edu.in/SitePages/University-resource-centre-events-agrarian-ecology-and-livelihoods.aspx).

10.9 Local Institutions and Mobilisation for Adaptive Skilling

nataka offers hope in this direction. ZBNF movement shows (Khadse et al. 2018) how peer-to-peer learning and reaching at a common internal logic can help avoid distress and accomplish sustainable production levels using available resources, without seeking outside capital.

Both production and consumption are nestled in the identity of 'small farmer' and in the rural landscape, as we saw in the introductory chapter, while urban areas remain predominantly consumption spaces. Nevertheless, the widespread indifference to and ignorance about the impacts of production and consumption activities seems to cut across both rural and urban areas. This perhaps explains why farmer producers and food consumers seem to comply with the discursive separation of food and farm policies, and with an unequal and unsustainable allocation of land, water and biodiversity. There is palpable lack of initiative for the establishment of informed mechanisms and local institutions to link local demand (e.g. schools and hospitals) with local production.

This shows that farmers' movements should go beyond seeking ventilator support in loan waivers, support prices, and subsidies. They should institutionalise community-wide adaptive skilling for a dynamic yet healthy rural–urban nexus and most importantly to resist being pushed blind-folded towards new technologies. From the study sites, it appears that protest movements generally emerge in production landscapes such as Mandya that showcase stagnated progress and not in the most precarious hinterlands like Yadgir. This is quite contrary to Omvedt's (1981) prediction that the new rural proletariat of peasants would trigger struggles for distributional rights.

Desai's (1979) take on the difference between farmers' movements among propertied and among poor farmers (similar to Balagopal's (1987a, 1987b) analysis on provincial propertied class) echoes this need to move towards a paradigm shift in the development imagination by movements, where smallholders—a large constituency among the poor, are prioritised. If not, ecological rent-seeking by capital chasers in urbanising accumulation economies will trigger Chayanovian hunger rent (see Sect. 2.2 in Chap. 2 for a brief discussion) in millions of smallholdings that fail to successfully bail out of farming before sinking into distress.

10.10 The City and the Peasant: Complementary, Competitive or Hegemonic?

The many shades of the urban–agrarian interface that the book unveils bring forth the challenges and opportunities in bridging the consumer–producer divide. Though the city as a consumption space where consumers and secondary producers congregate, offers opportunities for harmonious accomplishment of the twin goals of production (healthy food, livelihoods) and consumption (health and well-being), they seldom show this affinity, rather, they seem to foster an antagonistic relationship. Finding the means to correct this misconstrued relationship between the spaces of primary production, consumption and secondary manufacture is crucial not just to strengthen agrarian communities, but more importantly for the sustainability of human society as we know it.

The extent and intensity of urban utilisation of agrarian landscapes range from sourcing raw materials for regular consumption, manufacturing and construction to sourcing daily workforce or simply using them to dump city's effluents. An information vaccum at both consumption and production ends keeps the city-farm nexus either invisible or mutually antagonistic, with consumers and producers displaying a 'herd mentality' in passively emulating their peers.

When we segregate the peri-urban spaces of major cities and metros from those of small towns, complexity of the love–hate relationship that urbanism fosters with agrarian livelihoods unfolds. This can be seen in the patterns of cropping, migration, occupation and vulnerability across these diverse urban peripheries that currently host farm livelihoods. The pattern of farming that may be sustained in these agrarian peripheries varies and can be linked to specific enabling factors as discussed below.

Taking a cue from Dorin et al. (2013) and using the poverty trap lens. along with the family's engagement in farm and non-farm activities as well as income from those, it is possible to speculate various possibilities for small farmers. For the farmers of small-town Ramanagara, with reasonable financial surplus and biodiversity along with moderate indebtedness, it appears feasible to continue agriculture by choice, in a development trajectory. Farmers in Yadgir are caught in a Lewis trap with high indebtedness and negative surplus, highest ratio of farm to non-farm income and high share of on-farm labour. Bengaluru farmers may continue in farming as long as the already constrained land, water and labour permit their high value—high-cost production practices. Mandya's small-scale farming tied to canal irrigation and dependent on State support seems stagnant with depressed farm income at low liability levels.

Farmers in the outskirts of Bengaluru City hurry to feed the city markets with the wares they produce while simultaneously waiting for real estate sharks to buy their land. They appear to be fully engaged in farming, though detached from land and eager to bridge the economic distance from their kith and kin engaged in urban jobs. Perhaps as a reflection of this, it was more difficult for us to get farmers' time for interactions in the study taluks close to Bengaluru than in other sites. Farmers in remote Yadgir, largely unaware of the root cause of their concerns, passively accept their plight as an inevitable sacrifice at the altar of urbanisation for development.

Towards a Vibrant and Sustainable Urban–Agrarian Interface

Family farms are made up of members who stay and participate in agriculture in various ways—contributing to labour, capital or networks. The discussion so far indicates that sustainability of small family farms is a function of the relative size of land with respect to number of dependents, reliable non-farm income and presence of functional agro-ecologically informed local institutions.

The ecological and economic fissures in rural–urban exchanges will be visible to the agrarian society only if the terms of trade between farm and non-farm societies are made explicit. This envisages monitoring a dashboard of measures on farm and non-farm performance of family farms.[38] Ratio of aggregate family income to loans and input costs can keep track of financial viability of a farm. The proportion of purchased inputs in the total inputs used on a farm can indicate extent of market dependence. Given the low financial turnover in a small family farm, consumption expenditure, on-farm food production and the income elasticity of food consumption also need to be measured and monitored. The above-mentioned indicators along with the status of common natural resources including soil fertility can indicate the possible longevity of small-scale agricultural production.

Although it is clear that what is good for consumer health is essentially good for farmers and farmlands as well, the big question is—whether the State will take the minimum essential initiative needed to connect these obvious disjointed ends? For this, rather than forcing smallholders on treadmills of populist technologies, efforts are needed to first prioritise integrated interventions for soil moisture and soil fertility in farmlands using biodiversity of the surroundings. Secondly, regular procurement and aggregation of small surpluses by decentralised and diverse mechanisms are required. Finally, there is a need for policies that take into account the parallel repercussions of international agricultural trade on consumer health and farmer livelihoods.

The above integrative effort appears to be nothing short of an overhauling of India's mindset with regard to food and farm policies. Bridging the urban–agrarian rift envisages such innovative measures both from the State and society. In reality, this bridging of gaps can be initiated and catalysed by conversations between and across farmers, consumers, officials, people's representatives and researchers. Even as macroeconomists worry, this doesn't mean a ban on non-farm industries or a long slowing down of national economy. Instead, this bridging is about inclusive selection and prioritization of potential pivots of development and grass-roots employment.

Meanwhile, conflicts may flare up intermittently over access to quality resources of land, water and commons. The same resources that the agrarian economy needs for its expanded reproduction are also demanded by large capitalist farms, non-farm capital enterprises, public institutions and consumers.

Mishra's (1998) Growth Centre Theory which is widely used in developing countries for urban and regional development planning offers a micropolitan approach for rural transformation sans the rural–urban dichotomy. It is tantalising to imagine how micro-polises of ten-twelve villages with small urban centres having the required infrastructure for trade, commerce and cottage industries help forge rural–urban as well as farm and non-farm integration. Micro-polises of Gandhian imagination as espoused in Mishra's (1985, 1998) work stands for planned effort towards a strong bottom-up economy. Whether it is the micropolis, gram swaraj or a regional economy model, there needs to be a movement to imbibe the potential as well as limits of capitalisation. Farmers' struggles should be founded on a socio-economic logic woven around local agro-ecology and armed with creative options to combat the inequitable appropriation of nature's commons.

---

[38]Indicators simpler and realistic than those mentioned in literature like the Livelihood Farm Unit (Harriss 1987) and Labour Exploitation Index (Patnaik 1987).

Unless an informed urban–agrarian conversation opens up the pathways of adaptive skilling, there will be a small set of family farms that will be striving to supply high-value products to the rich and health conscious urban consumers through niche markets. The majority of others at the diametrically opposite end will survive by mass-producing cheap food, employing means which are harmful to themselves, to the natural resource base as well as to consumers. Unless this weakening bipolarity in farmer persistence is broken, agrarian concerns will persist as a cantankerous problem, trapping both the farmer constituencies in the uncertainties of non-farm informal sectors.

The fact that the whole model of development enterprise has to be recast for a lasting solution to agrarian concerns is seldom acknowledged. Equally unacknowledged is the fact that recasting the model has to begin and spread from the grass roots and not replicated from elsewhere. Fortunately, such sprouts are visible in the numerous small efforts scattered across the State of Karnataka.[39]

References

Aggarwal, N., Jain, S., & Narayanan, S. (2016). *The long road to transformation of agricultural markets in India: Lessons from Karnataka*. IGIRD Working Paper 2016-026.

Ambedkar, B. R. (1918). Small holdings in India and their remedies. *Journal of Indian Economic Society, I,* 1918.

Assadi, M., & Rajendran, S. (2000). Karnataka—Changing shape of caste conflict. *Economic and Political Weekly, 35*(19).

Balagopal, K. (1987a). An ideology of the provincial propertied class. *Economic and Political Weekly, 22*(50), 1544–1546.

Balagopal, K. (1987b). An ideology for the provincial propertied class. *Economic and Political Weekly,* 2177–2178.

Beinart, W., & Hughs, L. (2007). Environment and empire. In R. Luis (Ed.), *The Oxford history of the British empire, companion series.* Oxford University Press.

Buchanan, F. (1807). *A journey from Madras through the countries of Mysore, Canara, and Malabar* (Vol. 2, pp. 212, 291–195). London: East India Company.

Colatei, & Harriss-White. (2004).

Desai, A. (1979). *Peasant struggles in India.* Oxford University Press.

Deshpande, S. V., & Torgal, V. (1994). Administering land reforms in Karnataka. *Economic and Political Weekly, 29*(33), 2132–2134.

Dorin, B., Hourcade, J. C., & Benoit-Cattin, M. (2013). *A world without farmers? The levis path revisited.* CIRED Working Paper 47-2013.

Ducourtieux, O., Visonnavong, P., & Rossard, J. (2006). Introducing cash crop in shifting cultivation regions—The experience with Cardamom in Laos. *Agroforesty Systems, 66*(1), 65–76.

Epstein, S. (1973). *South India: Yesterday, today and tomorrow.* London: Macmillan.

Erappa, S. (2006). *Contract farming in Karnataka: A boon or bane?* ISEC Research Report: IX/ADRT/113.

Fan, S., & Chan-Kang, C. (2005). Is small beautiful? Farm size, productivity, and poverty in Asian agriculture. *Agricultural Economics,* 135–146.

---

[39]We here acknowledge the inspiring presence of active farmer organizations and supply chains working through Sahaja Samrudha, Honneru collective, Mandya organic co-operative society, Jaivik Krishi Society, Akshaya Kalpa, Safe Harvest, Navadarshanam, Buffalo Back, Shivganga organics and similar others around Bengaluru.

References

Food and Agriculture Organisation (FAO). (2012). Smallholders and family farmers. http://www.fao.org/fileadmin/templates/nr/sustainability_pathways/docs/Factsheet_SMALLHOLDERS.pdf.

Flachs, A., & Stone, G. D. (2018). Farmer knowledge across the commodification spectrum: Rice, cotton, and vegetables in Telangana, India. *Journal of Agrarian Change, 2018,* 1–21. https://doi.org/10.1111/joac.12295.

Foster, G. (1965). Peasant society and the image of limited good. *American Anthropology, 67*(2), 293–315.

Fukazawa, A.-H. (2002). *The medieval Deccan: Peasants, social systems and states sixteenth to eighteenth centuries.* Delhi: Oxford University Press.

Gowda, C. (2016, June 29). A nightmare called science city. *Bangalore Mirror.*

Groot, M. J., & Van't Hooft, K. E. (2016). The hidden effects of dairy farming on public and environmental health in the Netherlands, India, Ethiopia, and Uganda, considering the use of antibiotics and other agro-chemicals. *Frontier in Public Health, 4,* 12.

Harriss, B. (1987). Regional growth linkages from agriculture. *Journal of Development Studies, 23*(2), 275–289.

Himanshu, (2018). Too little, too late: apathy towards the rural sector. *Economic and Political Weekly, 53*(9), 25–30.

Hoffman, E., Jose, M., Nolke, N., & Mockel, T. (2017). Construction and use of a simple index of urbanization in the rural-urban interface of Bangalore, India. *Sustainability, 9,* 2146.

Jai Prabhakar, S. C. (2010). Socio-cultural dimensions of development in Karnataka. *CMDR Monograph Series No. 63.*

Jodhka, S. (2018). Rural change in times of 'distress'. *Economic and Political Weekly, 53*(26), 5–7.

Kadekodi, G. K., Kanbur, R., & Rao, V. (2007). Governance and the 'Karnataka model of development'. *Economic and Political Weekly,* 649–652.

Khadse, A., Rosset, P. M., Morales, H., & Ferguson, B. G. (2018). Taking agroecology to scale: The zero budget natural farming peasant movement in Karnataka, India. *The Journal of Peasant Studies, 45*(1), 192–219.

Khan, M. M. (1909). Imperial gazetteer of India. Provincial series. Hyderabad state.

Krishna, K. R., & Morrison, K. D. (2010). Histroy of South Indian agricuture and agroecosystems. In K. R. Krishna (Ed.), *Agroecosystem of South* (pp. 1–52). Boca Raton, FL, USA: Brown Walker.

Krishnamurthy, M. (2012). State of wheat. *Economic and Political Weekly, 47*(52).

Kritsman, L. N. (1984). Class stratification of the Soviet countryside. In Cox & Littlejohn (Eds.), *Kritsman and the agrarian marxist* (pp. 85–143). Routledge.

Kroeber, A. L. (Ed.). (1953). *Anthropology today.* Chicago: University Press.

Ladha J. K., Fischer, K. S., Hossain, M., Hobbs, P. R., & Hardy, B. (Eds.), (2000). *Improving the productivity and sustainability of rice-wheat systems of the Indo-Gangetic Plains: A synthesis of NARS-IRRI partnership research.* International Rice Research Institute, Discussion Paper No. 40.

Lenin, I. A. (1903). Riches and poverty, property-owners and workers in the countryside. In *To the rural poor* (pp. 377–390).

Marx, K., & Engels, F. (1848). The manifesto of the communist party. In *Marx/Engels selected works* (Vol. 1, pp. 98–137). Moscow: Progress Publishers.

Mishra, R. P. (1985). *Development issues of our time.* New Delhi: Concept Publishing Company.

Mishra, R. P. (1998). *Urbanisation in India: Challenges and opportunities.* India: Daya Books.

Mollinga, P. P. (1998). *On the waterfront: Water distribution, technology and agrarian change in South Indian canal irrigation system.* Wageningen.

Mukherji, A., Rawat, S., & Shah, T. (2013). Major insights from India's minor irrigation censuses: 1986–87 to 2006–07. *Economic and Political Weekly, 48*(26–27), 115–124.

Munster, D. (2015). "Ginger is a gamble" Crop booms, rural uncertainty, and the neoliberalisation of agriculture in South India. *Journal of Global and Historical Antrhopology, 71,* 100–113.

Naik, M. (1989). *Agrarian unrest in Karnataka.* New Delhi: Reliance Publishing House.

Negi, V. S. (2014). Where have all the small farmers gone! The story of agriculture and small Indian farmers. Focus on Smallholder Agroecology Series, 1.

Omvedt, G. (1981). Capitalist agriculture and rural classes in India. *Economic and Political Weekly, 16*(52).

Pani, N. (1997). Towards decentralized agrarian reforms: Lessons from Karnataka's 1974 experience. In Aziz & Krishna (Eds.) Land reforms in India: Karnataka promises kept and missed (Vol. 4, pp. 33–50). Sage Publications.

Pani, N. (2017). First nature and the state—Non-emergence of regional capital in Mandya. *Economic and Political Weekly, 52*(46).

Patnaik, U. (1987). *Peasant class differentiation: A study in method with reference to Haryana.* Delhi: Oxford University Press.

Pinto, A. S. J. (1994). Atrocities on dalits in Gulbarga-upper caste hold on police. *Economic and Political Weekly, 29*(16–17).

Rajan, M. A. S. (1997). Effects of land reform: What next? In Aziz & Krishna (Eds.), *Lana reforms in India: Karnataka promises kept and missed* (Vol. 4, pp. 83–84). Sage Publications.

Rice, K. L. (1897). *Mysore—A gazetteer compiled for government* (Vol. 2—Mysore by Districts, Vol. 1, pp. 575–599).

Saldhana. (2013). *Forfeiting our commons. A case for protecting and conserving Challakere's Amrit Mahal Kavals as livelihood-supporting, biodiversity-rich and ecologically sensitive grassland ecosystems.* Report submitted to Expert Committee of National Green Tribunal (South Central Zone).

Sampat, P. (2016). Dholera—The emperor's new city. *Economic and Political Weekly, 51*(17), 59–67.

Sanyal, K. (2007). *Rethinking capitalist development: Primitive accumulation, governmentality and post-colonial capitalism.* New Delhi, India: Routledge.

Sastri, K. A. N. (1940). Administration and Social Life under Vijayanagar. In *Madras University Historical Series: No 15* (pp. 217–220).

Satyan, B. N. (1966). *Mysore State Gazetteer, Gulbarga District.* Government Press.

Sethi, S. (2017). The bittersweet story of vanilla. Smithsonian.com. April 3, 2017.

Shah, T. (2011). *Past, present, and the future of canal irrigation in India.* India Infrastructure Report, pp. 69–89.

Shanin, T. (Ed.). (1971). *Peasants and peasant societies* (p. 230). Penguin Books.

Singh, S. (1997). *Taming the waters: The political economy of large dams in India* (pp. 270). Delhi: Oxford University Press.

Srinivas, M. (1976). *Remembered village.* Berkeley: University of California Press.

Stone, D. (2007). Agricultural deskilling and the spread of genetically modified cotton in Warangal. *Current Anthropology, 48*(1), 67–102.

Taylor, P. M. (1920). *The story of my life* (pp. 177). Oxford University Press.

Thimmaiah, G. (1997). New perspectives on land reforms. In Aziz & Krishna (Eds.), *Land reforms in India: Karnataka promises kept and missed* (Vol. 4, pp. 62–79). Sage Publications.

Upadhyaya, H. (2019). Will CAG reports of irrigation sector in 2018 help improve performance? *South Asian network on dams, rivers and people.* (https://sandrp.in/2019/01/28/will-cag-reports-of-irrigation-sector-in-2018-help-improve-performance/).

Vakulabharanam, V. (2005). Growth and distress in a South Indian peasant economy during the era of economic liberalisation. *Journal of Development Studies, 41*(6), 971–997.

Vasavi, A. R. (2016, March 20). The bitter reality behind the 'pro-farmer' budget. *LiveMint.*

Vasavi, A. R. (2018). The displaced threshing yard: Involution of the rural. In *Malcolm Adisheshaiah Memorial Lecture.*

Wallach, B. (1985). British irrigation works in India's Krishna basin. *Journal of Historical Geography, 11*(2), 155–173.

Wilks, M. (1810). *Historical sketches of the South of India, in an attempt to trace history of Mysore* (Vol. 1, pp. 73).

Worster, D. (1985). *Rivers of empire: Water, aridity, and the growth of the American West.* New York: Pentheon Books.

Index

A

Accumulation, 1, 8, 12, 18, 19, 29, 35, 38, 41–47
Adaptive skilling, 276, 277, 280
Adivasi, 96
Aeroponics, 119
Affluence, 46
Agglomeration, 104
Agrarian distress, 245, 246
Agrarian urbanisation, 183, 185, 189
Agriculturalist, 3, 16, 18
Agricultural Produce Marketing Committee (APMC), 142, 228, 233, 234, 240
Agroecology, 246, 250, 265, 271, 276, 279
Agro-pastoral, 79, 81
Agro-processing, 247, 272, 276
Agro-urban, 57, 67, 69
Airport, 121, 123, 127, 128, 138, 146
Alaamanes, 186
Anekal, 69, 121, 123–136, 138–140, 142–146, 148–150
Anganwadi, 68
Anicuts, 192, 207
Aquifers, 192
Arecanut, 166, 170, 172, 175, 192
Arkavathy, 129
Avare, 1231
Ayagar, 86–88

B

Baichbal, 79
Bajra, 224, 226, 227, 229, 232, 242
Banks, 204
Bannerghatta National Park, 160, 164
Bara baluti, 88

Bara butta, 82
Basavasagara dam, 220, 222, 226
Bedars, 218, 219, 239, 240
Begars, 255
Behavioral, 35
Below Poverty Line (BPL), 16
Bengaluru, 119–129, 131–133, 135–137, 139–144, 146, 147, 149–151
Bengaluru Metropolitan Region Development Authority (BMRDA), 123
Bevinkuppe, 188
Bhadra, 226
Bijapur, 220, 226
Biodiversity, 28, 33, 45
Biomass, 249, 258, 264
Biotechnology, 33
Black cotton soil, 250, 264
British, 84, 87, 88, 96
Bt Cotton, 12

C

Canal irrigation, 187, 192, 193, 195, 209, 222–227, 239–241
Canals, 185, 186, 192, 193, 197, 203
Capabilities, 35
Capital, 26, 29, 30, 38, 41, 48, 247, 248, 257, 264–266, 269, 273, 277–279
Caste, 250, 251, 254, 264, 266, 268, 274, 275
Castor, 187, 201
Caterpillars, 166
Cauvery, 90, 91, 93, 161, 162, 164, 186, 190–192, 208
Chandrike, 166, 167, 172, 180
Channapatna, 168
Chara Basaveshwara, 216, 217, 228

© Springer Nature Singapore Pte Ltd. 2019
S. Purushothaman and S. Patil, *Agrarian Change and Urbanization in Southern India*, India Studies in Business and Economics,
https://doi.org/10.1007/978-981-10-8336-5

284   Index

Chayanovian, 3, 18, 19
Child marriage, 232
Chitradurga, 59
Clusters, 54
Coalition theory, 31
Coastal, 55, 60, 65
Coconut, 131, 136, 140, 164–166, 170, 173, 175, 180, 186, 194–201, 203
Cocoons, 153, 156, 166, 167, 172, 173, 266
Collectivisation, 255
Commercialisation, 7
Commoditisation, 43
Common lands, 128, 129
Constituency, 25, 30, 33, 37, 44, 48
Continuum, 31, 37, 44
Contract farming, 257, 268
Co-operatives, 135, 149, 173
Copra, 187, 198, 202
Core-periphery, 247, 249, 269
Cotton, 219, 224, 227–229, 232–236, 241, 242, 248, 250, 251, 256, 264–266, 272
Credit, 204, 205
Cultural, 6, 10, 11, 15–17, 19–21
Cultural security, 28

D

Dairy farming, 128, 134, 135
Dasanpura, 129
Deccan, 77, 79, 82, 86, 87, 94
Decentralised, 34, 41
Depeasantisation, 272
De-ruralisation, 38
Deskilling, 276
Devanahalli, 59, 69, 121, 123–139, 141–146, 149, 150
Dharwad, 71
Dholera, 59
Disparity, 105
Dispensability, 30
Dispossession, 60, 61
District Domestic Product (DDP), 114
Diwan, 93
Domestication, 77, 79–81
Drip irrigation, 265
Drudgery, 6, 17

E

Ecological debt, 265
Ecological rent, 30, 34
Effluent, 248
Emancipation, 37
Entrepreneur, 29
Environmental economics, 10
Equilibrium, 6, 7

Eucalyptus, 131, 133, 134, 140, 144, 253, 272
Expertocracy, 15
Extension offices, 136

F

Fallow, 201, 257, 258
Fallowing, 159
Family farms, 25–28, 30, 32, 34, 37, 40, 42, 45, 49, 245, 259, 266, 269–27., 278, 280
Famine, 249, 250
Farmer Producer Organisations (FPOs), 268
Farm Yard Manure (FYM), 168–171, 229, 230, 258, 264
Feminisation, 8
Fertilisers, 14, 15, 229
Financial surplus, 269–272, 276, 278
Flowers, 121, 130–133, 136, 137, 140, 143, 145, 149, 151
Foeticide, 93
Food security, 14, 16
Foot loose, 47
Forced commerce, 16
Fruits, 126, 131, 137, 140–143, 145, 151
Fuel-wood, 195

G

Gazetteer, 71, 73
Gherkin, 267
Gini, 254, 271
Globalisation, 38, 45, 46, 48
Goa, 237
Goats, 197, 198
Godavari, 79, 228
Governance, 246, 248–250, 261, 276
Gram swaraj, 256, 279
Granite, 156, 160
Grapes, 134, 135, 137, 141, 144
Great global enclosures, 38
Green gram, 223, 224
Green revolution, 102, 103, 107
Groundnut, 223, 224, 238
Groundwater, 229
Gujjar, 265
Gulbarga, 67, 214, 216–222, 225

H

Haider Ali, 89
Hainu, 90
Handicrafts, 156
Hemavati, 186, 190, 191
Herd mentality, 278
Hingar, 90
Homestead, 1

Index

Horse gram, 131
Horticultural Producers' Co-operative
 Marketingand Processing Society
 (HOPCOMS), 141, 142, 148, 150
Housekeeping, 259
Hoysalas, 129
Human Development Index (HDI), 112–115
Hunger rent, 30
Hunsgi, 79
Hurusgundige, 216
Hyderabad, 55, 56, 67, 71, 73, 248–251, 255
Hydrology, 60
Hydroponics, 119

I

Identity, 28, 31, 48, 49
Import, 31, 47, 48
Impure peasant, 26
Inam, 94
Indebtedness, 256, 264, 270, 273, 275, 276,
 278
Individualisation, 34, 43
Industrial park, 220, 234
Inequality, 250, 253–256, 271
Inflation, 28
Influx, 56
Infrastructure, 102, 104
In-situ, 77, 80, 91, 93
Instability, 29
Institutional economics, 13
Intercrop, 83
Invisibilisation, 246
Involution, 6, 12, 27–29, 42, 44
Irwin Canal, 93

J

Jaggery, 186, 191, 195, 196, 201, 202, 208,
 266, 267
Jagir, 88, 94
Jobless growth, 63
Jowar, 223, 224, 226, 227, 229, 232, 234, 237,
 241, 242

K

Kadrapur, 216, 228, 229
Kagodu, 93
Kanakapura, 69, 153, 156–166, 168–178, 181
Karnataka, 7, 12, 17, 19, 21, 246, 247,
 249–256, 258–261, 263, 266–268, 272,
 274, 276, 280
Kempegowda, 129
Kharif, 251
Kisan Call Center, 171
Kodekal, 216, 223

Kodihalli, 188
Krishna, 79, 80, 90, 91, 93, 95
Krishna Raja Sagara (KRS), 191–195, 208, 252
Kumadavati, 161
Kumarappa, 196
Kurubas, 159, 219, 241

L

Lakes, 189, 190
Lambanis, 219
Land acquisition, 189
Land ceiling, 255, 257
Land distribution, 248, 255, 264
Land leasing, 219, 226
Landless, 9, 11, 18
Land reforms, 254–256, 264
La Via Campesina, 36
Leasing, 159
Limestone, 220
Lingayats, 219
Livestock, 186, 187, 197, 198, 203, 228, 230,
 235, 241
Lokapavani, 190, 192
Low External Input Sustainable Agriculture
 (LEISA), 36

M

Maadigas, 219
Maddur, 189, 192
Madiga, 159
Magadi, 69, 156–166, 168–178, 181
Maharashtra, 237
Maidan, 65
Maize, 131, 136, 140
Malaprabha, 93
Malnad, 65
Mandi, 266, 267
Mandya, 183, 185, 186, 188–204, 206–210,
 247, 248, 250–252, 254–257, 260–270,
 272, 274, 275, 277, 278, 280
Mangloor, 216
Mango, 156, 159, 160, 165, 166, 168–170,
 172, 174, 180
Maratha, 84, 88, 265
Marginalisation, 15, 37
Marginalized majority, 248
Marginal productivity, 28
Marxian, 26, 27, 29, 33, 36
Medieval, 82
Mega city, 57, 67
Melukote, 186, 191, 205
Metabolic rift, 11
Metamorphosis, 3, 4, 8, 21
Metropolis, 107

286 Index

Migrant, 124, 144, 146–148, 246, 251, 259, 271, 274, 275
Migration, 226, 231, 232, 236–242
Milch animals, 228
Millets, 227, 228, 242
Minimum Support Price (MSP), 103
Mining, 156, 160
Mobility, 259
Mola butta, 82
Molasses, 195
Movements, 251, 255, 265, 272, 277
Mughal, 84, 88
Mulberry, 126, 131, 134, 136, 137, 140, 143, 150, 151, 156, 159, 163–168, 170, 172–176, 192, 194, 198, 199, 203
Mungaru, 90
Mysore, 56, 64, 67, 71, 73, 248–252, 254, 272

N

Nagamangala, 69, 186–195, 197–201, 203–206
Narayanpur, 220, 222, 226
National Rural Livelihood Mission, 173
Nature's commons, 255, 279
Nayaka, 83, 217, 218, 221, 241
Need economy, 36, 38, 41, 42, 46
Neoliberal, 46, 47
Neolithic, 79–83
Net District Domestic Product (NDDP), 113, 115
Nexus, 49
Nizam, 248
Nutritional security, 28, 39, 47

O

Oddities, 101
Omnipresent, 44, 48
Open wells, 221, 223, 226, 227
Other Backward Caste (OBC), 159, 219, 254, 274
Outgrowth, 104

P

Paddy, 219, 223–229, 232, 233, 235, 239–242
Palegar, 86, 89
Paleolithic, 79
Panchayati Raj Institutions, 276
Pandavapura, 69, 186–195, 197–201, 203–207
Pandavas, 186
Path dependence, 250
Patidar, 265
Pauperisation, 30
Peasant, 1, 3–6, 8, 9, 11, 16–21, 245, 249, 269
Perishables, 248, 267, 272

Peri-urban, 5, 19, 20
Persistence, 3, 4, 6, 8, 14, 15, 19, 21
Pesticides, 136, 151, 229
Petit bourgeois, 245
Petty commodity, 63
Philip Meadows Taylor, 218
Physiocratic, 29
Planet of slums, 47
Plantations, 237
Politico-economic, 48
Polyhouse, 20, 132, 148
Poverty trap, 255, 278
Precariousness, 33, 37, 41, 269, 271, 274
Prisoner's dilemma, 61
Progressive farmer, 265
Proletarianisation, 43, 44
Proletariat, 277
Provisioning, 10
Public distribution system, 105
Pulse bowl, 265
Pulses, 126, 131, 134, 137, 140, 145, 226, 227, 232, 238, 240–242

R

Rabi, 251
Radical, 256
Ragi, 123, 126, 131, 134, 136, 137, 140, 147, 252, 253, 272
Raichur, 214, 220, 226, 239
Rainfed, 249, 252, 253, 256–258, 262 264, 265, 270
Rainfed farming, 226, 241
Raita Samparka Kendra, 136, 150
Raita Santhe, 266, 267
Raja kaluve, 161
Ramanagara, 153, 156–160, 162, 165–168, 170, 172–177, 179, 181
Reddy camps, 226, 239, 240
Red gram, 224, 229, 230, 232, 234, 265
Resilience, 42
Revolts, 37, 38
Rural middle class, 248
Rurban, 121, 125, 143
Ryotwari, 87, 88, 125, 188

S

Santhe, 140, 183, 200, 201, 267
Scale-neutral, 26, 35
Scheduled Caste (SC), 167, 219
Scheduled Tribe (ST), 167, 219
Self-exploitation, 25, 27
Self-Help Groups (SHGs), 140, 146, 149
Sericulture, 168, 170, 174, 176, 180
Sesamum, 187, 201

Index

Sewage, 62, 162, 164, 165, 177, 179, 181
Shahpur, 69, 214, 216–224, 228, 230, 231, 234–236
Shambhuvanahalli, 188
Share cropping, 35, 219
Sheep, 128, 197, 198
Shimsha, 186, 190, 192
Ship of fools, 47
Shorapur, 69, 214, 216–225, 227–231, 233–236, 240, 241
Siddihoskote, 124
Silk, 120, 151, 156, 157, 166–168, 172–174, 179
Silkworms, 172
Sink, 248
Small holders, 1–6, 8, 9, 11–16, 18, 21
Small town, 57, 67, 69
Social-ecological, 8, 10, 12–15, 18
Socialism, 256
Social network analysis, 71, 72
Societal commons, 255
Socio-economic pyramid, 3
Soil fertility, 249, 258, 260, 261, 279
Soil moisture, 258, 260, 262, 263, 276, 279
Soil nutrient, 264
Sorghum, 194, 265
Sovereignty, 36, 39
Srirangapattna, 190
Stree shakti sangha, 259
Subaltern, 183, 197
Subsidy, 13
Subsistence, 28, 29, 32, 33, 37, 38, 41, 42, 46
Sugarcane, 185, 186, 189, 192, 194–200, 203, 204, 208, 210
Sugar mills, 185, 186, 189, 191, 195, 196, 199, 201, 204, 210
Suicides, 48, 185, 197, 203, 204, 235, 236
Sultanate, 89
Suvarnamukhi, 161, 162, 164

T

Talathi, 68
Tanks, 186, 190–193, 195, 207, 217, 221, 222, 224, 226, 241
Telangana, 12
Tenant, 254, 256

Terrace farm, 1
T. G. Halli, 162
Thoobinkere, 188
Tipu Sultan, 95, 123, 186
Town municipal council, 123
Trade guilds, 120
Trade-off, 16, 18
Transition, 30, 42–44, 49, 54, 58, 65
Tribal, 31
Tube wells, 192, 193
Tungbhadra, 228

U

Unequal, 249, 277
University of Agricultural Sciences, 225, 229
Upper Krishna Project (UKP), 220, 222, 240
Urban-agrarian, 246, 247, 249, 277–280
Urbanisation, 15, 19, 21

V

Vaddars, 219
Veeravaishnavi, 190, 192
Vertical farms, 119
Vijayanagara, 82–84, 90
Vishwanathpura, 124, 129
Visvesvaraya Canal, 194, 195
Vokkaliga, 159, 189, 201
Volatility, 248, 276
Vrishabhavati, 161, 162, 164
Vulnerability, 15, 20

W

Welfare, 249, 250
Western Ghat, 79, 82, 95
Workforce, 4, 16

Y

Yadgir, 214, 216–222, 224–230, 232–242, 247–251, 254–265, 267–271, 273, 275, 277, 278

Z

Zamindari, 86, 87
Zemstvos, 26